Convention Sales and Services

Convention Sales and Services

Milton T. Astroff
Marketing Consultant

James R. Abbey, Ph.D.
Professor
College of Hotel Administration
University of Nevada, Las Vegas

Waterbury Press
2C Truro Drive
Cranbury, NJ 08512
(606) 395-1427

Printed in the United States of America

ISBN 0-9620710-0-5

Contents

Preface

Much has happened in the hotel-convention business since the first edition of this text. The industry has undergone many changes. More, perhaps, than in any similar period before it. If nothing else, the industry has achieved tremendous growth. Today the convention industry approaches $40 billion annually and is growing steadily.

With so much happening it was not difficult to determine what needed updating. Over the years we have maintained file folders for each chapter of the text. Into them have gone trade journal articles, scraps from newspapers, student and instructor comments, book reviews and seminar notes. Each of these folders became the basis for revised data, new ideas, clarifications and reworked segments. Readers who are familiar with the book will find the basic outline unchanged although the contents have been updated substantially. New photos and forms highlight the revised content. Each chapter has been updated to reflect the latest in research and practice.

This first edition of this book has been tested on the firing line in university classrooms and in hotel sales offices throughout the world and many ideas offered by early users have been incorporated into this edition. Most gratifying have been the critiques of seasoned industry professionals who have commented, "Yes, this is just the way it's done . . . large or small, those properties that are successful follow the procedures as layed out in your text."

It is hard to conceive of a new hotel going up today without plans for meeting facilities. However, the convention business requires more than just a physical plant. It is definitely a *people* business. The prizes go to those with the greatest expertise in the craft.

Convention Sales and Services was written to serve as a primer and guide for those who plan to be and those who already are involved in this exciting and promising segment of the hospitality world. All facets of the convention business will be discussed.

Part I offers practical insight into the different kinds of meetings and conventions, the types of organizations that stage such events, and the people who hold the key to site selection, and suggests how to reach and sell these important groups and people. Material includes how to analyze a hotel property to determine which segments of the market may be sold and serviced successfully and how to organize a staff to go after that kind of business. Practical advice is given on such subjects as negotiations and letters of agreement.

Part II deals with the vital convention service. Once the client has been sold on holding his or her event in the hotel, the staff must serve to allow the convention to flow smoothly. Each convention is a custom production, and skilled, knowledgeable hotel people are needed for its execution. Repeat business is essential for the success of any hotel, and professional convention service is absolutely necessary for a hotel to compete for its share of business.

The modern hotel executive must have a complete grasp of convention sales and service. This knowledge points the way to consistently high occupancy rates, filling in those empty calendar spots, those off-season times, those weaker days of the week. It offers an opportunity to go after the *kind* of guests you want, instead of just numbers.

No one can progress to executive ranks within the modern hotel field without a full understanding of the role such business plays in today's hotel plan. This lucrative market merits careful attention by students and those already in the field. *Convention Sales and Services* is offered to facilitate

your entry into and growth in the hotel industry.

Text Features

Our purpose throughout the book is to present convention management in a readable style with ample illustrations to facilitate comprehension and encourage retention of the text material.

End-of-Chapter Material. Review questions follow each chapter. These questions help the reader pull together and integrate the basic concepts of the chapter. In addition, the questions give the reader an opportunity to see how their own values will affect the way they apply the management principles.

Instructional Support Package. A comprehensive Instructor's Manual to assist teachers in the classroom use of the text is available. Each chapter in the Instructor's Manual includes a review outline, a list of key terms, a suggested lecture outline, suggested answers to the end-of-chapter discussion questions, and a test item file.

Part 1

Convention Sales

Introduction

Although no one is quite sure how or when they came about, conventions have become extremely important in today's business world. Business and professional people realized early the importance of getting together to discuss their problems and to clear up misunderstandings. Out of these early meetings came the massive convention business we know today.

A great many people have the misconception that a convention is just another vacation. But the basic purpose of a convention is not to assemble for fun and games but to exchange viewpoints and discuss matters of mutual concern.

When a convention is tied to a trade show, delegates expect to see and hear about the newest equipment and supplies in their profession or industry. They expect to have an opportunity to discuss personally with their suppliers the problems that have been troubling them.

Every field has its conventions: Professions, trade unionism, education, arts, commerce, politics, and fraternalism all rely on conventions to bring together the membership's cross section of ideas. The conventioneers congregate in hotel properties across the country to attend meetings and look over exhibits; invariably they come home better oriented toward their jobs and more certain of the goals of their organization.

What do conventions mean to a hotel? They can mean the difference between black and red ink in the profit column. Obviously, conventions play an important part in a hotel's overall sales effort. As much as 40 percent of total sales volume in major hotels is attributed to the influence of convention business; smaller properties count the effect at 15 to 20 percent.

Such group business is valuable to hotels for several reasons.

1. Conventioneers not only provide room revenue for the hotel, but, because they are more or less captive, they also use room service, hospitality suites, and laundry and valet services. The hotel's restaurant, lounge, drugstore, and barbershop also benefit.

2. Convention and group business allows a hotel to forecast advance booking. Since the length of each guest's stay is pretty much predetermined, employee scheduling is more accurate and labor costs are reduced.

3. Convention business can fill the gaps in the slack months. And thus better employee-employer relationships are maintained by eliminating the fear of slow periods and providing secure and steady working conditions.

4. Group business is an excellent builder for repeat business. With a convention, a large number of potential repeat guests become acquainted with your hotel. If they are treated well and are pleased, they will not only advertise by word of mouth, but they also will be likely to stay with you on other visits to the city.

And the only way to get this repeat business is through the development of an honest and fair rapport with convention groups. This means living up to all promises and obligations and providing excellent attention to detail and the service that is so necessary for the smooth running of the modern convention.

5. Should a trade show be part of the convention event, hotels find there is heavy demand for their suites and lounge facilities.
6. Spouses, more than ever, are accompanying delegates to conventions and this typically increases business in shops, health clubs and the like.

Outline

I. Marketing and Sales Promotion

    A. There Is a Difference
    B. Marketing Defined
    C. The Marketing Mix
    D. The Marketing Manager

II. The Convention and Meeting Business

    A. The Rolling Green Resort
    B. The Marketing Plan
        1. Analysis of Your Property
        2. Pinpoint Target Areas of Promotion
        3. Determination of Markets and Prospects
        4. Setting the Budget
        5. How to Reach Your Target Areas
    C. Rolling Green Revisited
    D. Importance of Convention Business

Marketing and Sales Promotion

Before charging off in an attempt to capture all the convention business it can handle, a hotel first should scrutinize its objectives. We all have probably been guilty of plunging headlong into an undertaking without thinking seriously where we were headed or why.

Perhaps it was the purchase of a new automobile or a household appliance offered at such a good buy that we just couldn't refuse. However, a few months later, when the cash was tied into our investment, problems began to appear. The initial excitement wore off and we begin to evaluate the rationality of our purchase. Too late? No, probably not. We are generally able to rationalize our poor, spur-of-the-moment decisions and justify our action. But we vow that the next time "such a good deal" is presented we will consider it thoroughly, weighing both the benefits and drawbacks of our investment.

The convention business is often viewed similarly by hotels "as such a good deal." Many properties have been guilty of investing in a convention sales program without formalizing a clear-cut plan of what they hope to achieve or how they plan to do it. The results can be costly shotgun advertising directed in the wrong places, fruitless sales calls, and groups that never rebook.

A true managerial approach to marketing should lead to realistic objectives that can be measured. A good plan, in fact, *demands* clearly defined objectives, with careful thought given to methods, policies, and procedures.

There Is a Difference

What is marketing? Many tend to lump sales, advertising, promotion, and merchandising and say that together they are marketing. Others say that marketing and sales promotion are interchangeable.

We want to make a clear distinction between marketing and sales. The terms are not synonymous. The title "marketing manager" has been wrongly posted on many hotel office doors. Few hotels actually practice marketing, having labeled their operations so only because of the recent popularity of the word. Many managers think marketing is nothing different from the age-old sales and promotion concept.

Marketing is more than sales; they are not equal. Being market-minded is much broader than being simply sales-minded. Marketing is strategic and directive. It is goal-oriented, and the goals are concise and measurable. Marketing precedes sales promotion and follows the sales transaction. It is the groundwork, the research, the plan on which sales promotion is based. Quite simply, marketing is the foundation on which sales are built. Theodore Levitt says:

> Strictly a sales oriented approach to doing business can be suicidal. The difference between selling and marketing is more than semantic. Selling focuses on the needs of the seller; marketing on the needs of the buyer.[1]

Selling, as seen by Levitt, is a product approach; marketing, a consumer approach. In the past, businesses could concentrate on their product effort, often ignoring the true desires of their client. But today, it takes more than sales to guarantee long-term survival. Businesses must look at the changing needs of the consumer.

Hotels that do not distinguish between selling and marketing are not likely to be maximizing their profit potential. The fact that the hotel industry is a service industry is well accepted. However, if managers become preoccupied with converting that service into cash and fail to identify the customer and his needs, the hotel may eventually end up possessing a product for which there is no customer.

Levitt points up the importance of planning a marketing approach by illustrating the shortsightedness of the railroads.

> The railroads are in trouble today not because the need (transportation) was filled by others (cars, trucks, airplanes), but because it was not filled by the railroads themselves. They let others take away customers from them because they assumed themselves to be in the railroad business, rather than in the transportation business . . . they were railroad oriented instead of transportation oriented; they were product oriented instead of customer oriented.[2]

Hotels must likewise guard themselves, lest they fall into the same trap as the railroad industry. Too frequently we see businesses with products to sell and no one to buy them. In the early days of innkeeping, the demand was greater than the supply. There were not enough hotel rooms to go around. It didn't matter what type of rooms were built because the customer had no alternative choices. A marketing plan that was customer-oriented was not needed to sell the product.

But the hospitality industry is a far cry from this state today. The city that once had a single inn now has four or five new hotels, each of them different. Where formerly the demand exceeded supply, the reverse is now true.

Sales in the hotel industry are composed of two parts: *room rate and occupancy*. For the last several years occupancy rates have been decreasing. Figure 1.1

1. From *Innovations in Marketing: New Prospectives for Profit and Growth* by Theodore Levitt, p. 55. Copyright © by McGraw-Hill, Inc. Used with permission of McGraw-Hill Book Company.
2. Ibid., p. 40.

7

Fig. 1.1. Trend of hotel room business: room rates, room sales, and occupancy. (Adapted from *Trends in the Hotel-Motel Business* (New York: Pannell Kerr, Forster and Company). Used with permission.

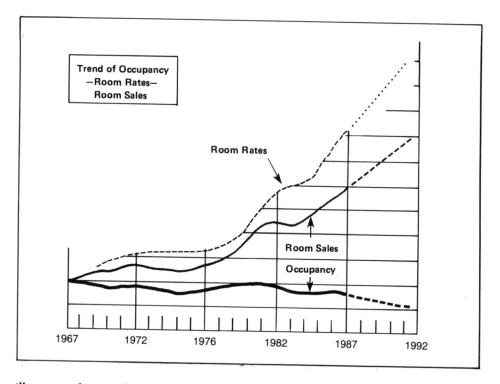

illustrates this trend. Note that room sales, the product of occupancy times room rate, have increased over the same period. The correct conclusion is that room rates have been increasing, offsetting the decline in occupancy.

Many industry leaders question how high room rates can go, maintaining that each rise in room rates brings a corresponding decline in occupancy. Other astute observers respond that rising room rates are only a symptom of a bigger problem, that of new facilities outdistancing demand. They point out that actually there has been no real decline in occupancy for the nation as a whole. The industry overall is selling more rooms, but the yearly construction of new rooms exceeds the room sales increase.

Because of this tremendous increase in rooms and a corresponding increase in competition, today's hotels and those of the future must make the distinction between marketing and sales. Hotels can no longer haphazardly allocate their monthly sales and promotion expense without a clear-cut plan and statement of objectives. The future belongs to those who are customer-oriented, those who are in the business of meeting the changing needs of the public, not just in the business of maintaining hotel rooms.

Marketing Defined

Having stipulated what marketing isn't, let us define what marketing is. The term *marketing* is a fairly new one, receiving wide usage only in the last thirty years. The expression is magical to some, frightening to others, and difficult to conceptualize to most. Both simple and complex definitions abound, yet marketing is not something explained, but something practiced.

Until recently, hotel marketing was never thought of in the same light as industrial marketing. It was not considered that a hotel might be similar to a consumer product. Now, the lodging industry is realizing that its problems are not unlike those of product companies. Thus many hotels are attempting to come to grips with what marketing means in an effort to apply marketing management principles.

The practice of marketing is not new. Many firms have recognized the importance of the customer and have successfully catered to his changing needs. The conscious application of the theory, however, is new, particularly to the hospitality industry.

Marketing is an encompassing function with many different elements that contribute to the salability of a product or service. A working definition, then, one that is explicit yet gives a framework to build upon, is: *Marketing is combining, blending, integrating, and controlling all those factors that have an influence on sales.*

The Marketing Mix

Marketing includes sales but is considerably more. It is that "more" that we are concerned with here; many refer to it as the *marketing mix*. The marketing mix is comprised of every factor that influences the sales effort, such as

1. *price*—room rates, menu prices, beverage prices, etc.
2. *packaging*—family plans, sporting events, the total gamut of amenities
3. *label*—the hotel's name, the ease with which it can be remembered
4. *color*—the resort's exterior and interior atmosphere
5. *size*—the number of guest rooms, meeting rooms, suites, etc.

6. *shape*—the inn's flexibility, whether large rooms can be divided into small ones.
7. *advertising*—where to promote: newspapers, trade journals, radio, TV
8. *public relations*—with the guest, the community, the hotel's purveyors, and its employees
9. *sales techniques*—external: direct mail, convention follow-up, referral systems; internal: selling at the front desk, in the dining room, and in guest rooms
10. *quality*—the reputation and image of the hotel

The Marketing Manager

From the preceding list, it can be seen that there are a number of factors besides sales that determine the profit picture of a hotel. It is the job of the hotel's marketing manager to plan, direct, and control all of these factors, including the establishment of programs, policies, and objectives. The marketing manager must know and understand the capital markets, break-even analysis, and cost-control concepts. His, or her, functions might include

1. establishing long- and short-range goals
2. analyzing the operation and how it compares with competition
3. identifying the markets and their potential
4. researching prospective customers
5. establishing a marketing budget
6. planning advertising and promotion packages
7. maintaining an accurate sales forecast
8. integrating all sales techniques to promote business
9. reviewing all services and facilities for needed changes

The marketing manager's job begins with planning. He must constantly plan new ways and activities to adapt to the changing needs of the customer. His duties to the firm are much the same as those of any other department head: It is his job to help provide continuity to the hotel and to improve its image. The marketing manager is part of top management and should be given full authority to coordinate and control all the marketing and sales promotion functions.

The Convention and Meeting Business

In this chapter we will present a practical step-by-step approach to planning a marketing program. This analysis will help you determine whether convention sales are actually a viable piece of business for your property. The market plan will be our base. We will refer to it often, so it is necessary for the reader to grasp the concept thoroughly.

From this beginning we will detail each aspect of the market plan, concentrating our discussion on the convention trade. Chapter 2, "Analyzing Your Property," will guide you into making such all-important decisions as, Will my property support group business? How much? What facilities do I have that I can capitalize on?

Chapter 3, "Defining and Locating the Market," will help you do just that. We will delineate the terminology used by the convention sales personnel and take a look at who holds meetings.

The characteristics of the association market, the corporate market, and other convention markets are described thoroughly in chapters 4, 5, and 6.

Chapter 7, "Organizing for Convention Sales," considers the sales department's position within the framework of the hotel. Here we will answer the questions, Who works in sales? How many salespeople do I need? What are their jobs? How do I set up my office for convention solicitation?

It has been said that nothing happens until a sale is made. This is true in the sense that the sale is our ultimate objective, but we might add that sales don't just happen—they are made. Chapter 8, "Techniques for Convention Sales," will provide you with the tools for making group sales. Direct mail, personal sales calls, and telephone calls are a few of the areas covered in this chapter.

Hopefully, your efforts have been fruitful. The meeting planner has visited your property and has decided to schedule his or her next convention at your hotel. Is that all there is to the sales process? No, now the details must be formalized. Chapter 9, the final chapter dealing with convention sales, discusses "Negotiations and Contracts." Although formal contracts are not used extensively today, informal letters of agreement between the hotel and the meeting group are customary.

The Rolling Green Resort

As a basis for study we offer the accompanying case study of the fictitious Rolling Green Resort. Place yourself in the position of the new sales manager. It is quite probable that this situation is similar to one you have experienced or will encounter.

The Marketing Plan

Your first action should be to outline a plan, a marketing strategy. In an article in *Resort Management,* a leading trade publication for the hospitality industry, Her-

---

The Rolling Green Resort   Case Study

The Rolling Green Resort is located on the banks of the Pritchard River forty miles north of St. Louis, a city with a metropolitan population of three million. This beautiful area is renowned as a vacation area, having high, wooded hills, picturesque fruit and dairy farms, country estates, historic battlefields, and a national cemetery. Forest Glen, a small community nearby, is a shopping center for the rural residents of the valley.

The resort is about two miles off U.S. 16, a main north-south highway with four lanes, which is fairly heavily traveled by tourists going south in the winter and north in the summer.

The inn has 320 rooms, all modern with private baths. A rather nice dining room overlooks the river. The kitchen is reasonably adequate. A ballroom that can accommodate 600 people is on the second floor, with a balcony toward the river. There are several rooms of various sizes in the basement, but they are used for miscellaneous storage, with one room serving as a day room for the hotel's staff.

Business the past year has been "just fair." Transient trade constitutes the bulk of the business. It is good in the peak summer months and for a few weeks in the winter. But business is just plain "poor" in the spring, fall, late winter, and during the holidays. Food sales are largely to the hotel guests; Forest Glen does not have sufficient population to provide very many customers.

Management of the resort is in the hands of an elderly gentleman who knows his hotel business but is unable to come up with any ideas to improve business. He has asked his board of directors for assistance.

You have been appointed sales manager after having served for two years on the sales department staff of the A & A Hotels Corporation.

PROBLEM: What efforts would you make to increase the resort's business?

---

bert Frank and Gary Adams cited five steps to take in formulating a marketing plan. Much of the following discussion on the market plan is from their presentation.[3]

Step #1—Analysis of Your Property

A frequent question a resort operator might ask when contemplating a marketing, advertising, and promotion program for his property is "Where do I start?" It is our

3. Herbert Frank and Gary Adams, "Marketing the Small Resort," Copyright *Resort Management*. Used with permission; further reproduction rights reserved except with written permission.

opinion that the most logical place to begin is with a written analysis of your property, the basic product you are selling. At first glance this may seem to be unnecessary, particularly for the operator who has run a property for several years, but we feel that the value of this exercise will become more obvious as our recommendations for formulating an effective marketing and advertising program are further delineated.

When making the analysis of your property, it is imperative that you do it as objectively as possible. This analysis will form the base of information from which virtually every marketing and advertising decision will be made, and any error in judgment here will almost certainly result in mistakes in your marketing and advertising strategy.

Among the important questions you should answer in analyzing your property are the following:

1. Would you be classified as an inn, hotel, motel, or cottage resort?
2. How established is your property?
   a. What percentage of your business is repeat business?
   b. What percentage of your business is from referrals by former guests?
3. What is the condition of your overall physical plant?
   a. Room condition, both plumbing and fixtures.
   b. Public space.
   c. Grounds.
4. What activities does your property offer to guests and how good are they in relation to your competition?
   a. Swimming pool (indoor and/or outdoor).
   b. Golf course (par 3, 9, 18, etc.).
   c. Tennis courts (how many?).
   d. Private beaches.
   e. Horseback riding.
   f. Lawn sports.
   g. Game room.
   h. Soaring.
   i. Fishing.
   j. Boating.
   k. Downhill skiing.
   l. Cross-country skiing.
   m. Skating.
5. What type of geographic location do you have and what are the historic, scenic, and amusement attractions in your general area?

6. What are the seasonal aspects of your property?
   a. Are you open year-round?
   b. What is your normal pattern of business by month?
7. Do you operate or lease a restaurant, dining room, and/or cocktail lounge?
   a. How good is your food and beverage operation in relation to your competition?
   b. Do you offer entertainment? What type?
8. Does your property have conference and/or group meeting facilities?
   a. What is the ideal-sized group for you to handle?
      What is the maximum size you can handle?
   b. Are you equipped to serve meals to groups in a room or rooms other than your restaurant or main dining room?
9. In general, how does your property compare with that of your competition?

Obviously much of the analysis of your property must be subjective. However, if good common sense is used and input is gathered from a variety of sources, including employees and guests, a solid information base can be established.

Step #2—Pinpoint Target Areas of Promotion

Our next recommendation is to pinpoint the specific target areas of promotion that are applicable to your operation. It is our view that there are basically five potential sources of business (target areas of promotion) that may involve promotion of one form or another. They are

1. individual guests
2. conference and group meetings
3. travel agents and tour operators
4. restaurant and lounge
5. functions

After determining from which of these potential sources of business you are actually drawing business, you should compile a dollar breakdown and percentage of your gross sales by source of business. The next step is to calculate as closely as possible the net income derived from each source. Admittedly, this is not the easiest thing in the world to do. However, it is an important factor to be considered when formulating the marketing, advertising, and promotion budgets because the profit factor obviously varies for each area of business. For example, an increase of $50,000 in your restaurant business certainly is not as profitable as a corresponding increase in room sales.

Finally, these gross sales and net income (by source of business) figures should be compared with those from the previous four or five years to determine the general trend or pattern of growth for each area of business.

Step #3—Determination of Markets and Prospects

Having defined specific target areas of promotion, their present importance, and their growth pattern, we can now move on to the interrelated questions of who your prospective guests are and where they come from.

The importance of determining who your prospects are and where they originate cannot be overstated. The answers to these questions will basically determine the direction of your marketing and promotion strategy.

The accuracy of the answers to these two questions will determine, more than any other factor, the eventual success or failure of your advertising and promotional efforts. The term *GIGO*, coined in the computer industry, aptly sums up this relationship between accurate information and results. For those who are not familiar with the term, GIGO stands for "Garbage In, Garbage Out." In short, if inaccurate information is used as input, inaccurate results will be obtained as output.

Given the five basic potential sources of business (target areas of promotion) outlined earlier, let us now examine how best to determine who and where these prospects are.

Individual Guests   We are continually amazed (and dismayed) at the number of small resort operators who do not know what percentage of their guest business comes from various geographic market areas. Lest you think us unsympathetic, let us assure you that we are well aware that "there just aren't enough hours in the day" for many resort operators and managers, and particularly, the very small operator with a limited staff. However, every property has its periods when things slow up a bit, and we urge that you "make time" during such periods to do some homework.

Registration and/or guest history cards contain the geographic information you are looking for (fig. 1.2). It then is merely a question of how best to extract and categorize this information. The information we feel to be most important is a compilation of the number of guests and number of guest nights by geographic area. Naturally, the smaller the geographic areas used as categories the better. For example, it is more useful to know that a guest came from Greater Boston than to know that a guest came from Massachusetts.

Armed with a good map (or several maps), you should break down and record registration cards, first by state and then by major metropolitan area. This may seem like (and, in fact, may be) an undertaking of monumental proportions if you are attempting to do this for the past year, which is the ideal procedure. If you

Fig. 1.2 Sample registration card will provide important geographic information. (Used with permission).

PLEASE PAY LAST AMOUNT

Hilton Inn St.George, Utah

1450 HILTON INN DRIVE
ST. GEORGE, UTAH 84770
(801) 628-0463

GUEST REGISTRATION   34725

Names_____

Address_____

City or Town_____ State_____ Zip_____

Firm_____

MAKE OF CAR	LICENSE No.	MODEL	STATE

MY ACCOUNT WILL BE PAID BY
☐ CASH   ☐ CHECK   ☐ CREDIT CARD_____
                                                          TYPE AND NUMBER
I AGREE TO THE CORRECTNESS OF THIS STATEMENT AND PERSONALLY ASSUME LIABILITY

SIGNATURE

X_____

REMARKS

NOTICE TO GUESTS: SAFETY DEPOSIT BOXES ARE PROVIDED FOR DEPOSIT OF VALUABLES. THE HOTEL IS NOT RESPONSIBLE FOR VALUABLES NOT DEPOSITED.

ARRIVED	DEPARTED	ROOM	RATE	CLERK	NO. GUESTS

feel you simply cannot spend the time to do this for the entire year, valuable information may still be gained by doing it for your strongest three months and a few of your slower months. One logical way to produce this geographic breakdown would be to do it on a daily basis, thus avoiding the confrontation with thousands of guest registration cards at the end of the year.

Some longtime operators may have a pretty good idea of where their markets are located, but we believe that even they may find this geographic analysis helpful and, perhaps, a little surprising, since the only constant in our business is change. Of course, the more accurate your information is, the sounder your advertising and promotion strategy will be.

Once you have established where your present guest business is coming from, you should turn your attention to the markets from which you presently draw very little but which may offer good potential. Much of your assessment of potential markets must be subjective, but you may be able to get useful information from local, regional, or state chambers of commerce and development agencies. You may also want to discuss this question with friendly competitors. You may "discover" that your competition is getting business out of a market or two where you are not active, markets that may prove worthwhile if given a little advertising and promotion.

It is equally important to know who your guests are. How old are they? Are they singles, married couples, families, middle-income, high-income, good drinkers, sports-minded, the "rocking chair set"?

This sort of demographic information could possibly be obtained by designing a brief questionnaire to be filled in by guests (offering an incentive such as a free weekend for a few of those filling out the questionnaire helps), but, more likely, you will have to make subjective judgments about the type of people your guests are. You should pay special attention to "profiting" your repeat guests since they are the cornerstone of your guest business.

The single most important word when attempting to define who your guests are is objectivity. The more honest and accurate you are in this, the more effective your advertising program will be. For example, if your property has attracted a strong middle-income, family-type clientele, but you feel that "given the proper advertising" you really could be getting a high-income, couples-only clientele, you are probably deluding yourself, unless you are planning to change your property significantly.

Restaurant and Lounge   Assuming that you want and/or need outside business for your restaurant and lounge operations, determination of markets becomes simply a matter of analyzing local preferences for decor, cuisine, and entertainment. The only advice we can give here is to experiment with different menus and entertainment and to forget about "portion control" drinks.

Meetings, Functions, Travel Agents, Tour Operators   Determination of markets or prospects as applied to these target areas differs from individual guest business in that to identify your prospects you have to reach them somehow with the information about your property. There are thousands of association, professional, social, and educational groups that meet regularly to share ideas and to plan for the future of their groups. In addition, corporations hold sales and planning meetings periodically. The size of such meetings varies widely from ten persons to thousands. Because there is such variety in types and sizes, any facility with meeting space can capitalize on this important market.

Step #4—Setting the Budget

Very occasionally, a client asks us, "How much should I spend on advertising? Am I spending too little, or perhaps too much?"

There are certainly no hard and fast rules in allocating a budget, and to some extent the attitude of the client determines whether the budget will exceed or drop below average ranges. Some hotel operators are promotion-minded; others are not. Those who are not are apt to retreat behind such arguments as "my best advertising is word of mouth," or "I had a bad year last year so I'll have to cut my advertising budget." And those who overbudget are sometimes carried away by overly optimistic projections of some of their fondly conceived plans.

Here are the items that should be considered as part of the advertising/sales promotion budget.

Media advertising—newspapers, magazines, guides and directories, trade papers, radio, TV, and outdoor

Production expense—cost of all layouts, photography, type composition, mechanics, and engravings

Brochures and collateral sales materials—color brochures, rate sheets, promotional fliers, special folders, displays

Direct mail-mail campaigns—postage, printing and stationery, and labor costs for sales correspondence

Miscellaneous promotion expenses—travel shows, travel expense applied specifically to promotional operations, matchbooks, souvenir giveaways, business entertainment

As a rule of thumb, media expenditures should be about 3 percent of gross sales; total advertising/sales promotion expense, including all of the above items, should be about 6 percent. Any attempt to limit this expense to less than 6 percent will usually reduce the media expense to less than 3 percent. Many resorts, carrying on an active campaign aimed at bolstering weak seasons, will spend a total of more than 6 percent, perhaps 8 percent. In weak periods, a much higher media allocation is justifiable.

Many resorts that employ people for strictly sales functions may attempt to treat expenses as promotional costs. We feel that these should be considered as sales costs, and must be budgeted over and above advertising and promotion costs, with definite controls to hold such costs in line with volume achieved.

Establish a Budget for Each Target Area of Promotion   Rooms business is obviously the most profitable factor of your operation. Therefore most of your budget should be allocated to building room sales. Food business is the least profitable, so don't overspend to build up weak food operations at the expense of room promotion. If your food operation isn't making it, advertising may help, but sometimes the answer is a fresh look at your operation—menu, prices, service, physical changes, etc.

Look at your figures for last year! Was it a profitable year? How much did you spend on advertising and promotion? Can you break the figures down to determine how much you actually spent for each target area of business? Did you spend your money in proper relationship to the fluctuating seasonableness of your business? Can you depend on good repeat business, or must you spend more money to attract new business?

In any event, you should budget a specific amount for each category of your business—room sales, restaurant and lounge functions, group meetings, tour operators, and travel agents. Obviously, there is no formula covering this allocation. It depends on your particular property and the volume you do in each category.

The budget should be set on a projected fiscal year basis. You should then break this amount into quarterly periods. Review your advertising plans, ads, and creative materials regularly with your advertising agency or advertising assistant, and be prepared to make periodic adjustments in your plans, based on good judgments on the trends of your business.

An advertising budget should not be changed every week or month, but should provide you with the basic figure around which you can deal flexibly with changing situations.

Step #5—How to Reach Your Target Areas

To refresh your memory, we identified what we feel to be the five basic target areas of promotion (sources of business) that would apply to most small resorts. They are

1. individual guests
2. conference and group meetings
3. travel agents and tour operators
4. restaurant and lounge
5. functions

Following are our general recommendations concerning the best ways to reach and sell prospects in each target area.

Individual Guests   As you probably can guess from the preceding general analysis of media, we believe that use of print media is the most effective promotion technique for generating individual guest business. Newspapers, magazines, and travel guides have proved their effectiveness for the small resort, and, depending on the variables outlined earlier, it is likely that one of these types of print media, a combination of them, or all three will produce good results for you.

Conference and Group Meetings   We mentioned previously that determination of markets or prospects for conference and/or group meeting business differs somewhat from that for individual guest business. Your basic markets for individual guest business can be quite well defined through geographic and demographic analysis of your present individual guest business. Once your individual guest markets have been well defined, it is reasonable to expect that media advertising, selected to match your geographic and demographic guest profiles, will succeed in producing business. But market definition for conference and/or group meeting businesses is more complex.

Geographic and demographic analysis is a useful first step in determining prospects for group meetings, but you should realize that it is just the first step. You may be able to define certain industries, organizations, and societies from specific geographic areas that have held meetings in your general area or even at your property, but there may be other equally attractive prospects that simply have never been sold.

Assuming that you have assembled a "prospect list" by industry and by geographic area, where do you go from there? The answer, in our opinion, is that you must establish a dialogue with these prospects.

The rather difficult problem now facing you is to determine specifically who makes the meeting decisions for each company or organization on your prospect list and what the best way is to reach him or her. Particularly for small meetings, the decision maker may have any one of 25 titles, which makes direct mail somewhat suspect. However, we feel the best general approach is to use a combination of direct mail, media advertising, and telephone calls to qualify prospects, and then to make personal sales calls where interest is shown.

Travel Agents and Tour Operators   The marketing situation for travel agents and tour operators is very similar to that for group meeting business. There are a number of trade publications reaching travel agents and tour operators that may work for you. Use a combination of direct mail and telephone calls to qualify your leads, and then make personal sales calls on those leads that show promise.

Restaurant, Lounge, and Functions   Restaurant, lounge and function promotion is basically a matter of evaluating the relative strengths of your local media. Newspapers, radio, TV, and poster distribution could all be effective.

Rolling Green Revisited

Having gone through the process of formulating a market plan, let's go back and apply these steps to our Rolling Green case study. To really have merit, a market-

20

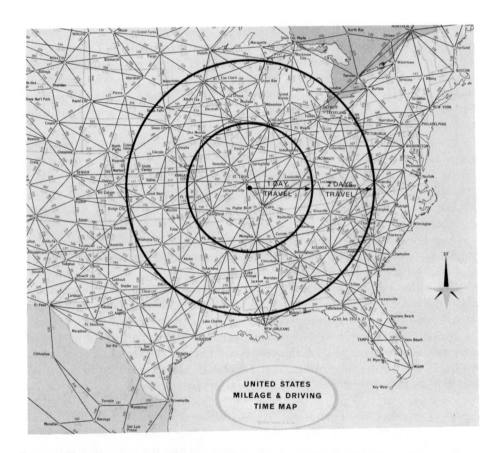

ing strategy must be workable and practical. In developing the case study we hope to give the reader a true feel for the importance of establishing a plan. A the same time, we will be laying the groundwork for the study and development of the convention and meeting market.

The suggestions in the case study should help to stimulate the summer demand for the Rolling Green Resort, but a different strategy should be employed for creating the off-season convention and meeting business. It is the selling and servicing of this market to which this book is addressed. With the Rolling Green Resort case study to prepare the way, the ensuing chapters will deal in detail with every aspect of the convention business.

Appendix E offers another marketing/sales plan. The reader is encouraged to compare it with the Rolling Green Resort plan.)

Rolling Green Revisited   Case Study

When you read the case study, you undoubtedly picked out many glaring shortcomings. There are areas obviously being neglected which could well be capitalized on. New markets need to be explored, requiring new channels of promotion. If you were to act immediately on these suppositions, failing to outline your objectives and to form a clear-cut plan, your efforts probably would fall short of maximizing the resort's market potential.

Your first move should be to assess the problem. As sales manager, you have been asked to counteract mediocre sales volumes and increase volume to improve the profit picture. Your overall objective might be to increase net profit by 5 percent the first year.

Analysis of Rolling Green Establishment
Examine the buildings and grounds. The resort has 320 modern guest rooms. There is a nice dining room, a ballroom for 600, and a kitchen to accommodate both. There is also a lower level with several unused rooms. Why aren't they used? What can you do to fill them?

Next, check the building exterior, parking lot, exterior lighting, and general landscaping. Are they all in good repair? Do they speak well of your establishment? Do the grounds give the observer a "clean" feeling? Is the exterior generally well kept, or is it run-down? A clean, respectable-looking establishment is most essential to the first impression.

What does the surrounding area offer? Are there scenic opportunities that are not being capitalized on? The historic battlefield, picturesque wooded area, and river activities might all be merchandised in a greater way.

Definition of the Market
To effectively increase sales it is necessary first to define the market to be approached. Individual guests are the main source of business. According to the information given, most of the business is summer transients, with a small pick-up for a few weeks in the winter. What is needed is a marketing strategy to extend this seasonal trade. Why the pick-up in the winter? Is it due to the Christmas season? The ski season? These questions need to be answered.

Conventions, group meetings, and tours should be considered as new sources of business for the off-season. The sales gaps could also be filled with banquet and function business. The nearby town of Forest Glen should not be overlooked as a source of banquet trade.

Determination of Characteristics of Present and Prospective Markets
Examination of the registration cards for the Rolling Green should reveal important demographic characteristics and geographic location of the resort's business. A chart, as shown in figure 1.3, might be drawn showing areas within a one- and two-day traveling distance from the resort.

A quick check will tell you the number of conventioneers, tourists, transients, and salespersons who come through the establishment. The length of stay also can be recorded. General observations made by employees should give a good idea of some of the interests of the average guest. From this data, specific plans of action can be formulated.

Setting the Budget

Once the nature of the markets is determined and the action to be taken specified, you should undertake the technical aspects of implementation. A budget needs to be determined for each source of business.

The *market survey method* brings into play all the market research you have done earlier. This is exactly what the name implies—a survey of the various kinds of business and a determination of the relative importance of each. Individual guest, convention and meeting, tour and travel, and function and banquet business are all markets that need to be considered, with an eye toward which ones need to be better developed. Here is a sample budget that might be constructed for the Rolling Green.

Individual Guest Sales

Newspaper advertising	$12,000
Rack brochures, amortized over 2 years	6,000
Crisscross advertising piece	4,500
	$22,500

Tour and Travel Sales

Travel agent blitz	3,600
Trade journal advertising	8,400
	12,000

Convention and Meeting Sales

Magazine advertising, including art costs	13,500
Convention brochure, including photography	3,600
Direct-mail advertising (4-piece mailing with reply cards sent out every 3 months)	3,900
Film presentation (16 mm)	6,000
	27,000
Agency Costs	18,000
Less Commissions	4,500
	13,500
TOTAL	$75,000

Reaching the Target Areas

Specific methods of implementing proposed plans now need to be evaluated and selected, along with the type of media to be used in the general promotion.

If business seems to come from certain areas, such as Chicago, Kansas City, or Indianapolis (fig. 1.3), a special effort should be made to increase promotion in these areas. Media advertising and direct mailing to previous guests could be used effectively.

The interests of the guests is a very important facet to consider in marketing strategy. If the Rolling Green's guests show certain interests, such as fishing or hiking, your promotional attempts should be aimed at appealing to them, perhaps through advertising in selective publications.

Importance of Convention Business

As sales manager of the Rolling Green, it would be prudent for you to assess how profitable conventions might be for your operation. After all, if the revenue does not justify the expense, it would be foolish to make a concerted effort for the convention market.

Group business is comprised of two major segments: corporate meetings and association meetings.

According to the most recently published figures by *Meetings and Conventions* magazine, more than 197,000 association meetings (international, national, state, and regional) are held annually. In addition, associations sponsor numerous educational seminars annually. Attendance at these association meetings and seminars is in excess of 31 million.

The corporate market is even larger, with more than 706,000 corporate meetings held annually in hotels and motels throughout the country. These meetings, for training directors, salespersons, distributors, dealers, and management personnel, range in size from a dozen persons to several thousand.

The expenditures by these groups are staggering. Of the three types of visitor groups—conventioneers, businesspeople, and vacationers—conventioneers are the heaviest spenders. A study done by the San Francisco Convention and Visitors Bureau and the Institute of Business and Economic Research (fig. 1.4) shows that conventioneers contribute an average of $612 per visit to the local economy. Of every dollar spent by convention-goers, nearly 50 percent was spent in the hotel for lodging and restaurant expenses, and probably an additional 15 percent could be allotted to entertainment and retail shops within the hotel.

Meetings and Conventions magazine has estimated the total dollar effect of the corporate market to be over seven billion. That's a big chunk of business, and it should be obvious by now why group meetings play such an important part in a hotel's sales efforts.

Clearly, conventions would mean dollars for the Rolling Green Resort.

24

Fig. 1.4 Spending by visitor group. (Courtesy of the San Francisco Convention and Visitors Bureau and the Institute of Business and Economic Research).

SAN FRANCISCO CONVENTION AND VISITOR STUDY

SPENDING BY VISITOR GROUP

	Convention-Goers	Business Only	Pleasure-Vacation
Average Total Spending per Trip (Adjusted for inflation)	$612.37	$359.77	$481.81
Average Stay (days)	5.02	5.15	3.94

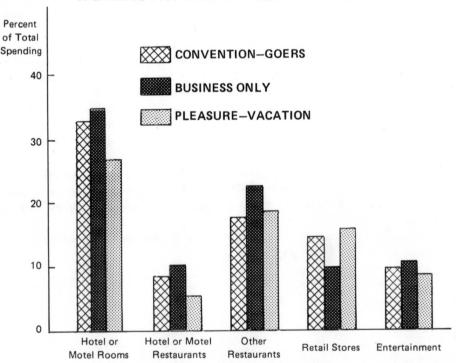

SPENDING PATTERN BY VISITOR GROUP

Study Questions

1. Convention business has been cited throughout this chapter as an important segment of a hotel's overall marketing plan. List several reasons why group business is valuable.

2. Marketing is not synonymous with sales. Distinguish between the two and give reasons why the distinction must be made.

3. Discuss the relationship between room rates, occupancy, and room sales within the context of future hotel room demand.

4. What is meant by the marketing mix?

5. List the five steps in formulating a market plan and apply them to a hotel you are familiar with.

6. What five basic target areas were mentioned by Frank and Adams? Discuss the best ways to reach and sell each of these prospects.

7. Figure 1.4 showing the spending pattern by visitor groups reveals an area where hotels are not capitalizing on their convention trade. Study the chart and point out this problem area.

1 paragraph

Outline

I. Group Size

    A. Function Rooms
    B. Equipment Needs
    C. Several Meetings Simultaneously

II. Sell What You Have

III. Physical Appearance

IV. Property Analysis Checklist

2

It is a rare hotel property that cannot house *some* kind of meeting. But it makes sense to analyze your property to determine which types of meetings would be best for your hotel. Which kinds of events can you serve well? Which kinds fit best into your marketing plans? There are many factors to be considered, but you should keep in mind that it is better to go after meetings you can handle efficiently and well than to go after anything you can possibly sell.

Throughout this book, the term *property* is used within the context of hotels. We recognize, however, that hotels come in many styles and shapes, and that many different names are given to properties that house conventions. In addition, hotels are not the only facilities chosen by meeting planners. Meeting sites include:

1. resort hotels
2. commercial hotels
3. suburban hotels
4. airport hotels
5. large motels and motor hotels
6. condominium resorts
7. cruise ships
8. universities
9. company meeting rooms
10. specialized meeting centers

The concepts presented throughout this book may be applied to any of these facilities.

Group Size

Certainly, a prime consideration in analyzing your property is the group size. After all, your guest rooms and meeting rooms have to accommodate the group. So, unless you are working with other hotels, the number of guest rooms and the number and size of your meeting/public rooms will automatically rule out the solicitation of groups above a certain size.

A management decision is called for at this point. Some hotels will sell out completely to a convention event, while others feel that this is not desirable. If a hotel normally caters to a business clientele or casual travelers, the management might prefer to hold back some of the guest room capacity to accommodate regular trade. There is a certain risk in sending a regular customer away, even if you arrange for him to stay at a nearby hotel. He may resent it, or having sampled your competitor, may elect to stay there in the future.

It is very hard to determine a blanket policy on the proper percentage of room capacity that can be committed to a convention. The *location* of the hotel is an important factor. Do you get walk-in business on a fairly regular basis? At some hotels almost all business is based on advance reservations, with little off-the-street business. This is generally true of resort properties. Downtown or airport locations enjoy more drop-in business for obvious reasons.

The *time of the week* for a proposed meeting is another key factor. A hotel like the Essex House in New York City enjoys much commercial business that keeps it busy from Mondays to Thursdays. So a meeting scheduled to begin on Friday and run through the weekend would meet with an enthusiastic welcome. Most managers would gladly commit themselves fully for all the room reservations they could get under such circumstances. On the other hand, a resort property may enjoy high occupancy on the weekends and so would be happy to delegate all its rooms to a weekday group.

Take note, too, of the *kind of meeting organization* involved. If you are going to commit a high percentage or all of your rooms to an event, you need some assurance that the rooms will be occupied. As we shall discuss later, association conventions are attended at the members' option, so the exact number attending varies. On the other hand, the number attending a corporate meeting is more dependable. The number told to turn up usually does.

Making a decision on room commitment is a two-edged sword. If you commit all or most of your rooms to an association, you may find yourself turning away regular business as you exceed your capacity. If you hold back some of these rooms, you have the extra capacity for regular customers or for a heavier association turnout. But you could find yourself with vacant rooms on your hands. Hopefully, by the reservation cutoff date you will be full or will be able to make a better judgment on whether to hold the rooms or to release them. In any case, the size of the group plays a very important role.

Function Rooms

The number of meeting rooms you have available for any function also must be considered in your analysis. Some meetings, such as a lecture, require little more than a large auditorium-type room. There may not be even a single food function. Other types of meetings, such as most conventions, require a variety of rooms. Perhaps a large auditorium setup, an exhibit hall, and several small rooms for workshops or committee meetings will do it. Rooms for food functions generally will be needed. Your property just may not have such facilities or enough of them. How-

29

Fig. 2.1 The American Management Association meeting room at the Boca Raton Hotel in Boca Raton, Florida, designed to the specifications of the AMA. It is regarded as one of the best meeting rooms in the world for business meetings. (Courtesy of the Boca Raton Hotel and Club).

ever, a number of hotels do a great deal of business with meeting planners who require no exhibit space at all or just a number of small rooms.

It is vital that you examine your property coldly and objectively to determine what it is best suited for. You and your property are better off not selling something you cannot serve satisfactorily.

Many hotel people judge capacity solely by the capacity of their largest room or largest two rooms. But there is a great deal of meetings business that needs only small rooms, perhaps a number of them, near each other if not actually adjoining. Suites can be used quite easily for such meetings. And don't forget other types of rooms that can be pressed into service—sample rooms, indoor tennis courts, and card rooms, for example.

William Cox, architect for the Boca Raton Hotel in Boca Raton, Florida, said in a speech at an American Hotel & Motel Association meeting that his firm studied a number of hotels throughout the world in an attempt to arrive at an ideal design and layout of function rooms for a convention-oriented property.[1] He concluded

1. William Cox, "Design Guidelines for Convention Resorts," (Highlights of meeting of the American Hotel & Motel Association's Resort Committee).

that to achieve maximum guest comfort a different type of facility would be needed for servicing groups than for catering to individual guests.

His firm's study identified two general types of facilities: (1) older properties with many small- and medium-sized function rooms that lacked the flexibility to service larger groups and (2) newer hotels with fewer small rooms and one or two large halls designed for banquets but not suited for training meetings.

After thorough research, Mr. Cox recommended the following design guidelines to the Boca Raton management:

1. A large hall capable of seating and feeding at one time the total number of guests the house is designed to accommodate.
2. Meeting rooms for groups ranging in size from 20 to 100. The total area of these rooms should equal or exceed that of the banquet hall.
3. Large and small meeting rooms that can be partitioned easily and quickly to adapt to individual group requirements.
4. Built-in audio and visual aids in each meeting room, with individual control stations in each possible subdivision of the space. The speaker should be able to control lights, sound, and projection from a single station.
5. Stage facilities in the main banquet room for the production of musical shows or a single performer.
6. Exhibit space with adequate electrical service, water, and gas. Another special requirement: Doorways must be high enough and wide enough to accommodate a tractor-trailer.

Certainly the function room criteria outlined by Cox can apply to any property seriously considering the convention business. Whether you are adding new convention facilities or merely analyzing your present function space, these guidelines should be studied.

A survey done by Jack Knight, managing director of the Kingsmill Inn in Williamsburg, Virginia, is also worthy of examination. Knight asked 300 meeting planners this question: *What aspects of a meeting facility do you consider most essential to the success of serious business meetings?*

The results of this questionnaire are shown in figure 2.2. The most common concerns expressed by meeting planners are ranked according to the frequency mentioned.

Equipment Needs

Hotels vying for convention business also must inventory the equipment requirements for servicing groups. Function rooms often are not sufficient within them-

Fig. 2.2 Ranking of the most important criteria in servicing business meetings, from a survey of 300 meeting planners. (From "What Do Conference Planners Really Want?" *Resort Management*, Used with permission).

Ranking of 300 meeting planners' responses to the question, What aspects of a meeting facility do you consider most essential to the success of serious business meetings?

1.	Front desk attitude (registration and staff courtesy)	81%
2.	Conference coordinator (resort staff)	76%
3.	Meeting room comfort, including decor, atmosphere, and business environment	67%
4.	Meeting room acoustics and lack of distracting noises	63%
5.	Meeting room lighting, audiovisual equipment, and supplies	62%
6.	Follow-through by resort staff	61%
7.	Abundant recreation and easy acess (golf, tennis, game room, etc.)	58%
8.	Check-out procedures	51%
9.	Wake-up and message service	34%
10.	Laundry and valet service	23%
11.	Provisions for female conferees	18%
12.	Food service—quality, speed of service	18%
13.	Properly handled coffee breaks	16%
14.	Adequate restrooms	15%
15.	Sightseeing and ladies' program	13%

---

selves. Today's meeting planner also considers the suitability of the hotel's equipment when he or she is selecting a site. Chairs, tables, platforms, audiovisual equipment, and electrical outlets are just a few of the requirements designated by most executives. Part II of this text, "Convention Service," deals in depth with the equipment used for servicing groups. Size, quantity, and specifications are presented for every type of equipment used.

It is wise for a hotel to prepare a printed list of its group business equipment. Kinds, quantity, and locations should be noted. In addition, the hotel should prepare a list of equipment that can be obtained from local suppliers; a checklist format is particularly desirable. This itemization can serve both as a selling tool when presented to the meeting planner and as an inventory list for the hotel.

Several Meetings Simultaneously

There are more small meetings than large. More than 75 percent of all corporate meetings have fewer than 100 in attendance. If you are to do much business in the convention field, you must be able to house more than one meeting simultaneously.

Naturally, this is not the case when you virtually sell out the house, but most often the function book[2] fills up with a number of more modest events.

Handling several smaller meetings calls for careful planning. You may not be negotiating with both groups at the same time, so you must take care not to commit all your public space to one group, leaving you with no facilities for the other. Traffic patterns must be carefully planned to avoid confusion and congestion. Give thought, too, to the proximity of very different kinds of groups. Holding a training session next door to a college reunion is asking for trouble.

You may find it extremely profitable to go after smaller meetings. To begin with, there are more of them. And smaller meeting organizers are generally not as demanding of price and concessions, often can offer much repeat business, and tax your staff less in serving them.

It is most helpful to come to some kind of decision as to what kinds of meetings you want to handle and can handle well. It will make your sales and marketing job much easier to execute.

Sell What You Have

Of course, considerations other than meeting room size and equipment should be examined. Many kinds of meetings cite other characteristics of the hotel to stimulate attendance. This is obviously true of resort properties. Geographic location is another non-meeting feature that could make your hotel attractive.

If you can find out *why* a meeting is being held, you can go after the business more intelligently. A workshop sales training session may be easy to sell for an airport or downtown hotel.

But such locations might be most difficult to sell if there is an incentive aspect in attending the meeting. Many corporations offer trips to their employees as an inducement for increasing sales; automobile dealerships, insurance companies, and appliance distributors are noted for this. With no slur intended, a meeting held in downtown Philadelphia or at O'Hare Airport holds no incentive attractiveness. You should be able to see at this point that a representative from a Miami or Las Vegas property would be more likely to end up with the business.

On the other hand, a quick meeting to train the sales staff about some new development may be just the thing for that Philadelphia or Chicago hotel to sign up

2. The function book is the master listing of all activities scheduled in the hotel. Chapter 7 offers a thorough discussion of the control and importance of the function book.

with little hassle. A suburban motel may be able to capitalize on the freedom from distraction that its location offers.

Physical Appearance

Every hotel should evaluate its appearance and condition. Physical appearance to a great extent determines the sales promotion used. Meeting planners form a positive or negative first impression from appearance. A hotel with a neat, eye-catching appearance is a step ahead of a more lackluster competitor.

With this in mind, many new hotels are employing the wide-open atrium design (fig. 2.3). Hyatt, Marriott, Hilton, and others are building with aesthetics in mind. Waterfalls, gardens, and landscaping are becoming common in lobby areas. The approach is to blend the building into the landscaping, giving the effect of a city within a city.

What factors should be considered in evaluating your property? Externally, the entrances, grounds, and exterior construction should be assessed with a critical eye for improvement. Internally, the guest rooms, function rooms, public space, and lobby areas should be taken into account. Factors for evaluating each area include traffic flow, accessibility, eye appeal, and compatibility with surroundings.

Try this exercise. Place yourself in the role of a convention organizer. Write down the characteristics of your event. What features would you look for in a hotel site? Write them down.

Now place yourself in the position of a company sales manager in need of a meeting site for a national sales staff of 200 men and women. Rough out a program. What kind of facility do you want? What kind of location? Downtown or secluded off-season resort? What are the effects of transportation on your selection? Is price a factor?

A training director has other needs. Where would you set up for frequent meetings of just thirty persons or so? You want quiet and freedom from distractions. You need much audiovisual support. Easy access is a must.

Now swing back to your role as hotel convention sales manager. What is your property best suited for? Are you going to be the kind of salesperson who admits to selling anything you can talk someone into signing? It just doesn't work for the long haul, especially in the convention business, where you want—and need—repeat business. It costs too much to get the customer the first time not to try to get him again and again.

The answer lies in frank and brutal appraisal of your property. There is a base of honest sales appeal for *every* property. If this were not so, the new and glamo-

Fig. 2.3 Wide-open atrium construction used in many newer convention hotels. This is the Atrium at the Hyatt Regency O'Hare. (Courtesy of the Hyatt Corporation).

rous hotels would do all the business. Back up your word! An honest approach to your property is the only answer—make your property sound like something it isn't, and you are only fooling yourself, certainly not the experienced meeting planner.

Property Analysis Checklist

Following is a sample property analysis checklist. The first step in a market plan is to analyze your product. Whether you are selling shoes, automobiles, or the services of a hotel, you must know exactly what you have to offer. *Do this in writing.* While it may seem superfluous to write everything down, only when you know your property thoroughly can you effectively sell it.

What is my property?
- [ ] resort
- [ ] hotel
- [ ] inn
- [ ] hotel-condominium
- [ ] motel

How large am I?
- [ ] number of guest rooms, types
- [ ] number of guests I can accommodate
- [ ] number of restaurant seats
- [ ] meeting space availability, banquet rooms, exhibit area
- [ ] how many guest rooms can be assigned to group business

Where am I located?
- [ ] distance to airport, downtown, other modes of transportation
- [ ] distance to industrial centers, major attractions
- [ ] by what highways do my customers arrive
- [ ] how large is the city
- [ ] how large are neighboring cities
- [ ] closest competitors: names, distances, and number of rooms

How established is my business?
- [ ] what percent is repeat
- [ ] what is my image in the community
- [ ] what is my position in the market place

☐ what months, days, and hours is my business best
☐ how much is referral business
☐ what upcoming changes might affect my business
☐ is business seasonal

In what condition are my facilities?
☐ age: old and run-down or modern and clean
☐ condition of exterior, main entrance, parking area, grounds, lobby
☐ condition of guest rooms, hallways, public space, recreation areas
☐ how much is spent on maintenance and repairs
☐ condition of furnishings, mattresses, linen, audiovisual equipment

What recreation facilities are offered?
☐ golf course, swimming, lawn sports, boating, skiing, tennis
☐ what facilities are nearby
☐ what new facilities might be considered
☐ historic, scenic, and amusement attractions in the area
☐ what is the atmosphere—quiet, ritzy, fast-moving
☐ what natural advantages do I have, man-made attractions, unique features

How good is my restaurant and lounge?
☐ menu, specialties, food quantity, coffee, salads, soups
☐ decor, glassware, china, silver
☐ quality- and quantity-control procedures
☐ am I using the right-sized glasses: wine, rock, highball
☐ how good is competition's food, entertainment, service

How service-minded are my employees?
☐ front desk, cashiers, maids, waitresses
☐ how many complaints and compliments, and their frequency
☐ employee relations, employee training, suggestion box
☐ organizational structure: each employee with one boss

What conference and meeting facilities do I offer?
☐ what is the ideal-sized group, what is the maximum-sized group
☐ meeting equipment available: tables, chairs, audiovisual, risers, exhibits
☐ how many function rooms; how flexible are they
☐ outside services available: manpower, ground handlers, audiovisual
☐ what overflow facilities are available for large groups
☐ how many meetings and/or food functions can be held concurrently
☐ are sound systems and lighting adequate

Every property has its appeal. Sort out the true attractions from the nonsense. If you can't find any sales appeal at all, maybe you shouldn't be selling. Certainly some hotels are better suited for the convention business than others. Find your place in the market. Study the competition. Your physical condition and theirs. Your clientele and image and theirs. Your location and theirs. Your rates and theirs.

You may be in the right part of town or in the right part of the country. You may be isolated or at the crossroads. You may offer a group the option of being the only meeting in the house, which pleases some. You may offer a glamorous resort at low off-season rates, which may appeal to others.

Analyze your property—from the viewpoint of different kinds of customers. Concentrate on selling those types that will accept what you offer. Concentrate on that and you'll achieve your share of success.

Study Questions

1. What kinds of questions should a hotel sales manager ask before going after a particular piece of convention business?
2. From the study done by Jack Knight of the Kingsmill Inn (fig. 2.2) what are the most essential criteria in servicing conventions?
3. Apply the "property analysis checklist" to a hotel property you are familiar with. Make recommendations and applications by tying this into the market plan you formulated in study question five of chapter 1.

I. Definitions

    A. Convention
    B. Conference
    C. Congress
    D. Forum
    E. Symposium
    F. Lecture
    G. Seminar
    H. Workshop
    I. Clinic
    J. Panel
    K. Institute
    L. Exhibition
    M. Meeting
    N. Usage Not Precise

II. Who Holds Meetings?

    A. Associations
        1. Trade Associations
        2. Professional and Scientific Associations
        3. Veterans and Military Associations
        4. Educational Associations
        5. Technical Societies
    B. Fraternal Organizations
    C. Corporate Organizations
    D. Nonprofit Organizations
        1. Governmental Agencies
        2. Labor Unions
        3. Religious Groups
    E. Insurance Groups
    F. Where the Delegate Spends Money

Hotel people should be experts at the hotel business. If you go after the convention part of the hotel business, you owe it to yourself, your employer, and your clients to be quite expert at it. The more you know about conventions, the more able you are to help your clients achieve the kinds of meetings they want.

Such assistance does not go unnoticed by meeting planners. They'll come back to the scene of a successful event. And knowledgeable planners often will follow an expert hotel person from property to property. Develop the reputation for expertise and your following will be loyal. This is especially true of the convention field.

Definitions

Meetings fall under many names. It would indeed be simpler if all such events were just called *meetings*. After all, that's what they basically are. But that's not the way it is. There are a number of not-quite synonyms for the term, with nuances of difference.

It is important for hotel people to understand these differences in order to fully grasp the kind of event the client is trying to produce and to help him or her carry it out. Much of it has to do with the projection of a desired image. For example, a *seminar* connotes something more cerebral than a *convention*. A *conference* in Chicago may be termed a *congress* in Geneva. A *workshop* conjures up a picture of a small group in shirt-sleeves, while a *lecture* promises a more formal presentation to a passive audience. In the interest of simplicity, we refer to the *convention* business, but we are actually dealing with the entire spectrum of meetings of all types.

Convention

The most commonly used term in the field is *convention*. The dictionary tells us that a convention is a meeting of delegates for action on particular matters. These may be matters of politics, trade, science, or technology, among others.

Today's convention usually involves a general session and supplementary smaller meetings, most commonly committee meetings. Conventions are produced both with and without exhibits. Most conventions have a repetitive cycle, the most common of which is annual. Market reports, revealing of new products, and mapping of company strategy are common objectives of a convention.

The general session usually requires a ballroom or large auditorium, where information is given to the whole group. Specific problems then are discussed in smaller groups using a number of small break-out rooms.

Conference

A *conference* is a near-synonym for a convention, usually implying much discussion and participation. The word convention is used more frequently in trade circles for regular meetings of a general nature. The term conference is used frequently in technical and scientific areas, although it is used in trade as well. The differences are primarily those of semantics rather than execution. A conference program commonly deals with specific problems or developments and may or may not have smaller break-out meetings. Conferences may be small or large in attendance.

Congress

The term *congress* is most commonly used in Europe and in international events. It usually refers to an event similar to a conference in nature. Oddly enough, only in the United States is the term used to designate a legislative body. Attendance at a congress varies a great deal.

Forum

A meeting featuring much back-and-forth discussion, generally led by panelists or presenters, is often called a *forum.* Much audience participation is to be expected, with all sides of a question aired by both the panelists and the audience. Two or more speakers might take opposing sides and address the audience rather than each other. Generally a moderator will summarize points of view and lead the discussion. The audience is usually allowed to ask questions, so table microphones often must be supplied by the hotel.

Symposium

The format of a *symposium* is very similar to that of a forum, except that conduct tends to be more formal in a symposium. Whether by individuals or panels, the method is one of presentations. Some audience participation is anticipated, but there is generally less of the give-and-take that characterizes a forum.

41

Fig. 3.1 Conference seating arrangement with a raised head table. This is the Ballroom at the Hyatt Regency San Francisco in Embarcadero Center.

Lecture

The *lecture* is even more formal or structured, using individual presentation, often by just one expert. It may or may not be followed by questions from the audience. Lectures may be just about any size, of course.

Seminar

The *seminar* format tries to get away from the idea of a presenter or presenters addressing an audience from a platform. A seminar usually involves much participation, much give-and-take, a sharing of knowledge and experience by all. It usually is under the supervision of a discussion leader. This format obviously lends itself only to relatively small groups; when such a meeting grows, it generally changes to a forum or symposium.

Workshop

The *workshop* format calls for general sessions involving only small groups that deal with specific problems or assignments. Whether or not the term is used, the workshop format is commonly used by training directors for skill training and drills. The participants actually train one another as they share new knowledge, skills, and insights into problems. Obviously, it is characterized by face-to-face dealing, with a great deal of participation by all.

Clinic

Used a great deal in training activity, the *clinic* offers drills and instruction in specific skills. It is almost always limited to small groups.

Panel

The *panel* calls for two or more speakers offering viewpoints or areas of expertise. It is open for discussion among the panelists, as well as with the audience. A panel is always guided by a moderator and may be part of a larger meeting format.

Institute

Conferences, seminars, and workshops are often offered by an *institute,* which is frequently established within a trade or profession to offer extended educational and training opportunities. The term is often used to suggest further meetings on the same topic. For example, an institute might offer continuing training programs every quarter of the year.

Exhibition

The *exhibition* format is used for display, usually by vendors of goods and services. It may be an adjunct of a convention or conference, or it may stand on its own. Other terms used interchangeably are *exposition, show,* and *trade show.* In Europe such exhibits, generally without any other type of program, are called *trade fairs.*

Meeting

All the terms we've defined represent meetings of a sort. When none of the terms seems to apply, the event can always be called simply a *meeting.* This is particularly true when all the attendees are members of a single organization meeting to discuss organizational affairs. The subject could just as accurately be termed the meetings business as the convention business.

Usage Not Precise

Why bother with such terminology at all, especially from the hotel viewpoint? Many clients use the terms inaccurately and loosely, so why not simply call them all conventions or meetings?

The answer lies in the efforts toward professionalism. Proper terminology is an important communication aid, and accurate communication is very much needed in the convention business. Certainly those in the field should understand all such terms and use them correctly.

It is important, however, to recognize that such terms are not scientific terms, but loose, descriptive ones. They can help people work together to achieve a tone or image at an event, and in that sense, they are important.

Who Holds Meetings?

Once you have decided that convention business, whatever the terminology, is worth going after, the next question deals with locating the people and organizations that hold meetings.

Associations

The most visible convention organizers are the many associations throughout the country—indeed, throughout the world, because many of them are truly international. Associations vary in size and nature. Their scope ranges from small regional organizations through statewide associations to national and international ones.

Perhaps the best-known group to hotel sales managers is the American Society of Association Executives (ASAE). This group's membership consists of meeting planners and key decision makers who play major roles in the selection of cities and hotels for their conventions.

Trade Associations

Trade conventions are usually considered the most lucrative form of meeting business because their memberships are composed mostly of executives who have made it in business. Such conventions are often held in conjunction with exhibits.

A good example of such a group in the hospitality industry is the National Restaurant Association, which meets annually in Chicago with more than 110,000 in attendance. Big industrial suppliers of kitchen equipment and restaurant supplies do a great amount of entertaining during the convention.

It is a rare trade that doesn't have at least one association. Many have several national ones, involving different levels of the trade. It is common for the manufacturers in a trade to have their own association; the wholesalers and distributors to have theirs; and the retailers, still a third.

The photographic industry shows this pattern. There is the Photographic Marketing Association, whose members are retailers and photofinishers. They hold an annual convention of national status and a regional one six months later. The National Association of Photographic Manufacturers is a smaller group made up exclusively of domestic manufacturers. All members meet once a year and boards and committees meet more frequently. The Photographic Manufacturers and Distributors Association has a broader membership base made up of foreign and domestic companies. In addition, there are a number of regional associations of independent camera dealers that hold regional exhibits and meetings. All of these organizations are trade associations.

Professional and Scientific Associations

The numerous associations in the professional and scientific fields also are inveterate meeting holders. Their subject range is far and wide, but they share a love for meetings and conferences. Each profession has its national association, as well as state chapters.

Organizations such as the American Medical Association and the American Bar Association are well known to almost everyone. The Hotel Sales Marketing Association (HSMA) is a good example of a professional group in the hospitality industry. Hotel salespeople meet annually for a major get-together and hold a number of regional and state workshops throughout the year.

Veterans and Military Associations

Meetings are held by both "active-status" and veteran reunion groups of the military associations. These groups have been known to get quite rowdy but are often good spenders. Such groups have large annual conventions and usually are interested in a resort-recreation atmosphere.

Educational Associations

Elementary, high school, and college teachers and others affiliated with academic programs are prime sources of convention business. They hold a number of national meetings, and every state has a teachers association of some sort as well. Even educators in the lodging and foodservice industry have their own association, the Council on Hotel, Restaurant and Institutional Education (CHRIE).

One aspect of the educational group business that makes it particularly attractive to many hotels is the time of year these groups meet. While they are not excessive spenders, they frequently meet during the slow summer months. Figure 3.2 shows a month-by-month breakdown of the corporate and association convention business. Educational associations meeting in the summer months are excellent sources of business, providing meetings when hotels most need them.

Technical Societies

Associations also are found among technical professions. The Society of Motion Picture and Television Engineers holds two national conventions a year. The Professional Photographers of America holds a national event annually, and most states have versions of the society that hold annual conventions of their own.

Think of any profession or career and you'll find at least one association. Librarians, teachers, hospital administrators, engineers—all have associations.

Fraternal Organizations

There are organizations outside the professional and business worlds that also have their events. National fraternities and sororities generally confirm their annual meetings two to three years in advance. Like educational associations, they often meet during the summer months and so are a prime market for hotels with a slow third quarter. The meeting planners for these national organizations generally are paid executives.

The annual flower show and stamp show in New York City are mammoth exhibits attended by tens of thousands. There are many others. You have heard of

Fig. 3.2 Monthly convention meeting pattern. Chart has particular importance for selling fraternal and educational associations, which normally meet during the slow months of July and August.

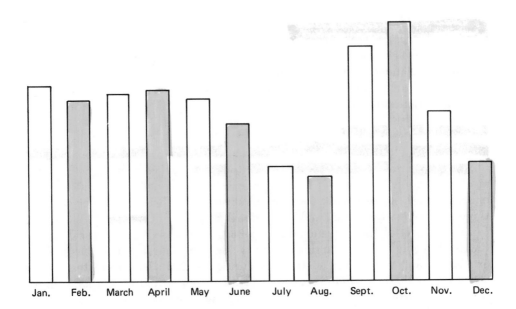

| Jan. | Feb. | March | April | May | June | July | Aug. | Sept. | Oct. | Nov. | Dec. |

the American Legion, the Daughters of the American Revolution, the American Association of University Women. There are gun clubs, bridge clubs, and bowling leagues, to name but a few.

A European hotelman once remarked to us that it was his impression that every American felt a compulsion to belong to at least one organization. Each organization meets in a regular cycle as part of its raison d'etre, holding and stimulating attendance with that great yearly affair.

Corporate Organizations

Less visible, but of extreme importance, is the corporate meeting. Corporate meetings can be likened to an iceberg: A small tip protrudes above the surface while a huge mass floats beneath it. Companies often have no need or desire to publicize their meetings, but meet they do. And often. They hold small meetings, large meetings, and middle-sized meetings. Modern thought among business executives stresses communication, and one of the fundamental methods of intra-company communication is the meeting.

Corporate meetings are very different from association meetings. They have to be sold differently and serviced differently, as we shall discuss in chapter 5. Company meetings are a prime part of the conventions market, and probably are the most rapidly growing segment.

Attending conventions and conferences is very definitely a part of professional and business activity. Such expenses as transportation, lodging, food, entertainment of clients, and registration fees are tax-deductible as business or professional expenses. Companies that stage meetings for dealers or their own staffs also may deduct the cost of such events as business expenses. This has been a strong stimulant to meetings and conventions. It is also a strong factor in site selection, as those who attend look to such business trips as quasi vacations as well.

Nonprofit Organizations

There are many nonprofit organizations that just don't fit into the above slots, but they take no back seat when it comes to meetings.

All of us have witnessed political conventions on television. The camera shows us only the main assembly floor, but give some thought to the demand for smaller meeting rooms, suites, food functions, and so on. The traditional "smoke-filled room" is invariably in a hotel.

The story is repeated on a more modest scale on the state and regional levels. The same is true of labor unions, fund-raising organizations, foundations, and educational institutions. All add to the market. Some hotels do a fine amount of business with weekend seminars on sex and marital problems, women's role in the new world, and social problems, to mention a few.

The meetings of nonprofit organizations are just like those of the associations. We list them separately, but they are sold and serviced just like their cousins, the trade and professional associations.

Governmental Agencies

Many branches of the government have a need to hold meetings off government premises. Sometimes these meetings deal with government employees, and other times with the public. The Department of Agriculture, the Department of Commerce, the World Health Organization, and other United Nations affiliates are frequent meeting planners. They straddle the line between business associations and quasi-governmental agencies.

These agencies are funded in a variety of ways. Chambers of Commerce are usually membership organizations that are privately funded. The Department of Agriculture, of course, spends public money. The labels are not important so long as you understand how they operate, what their meeting needs are, and how you can sell and serve them efficiently.

(A word may be in order here. There is a love for abbreviations among some associations and governmental agencies that can drive the outsider up the wall. Each association seems to feel that the world is focused on it and that everyone knows what XYZ stands for. It also leads to crossed lines. Take AMA. It can refer to the American Medical Association or the American Management Association, both of which are prolific meeting holders. It takes but a note of caution. You have to listen carefully and take good notes. Be careful to take nothing out of context. After awhile, you'll talk in abbreviations and acronyms, too.)

Labor Unions

Labor unions have become one of the most important economic forces in the world. The largest unions are in the construction, manufacturing, mining, and transportation fields. Figure 3.3 lists the more prominent unions in the United States and their approximate memberships.

Labor unions are organized on four levels: local, state and regional, national, and international. Each level represents countless meetings and conventions, providing a ripe market for hotels. Most union members spend slightly less than the average convention delegate, but they still provide hotels with a sizeable piece of business.

Large labor union conventions are similar to political conventions. They are held every year or every other year and include committee meetings, debates, speeches, and guest speakers. Broad policy and union direction decisions are made and union officials are elected. A convention held every two years governs the membership of the international AFL-CIO. Delegates are sent to this convention from their national unions in accordance with membership size.

Religious Groups

Other nonprofit organizations holding a number of meetings are the many religious denominations throughout the country. Like some other nonprofit groups, they are not traditionally big spenders, but they are nevertheless a viable market. Denominations have become frequent sponsors of seminars and ministerial workshops, in addition to their larger regional and national meetings. Their events frequently begin on Monday and close on Thursday, providing weekend resort properties with business during their slack mid-week periods.

Fig. 3.3 Approximate membership of U.S. labor unions. (From the U.S. Department of Labor).

Name	Membership	Name	Membership
Actors and Artistes of America, Associated	63,000	Musicians, American Federation of	315,000
Air Line Pilots Association, International	27,639	Newspaper Guild, American	32,525
Allied Industrial Workers of America, International Union	86,000	Oil, Chemical and Atomic Workers Int. Union	172,000
Amalgamated Clothing Workers of America	385,000	Packinghouse Workers of America, United	2,600
Bakery and Confectionery Workers International Union of America (Ind.)	145,836	Painters, Decorators and Paperhangers of America, Brotherhood of	207,844
Boilermakers, Iron Ship Builders, Blacksmiths, Forgers and Helpers, Int. Brotherhood of	132,000	Papermakers and Paperworkers, United	389,427
Bricklayers, Masons and Plasterers International Union of America	149,000	Plumbing and Pipe Fitting Industry of the U.S. and Canada, United Association of Journeymen and Apprentices of the	228,000
Bridge, Structural and Ornamental Iron Workers, International Association of	146,900	Post Office Clerks, National Federation of	32,965
Building Service Employees Int. Union	230,000	Printing Pressmen and Assistants' Union of North America, International	123,000
Carpenters and Joiners of America, United Brotherhood of	820,000	Pulp, Sulphite and Paper Mill Workers, International Brotherhood of	165,000
Communications Workers of America	443,275	Railroad Trainmen, Brotherhood of	12,000
Electrical, Radio and Machine Workers, International Union of	165,000	Railway and Steamship Clerks, Freight Handlers, Express and Station Employes, Brotherhood of	238,355
Electrical, Radio and Machine Workers of America, United (Ind.)	290,000	Railway Carmen of America, Brotherhood	103,922
Electrical Workers, Int. Brotherhood of	956,579	Retail Clerks International Association	633,211
Engineers, Int. Union of Operating	200,000	Retail, Wholesale and Department Store Union	643,000
Federal Employees, Natl. Federation of (Ind.)	85,000	Rubber, Cork, Linoleum and Plastic Workers of America, United	182,949
Garment Workers of America, United	25,000	State, County, and Municipal Employes, American Federation of	529,035
Garment Workers' Union, Int. Ladies'	450,000	Steelworkers of America, United	1,400,000
Hod Carriers', Building and Common Laborers' Union of America, International	465,900	Street, Electric Railway and Motor Coach Employes of America, Amalgamated Assoc. of	143,700
Hotel and Restaurant Employees and Bartenders International Union	458,029	Teachers, American Federation of	248,521
Laundry, Cleaning and Dye House Workers International Union (Ind.)	225,000	Teamsters, Chauffeurs, Warehousemen and Helpers of America, International Brotherhood of (Ind.)	1,854,659
Letter Carriers, National Association of	220,000	Telegraphers' Union, The Commercial	30,000
Locomotive Engineers, Brotherhood of (Ind.)	37,000	Telephone Unions, Alliance Independent (Ind.)	50,000
Locomotive Firemen and Enginemen, Brotherhood of	27,000	Textile Workers of America, United	52,000
Longshoremen's Association, International (Ind.)	60,000	Textile Workers Union of America	174,000
Longshoremen's and Warehousemen's Union, International (Ind.)	58,000	Tobacco Workers International Union	33,565
Machinists, International Association of	757,564	Transport Workers Union of America	150,000
Maintenance of Way Employes, Brotherhood of	142,289	Typographical Union, International	115,273
Marine and Shipbuilding Workers of America, Industrial Union of	21,000	United Automobile, Aerospace and Agricultural Implement Workers of America, International Union	1,900,000
Maritime Union of America, National	45,000	United Mine Workers of America (Ind.)	95,000
Meat Cutters and Butcher Workmen of North America, Amalgamated	528,631	Utility Workers Union	60,000
Mine, Mill and Smelter Workers, International Union of (Ind.)	200,000	Woodworkers of America, International	91,000

Fig. 3.4 Breakdown of the approximately one hundred twenty-five dollars that the International Association of Convention and Visitor Bureaus determined was spent by the average association meeting delegate per day at national and international conventions. (Adapted with permission from the International Association of Convention & Visitor Bureaus' Delegate Expenditure Study 1986).

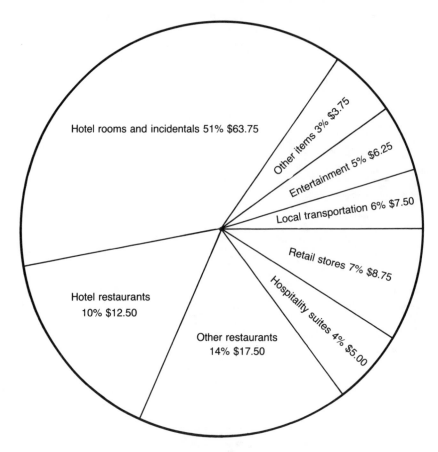

Hotel rooms and incidentals 51% $63.75

Other items 3% $3.75

Entertainment 5% $6.25

Local transportation 6% $7.50

Retail stores 7% $8.75

Hospitality suites 4% $5.00

Hotel restaurants
10% $12.50

Other restaurants
14% $17.50

Insurance Groups

Another important client for the hotel sales manager is the insurance meeting planner. Insurance groups frequently sponsor incentive trips for their top salespeople. While it is free to the delegate, the incentive trip is not planned exclusively to provide recreation; most insurance companies schedule training and sales technique workshops in conjunction with such trips.

Insurance companies frequently require more advance planning than other industries because the incentive trips must be promoted a year in advance. The size and duration of insurance meetings vary widely, thus providing potential for both the large hotel and the small inn. Consequently, insurance clients are important contacts to be developed.

Where the Delegate Spends Money

The International Association of Convention and Visitor Bureaus (IACVB) recently surveyed the meetings field. Its study was to determine how much money the delegate spends during a stay in a city and how he or she spends it. While the figures are only averages and not as specific as the San Francisco study mentioned in chapter 1, they are representative of most convention cities. It is also important to note that only association delegates were surveyed; corporate delegates could be expected to spend five to ten dollars more, as many are on expense accounts.

Figure 3.4 shows a breakdown of delegates' daily expenditures. The IACVB survey found that the total daily expenditure for national and international conventions was about one hundred twenty five dollars.

Study Questions

1. Why is it important for hotel people to understand the differences between various types of meetings after all, aren't all the definitions synonymous?

2. Distinguish between a congress and a conference, a symposium and a workshop, an exhibition and a seminar.

3. Outline steps you would take to reach educational associations and specify why such groups are particularly important to hotels.

4. Discuss the role of abbreviations and acronyms in the convention field. What problems are associated with their use?

5. Figure 3.4, like the San Francisco study in chapter 1, points out a glaring lack of internal sales promotion in that the convention delegate spends more in restaurants outside the hotel than those in the hotel. What sales promotion techniques might be used to induce the convention delegate to spend on in-house restaurants?

Outline

I. Revenue Procedures

II. What Do They Look For?

III. Kinds of Association Meetings

    A. Annual Conventions
    B. Regional Conventions
    C. Conferences
    D. Seminars and Workshops
    E. Board and Committee Meetings

IV. Characteristics of Association Meetings

    A. Cycle and Pattern
    B. Geographic Restrictions
    C. Lead Time
    D. Kind of Sites
    E. Attendance is Voluntary
    F. Convention Duration
    G. Price

V. Who Makes the Decision?

    A. Association Executive
    B. Association President
    C. Committee Chairperson
    D. Board of Directories
    E. Local Influences

VI. How Do You Find Associations?

    A. Directories
    B. Specialized Periodicals
    C. Meeting Associations
    D. Hotel Records

4

In the preceding chapter we delineated the types of meetings and introduced the groups that hold meetings. This chapter and the next two will deal in detail with the d:fferent types of meeting groups: association, corporate, nonprofit, incentive travel, government agencies and so on.

There are about five thousand national and international associations in the United States and about fifteen thousand more on the state and regional level. Each holds a variety of meetings every year. Picture some eighteen million delegates at more than nine thousand national and international conventions and thirty-seven thousand state and regional conventions. Add more than three million at some two hundred thousand educational seminars.

It comes as no surprise, then, to learn that associations spend more than $5 billion a year on such meetings. That's a lot of business, and it warrants careful study of the kinds of meetings associations hold and how you can go after your share of the pot.

Revenue Producers

The convention is of extreme importance to the association. In most cases, it is the group's principal source of revenue. Membership dues range from twenty-five dollars or so a year to several thousand dollars in more affluent associations, but almost every association uses its conventions and meetings as prime sources of money.

Associations earn money from conventions in several ways. One is with exhibits. The group may pay for an exhibit hall or get it free in exchange for the large number of guest rooms booked. It also pays a decorator about fifteen to twenty-five dollars for the decor of each booth unit. But, in turn, the association charges exhibitors anywhere from $300 to $800 for the space.

Registration fees at such events also add to the association's coffers. Sometimes the registration fee is just a few dollars, but it can run to several hundred. It is not uncommon for a convention "package" to cost the delegate several hundred dollars, including a number of meal functions. Not every person attends every event, which adds more to the profits of the convention since the hotel is paid only for the actual number of meal tickets collected or the number of meals the meeting planner guarantees.

Associations earn additional money from the advertising in their publications and programs. And when a participating company sponsors a segment of the program and picks up the tab, the association's costs are further reduced.

Thus, when you consider how important conventions are to membership retention and revenue production, it becomes apparent that these events are ab-

Fig. 4.1 Characteristics of the association meetings market. (By permission of *Successful Meetings* and the International Association of Convention & Visitor Bureaus).

---

annual association meetings expenditure

(based on the national average per delegate as determined by the international Association of Convention and Visitors Bureaus' 1986 Convention Delegate Survey)

	1985 Results	U.S. Cities Only		% Increase
		1985	1986	
Average total expenditure per delegate	$419.26	$453.46	$477.49	5.3
Average daily expenditure per delegate	105.05	122.56	125.66	2.5
Average length of stay per delegate	4.0 nights	3.70	3.80	2.7
Average travel party size	2.5 people	1.80	1.65	−8.3

all meetings and trade shows by attendance

- 50% of all *national* meetings and trade shows have attendances of *300 or less*
- 51% of all *regional* meetings and trade shows have attendances of *300 or less*
- 48% of all *state* meetings and trade shows have attendances of *300 or less*
- 80% of all *national* meetings and trade shows have attendances of *1,000 or less*
- 83% of all *regional* meetings and trade shows have attendances of *1,000 or less*
- 85.4% of all *state* meetings and trade shows have attendances of *1,000 or less*

site selection statistics

Following is a breakdown of areas most commonly used for association meetings and trade shows:

- 51% metropolitan
- 9% resorts
- 40% resorts and metropolitan
- 80% rotate between 3 or more areas
- 12% of all U.S. based associations have met or plan to meet outside the continental U.S.
- 9% of state groups have met, considered or plan to meet outside their respective states

---

solutely essential for the well-being of an association. They constitute a major effort on an association's part, and they are planned and conducted as such.

What Do They Look For?

Site selection is quite important to the success of a convention. Mike Welch, executive director of the Credit Union Executives Society of Madison, Wisconsin, has said:

> We look for good facilities, pleasant weather, an attractive location, and a city that's near the largest concentration of members. We also consider who else is going there and when. For instance, when our annual convention is taking place in a city, we don't want to go there for a seminar within the same year or two.[1]

1. Barbara Leonard, "Regional Seminars: Specialized Communication," *Association and Society Manager* Copyright Barrington Publications, Inc., 825 S. Barrington Ave., Los Angeles, Calif. 90049.

Figure 4.2 Factors Considered Important to Association Meeting Planners in the selection of a facility/hotel. Although the purpose of a meeting ultimately determines the facility selection criteria, the table below gives insight into general factors of importance to the association meeting planner. (Source: The Meetings Market Study conducted by Meetings and Conventions Magazine.)

Factors Considered Very Important	Association Planners	
	For Major Conventions	For Other Meetings
Number, size and caliber of meeting rooms	88%	53%
Number, size and caliber of sleeping rooms	74	38
Quality of food service	72	57
Efficiency of check-in/check-out procedures	56	41
Assignment of one staff person to handle all aspects of meeting	52	36
Availability of meeting support services and equipment such as audio-visual equipment	50	33
Previous experience in dealing with facility and its staff	44	34
Availability of exhibit space	44	6
Number, size and caliber of suites	24	9
Convenience to other modes of transportation	22	18
On-site recreational facilities, i.e., golf, swimming, tennis	22	9
Proximity to shopping, restaurants, off-site entertainment	20	9
Proximity to airport	17	23
Provision of special meeting services, such as pre-registration, special equipment, etc.	14	6
Newness of facility	6	3

Price, too, becomes relevant. What else do the planners look for in making site selections? (fig. 4.2)

An Attractive Location

"Attractive location" doesn't necessarily mean a resort or playground. A location may be attractive to different groups for different reasons. Perhaps a site is very convenient for travel. Chicago enjoys a great deal of convention business because of its central location and great number of airlines and flights. That's very important to many busy groups.

Other groups may like to combine the show with other business. Your city may be in the heart of their business world. Attendance is also easier to stimulate if people don't have to travel too far. Easy driving distance may mean an extra 10 percent registration.

Many groups do like resort locations. You may be able to offer that, or perhaps you are located in great tourist country. It may be the beauty of the scenic Poconos, or the theater and shopping in New York City. Famous and challenging golf courses draw others. In short, you have to offer something attractive to a particular group.

Adequate Meeting Space

The organizer is always concerned about your ability to house the general assembly and smaller sessions. He or she is interested in space for workshops and committee meetings, as well as your ability to handle food functions comfortably without encroaching on the meetings.

Adequate Exhibit Space

As we discussed, exhibits mean money for the association and an attraction for the members. The planners look for adequate exhibit space, located conveniently to housing. Hotels with their own exhibit facilities obviously have an advantage. When larger exhibits require exhibition halls, the preference is for setups near the hotel. Delegates prefer not to have to travel between hotel rooms and exhibit and convention areas.

Enough Guest Rooms

We don't know a single convention organizer who doesn't prefer to house the entire group in a single hotel. Suites are needed in addition to singles, twins, and doubles. When a single hotel can't house the entire group, two or more hotels in close proximity are the most desirable.

Service

Last, but probably most important, the meeting planners look for service. They want some assurance that you have an experienced staff that is interested in doing a good job. Each convention event is a custom job and many things can, and do, go wrong. Convention planners live with such hazards and justly feel that your staff should have the expertise and the desire to keep the show moving. Service is what brings repeat and recommended business.

Kinds of Association Meetings

The first kind of association meetings to come to mind is the *annual convention*. Certainly this is the most visible, but there are other occasions to meet. Lots of planning is required in staging a convention. *Board and committee meetings* are often scheduled for this purpose and may require the meeting room of a hotel property. In addition, *regional conventions, conferences, seminars, and workshops* are conducted throughout the year by most associations. (fig. 4.3)

Annual Conventions

It is a rare association that doesn't have an annual convention. And simple arithmetic in the opening paragraphs of this chapter shows that many have more than one convention a year. The annual convention is a ritual in associations of all types —national, state, and regional.

Attendance varies, of course. Some conventions are truly huge affairs. The Chemical Society draws between 20,000 and 30,000, yet many have fewer than 100. The mean attendance figure is nearly 400 people. They vary only in scale, maintaining similar philosophy and motivation.

More than half of the annual association conventions are held in conjunction with a trade show or exhibit. This is especially true of trade and technical societies. Exhibits are a financial boom to associations, as we've discussed, but conventions are also extremely important to the exhibitors.

There are conventions without exhibits, of course, and it is also not unheard of for a convention to stage a major program with exhibit in one hotel and another program without exhibit in another. And sometimes, an event may be held in a city because of the presence of another convention with an exhibit.

Most annual conventions have a main session attended by everyone and a number of smaller meetings of committees or task forces on specific assignments. Sometimes the general session runs concurrently with the exhibit hours; sometimes they run in tandem so as not to compete for members' attention.

It is a rare convention that doesn't include food functions. As we said, many groups sell a complete convention package that includes registration fees and prepaid tickets to all food functions and special events.

You can see at this point that a convention, especially a large one, calls for a number of rooms of different kinds. You need large rooms for the general assembly, the exhibit, and the food functions; smaller rooms for committee and board meetings, workshops, and smaller food functions; and suites and similar rooms for hospitality centers.

Often a hotel cannot handle an entire convention because of its size, so several hotels may band together to sell an association as a team. The hotel business is odd in that strong competitors often become partners in a project, and both enjoy additional business as a result. Even a piece of a convention event may be profitable, as well as giving the hotel a foot in the door for future business.

Fig. 4.3 Summary of types of Association meetings other than the major convention. (Source: The Meetings Market Study conducted by Meetings and Convention Magazine.)

Type of Meeting	Average # Planned	Average Attendance	Average # Days Duration	Average # of Months Lead Time
Board Meeting	4.2	36	1.9	5.1
Educational Seminars	11.3	122	2.3	6.2
Professional/Technical Meetings	7.3	132	2.4	6.6
Regional/Local Chapter Meetings	10.9	169	2.6	6.1
Other Meetings	8.7	172	3.0	8.6
TOTAL	18.2	120	2.4	6.5

There is another variation of the national convention—the exhibit without convention program. These events, often called *exhibition* or *exposition*, sometimes are not even sponsored by an association but by individual entrepreneurs or companies. These events can bring you business even if you cannot house the exhibit itself. Many an exhibition becomes the focal point of the industry or trade it serves and gives exhibitors the opportunity to hold sales meetings and dealer meetings in conjunction with the event.

Regional Conventions

The major difference between a regional convention of a national organization and one staged by a state or regional association is sponsorship. A state association usually holds an annual meeting for its members within the state, although in recent years state organizations have ventured beyond state borders on occasion (fig. 4.1). Many national associations, even those with affiliated state chapters, hold regional conventions to supplement their national ones. As a rule, the regional event is smaller than the national one both in attendance and size of the exhibit. Again, some regional conventions have exhibits and others don't. There is no rule of thumb.

The major difference, as far as hotel people are concerned, has to do with who makes the decisions about when and where the event will be held. Both state and regional conventions are an important source of business for both large and small hotel properties.

Conferences

Associations have become frequent stagers of conferences, primarily to supplement the annual convention program with a specific program made timely by new developments. The energy crisis of 1974 precipitated a number of conferences in many industries.

The number of conferences held within an industry varies, of course. They have become commonplace in the technical, scientific, and professional worlds. A breakthrough in an electronic process or medical treatment or a change in corporate law or tax structure would bring on a rash of conferences.

Seminars and Workshops

Closely allied to the conference, but on a more modest basis, is the seminar. Association seminars are usually tied in with training and continuing education, such as the training of apprentice craftsmen, the updating of scientific and engineering personnel, or the presentation of marketing developments within an industry. Such seminars usually travel around the country handling small groups. This kind of business is within the scope of almost any hotel property.

Board and Committee Meetings

Association business regularly calls for smaller meetings. The board of directors may meet on a regular basis, and not necessarily in the city of the association office. These meetings are often set in attractive locales as a way of attracting outstanding people to serve, since they are not paid. Attendance at board meetings may range from 10 or 12 up to 200. The hotel that is chosen for such meetings is in a prime position to sell the property for the big national convention.

Committee meetings may range in size from ten to fifty people and are held at varying rates of frequency. These events, too, can be serviced by hotels of any size so long as they are geared for meetings.

Characteristics of Association Meetings

Association meetings of all types follow fairly neat patterns; understanding these patterns will help you sell them intelligently.

Cycle and Pattern

Conventions are held on a regular time cycle. The most common is annual, although there are associations that hold two conventions a year and some that convene only every two years. The one-year cycle is often supplemented in a national organization with one, two, or even three regional conventions on a smaller scale.

Conventions are more commonly held during the early part of the week. They most frequently begin on a Sunday, or possibly a Monday, and run through Wednesday or Thursday (fig. 4.4). A group that meet at the end of the week or on the weekend often receives a warm welcome and attractive deals from hotel people.

A strong geographic pattern is also indicated. Most associations alternate between the East and West in site selection. The most popular variation calls for a midwestern city every two years, with eastern and western cities alternating during the other years. Typical examples follow.

	1983	1984	1985	1986	1987
National Conventions					
ABC Assn.	New York	Los Angeles	Washington, D.C.	Denver	Boston
XYZ Assn.	Chicago	New York	St. Louis	Las Vegas	Milwaukee
Regional Conventions					
ABC Assn.	San Diego	Atlanta	Phoenix	Miami	San Francisco
	Cleveland	Kansas City	Cincinnati	St. Louis	New Orleans
XYZ Assn.	Los Angeles	Dallas	Philadelphia	Boston	Miami
	Atlanta	Seattle	San Diego	Detroit	Los Angeles

The important factor is the area of the country, not the specific city. The pattern may call for a Midwest location, which could be St. Louis, Chicago, Cincinnati, or others. The Southeast could be served with Atlanta, Miami, Tampa, or Memphis. Much depends on the geographic interests of the association members. If there is no special interest factor, the site selectors attempt to provide an interesting place to serve as an additional attraction.

The scheduling of regional events calls for a frank recognition that some members will not travel too far for the event. One association executive told us that his records show that a hard core of regulars comes to the convention every year no matter where it is held. This group is supplemented by members who come from

Fig. 4.4 Monthly and daily meeting
pattern of associations. (By permission of
Successful Meetings).

when they are held

Rated by the *number of events,*
these are the most active convention
months in order of importance:

• October • May • April •
• June • September •

Rated by the *number of attendees,*
these are the most active convention
months in order of importance:

• October • September • March •
• February • January •

STARTING DAY OF MEETING
(Percentage of Total Market)

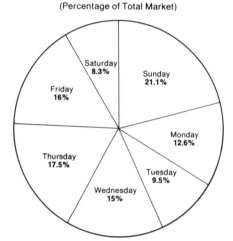

within some three hundred miles. Obviously, he holds regional conventions to keep
his members involved. Perusal of the meeting pattern should show you when the
group next would consider your part of the country.

Geographic Restrictions

Many state organizations, as part of their constitutions, have limited site selection
to their own states. This is also true of regional organizations. There may be further

restrictions because of the narrow interests of the program or the nature of the association's business.

There has been some deviation from such limitations in recent years. One device that association executives have used to break out of the pattern is a reciprocal agreement with another state organization. Thus a Colorado chapter might meet in Massachusetts one year and the Massachusetts chapter would meet in Colorado. This satisfies the political aspects of catering to local businesses while providing a novel site to stimulate attendance.

Similarly there have been restrictions on national associations to meet within the United States. But that, too, is breaking down, and a number of associations have booked in Europe. The trend-setting American Society of Association Executives has held events in Paris and Montreux, Switzerland.

Legislation recently was passed, however, that restricts the tax deductions for such overseas meetings. One expectation of those who oppose such limits is that future business and association groups from Europe will come to the United States. The closer relative values of national currencies in recent years makes this a less remote possibility than previously.

Lead Time

Association conventions are planned well in advance, with two to five years the norm. Even decisions finalized two years in advance are the result of research and discussion that took up to five years. The larger the convention, the greater the lead time. Meeting planners are well aware that every hotel is not suitable for their convention; this is especially true of the larger ones. They want time to visit the site, check with past clients, and check other alternatives before making the decision.

This long lead time can be frustrating for the new hotel or the new hotel sales manager, but it is the pattern for association conventions. And the clear pattern enables you to decide when you can best propose your property to have the best chances of success.

Kind of Sites

Association business does not all go to the same kind of property (fig. 4.1). This is hardly surprising, considering the many kinds of associations and societies and the many types of meeting events. Requirements and preferences could scarcely be expected to be uniform.

The kind of site selected generally reflects the group's size, complexity, degree of sophistication, and members' affluence. Obviously, a 200-room hotel would not be considered for a 500-person convention, unless it is in cooperation with other hotels. The basic requirements must be met—an auditorium for the main assembly, exhibit space if needed, support rooms for committees' and exhibitors' meetings.

We have discussed geographic considerations. Add to that the ease of transportation and how the association executive feels about it. It is hard, for example, to find a more accessible place than the hotels near O'Hare Airport at Chicago. If the executive believes that such a site would draw more attendance, he or she may choose it.

There are other geographic factors involved. Many convention organizers want the vacation element working for them. How many extra registrations can a site like Miami or Las Vegas or Colorado Springs draw? That's the name of the game. There are many ways to enliven a regularly scheduled convention. Good, stimulating programming is the ideal way, but it's very hard to execute. It is often easier to stage the event at a lovely resort and keep your people happy by exposing them to la dolce vita.

Sports play a role in site selection. Golf, tennis, swimming, and boating are factors considered by convention planners as they analyze their people. Some fervent golfers on the board of directors may very well swing the decision to a property with a famous course and favorable climate.

If you examine past choices, you may find the pattern. It varies from group to group and the successful salesperson is the one who discerns the key to the group. Find out what turns them on and see if you can supply that ingredient at your place.

Attendance Is Voluntary

It should be clear by now that the association convention planner has to *attract* members to the annual event. One might think that business and professional interests would suffice as a magnet. Undoubtedly they do draw a certain number, but there are an indeterminable number of fence sitters. Should they go this year or should they skip it? This is where site attraction plays such an important role, and the meeting planner is aware of it.

The option to attend is the member's own. He may demand that both his business needs and his vacation desires be satisfied. If your property or region has some tourist attractions, you should make sure that it is part of your presentation. Whether it is the opera at the Lincoln Center or shopping at Saks Fifth Avenue, antique hunting in the Poconos, or gaming at Las Vegas, a hotel's attraction is more than just its decor and facilities. Learn what positive aspects of your property you can project. Sales may depend on it.

As a bonus, records show that spouses come too when the site is attractive. That results in double-occupancy revenues and longer stays. Vacations with tax-deductible expenditures also help turn out the members.

Convention Duration

The average duration of a convention is three to five days (fig. 4.5). This is generally true for the national events, although smaller affairs may last only two to three days. Seminars, committee meetings, and such can last just a day or two. Most conventions with exhibits meet for no fewer than three days. There is additional business to be picked up, as many exhibiting firms hold sales meetings just before the event. This is true, too, for the association's board of directors and many committees.

Price

Your rate schedule is an important consideration to the association executive. We refer to your guest room rates, not so much to your charges for meeting rooms, food functions, etc., although they will be reflected in the overall registration fee and charges for individual events. Guest room rates must be aligned with the kind of people expected to attend. This is where the full range of hotels comes into play.

Many a convention organizer sticks with the traditional downtown hotels because of price. The older properties, built years ago at lower costs and lower mortgages, often offer lower rates. That means nothing to some associations. But to others, it can mean the difference between choosing your property and rejecting it. Price can be a factor. Keep in mind that it is not always an important one, even though it is always brought up.

Here, too, some study of where the group has met will help. If its history discloses successful years at places like the Fairmont in San Francisco and the Plaza in New York, you can feel pretty sure that the convention organizer wants the best places for his people and that they are accustomed to paying the price. On the

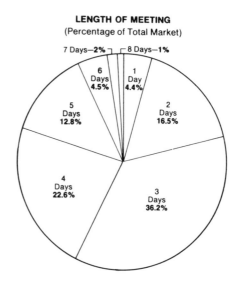

LENGTH OF MEETING
(Percentage of Total Market)

7 Days—**2%** ⌐ 8 Days—**1%**

6 Days **4.5%**

1 Day **4.4%**

5 Days **12.8%**

2 Days **16.5%**

4 Days **22.6%**

3 Days **36.2%**

other hand, one convention executive told us that his people were middle-level employees who traditionally paid their own way to the convention. When he booked at a more expensive place, he invariably received an increased number of complaints from members.

There is no right price level. It must suit the group you are trying to sell. Or, more accurately, it must suit the picture the association executive has of his people.

Who Makes the Decisions?

Selection of the convention site—both city and hotel— is a two-step process. The first is screening all suggestions and solicitations; the second is the final approval. We have separated the two because not all people involved are active in both phases.

Association Executive

Almost every association has a permanent executive staff member. His title may be executive secretary, executive vice president, or executive director. Generally, he is the administrator of the association, and a very important person to hotel people. Your sales efforts start with him. A well-run sales staff of a hotel or convention bureau will treasure a file on each association and its key people; the list always starts with the executive secretary. (fig. 4.6)

(The "he" in this discussion is purely for convenience. The executive secretary may be a woman, and female executives are by no means restricted to associations with primarily women members or activities. If an inquiry comes in from a female "executive secretary," don't assume that she is a clerical assistant to the boss man. Those days are long gone.)

Small associations often cannot afford a full-time executive. Such organizations are serviced by *multiple association management organizations.* Such firms function as the executive and office staff for a number of associations that otherwise would have to make do with volunteers. In this way the associations enjoy professional management at costs they can afford. In such cases, you may find yourself dealing with one man or woman responsible for several possible convention bookings.

The executive secretary is a key person for the initial screening of suitable convention sites and swings great influence over the final selection as well. After all, this executive has the continuity in office that the elected association officials do not have. The elected officials may serve for a year or two and then pass the reins on to the next team. But the executive secretary continues in office, and does so with the backing of the key members of the association.

The executive doesn't work alone, however, especially in the larger organizations. Since much of the administrative work has nothing to do with the convention activities, the executive often has a staff member specifically assigned to convention planning. In the largest organization, this person may have a staff of his own. This convention planner thus is another person you should consider as very important when you make your presentation. He or she reports to and works closely with the executive secretary. Often the executive appoints a site selection committee. This group visits cities and hotels and is responsible for securing convention space arrangements for the association.

There are independent companies that fill this role, too. Convention management companies either receive a fee for the work or a percentage of the registration fees as an incentive to stimulate attendance. Such management firms obviously are very important to the hotel people; they influence site selection and are also the people who work with the hotels to execute the meeting.

Association President

The power of a president varies greatly among associations. As mentioned, the president usually serves for a year or two. He or she may serve as an honorary figurehead or may flex a great deal of muscle. He or she shares in the initial screening of a selection site and is certainly in on the final decision.

When you build your card file on association personnel, make sure to take notes too on the vice-presidents. They are next year's presidents. Make your friends early and reap the harvest later.

Committee Chairperson

Certain committee heads get involved in the initial suggestions and screening. This depends on the nature and structure of the organization and the subject of the event. They most definitely are a factor in site selection for seminars dealing with their committee's subject matter.

You can see that a fair number of hands get involved in the original list of proposed places and in the preliminary screening to narrow down the choices. Your elimination in the final selection may mean loss of business that year, but you may well be in line for a booking when the cycle brings the association back to your part of the country. There may also be some consolation prizes in the form of selection for lesser events like committee meetings or seminars.

Board of Directors

The final list is usually presented to the board of directors for the final selection. It is worth emphasizing that the recommendations of the executive secretary usually are accepted. Some get their way all the time; some must deal more politically and tactfully. But the executive remains the single most important person you must sell to get association business. He may not rule autocratically, but he manages to get his way most of the time. You may lose the business at the directors' meeting, but without the support of the executive secretary, you never even get that far. Generally, *all* the finalists meet with the executive's approval.

Local Influences

It is common practice in many scientific and technical societies for local chapters to bid for the national event. That is not to say that they *bid* in the sense of offering money. Rather, they request the honor of playing host to the national group and

Job Title	Association Planners
Director	25%
Executive Director/Managing Director	24
Secretary/Executive Secretary of the Association	13
Vice-President	9
Meetings/Conference Coordinator	9
President/Chairman	8
Manager	6
All other titles	6
TOTAL	100%

offer their efforts to make the convention a success. This is especially true with international societies.

Hotel sales people are aware of this practice. We know of many cases in which a local delegate to an international congress has been approached by a convention bureau or hotel. An appeal is made to his local pride or nationalism, and any other emotions that can be brought to bear. It is not uncommon, in such cases, for the hotel or bureau to bear the costs of the delegate's travel, a hospitality suite, and the presentation to the board. It is also wise to assure the delegate that, should the society agree to meet in his home area, the bureau or hotel would supply all clerical support personnel to enable the delegate to fulfill his role of host.

It doesn't always require such effort. Appeals to local delegates or chapters often bring results merely because of civic pride and a desire to help local businesses. Look around your city and make friends with people in local association chapters. At the very least, you may pick up a local banquet or one-night meeting.

It is important when you enlist the aid of local members to impress upon them that you and your establishment are fully capable of handling the business. They may very well feel uncertain about the wisdom of getting involved and perhaps fear the embarrassment of a debacle at the national convention. But then you have to convince any prospect at any level that you and your staff are competent and interested in doing a good job. Those are the two key points you must make over and over—that your staff has the *expertise* and the *desire* to do whatever must be done to execute the meeting properly.

How Do You Find Associations?

Associations are readily located, fortunately. The national ones seem to be clustered in a relatively few cities. New York, Washington, and Chicago lead in the number of associations. Other major headquarters cities include Philadelphia, Austin, Indianapolis, Los Angeles, Milwaukee, Oklahoma City, and Richmond.

Directories

Several volumes offer detailed listings of associations. One is *Who's Who in Association Management*, published by the American Society of Association Executives, 1575 Eye Street, N. W., Washington, D.C. 20005. It sells for $80.00 and lists approximately seven thousand associations. The list is available for direct mail rental under certain circumstances. It is a valuable reference.

Another is the *National Trade and Professional Associations of the United States and Canada and Labor Unions*. This offers some seven thousand listings. The publisher is Columbia Books, 1350 New York Ave., Washington, D.C. 20005. This publisher will rent the list for direct-mail use and will supply various breakdowns and services at prices quoted on request.

The *Encyclopedia of Associations* (and its companion, *Geographic Index of Associations*) is published by Gale Research Company, Book Tower Building, Detroit. The price is one hundred ninety-five dollars, plus one hundred seventy-five dollars for the geographic index.

The *Nationwide Directory of Association Meeting Planners* provides the names and titles of over 10,000 meeting planners of 6,500 major associations. The directory features the number of meetings held yearly, months in which meetings are staged, approximate number of attendees, and geographic location of meetings including type of facilities used. It may be ordered from Bayard Publications and sells for $160.00.

National Associations of the United States lists all the national associations, membership totals, and officers and addresses. It may be obtained by writing to the Superintendent of Documents, U.S. Government Printing Office, Washington, D.C.

Successful Meetings magazine (known for many years as *Sales Meetings*) publishes two directories. The *Directory of Conventions* lists more than nineteen thousand coming events in the convention field. It offers such excellent details as convention sponsor, dates, whether there is an exhibit, estimated attendance, headquarters facilities, name, title, and address of the executive in charge, and reports on the scope of the meeting. It costs one hundred five dollars and has an annual supplement.

The second publication is *The Exhibit Schedule*, which includes more than eleven thousand listings of major exhibits around the world. It includes full data, as in the *Directory of Conventions*.

Successful Meetings magazine also offers a most useful marketing service for the hotel field, called *SM/Databank*. The magazine has stored data on the history of more than three hundred thousand meetings held by some twenty-eight thousand associations over the past twenty-five years. It has key-punched in data dealing with events planned by associations. A hotel person may obtain information about prospects that fit his preferred client profile, such as time of week in which a group meets, time of year, geographic pattern, size of the group, whether it has exhibits, where it has met previously and where it is scheduled to meet in the future.

It is a valuable service in building a prospect file for sales campaigns. The cost is $350.00 for the setup fee and approximately $5.00 for each *tip sheet* (see Figure 8.8) on a particular group.

Specialized Periodicals

There are a number of periodicals that serve the market, with their advertising directed to convention organizers. Some go only to association personnel; others are distributed to both association and corporate personnel.

Association Management is published monthly by the American Society of Association executives. Its circulation consists of the members of this prestigious organization. The list is available for rental for direct mail under special circumstances. The Association Directory & Buying Guide list members with address and telephone number which makes it most useful. Vendors may join the society as associate members.

Association & Society Manager is published every other month. Its circulation includes full-time managers of societies and associations as well as volunteer/member part-time managers, plus other reader types. A sales lead service is available to advertisers.

Successful Meetings is a monthly magazine whose circulation includes association personnel. Advertisers receive the SM Convention Research Bulletin published weekly, supplying information about groups planning meetings. Included are names and addresses of key people involved in site selection. Successful Meetings also publishes the SM Tip Flash, which supplies advertisers with additional sales leads. The list may be rented for direct mail. The magazine also offers all sorts of breakouts through the SM/Databank discussed previously.

Meeting News is a monthly tabloid newspaper. Its circulation includes association personnel, too. The tabloid uses a reader service card to key ads and to supply sales leads. In addition, the New Names service given to advertisers lists meeting planners who are in that function for less than one year.

Meetings & Conventions is a monthly magazine whose circulation also includes association personnel. Its circulation is available for rental for direct mail. Advertisers benefit from the reader service card system plus a sales lead service in the association and corporate fields.

Medical Meetings is a publication that concentrates in a specific segment of the convention and meetings field. Their circulation is formed from medical societies and associations, biomedical corporations, hospitals and medical centers and government and foundation organizations. They, too, offer a reader sales lead system.

These are prominent publications but not the only ones. Others are listed in Appendix A. Information as to the particular segment of the market served can be obtained from the publishers.

Meeting Associations

Another excellent method of reaching the association market is through meeting planners' associations. Just as teachers, doctors and lawyers have their associations, so do meeting planners. Following is a list of major meeting associations, their addresses and a brief description of their membership characteristics. A more complete list of convention-oriented groups is given in Appendix A.

American Society of Association Executives
1575 Eye Street N.W.
Washington, DC 20005
Membership: professional and trade association executives.

The American Society of Travel Agents
4400 MacArthur Boulevard N.W.
Washington, DC 20007
Membership: domestic and international agents and allied members from airlines, cruise lines and hotels.

Association of Independent Meeting Planners
5103 Wigville Road
Thurmont, MD 21788
Membership: Independent contractors who plan conventions and meetings of all types.

Exposition Service Contractors Association
1516 So. Pontius Avenue
Los Angeles, CA 90025
Membership: Exposition service contractors and suppliers to the industry.

Institute of Association Management Companies
5820 Wilshire Boulevard

Los Angeles, CA 90036
Membership: Companies providing full association management services to two or more organizations.

Health Care Exhibitors Association
5775 Peachtree-Dunwoody Road
Atlanta, GA 30342
Membership: Companies involved in marketing products and services in the health care industry.

Insurance Conference Planners Association
18 Chestnut Street
Worcester, MA 01608
Membership: Meeting planners for insurance companies.

International Association of Auditorium Managers
500 N. Michigan Avenue
Chicago, IL 60611
Membership: Managers of auditoriums, arenas, theaters, stadiums, convention centers.

Meeting Planners International
1950 Stemmons Freeway
Dallas, TX 75207
Membership: Meeting planners and suppliers.

National Association of Exposition Managers
344 E. Garfield Road
P.O. Box 377
Aurora, OH 44202
Membership: Exposition and trade show managers; and suppliers.

Professional Convention Management Association
100 Vestavia Office Park
Birmingham, AL 35216
Membership: Meeting planners within the health care industry; and suppliers.

Hotel Records

If you are newly assigned to a hotel convention staff, one of the first things to do is to closet yourself with the function books and other records from the past few years.

Much can be learned from them. How many groups met in your house but never returned? How many did not return merely because no one ever asked them? It is amazing how many times business is lost because no one followed up and pressed for more business.

Your hotel records will also offer clues to personnel changes. If a group didn't return, a new executive secretary could offer another chance. You could call and indicate that his group had met successfully at your hotel and perhaps persuade him to book it again. You also should try to find out where the previous executive is now located. After all, he had selected your hotel previously and may be amenable to doing so again. No sales staffer should rely on a past customer's memory to bring him back. Sales life is not that easy. You must go after them.

But remember that the easiest prospect is a satisfied past customer. If the meeting went well, you have an excellent prospect. If it did not go smoothly, it is imperative to find out why. It could be something that you must prevent from happening with other clients, or it may be something that you have already corrected and could then press for business. Some of the best business relationships result from clearing up past grievances.

Your hotel records also may offer a clue to other prospects gleaned from local small bookings. A dinner meeting handled solely by the banquet manager may indicate only a local chapter. But this small bit of business of dinner for twenty or so may be just the Trojan horse you need to penetrate the state or national parent organization. Much can be learned from the members themselves. At the very least, a follow-up phone call will increase the chances for more local business.

It is important not to get discouraged and to realize that much association business must be cultivated over the long haul. The road to that major booking may have gone through many minor bits of business before scoring on the big one, or before scoring at all. Maintain a good follow-up system and keep after target associations, and you'll get your share of the harvest.

Study Questions

1. Conventions are extremely important to associations for financial reasons. Explain why.
2. What do associations look for in their site selection? What kinds of meetings do they hold?
3. Why are resort sites frequently used by associations? Attendance for association conventions is voluntary. What implications does this have for the hotel's sales promotion efforts? How important is price to the association executive?
4. What individuals in the association make the site selection decision?
5. List sources for locating associations.

Outline

I. What Do They Look For?

II. Kinds of Company Meetings

    A. Sales Meetings
    B. Dealer Meetings
    C. Technical Meetings
    D. Executive Meetings
    E. Training Meetings
    F. Public Meetings

III. Characteristics of Company Meetings

    A. Time Cycle
    B. Lead Time
    C. Geography
    D. Kind of Site
    E. Attendance
    F. Duration
    G. Exhibits
    H. Meeting Room Requirements
    I. Repeat Business
    J. Meeting Planning Decisions
    K. Multi-Booking Potential
    L. One Meeting—One Check
    M. Meeting Business Brings Other Business

IV. Who Makes the Decisions?

    A. Full-ime Meeting Planner
    B. President
    C. Marketing and Sales Executive
    D. Advertising and Sales Promotion Manager
    E. Other Corporate Executives
    F. Marketing and Sales Services Manager
    G. Passenger Traffic
    H. Training Director
    I. Meeting Specialist

V. How Do You Find the Organizations and the Right Person?

    A. Special Meeting Publications
    B. Business Publications
    C. Trade Directories and Publications
    D. Trade Associations
    E. General Business Directories
    F. Local Branch Offices
    G. Lateral Referral and Penetration

Today's corporation is a complex organization. The geographic marketing range has grown to the point that most companies now market nationally or internationally. The structure of larger companies is more detailed and multifaceted than ever before.

Modern executives received their training with such companies in mind, and they have had drilled into them over and over the vital need for *communication.* Meetings remain a most basic form of communication within the company, and radiating out from the company through its network of distribution around its world.

Of course, the hotel marketing executive is concerned solely with those company meetings that take place off company premises. There are enough of these, however, to satisfy any enterprising hotel sales staff.

If the association convention business represents the best-known and most visible segment of the meetings field, corporate meetings probably offer the greatest potential for growth. The present volume is actually greater than the association business, but it is decidedly not as visible. Company meetings are varied, and controlled by a wider variety of company personnel, and they are certainly harder to dig out. But they offer a great deal of group business potential that is absolutely impossible for any hotel to ignore.

Fortunately, hotel marketing people do not have to decide which segment of the market—associations or corporations—to sell. They can handle both kinds with the same property. The two are a digestible mix, and a successful property enjoys its share of both kinds. The ratio of each, or even the priority given to each type, really reflects upon the kind of property you have, what you are equipped to handle, where you are located. Examine your hotel with an eye to what corporate meeting planners want and the kinds of meetings they hold.

As you read this chapter, you will find many similarities between the association meetings market, discussed in chapter 4, and the corporate market. While similar, they are not the same. At the risk of being redundant, we have chosen to separate the two in an effort to delineate clearly the most effective selling approaches used in reaching each market.

What Do They Look For?

The factors that make a hotel attractive for association events hold true for most corporate meetings as well. Do keep in mind that corporate meetings vary a great deal in size and scope. (fig. 5.1)

Fig. 5.1 Factors considered important to corporate meeting planners in the selection of a facility/hotel. (Source: The Meetings Market Study conducted by Meetings and Conventions Magazine)

Factors Considered Very Important	Corporate Planners
Quality of food service	79%
Number, size and caliber of meeting rooms	64
Efficiency of billing procedures	52
Number, size and caliber of sleeping rooms	49
Efficiency of check-in/check-out procedures	48
Assignment of one staff person to handle all aspects of meeting	46
Availability of meeting support services and equipment, such as audio-visual equipment	44
Previous experience in dealing with facility and its staff	39
On-site recreational facilities, i.e., golf, swimming, tennis	27
Convenience to other modes of transportation	26
Proximity to airport	24
Provision of special meeting services such as pre-registration, special equipment, etc.	18
Availability of exhibit space	16
Number, size and caliber of suites	12
Proximity to shopping, restaurants, off-site entertainment	12
Newness of facility	8

Convenient Location

Location is very important to the corporate meeting planner. Travel means company money, and the time spent traveling and at the meeting itself means time off the job. That's a prime factor. Thus a convenient location is a very strong sales asset. Company meeting planners frequently use downtown hotels, airport hotels, and certain suburban locations, especially for regional sales meetings and training sessions.

Attractive Location

Most business officials have a clear idea of their company's image, and they want to meet in a hotel that will be consistent with that image. This does not necessarily mean a posh place, but, all things being equal, the decision will go to an attractive property or locale.

This is absolutely essential in sites for incentive trips. It goes without saying that the hotel and the area or country must have strong tourist attraction. It wouldn't be a prize to work for if it didn't have a strong appeal. The approach for incentive meetings is quite different from that of sales meetings, but the two are often intertwined. A working sales meeting requires solely a *suitable* hotel site; an incentive meeting requires a most *desirable* one.

Enough Guest Rooms

No company likes to split up its staff at a meeting. The chance of "losing" attendees during the walk or cab ride to the meeting site frightens every company meeting planner. Companies show a strong preference to housing everyone under the same roof. This is a difficult problem to overcome if you can't offer it but your competitor can. Sometimes several hotels combine in a presentation to very large groups, but the first choice invariably goes to the single hotel that can house the entire group.

Adequate Meeting Space

It is hard to hold a meeting efficiently if the meeting rooms are too small—or too large, although surplus area may be screened off. When you go after company business, discuss in great detail the rooms needed. The main room may need support from a number of small rooms. If your layout shows these nearby, you have a strong selling point.

Security

Corporate meetings are private affairs, to a far greater extent than most conventions. The discussions are not meant for the ears of people outside the company. Folding vinyl partitions leave corporate planners cold, and meeting rooms right off busy lobbies are difficult to control. If you arrange a layout off the traffic pattern of the hotel, stress it in making your case. And if it will be the only group meeting in the hotel, you have another positive sales point.

Service

Companies meet for good reasons, and they don't want anything to interfere. They want service—good service. They want everything that was promised, and on time. The reward for supplying such service is repeat business. With the exception of incentive programs, corporate business holds the most promise of repeat business. Good service breeds confidence, and that brings in the bookings. Most company meeting planners mention service first when asked what they look for in a meeting site.

Kinds of Company Meetings

Corporate meeting business has been increasing more rapidly in recent years than any other market. Hundreds of thousands of meetings are held all over the country throughout the year, and the spectrum of meetings attended is broad. Among the prevalent types of company meetings are

    sales meetings
    dealer meetings
    technical meetings
    executive meetings
    training meetings
    public meetings

Each will be considered in detail.

The kinds of companies holding meetings are also broad and diverse. Insurance companies, banking and investment groups, automobile companies, and industrial and manufacturing concerns are just a few of the prospects for the corporate meeting business. While the selling and servicing of the corporate market is similar to associations, there are several differences.

Sales Meetings

The best-known company meeting and, without doubt, the largest sector of the corporate meetings market, is the sales meeting. The very nature of a national sales organization makes it a natural for meetings. These events are scattered throughout the country, with new products and new sales developments appearing all the time. There is a constant need for sales management to meet face to face with the sales team, and it goes on at every level. There are national sales meetings with everyone present. There are meetings of regional sales managers. There are regional sales meetings run by regional sales managers.

Attendance at national sales meetings averages about one hundred fifty to two hundred, and the meetings last three to four days. Regional sales meetings are smaller, averaging about fifty or so in size, and usually go on for two to three days (fig. 5.2).

The reasons for sales meetings are many. Often a meeting will deal with several company objectives. The annual sales meeting may involve new product introduction, new company policy, and suggested sales techniques to overcome problems, or it may be simply a morale builder and stimulator to cap a successful year and to start work on the next one. Sales meetings come in all sizes and shapes, and all of them mean good, regular, repeat business for hotels.

Sales meetings are generally staged and controlled within the sales and marketing departments of each division of a company.

Dealer Meetings

A sales executive and his staff often hold national and regional events to meet with dealers or distributors. New product introduction is very important in these meetings too. The introduction of new sales and advertising campaigns calls for carrying the message out to the hinterlands. The very heart of the American sales and marketing philosophy is to sell your own staff first and then your distributors and dealers and their staffs, and to work them up to new levels of enthusiasm. The advertising slogan or jingle or song is the business equivalent of the old school song. This results in many meetings around the country.

As in the case of sales meetings, dealer meetings can be very small, such as a cocktail reception for a dozen or so one evening, or great affairs involving thousands and running three to five days. The Ford Motor Company spent several million dollars for a live Broadway-type stage presentation, combined with multi-media presentation, at the large Las Vegas Convention Center. The affair called for several days of rehearsals and two weeks of back-to-back charter flights of dealers from all parts of the country. The production was worthy of any on Broadway, yet had a run of only two weeks.

Technical Meetings

The need to update technical personnel increases every year. The volume of technical development and innovation is hard to envision. A presentation by well-known convention speaker Joe Powell graphically displays the technical and scientific progress made since the beginnings of man. The graph curve remains almost horizontal over eons of years, starts moving up in the modern era, and just about goes straight up for the current century.

In only the last 75 years—just three generations—man has created the automobile, the airplane, the spaceship, the laser, the transistor. An engineer or scientist cannot afford to stop learning or he will soon be obsolete. To give you some idea of the scope, General Electric has some thirty thousand engineers, representing an enormous investment in technical talent that requires constant updating.

Company technical meetings often take the seminar and workshop formats. Independent consultants, educators, and even vendors are invited to demonstrate and lecture.

Executive Meetings

Just as sales staffs and technical personnel meet, so do all levels of executives. Far-flung organizational charts mean that even at the very top of a company or division, there is a need for peers to get together for discussion.

Such meetings may be regular events, such as board of directors meetings, or they may be called in response to a situation. These are usually relatively small meetings, but they call for the finest in accommodations and service. An important characteristic of such meetings for hotel people is that each attendee is a potential customer for meetings within his or her own division or company.

Executive meetings follow no special location rule, running the gamut from the most easily reached downtown or airport location to remote resorts or lodges. Such meetings most commonly last two days.

Training Meetings

Training of personnel—on all levels—is an important activity of the larger corporations. Companies may conduct training in such skills as running office machines, typing, and stenography, and in such technical skills as welding, machinery repair, and maintenance. Sales personnel frequently receive training, as do executives. These latter training programs may involve the newly recruited college graduate, the middle-management level, and on into special programs to develop the next executive strata.

Much training activity—particularly for clerical and blue-collar personnel—is conducted on company premises; much of it is actually on the job. About half of the training directors across the country, however, also conduct many programs off the company premises, and on a regular basis. The average number indicated was eleven times a year. The numbers involved each time are small. Most training groups number fewer than fifty, and most are nearer thirty (fig. 5.2). Groups of ten to fifteen are not all that rare. These meetings usually run from three to five days.

These meetings can be handled by quite small hotels. That is not to say that training directors are satisfied by just any facility; they have firm criteria. They do, however, deal with small groups that are easily accommodated. Requirements frequently mentioned by training directors are meeting rooms with permanent walls instead of screen dividers, reasonable soundproofing, dependable sources of audiovisual equipment, rooms that lend themselves to audiovisual use, easy access to meeting rooms without much distraction from other hotel activities, and prompt service for food functions like coffee breaks and lunches.

Training directors do not need prestigious locations and impressive surroundings. They are more likely to choose hotels that are convenient to airports, highways, and parking. They make excellent customers because they tend to come back to hotels that worked out well, having no need to change locations to stimulate attendance or interest. Dependability, reasonable prices, and good service all count a great deal toward repeat business.

Many hotels and motels have done well with this kind of business, to the point of having almost permanent commitment of certain meeting rooms and a constant use of a minimum number of guest rooms by a single company. Chain operations, too, find such business good because training requirements often call for similar setups by a team in central locations around the country.

Regular business bookings can be picked up too when personnel become acquainted with a property while attending a training session.

An odd characteristic of training meetings is the reluctance to use the term *training*. At some levels, notably the lower ones, employees look for training and frequently will stick with an employer that offers it. But sales and middle-line people at times resent the implication that they *need* further development. This situation is dispelled by the use of tact and common sense, so don't be surprised to see *workshops, seminars,* or simply *meetings* being booked by training directors.

Public Meetings

Companies find it necessary at times to hold meetings for non-employees. One that comes to mind immediately is the annual stockholders meeting. Sometimes this is a mere formality attended by a handful; at other times it is a fairly active one-day event involving a goodly number, with lunch and coffee breaks. These seem to vary with the economic climate.

Public relations and industrial relations departments hold meetings and exhibits to tell their stories. They, too, add their bit to the growing number of corporate meetings.

Characteristics of Company Meetings

It is easy to analyze a meeting. Any meeting should have a clearly recognized objective or objectives, a logical attendance group, and a site and structure to suit the event. When we discuss characteristics of company meetings, keep in mind that we are talking about many different *kinds* of meetings—all sizes and shapes, instigated by a variety of causes, planned and executed with rare exception by a number of people.

But this very difficulty in describing a "typical" company meeting should be most encouraging to hotel staffs. It is a most unimaginative hotel salesperson, or a particularly primitive hotel property, who cannot come up with some part of this market that can be sold and serviced. This is the time to ignore what you lack and concentrate on what you *have* to select that portion of the market that you can call your own. Think in terms of your own sales campaigns and the kinds of hotel properties that can handle the situations discussed in this chapter.

Time Cycle

Some company meetings have a clearly noticeable cycle, such as the annual sales meeting or the annual stockholders meeting. Incentive programs are also on a steady cycle, usually annual. Other than these, company meetings seem to follow a demand schedule instead of a fixed-time cycle. A meeting is planned and executed when the need arises. After all, a company meeting doesn't require all the time needed by associations to build attendance. A simple directive issued by the top brass assures the meeting of the desired attendance.

Lead Time

The planning period for company meetings is relatively short, rarely longer than a year. In the case of incentive trips, some consideration about general area may be made some fifteen months in advance, and in the case of great numbers, the time may stretch to two years. But that is still much shorter than that used by associations in planning conventions.

The annual sales meeting is usually planned a year in advance. Corporate structure in this decision making is simple. Some middle-level person, or perhaps two, will suggest, investigate, and screen properties and pass along the recom-

Fig. 5.2 Corporate meetings market data. (By permission of *Successful Meetings*).

corporate meetings

Corporate meetings fall into various categories. SM provides you with a breakdown of the types most companies participate in:

- National Sales Meetings
- Regional Sales Meetings
- Training and Development Meetings
- Distributor and Dealer Meetings
- Executive Conferences
- Stockholder Meetings
- Management Development Seminars

number of meetings held annually

These figures are based on studies of U.S. based corporations that market nationally. Only those meetings held off-company premises in public facilities are included in figures.

National sales meeting 17,000
Regional sales meeting 102,000
Training and development
 meeting 274,000
Distributor and dealer meeting 88,000
Executive conference 91,000
Stockholder meeting 16,000
Management development
 seminar 5,000
*TOTAL ANNUAL
CORPORATE MEETINGS* 593,000

annual corporate expenditures on off-premise meetings—

Studying the corporate meetings expenses, SM's current findings reveal these figures:

- **National meeting** expenditures were at the rate of $136.20 per man per day . . . averaging $89,700 per meeting . . . totaling $1,525 million per year.

---

corporate meeting statistics

type of meeting	range of attendance	length of meeting
National sales meeting	183 average	3.6 days
Regional sales meeting	54 average	2.4 days
Training and development meeting	29 average	1–7 days
Distributor and dealer meeting	All company distributors	1–3 days
	Determined by subject	
Executive conference	for consideration	2 days
Stockholder meeting	Varies with corporation	1 day
Management development seminar	15 average	6 days

- **Regional meeting** expenditures were at the rate of $57.90 per man per day . . . averaging $6,700 per meeting . . . totaling 686 million dollars annually.

All other corporate meetings figured $2,841 million total annual expenditure, with an overall annual expenditure of $5.052 billion.

(includes all meeting costs encompassing audio visual and transportation)

when they meet

SPRING: (Mar., Apr., May) 24,742
SUMMER: (June, July, Aug.) ... 22,034
FALL: (Sept., Oct., Nov.) 25,549
WINTER: (Dec., Jan., Feb.) 25,046
(based on sm's reader's companies)

size of meetings

- 38,743 are less than 100
- 6,578 have attendance from 101-200
- Over 200—6,456

CORPORATE MEETING PLANNERS
(Where They Meet)

NUMBER		
19.327	EAST **33.7%**	
16.120	MIDWEST **28.2%**	
11.922	WEST **20.8%**	
9.924	SOUTHWEST **17.3%**	

0   10   20   30   40   100%
PERCENT

---

mendation to one executive who generally makes the final decision. In some companies, one person does it all, which certainly can shorten lead time. There are many variations, of course.

Most other company meetings have a very short lead time—three to six months is typical. Every company meeting planner can recall instances when it seemed like the meeting was needed for tomorrow. There is one kind of company meeting that we refer to as a *crisis* meeting. That follows when someone says, "Let's get everyone together as soon as possible and talk this thing out!"

It is too late to start selling your property at that point. If you had been in there selling, or had enjoyed some business from the company before, you might get a chance at this business. Certainly, there is no time for anyone to shop around.

The meeting calls for fast action and it generally goes to a place the company has used before or to some wide-awake salesperson who had been in there pitching at the time.

It is such types of corporate business that must fill the gap when the convention function book is less than filled. The unexpected sales meeting, the crisis that calls for facing dealers or distributors, the new modification for which service personnel must be trained—all these bring opportunities for business meetings. These are meetings executives don't discuss when you talk to them. You must sell them on the idea of using your facility when the need next arises, and hope you've made enough of an impression that they'll remember.

Geography

There is no general geographic pattern to company meetings. To begin with, there is often no reason to vary sites to attract attendance, as is the case with associations. When the vice-president of sales calls a meeting in Chicago at the first of the month, it is not surprising to find the sales staff in Chicago at that time.

There is also no reason not to go back to the same hotel if it served well. The main reason for another selection may very well be mere boredom on the part of the meeting planner of his or her boss. It really depends on the kind of meeting. The annual meeting, with much hoopla and singing of the company song, may call for a variety of sites from year to year, but the hastily organized tactical meeting doesn't. In fact, a strong case can be built for repeating at a hotel proven dependable by the last meeting, or at least for some hotel that had been pushing for the business.

Training directors, in particular, prefer to deal with the same hotel over and over again. Some feel that with only small meetings to offer, they reach the status of *important customer* only through the promise of repeated business. Most training directors feel the need for distraction-free, classroom-type isolation, with a good supply of audiovisual equipment and service. Once having worked out such an arrangement with a suitable facility, they are understandably loath to change.

There is some geographic factor involved, but it is the most obvious one. An Atlanta hotel obviously will have a better chance at getting a regional sales meeting for a staff covering the southeastern states than will a hotel in Boston or St. Louis. Time, the cost of transportation, and convenience are all factors reflecting geographical location.

Imagine the assignment given to a company meeting planner to arrange for a series of regional meetings for a national sales staff. He, or she, might plan to use hotels in New York, Chicago, Seattle, Los Angeles, Dallas, and Atlanta. If you have a hotel in any of these general areas, geography will work for you and give you a chance at the business in your sector. But the planner is also free to meet in Houston instead of Dallas, in St. Louis or Milwaukee instead of Chicago, in Boston or Philadelphia instead of New York, and so on.

This is where the selling comes in. The hotel sales staffer must present the hotel positively, turn what might seem like a liability into an asset. If Kansas City is less glamorous than New York, it is more centrally located. If your property is not downtown, it offers fewer distractions and easier access by automobile and free parking. If it is downtown, it offers more off-meeting-time opportunities for entertainment. Salespeople should concentrate on their properties' positive factors, instead of being haunted by the shortcomings.

Company meetings, unlike many association conventions, rarely have regulations against meeting anywhere. The company president or board may favor some types of sites and frown on others in keeping with the image they want to project, but that's not quite the same as restrictions written into the constitution. Company policies, and company presidents, have been known to change with little notice. The images of areas and of the hotels themselves change. The efforts of convention bureaus, chambers of commerce, and local businesses often bear fruit in bringing about policy changes regarding site selection.

Kind of Site

What kind of hotel does a company prefer? The answer has as many variations as there are companies and kinds of meetings. A meeting planner should select a site so as to benefit from its locale and the hotel's attractions. There is really no one kind of hotel for all occasions. The hotel that would be good for an incentive trip or annual dealer meeting may not be the wisest choice for that crisis meeting or training session. (fig. 5.3)

This is not to say that you could not serve any meeting you can house comfortably. It merely reflects our feeling that a smart meeting planner chooses a site carefully. The mood and tone of the meeting is immediately indicated by the setting. There may be factors working against the ideal choice, and a small, elite group of executives may meet in a very ordinary downtown installation, in which case the planner has done nothing to help set the tone for the meeting.

If you are interested in a successful sales and marketing career, you want to help your customer achieve the kind of meeting he or she wants. You know what goes well in your establishment. Try to get those meetings. Let the ones that get away be those that really should be held in some other type of hotel.

Give careful thought to the kind of meetings most suitable for your hotel. Is yours a downtown hotel? Then stress its convenient location, especially when some people participate in only part of the program. Comfortable and familiar, the downtown hotel is a frequent choice, especially for sizable groups.

Is yours a suburban hotel/motel? Then it can provide easy access by auto and easy, free parking. Stress its informal, relaxed atmosphere, and the fact that the meeting is most often the only one in the house.

Airport location? The obvious advantage is convenience when air transportation is used. In addition, it has all the features of the suburban hotel. Once small properties, airport hotels come in all sizes these days.

Resort? This is the obvious choice for incentive meetings, but is also often chosen to get away from the distractions of the city. Resorts in the off season offer excellent rates, charm, exclusivity, industrial security, physical beauty, and a good image.

These are but a few benefits and characteristics of each type of property. You should be able to add to the list. The key is to present your property as the one that fits the meeting planner's event.

Attendance

One characteristic of corporate meetings that makes them popular with hotel people is the predictable attendance. Whether stag, using single occupancy or twin rooms, or with spouse, meaning double occupancy, attendance is reliable and nearly always mandatory. A rooming list submitted before the event is usually accurate. Barring mishap or illness, no-shows are minimal. In many cases, you can arrange for a full guarantee and all rooms will be paid for.

Care should be taken to get a VIP list. It can be embarrassing to everyone to have that fledgling sales trainee in the fine corner room and the vice-president of sales in a minimum single. If no VIP list is submitted, bring up the subject yourself and help your customer create one. If no need exists for him, fine. But check it out and at least flag a few names for preferred treatment. Those executives are the ones whose comments may determine whether you get the group again.

Duration

Most corporate meetings are short. Some are limited to a single day and others may run as long as five days, but three days are about the most common. Arrival on the previous evening is popular so that the meeting can start early the next morning. Cocktail receptions and/or brisk action at the hotel bars add to the profits to be derived from corporate meetings business.

Take care to coordinate the final day meeting program with your policy on check-out time. Plan ahead. If you can't gracefully extend the normal check-out time, perhaps you can arrange to check all the luggage with the bell captain or arrange for all luggage to be placed in just a few rooms before the check-out deadline. If you don't look ahead and decide how you will cope with the many requests at the last minute (or even with the entire group checking out late without even discussing it with you), your staff will be forced to improvise. And they may not always handle it as you would like.

Don't bury your head in the sand. Bring the matter up with the meeting organizer even if he doesn't. State your policy and suggest how to arrange matters. You can arrive at an agreed-upon arrangement. At the very least, you have alerted the planner to a potential problem.

Exhibits

The exhibit is a trademark of the association, for the most part. Corporate meetings, however, frequently have exhibits too. It is not uncommon, for example, for such meetings to display new product lines or to use live presentations on a grand scale. Thus you can expect requests for stage facilities and exhibit space when servicing corporate conventions.

Meeting Room Requirements

There is a need for large and small meeting rooms. Naturally, this varies from event to event. Some meetings call for small commitee-type rooms. In many training set-ups, the main group breaks into smaller ones of as few as ten people who meet separately for awhile, then reconvene in the main meeting room. Most meeting organizers prefer such *break-out rooms* to be right at hand.[1]

1. Break-out rooms are used when a large assembly divides into smaller groups following a general meeting or teaching session. Chapter 13 gives an extensive discussion of types of meeting rooms.

Types of Facilities at Which Meetings Were Held in the Past Year	Corporate Planners
Midtown hotel	58%
Suburban hotel	45
Resort hotel	44
Airport hotel	27
Privately-owned conference center	17
Suite Hotel	9
Condominium resort	9
University-owned conference center	5
Cruise ship	3
TOTAL	*

*Total is greater than 100% due to multiple mentions.

If your hotel has such rooms in the same wing of the building, you have an advantage when you solicit such business. It leaves something to be desired if the group has to huddle around a few tables in different parts of the main meeting room. It certainly would be difficult to attract such a group under those circumstances if the competition can offer more suitable arrangements.

Repeat Business

Do a good job for the meeting planner and you stand a good chance of getting repeat business. When you consider the relatively short lead time of some meetings, and the stress under which some are rushed into being, you can understand why such clients like to repeat in proven hotels. They don't need the change of scene to entice attendees. And they sleep better when they are confident that they are in good hands. Then they can concentrate on the problems that caused the meeting to be called in the first place.

Meeting Planning Decisions

Some companies have meeting planning staffs that serve the entire company, but that is rare. A division that does a heavy amount of such work may have full-time meeting planners, but even then it is common for another division to execute its own meetings with little or no consultation and no help from the other section. This means that a very busy meeting specialist may set up many sales and dealer meetings but have nothing at all to do with training meetings.

Translated into sales effort by hotel people, this means that if you are selling one division or department of a company, there may also be possible business elsewhere in the same organization. Think of a large company like RCA. You may get all the business from one sales department and none from another sales department, even within the same division and city. The latter may have little or no contact with those in their own organization who have used your hotel. Think of such large organizations as having a number of sales prospects for you (fig. 5.4).

On the other hand, selling within a corporate structure is relatively easy because decision making is concentrated. It may be entirely the responsibility of one man or woman, or perhaps two. If you sell those people, you have sold the business. The larger meetings, especially the incentive ones, usually call for screening and suggestions to a top executive who may make the final selection. Even then, this applies more to the area than a particular hotel.

Remember that most large corporations have a *number* of people capable of making the decisions for their meetings in different parts of the company. Such decisions may be made for the company as a whole, for a division, or just a single department.

Multi-Booking Potential

What appears to be a single meeting may be repeated in several parts of the country. This is a great situation for hotel chains. One person may order meetings in a number of locations, and one person may handle the logistics of all the meetings. There is often enough flexibility in the designation of the cities to be used that a chain may sell dates in a number of different properties. The appeal to the meeting planner is that he, or she, appears as a bigger and more important customer; he only has to explain his needs once and have them duplicated in different hotels.

What does this mean to the single-location hotel? In order to compete with a chain effort, the individual hotel must present a good case for being the best choice in the city. Ideally, that image would be so strong that a meeting planner normally using a chain would break that pattern when it comes to your city.

Many wise hotel salespeople cooperate with their counterparts in independent hotels in other cities. They recommend each other to combat chain competition. They try to get the meeting planner to buy from independents as often as possible, and to make it easy for that to happen by recommendations. One outgrowth is the hotel representative who, with a stable of independent hotels, can offer the same kind of "one-stop shopping" as do the chains. The subject of *independent hotel representatives* is thoroughly discussed in chapter 7.

90

Fig. 5.4 Adapted organizational chart of large manufacturing company showing the wide variety of meeting planners and decision makers possible within a corporate structure.

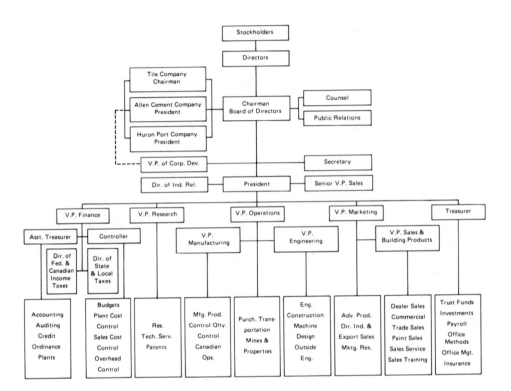

One Meeting—One Check

It is nice for a hotel to have all but the little items paid for in one fat check. That's one appeal of corporate business. Many companies pay all the expenses for their employees; others have different guidelines. You must discuss with the meeting planner what he or she will approve for payment on the master account and what the individual must pay for upon checkout. Your front desk must be informed. Your credit manager may want to do some homework on the customer-corporation and may choose to propose a schedule of payments beginning with a deposit. As a general statement, corporate meeting business is paid for en masse. And that's nice business.

Meeting Business Brings Other Business

Hosting company meetings offers the opportunity to promote other business. Without doing a thing except helping to execute a smoothly functioning meeting, you can pick up future business.

Each person attending the meeting has sampled your hotel. If the impression is favorable, you may become the first choice whenever that person stops in your city. Or you may benefit from recommendations of your hotel to others both in and out of the organization. Remember, too, that most association boards of directors include businesspeople who hold their own organizational meetings.

Word of mouth advertising is most effective, but it is a two-edged sword. Perform well and those tongues wag in your favor. Mess it up and you unleash a powerful force against you. When things go wrong at a meeting, and there are times when they do, take care how you handle the situation. Each such occurrence offers, along with the headaches, the opportunity to show expertise under fire and to win future customers. Don't be tagged as another house in which everything seems to go wrong and no one seems to be able to cope with it.

Who Makes The Decisions?

We have already discussed how varied the decision making can be. Nevertheless, no sales effort succeeds unless it is directed at the person or persons with the authority to make the decision. The convention sales picture is no different. Your story may be a good one, but it will be to no avail unless it is told to the right person.

Who is the *right person?* Not only does this vary from company to company, but it may vary from year to year within the same company. But some titles do keep coming up, and they certainly represent a starting point for sales penetration.

Full-time Meeting Planner

There are companies with centralized meeting planning activity. In such cases, you deal with a full-time meeting planner. Hopefully, this should make your job easier because you are dealing with an experienced, knowledgeable pro who knows what he or she wants and how to go about getting it.

It is easier to deal with someone who knows what he wants. It can even protect you from overlooking something in the arrangements. Both parties really want the same thing—a smoothly run meeting—and it helps if both parties are experts. Build

92

Fig. 5.5 Meeting planner's corporate position. Most corporations do not have professional meeting planners therefore in prospecting for business it is wise to know the common job titles of the corporate decision makers as summarized below. (Sources: The Meetings Market Study conducted by Meetings and Conventions Magazine.)

Meeting Planner's Corporate Position

Job Title or Position	Corporate Planners
Sales/Marketing	37%
Corporate Administration	35
Advertising/Sales Promotion/Public Relations	13
Meeting/Exhibit Planning	7
Personnel/Training and Development	5
Travel/Traffic	1
Manufacturing/Operations	1
Other	1
TOTAL	100%

a reputation for competence and fair dealing among the pros and you are well on your way to a successful sales career in the convention field.

There are several organizations of active meeting planners. They are listed in Appendix A. You should get to know these people very well.

President

Smaller companies do not have enough meeting activity to warrant a full-time planning employee. In many such companies, the decision maker is the president himself, or some counterpart such as a partner or chairman. It is understandable that the president of a larger corporation like General Motors will not be involved in such decisions, but the president of a company employing several hundred people might get involved in the national sales or dealer meeting. Never worry about making contact too high up the corporate ladder. If he or she isn't involved personally, a president is seldom hesitant about telling you who the right person is. Getting the approval or the recommendation of the president should do you no harm when you deal with the subordinates.

Marketing and Sales Executive

Marketing and sales executives are key people. The exact title may be *vice-president, sales* or *marketing director* or *manager,* or *product manager.* They may operate on a national, international, or even a regional basis. The bulk of corporate meetings involves the important areas of sales and marketing, so it makes sense to zero in on these people.

You probably will not find these executives in meeting planning societies. They don't think of themselves as meeting or convention planners. But they do plan a great many of them, or, more accurately, are involved with them. They call the meetings, control the kind of meetings they want, and often decide where and when they will take place. That makes them very important people for you.

Advertising and Sales Promotion Manager

One step down the corporate ladder is the *advertising* or *sales promotion manager.* One person may carry both titles because the work is interrelated. In addition to the usual duties, such middle executives frequently handle meeting planning functions. There is no relationship in such assignment to the size or type of company. If the company does not have a full-time meeting planner, the task is assigned to some departmental or divisional manager, and since it involves marketing activity, the advertising or sales promotion manager is often selected.

At the very least, such middle managers get involved in the initial screening of a site and play a role in the planning and execution of a meeting. They could be your first hurdle. You need them to recommend your property. In some cases, that is sufficient; in others, the final selection is made by their boss—the vice-president or sales and marketing director or manager. Some people freely admit it when their authority is limited, but some find it too painful to their egos to do so.

It helps you to know who the final decision maker is, but you have to pay attention to the level that screens, too, or you may never get to the final selection stage. Make sure that your presentation summarizes your strong points very clearly so that they may be passed along in discussion with others.

Other Corporate Executives

Not all meetings stem from marketing divisions. Other executives get involved with staging meetings and therefore site selections. They carry titles like *manager of corporate relations, public relations, industrial relations, or communications.* Such personnel may very well be active in sales and marketing, too. Corporate organizational charts seldom indicate anyone as meeting specialists, yet many executives are. The executive in charge of meetings may have that assignment for a period of time and then it may pass on to another.

People with these communications-type titles get involved with meetings even when the basic sales and dealer meetings are managed by someone else. Press receptions are an example. Some are quite involved, while others are little more than an afternoon cocktail party or an evening banquet.

Meetings involving stockholders or the public, such as in community affairs, may also mean business for you. As a rule, such meetings are local and don't involve much in the way of guest room business.

Marketing and Sales Services Manager

As sales and marketing staffs grow in size and sophistication, many of them establish sales service positions. These are generally support activities for sales departments. Thus here is another title to research. Sales and/or dealer meetings are often assigned to sales services personnel, especially when the purpose of meetings is to train dealers' personnel.

Passenger Traffic

Many companies maintain a travel desk, which handles arrangements for employee business travel. When an executive or salesperson needs plane or hotel reservations, he or she requisitions it through the passenger traffic personnel. Sometimes such offices get into the meetings activity; it is surprising that this does not happen more frequently. In any case, such personnel commonly negotiate with a hotel or hotel chain for a *commercial rate,* a rate guaranteed to all personnel of that company.

Training Director

Training activity of large companies is a good source of business. These are generally small meetings, and the training calendar frequently schedules repeat business. The average training director plans about a dozen meetings a year off company premises. (This is in addition to any semi-permanent arrangements for meeting rooms used as classrooms.) Training groups are usually twenty-five to fifty people meeting for three to five days.

Training directors may be active only with a local hotel or they may arrange meetings in central locations around the country. They use a wide variety of hotel types. Airport and other suburban locations are popular because of ease of access and parking. However, small resorts are also used in the off season, especially when complete control over the group is desired. Sessions at off-season resorts are secluded and captive, but pleasantly so. Resort sites are often used when executive development programs call for more prestigious sites. Small ski lodges can handle this type of meeting with little trouble; they are a popular selection during the shoulder (slow part) of the season.

Training directors may also choose to meet at one of the number of conference centers that are becoming more common. These are specially designed establishments that cater solely to meetings and include guest rooms and meeting rooms. Some were built from design up; others are renovated mansions. They usually concentrate on small meetings because of size limitations.

Training departments usually make their own arrangements for meetings, even in cases where the company already has a setup for sales meetings. You very well may sell the sales department on its meetings but still have to sell another group if you want the training sessions.

Being avid users of audiovisual techniques, training directors have their own criteria for site selection. These requirements do not differ from those of most small meetings, but training directors are less likely to be permissive about such things as dividing walls, low-hanging chandeliers, and nearby distractions in the hotel. Actually, these specifications are similar to those that any good, experienced meeting planner wants.

Training directors often are hampered by lower budgets than those of sales departments. So they make good use of secondary hotels, off-season rate breaks, and all-cost packages. Training people are good prospects for smaller hotel properties.

Meeting Specialists

Companies, like associations, often use outside organizations to help stage meetings. As you might expect, these specialists get involved only in larger corporate meetings. Travel organizations are called in at times, especially for incentive programs. Such organizations are important sources of business.

And there are meeting specialists who stage their own series of seminars. They may be small companies on their own, but their hotel bookings make them frequent clients.

How Do You Find the Organizations and the Right Person?

It's a great big business world out there, and while you may be eager to just get out there and knock on doors, that isn't the recommended use of time. Once you have a picture of the kind of corporate executive you are looking for, there are a number of ways for you to reach some of them.

Special Meetings Publications

The corporate meetings business is served by several publications that have literally done your job of sorting out those executives interested in meetings. It is hardly a surprise, therefore, to find that the advertising in these publications appears to be an industry rundown of the leading convention hotels. These magazines also offer advertisers sales-lead services giving the names of and data about likely prospects.

The three leading publications were discussed in the previous chapter on associations. The three *Successful Meetings, Meeting News,* and *Meetings & Conventions,* have most of their circulation in the corporate area. A complete list of trade magazines and their addresses is given in Appendix A.

These publications offer a direct route to prospects through advertising, list rentals for direct mail, and sales-lead services.

Business Publications

There are other publications of interest to hotel marketing people, although they do not specialize in conventions. This is because they either deal with related editorial subjects or reach the kind of executives who are important in making meeting decisions.

The most relevant is *Sales and Marketing Management.* As its name implies, this publication serves sales and marketing executives, who, as we've said, are often involved with meetings.

General business publications must be considered as well. We do not pretend that these publications go only to those executives who are involved with meeting decisions, but their circulations do reflect a profile that parallels the picture we have drawn of meeting planners. Thus the approach through publications such as *The Wall Street Journal, Business Week,* and *Fortune* is a very broad one and not at all directional.

The high expenditures required for such publications, the buckshot aspect of such circulation, and the absence of sales-lead services all tend to keep hotel advertising in them to a minimum. But they do reach that important sector of the market involved with corporate decisions.

Trade Directories and Publications

It is possible to develop sales leads by working your way through a specific industry. If your records indicate meetings of similar companies, it may be that industry is a fertile field for more business. The insurance industry is a prolific meeting group. There is even an association of meeting planners solely within that field. Other individual trades and industries may offer names of companies similar to those that have met in your hotel. It may seem like cold calls, and it is, in some respects, but it may do for a new mailing list.

Dun and Bradstreet's Million Dollar Directory is a list of the nation's largest businesses and their officers. It is published by Dun and Bradstreet, 99 Church Street, New York, New York.

Poor's Register of Directors and Executives is a similar publication put out by Standard and Poor's Corporation, 25 Broadway, New York, New York 10004.

Thomas Register of American Manufacturers is published by Thomas Publishing Company, 461 8th Avenue, New York, New York.

Scientific and Technical Societies in the U.S. and Canada is published by Canadian Business Magazine, 300 St. Sacrament Street, Montreal, Quebec, Canada.

The National Association of Businesspersons is published by the U.S. Department of Commerce. Listed are the names, addresses and chief executives of associations of business firms. This publication is available from the Superintendent of Documents, U.S. Government Printing Office, Washington, D.C.

Best Insurance Reports, published by A. M. Best Company, Ambest Rd., Oldwick, N.J. 08858, lists some ten thousand executives of life insurance firms.

Insurance Almanac is published by the Underwriter Printing and Publishing Company, 116 John Street, New York.

The *Directory of Corporate Meeting Planners* lists 12,000 meeting planners, with address, phone number, number of meetings, and when and where. It is available from the Salesmans Guide Inc., 1140 Broadway, New York, NY 10001.

Trade Associations—Local Business Directories and Branch Offices

If you feel that a specific industry might be worth following, call on the executive secretary of its trade association. You should be calling on him anyway for his own association business, but he can also be a prime source of leads. He can pinpoint the larger companies in the trade and those in your part of the country. His trade directory could be a good source of leads and a good addition to your mailing list.

Many meetings are held in the principal locale of the sponsoring company. It makes sense, therefore, to study directories of businesses within your city, state, or area of the country. Chambers of commerce could supply such lists.

Don't neglect to solicit the local branches of national organizations. You may be told that meeting decisions are made at the national headquarters, but don't ignore these local people. It is common for a corporate meeting planner to ask a local district manager about a suitable hotel in the area. The order may come from corporate headquarters, but the important input could come from your own area.

In addition, local branches often hold meetings of their own, albeit smaller ones. Local dealer meetings, training sessions, and regional sales meetings are often within the responsibility of the regional sales manager. Going after the regular commercial business of a branch sales office may give you a chance at some group business as well.

Lateral Referral and Penetration

Many hotel people are content when they get meetings business from a large corporation and feel they are getting all they can from that firm. But there may very well be more business to be had from the company.

As we have said, some companies are so large that people in one sector have little or nothing to do with those in other sectors. So if your piece of business came from a product manager in one division, give serious thought to following up with everyone who has the title of product manager in that and other divisions of the company.

The operating structure of the company may be uniform throughout, and if the product manager in one instance has the meetings responsibility, it is likely that others would too. If not, you have lost little because that person would be able to point you to the right one. Your case is stronger if you can get a recommendation from your original product manager customer. Even if he or she doesn't know the others personally, an endorsement from within the firm should carry weight.

Such lateral referrals and complete penetration of all sectors of a large firm is the sign of a successful hotel sales manager.

This will also help your prospects for business in other companies. You will gain an insight into corporate structure that will help you to analyze other companies in the same industry. The structures are generally similar. It certainly provides you with a good starting point by knowing the titles you are seeking. Understanding the corporate setup and who most likely has the meetings chore gives you a big leg up to penetrating and selling corporate business.

Study Questions

1. There are many similarities between association meetings and corporate meetings, but there are also clear distinctions. Contrast the two by comparing figure 5.2 with figure 4.1. Consider lead time, attendance, kind of site, exhibits, time cycle, etc.

2. Company meetings come in many sizes and shapes. Suppose you are the sales manager of a small property with limited meeting facilities. What kinds of company meetings would you go after and what methods would you use to reach the decision makers?

3. Discuss the multi-booking potential of corporate meetings.

4. As with associations, finding the person who makes the decisions is of utmost importance in corporate meeting solicitation. Why is this problem so acute in the corporate meetings market? List the probable decision makers in the corporate structure.

5. What role do local chapters and local business offices play in the determination of meeting sites?

Outline

I. Other Group Business

    A. Nonprofit Organizations
    B. Government Agencies
    C. Incentive Meetings
        1. Their Importance to the Hotel
        2. Role of the Travel Agent
        3. Commissions
    D. Promoting Weekend Conventions

II. New Developments

III. Working with Other Organizations

    A. Convention Bureaus
    B. Publicity

6

Other Group Business

Two other areas in which you can find meetings business are nonprofit organizations and government agencies. The structures of these organizations are quite similar to those of associations and corporations when it comes to meeting planning, so there is no need to repeat all the principles of selling to such organizations.

Nonprofit Organizations

Many organizations cannot properly be termed associations. But they are structured in similar fashion in that they have members, are nonprofit, and were created to accomplish some common purpose, even if the purpose is merely pleasure. Naming a few types may be the easiest way to illustrate this diffuse market.

Political clubs and parties frequently need hotel meeting accommodations. So do labor unions. These groups have regular conventions, as well as meetings called as the need arises.

Church groups, school groups, garden clubs, alumni groups, athletic organizations, the Boy Scouts and the Girl Scouts, charitable fund-raising organizations—all schedule meetings and/or conventions. At the very least, they have regular gala affairs that could serve your banquet department well.

Selling such organizations is much the same as selling trade associations. There are permanent employees, volunteers, and a board of directors. Some people will screen suggested meeting places and pass along the final suggestions to a board for final selection. Lead time tends to be shorter than for most trade associations, many of which plan five years or more in advance. A lead time of one or two years is the most common for nonprofit organizations.

It is hard to find a central source of such organizations since there are so many kinds. Start by soliciting local chapters of national groups, and stay alert for autonomous local groups, such as those affiliated with churches and schools. The records of convention or tourist bureau may be of some help.

Keep in mind that most local committees are made up of volunteers, so it is a good policy to assure them of your aid should they succeed in getting the national organization to schedule its event in their home town. The prestige will be theirs, but you must extend help for the chores associated with being the host chapter. Such encouragement might get them to push their home town for consideration.

Once you are past the local chapters and have penetrated the national organization, you may very well find there are experienced meeting planners on the staff.

Some of these national organizations do much convention work. They will work with you in the manner of association staffs, especially if you have been successful in getting the local chapter to request the position as host chapter.

Don't be reluctant to point out to your local people the economic benefits to the community when a convention is held there. Research has indicated that delegates to regional and state conventions each account for expenditures of about one hundred five dollars a day for three or four days.

There are some directories from which a list of nonprofit meeting groups can be compiled. The *Guide to American Directories* and the *Guide to American Educational Directories* are published by the Klein Company, New York, New York.

A pamphlet specifically keyed to the educational meeting market is *Educational Associations and Directories*. It gives the names and addresses of educational offices and may be obtained from the Superintendent of Documents, U.S. Printing Office, Washington, D.C.

Leland's Annual Fraternity-Sorority Directory is issued each January by Leland Publishers, Inc. It lists the officers of national sororities and fraternities.

The Blue Book of College Athletics identifies personnel in the athletic departments of universities and colleges throughout the United States. This directory can be secured from the Rohrich Corporation, Akron, Ohio.

Government Agencies

Many hotel people overlook government agencies as a source of convention business, but they are one. This is especially true of agencies that deal with business groups, such as the Department of Agriculture and the International Food Organization of the United Nations.

It is hard to generalize about the kind of business that comes from agencies. It does vary a great deal, as does the interest in different parts of the country. We are strong believers in fishing expeditions. Go into any local government office and ask the supervisor about meetings held by his department or any emanating from the national or state office. It takes patience and work, but you may be able to add a number of prospects to your lists. Some chambers of commerce are funded by local governments, and some are independent membership organizations, but all are sources of meetings business.

If the people expected to attend such meetings are government employees, it would help if you learned what the current per-diem allowance is for your city. Government employees are given a fixed amount of money for each day of travel away from the office. It is seldom a generous sum, and employees often add to it out of their own pockets. It helps in pursuing such business if you can offer a meeting package of lodging and meals that is covered by the allowance.

When going after government business, you will find that it is not too much different from corporate setups. You deal with organized strata of executives. When you get to the person of authority, you can close the deal. You can expect many small meetings, on short notice, just as in corporate business.

Be sure to contact your local legislators to enlist their aid in pushing for meetings of government agencies in your town. A suggestion by a legislative committee member helps in such matters. They have to meet somewhere; why not in your hotel?

One exceptional source for reaching the government market is the Society of Government Meeting Planners. There are presently Chapters of SGMP in Seattle, Chicago and Washington, D.C. Its membership is open to meeting planners at all levels of the government as well as hotel salespeople and suppliers.

Allied members have access to membership lists and may attend monthly meetings.

Incentive Meetings

What is incentive travel? It is a *travel award*—often a deluxe tour package—offered as a reward to employees who put forth extra effort according to criteria established by the program sponsors.

Travel award programs are frequently established for automobile dealers, appliance distributors, insurance salespersons, and other employee and customer groups to which motivation is important for performance. The insurance industry and appliance and television manufacturers are the heaviest users of incentive travel.

Travel incentives have been used to improve morale, reduce employee turnover, and achieve special sales targets. They have been recognized as effective motivators.

The economic environment has a great impact on the degree of incentive travel. When times are tough it becomes critical to motivate employees. Because of the energy shortage, people in businesses are finding it necessary to work harder to have profitable operations. Incentives have proven to increase employee and distributor participation in moving products and services.

104

Fig. 6.1 A Plan for Marketing to Incentive Planners. Source: "The Incentive-Travel Market: How To Reap Your Share," by Robert C. Lewis, The Cornell Hotel and Restaurant Administration Quarterly in the *The Group Market: What It Is and How to Sell It, Hotel Sales Marketing Association.* Use with permission.

A PLAN FOR MARKETING TO INCENTIVE PLANNERS

1. Create and maintain a favorable image with incentive planners' client companies through (a) appropriate advertising, (b) direct mail to key management personnel, and (c) performance when booking and servicing incentive travel groups. NOTE: This is not a "selling" job; the objective is to develop awareness and build an image. As previously noted, this is a very minor part of a hotel's input; thus, it does not justify large expenditures. The main emphasis must be on part (c).

2. Alert hotel managers to the specific needs of incentive travelers. This can be done by:

- Educating managers about how incentive travelers are different (e.g., they are reward winners and this trip was their incentive; winners repeat and need new and different experiences; they want to be treated like vacationers rather than conventioneers; they want hotels to be flexible in accommodating them as individuals);

- Instilling in managers a willingness to be flexible, in place of rigid conformity to policies;

- Maintaining high standards in service and product, especially during site visits, in terms of marketing as well as operations;

- Appointing one person per hotel to deal exclusively with incentive planners and clients. This person should have flexibility in and authority over pricing and operations.

3. Train office personnel to refer inquiries (politely and professionally) to those who can handle them properly. Train those charged with incentive marketing to follow through promptly and efficiently.

4. Prepare and circulate materials addressed specifically to planners . . . . Regardless of its format, this material should reflect the personality of the hotel, its understanding of incentive travel, and its ability to fulfill travelers' needs completely.

5. Prepare incentive promotional collateral for planners to distribute to their clients.

6. Segment the incentive-planner market by extent of experience, as well as on the basis of planners' specific needs and client rosters, and market to each segment and its clients accordingly.

7. Deliver what is promised even if it means additional cost. Incentive planners remember; they would prefer to use one hotel and one company over and over if they know they could depend on the company to please the clients who are their bread and butter.

8. Develop a comprehensive marketing plan for incentive sales. This takes time and effort and should include input from key personnel.

9. Conduct research focusing specifically on key incentive planners who are known users of your hotels, and apply the research as a benchmark for follow-up feedback from planners when they use one of the hotels. The goal of this effort should be to verify that the needs and wants of the planners are being satisfied.

Their Importance to the Hotel

Incentive travel now accounts for some 10 percent of the large premium and in-centive industry. (Gifts given to employees besides travel include television sets and other appliances.) The measurable portion of the incentive travel business totals some half-billion dollars annually, and it's still growing.

Also of importance to hotels is the tendency of such travel to include spouses of sales staff members (dealers' spouses are always part of the deal). Sales psychologists are convinced that spouses are important to the success of the employees. (*Spouse* is a well-chosen word because today many a sales staffer is a *saleswoman* instead of a *salesman.* The accompanying spouse, in increasing numbers, may be a husband.) Spouses are included because the company wants them to feel they are part of the team, helping to meet the goal while showing tolerance for the time de-mands placed on the hustling salesperson.

Eric F. Green, a CPA with Harris, Kerr, Forster & Company, says of spouses and the importance of incentive travel to the hotel:

> The fact that spouses usually accompany the winners of incentive travel awards enables such business to contribute to an increase in the double occupancy rate of a hotel, something which, in itself, has a favorable effect on operating results. Also, the award winners, realizing they will not have to pay the basic expenses of the trips, may spend their own money quite liberally on extras such as gift items and types of recrea-tion and entertainment too lavish to be included in the awards. Another good aspect of incentive travel plans is that such business can be depended upon to boost a hotel's occupancy on weekends and at other times which may be slow periods.[1]

Such travel incentive programs are always tied in to hard-sell merchandising programs, but with the hard sell slipped beautifully into the velvet glove of a de-lightful vacation trip. We see the psychology of a group of "winners" enjoying a trip "earned" by performance, paid for by the supplier (benefactor) being catered to far beyond the experience of the ordinary tourist.

Obviously, incentive trips call for a desirable vacation setting. All the tourist attractions come into play here—be it a natural attraction, an ideal climate, excite-ment, or even some tie-in with the industry or company. The visit to the factory may seem trite, but it often is worked into the itinerary. What is ordinary and trite to some groups may be exciting and stimulating to others.

The experienced incentive program planner analyzes his people carefully to decide what kind of site and program will draw interest from the greatest number. It may be a big-city trip, a trip abroad or to a Caribbean resort, or an exciting visit

1. Eric F. Green, CPA, Partner, Harris, Kerr, Forster & Company, "A Good Time for In-centive Travel Plans," *Transcript.*

to a playground like Las Vegas. A Pocono resort, a ski lodge in Colorado, or a country club with a famous golf course may be just the thing for a smaller group.

It is a rare company that does not take the opportunity to hold some sort of meeting, however brief, in the victorious climate of a rewarding trip for the qualifying sales staff or dealer group. These meetings serve to remind the attendees that they have profited a great deal by the goods and services successfully sold. It is also a most opportune time to present new products or new advertising and promotion campaigns, and to generally promote good will among the company's very best customers.

Much less is called for in the way of meeting facilities for incentive groups than for a convention or conference. And the meeting business that is conducted is less complex. Usually a general assembly hall and banquet facilities will suffice. The accent is on the vacation activities, and the business connection is definitely of the soft-sell variety. Almost any resort property should be able to handle this type of business.

It is a rare incentive trip that runs beyond a week, or less than five days.

Contacts and leads for the incentive market can be developed through the Society of Incentive Travel Executives (SITE). SITE sponsors an annual trade show called the Incentive Travel and Meeting Executives Show, where incentive travel suppliers such as hotels, attractions, and airlines exhibit their products. SITE also publishes an annual directory of incentive travel executives.

Role of the Travel Agent

"We have noticed a definite trend in agency-produced business-travel agents are getting more involved in group business, primarily with corporate accounts."[2]

There are many details that need to be taken care of before an incentive program gets off the ground. Many of the larger companies that sponsor incentive travel have their own travel managers who make all travel and hotel arrangements for the group. Smaller companies or associations that have found it unfeasible to employ a specialist have called on outside travel agents to coordinate their travel and meeting needs. (fig. 6.2)

The National Passenger Traffic Association also reports that travel agencies are becoming increasingly involved in convention service and incentive planning.

2. Edmund Sansovini, executive director for sales and marketing for the Boca Raton Hotel and Club, quoted in "Yes, We Use Travel Agents," *Resort Management.*

Fig. 6.2 Use of travel agents by association and corporate meeting planners to plan meetings. (Source: The Meetings Market Study conducted by Meetings and Conventions Magazine)

Question: Do You Use Travel Agents to Help Plan Off-Premises Meetings?

	Total Corporate Planners	Total Association Planners for Meeting Other than Major Convention
Yes, used travel agent	58%	25%
No, did not use travel agent	42	75
TOTAL	100%	100%
Average # of meetings used travel agent:	6.7	7.3
Travel Agent Services Utilized		
Airline ticketing	98%	97%
Hotel room reservations	55	26
Hotel recommendation	31	17
Provide maps, brochures, etc.	30	12
Producing itineraries	23	21
Site inspection	20	15
Hotel selection	13	8
Destination selection	9	4
Destination recommendation	9	6
Other	2	4

In fact, many of the larger corporations have dropped their in-house travel departments. Specialized *group travel organizations* have been the outgrowth of this trend.

E. F. MacDonald is generally regarded as the innovator in incentive travel. Working as a stock boy in a luggage factory, he observed an NCR representative picking up merchandise. He learned the luggage was intended as incentive prizes for dealers. He conjectured that if luggage could be used as an incentive, so could travel. From this was born the specialized incentive travel agent. E. F. MacDonald was soon joined by other firms. S. and H. Travel Awards, Maritz, Diners-Fugazy, and others have moved in to capture a share of this growing market.

These agencies see to the details of the incentive program. They negotiate with airlines and hotels and then package the transportation, lodging and meeting accommodations, meals, tours, and entertainment. They often prepare the promotional literature and may even get involved in setting the goals of the program.

Before the group arrives, the travel agent visits the site and reviews with the hotel the arrangements for servicing the group. The agent sees the group through its stay, serving as the middleman between the group and the hotel. In essence, then, the travel agent serves as a bona fide meeting planner, seeing to the needs of the group he or she represents.

Commissions

A highly controversial subject between hotels and travel agents is the question of commissions on convention business. Generally, a hotel will pay a commission of approximately 10 percent to an agent who books an *independent* or *tour guest* into a hotel. However, *convention rates* are usually quoted *net* and not commissionable further.

What this means is that the hotel will not pay a commission to a travel agent for booking a convention delegate. The airline and ground handler, on the other hand, do pay a 10 percent commission for a convention air tour package.

Promoting Weekend Conventions

Resort hotels and commercial hotels have different peak and valley periods. Resort properties traditionally find themselves busy on weekends, but slow on weekdays, while the opposite is true for downtown hotels (fig. 6.3). Resorts have countered the trend by using conventions to pick up the slack during their shoulder period. This avenue, however, has not been so freely open to city hotels since conventions seldom meet during the weekends. While downtown hotels maintain a respectable occupancy level throughout the week, the weekend slack drags the average occupancy down to a point that is often discouraging.

City hotels thus make special efforts to promote weekend convention business. The following suggestions will help to increase the average occupancy and net income of commercial hotels:

1. Delegates who are meeting during the week are excellent weekend prospects, and efforts should be made to persuade them to *prolong their stay*. Place a list of weekend events in every room.
2. *Promote the city*. Inform the meeting planner of the many attractions available on weekends that may not be so readily attended on weekdays. Convention bureaus can often assist with direct mail campaigns and brochures pointing out the advantages of holding weekend conventions.
3. Package *special events* as part of the convention program. Sporting, theater, and musical attractions tied in as a convention tour may be used to lure weekend group business.
4. Suggest that the meeting double as a *vacation*. Delegates might be encouraged to bring their families, combining business with an educational trip.
5. Be honest with the meeting planner. The convention staff is generally able to

Fig. 6.3 Typical daily occupancy pattern of a commercial hotel. Note need for promoting conventions and meetings on the slow weekend days.

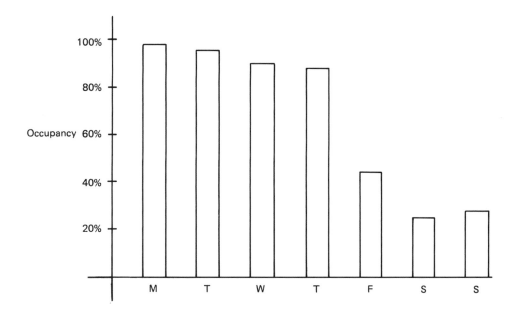

do a better job on weekends, giving its *undivided attention* to groups meeting then. Also, it is easier to be more generous with complimentary rooms, suites, and public rooms on weekends.

6. A strong selling point to corporate meeting planners is the suggestion that a weekend convention *will not cut into the normal work week* of their people.

7. *Reduced rates* are prime inducements for drawing weekend meetings at city and suburban hotels. A survey of both corporate and association meeting planners on the question of weekend inducements was conducted by *Meetings & Conventions magazine.* The results showed the most effective way to encourage weekend group business is through the use of lower rates.

Working with Other Organizations

The hotel staff cannot handle all the service requests made for an average convention, so outside organizations enter the picture. Convention decorators, drayage companies, florists, printers and duplicators, photographers, ground handlers, and audiovisual specialists are a few of these outside organizations. Receptive agents, those who perform such services for delegates as guided tours and local transportation, are also extremely important to the success of a convention.

And local talent agencies for live entertainment, program bureaus for speakers, temporary personnel, and model agencies also play small but important roles in modern conventions. An experienced convention sales and/or service manager has a book of such companies in the area that have proved to be resourceful and reliable.

Not only must the client be assisted in searching out and dealing with local supply and service companies, but he must also be assisted in establishing credit with such new suppliers. If such credit cannot be established in some cases, provision must be made to pay in cash.

We strongly believe that a business should not lay out any money for a client on which there is no profit markup. Following such philosophy, then, the convening organization should be encouraged to deal directly with these outside supply and service organizations. The hotel may be instrumental in finding such companies, recommending those with a history of reliability, and expediting such efforts. But try to have such billing done outside the hotel's billing arrangements. This is easily done when the association is dealing through a convention management company.

Convention Bureaus

A Bureau's function is to bring conventions, trade shows and tourists to their respective areas. A secondary objective is, of course, to offer those services which necessarily follow the attraction of conventions, trade shows and tourists. To accomplish this most Bureaus operate on either a formal or informal departmental basis in that conventions and trade shows represent a special sales activity that is handled by a department or section of the Bureau along with the accompanying services relating to it. On the other hand, the tourism effort and its services are generally handled by another department of the Bureau.

Bureaus actively sell not only their Convention Centers but also the individual hotel and motel properties that are required or could be used by convention, conferences or trade show groups.

A Bureau should be the nucleus for the sales effort in the visitor industry for that community and should also represent the point of "one stop shopping" for any prospect or client contemplating holding a convention or trade show in that city. A Bureau must be impartial in its representation of its facilities if it is to be successful in its position of the tripartite relationship. That relationship consists of the Bureau representing the convention meeting group to its facilities and conversely the Bureau representing the convention and meeting facilities to the group using them.[3]

If the city or area has a convention bureau, the hotel staff has an ally. Many of the outside service organizations referred to earlier may be procured through the convention bureau's files and experience. The original sales contact and presentation may very well have been made in close cooperation with the convention bureau staff.

The convention bureau's role is to attract convention business to its city or area. It makes sales efforts to get such business, especially when the convening group is large enough to necessitate the use of several hotels. The bureau also assists in executing conventions, often supplying registration clerks, guides, women's program personnel, etc. Most convention bureaus also provide a *housing bureau* for placing delegates in the city's hotels when large conventions are booked. (This is discussed in chapter 11.)

The convention bureau's sales office is set up similarly to a hotel sales office, but on a larger scale. In a nutshell, its job is to sell the city, bring conventions to the area, and make the stay both productive and enjoyable. The bureau goes after convention business. Its staff is aware of the capabilities of the hotels in the city and may advise convention planners on the ones best suited for the event. The convention group may have decided to hold next year's event in a certain *city*, and only later is a *hotel* selected. The convention bureau staff may have played a role in getting that show into town, and may work with the hotel sales staff to close the sale.

Thus the bureau actually functions as an extension of the hotel's sales staff. It often receives a statement from an association saying that the city has been selected for the convention. The bureau then sends out a convention lead form to the hotels (fig. 6.4).

Convention bureaus are structured in different ways. Some are membership organizations to which hotels, transportation companies, restaurants, and local merchants turn in order to organize efforts to bring in convention business. Others are funded with local government money, and may also work to promote general tourism. In some cases, they operate exhibition halls that were built with public funds.

The bureaus we have dealt with invariably have excellent records of association conventions. This is just about the *first step* you should take in your search for

---

3. Quoted from correspondence with William F. Snyder, president of the Anaheim Visitor and Convention Bureau, on the role of his organization.

Fig. 6.4 Convention lead form sent by convention bureau to hotels in the city advising them of an upcoming convention. (By permission of the San Francisco Convention and Visitors Bureau).

SAN FRANCISCO
CONVENTION & VISITORS BUREAU
1390 MARKET STREET, SAN FRANCISCO, CALIFORNIA 94102

<u>CONVENTION LEAD FORM</u>

Date xxx

TO	All major hotels
FROM	Matt Miller
GROUP	XYZ CORPORATION

CONTACT   Mr. John Jones   TITLE   Convention Manager

ADDRESS   6000 K Street, N.W.

CITY   Washington, D.C.   20097   PHONE   (202) 123-4567

ATTENDANCE   500   NO OF ROOMS   350

EXHIBIT SPACE NET SQ FT   4000

REQUESTED DATES   February 3-6, February 10-13, 1989

                arrivals 2/2 or 2/9; departures 2/7 or 2/14

MEETING REQUIREMENTS

```
    2/2 or 2/9  6 p.m. reception for 500 people
    2/3  "  2/10  8 a.m. breakfast for 150
                  12 noon lunch for 500
                  9:00-5:00 general session for 500 theatre style
    2/4  "  2/11  9:00-12 noon five workshops for 100 each theatre style
                  afternoon free
    2/5  "  2/12  9:00-12 noon general session for 500 theatre style
                  12 noon reception & lunch for 500
                  2:00-5:00 five workshops for 100 each
    2/6  "  2/13  9:00-12 noon general session for 500 theatre style
                  7 p.m. reception & dinner dance for 500 people

    San Francisco is definite; hotel selection within three months
```

Please copy the Bureau on all your correspondence

HISTORY
```
    1985  New Orleans  476 registered; 327 rooms used
    1986  Las Vegas    498 registered; 319 rooms used
```

business. Your convention bureau executive could fill you in on the history of the associations that have met in your area or those that are considering meeting in your area but decided in favor of another site.

If your area has a convention bureau, it most likely is a member of the IACVB —the International Association of Convention and Visitor Bureaus. If so, you are most fortunate because the IACVB can offer you a wealth of detailed, confidential information. Each IACVB member files and receives reports dealing with convention performances and characteristics of all associations that convened within a member's city. This data includes promised attendance and actual figures, prices paid, concessions granted, and almost anything else you want to know about a prospect. When you track a convention over the last five years or so, a pattern emerges that enables you to decide whether you have a good chance to get such business and how to go after it.

The convention bureau also serves as a coordinator when the size of the event makes it mandatory to present the sales proposal as a group and to house the delegates in a number of hotels. The first objective is to sell the organization on the wisdom of coming to your city or area. How the delegates split up within the hotel group is of secondary consideration. There is a famous recipe for rabbit stew that begins, "First—catch a rabbit!" Catching big game requires the efforts of a number of competitor/associates. But such team work enables you to cash in on events that otherwise are too large for your facility.

Promotion among local schools, organizations, and merchants may be coordinated with the convention bureau to everyone's benefit. The convening group feels the welcome extended beyond the hotel to the entire community. And local businesses recognize that they too are a part of this convention business.

Preconvention and post-convention tours are another source of business. If you have local attractions, the hotel can be instrumental in stimulating business for them by publicizing the tourist features. It helps the hotel sell itself as a convention site and helps the local attraction draw additional attendance. Guests leave with favorable impressions of the hotel and the hotel and the community because they had a good time.

Publicity

Local media don't really fit the definition of a convention service organization. You just don't need to use the local newspaper or radio station except when local attendance can be stimulated by local advertising. But the media can play a role, nevertheless. They constantly look for local color stories. If you can bring your client and local news people together, the resultant publicity will be appreciated by the client, will help the hotel, and will help to keep civic support for such business activity.

Study Questions

1. List several types of nonprofit organizations. What sources can be used to locate their meeting planners?

2. Incentive meetings are becoming increasingly popular. Discuss incentive travel, the types of meeting sites preferred by such groups, and the group travel organizations that specialize in this business.

3. Discuss the role of the travel agent in group business, including the issue of commissions.

4. Downtown hotels have different peak and valley periods than resort hotels. Commercial hotels typically are slow on weekends. Cite several possible methods of promoting weekend conventions.

5. Define the role of the convention bureau in selling conventions, including references to the International Association of Convention and Visitor Bureaus (IACVB).

Outline

I. Sales within the Hotel Framework

    A. Marketing Objectives
    B. Sales Structure

II. Sales and Marketing Staff

    A. Positions within Sales
    B. Differences between Large and Small Properties
    C. Independent Hotel Representatives
        1. What the Hotel Representative Does
        2. How to Choose a Hotel Representative
        3. How to Work with a Hotel Representative
    D. Banquet Department
    E. Convention Services

III. Sales Records and Filing Systems

    A. Three Methods of Filing
    B. Elements of the Filing System
        1. The Master Card
        2. The Letter Folder
        3. The Tickler File
    C. Examples of Filing Systems
        1. Aladdin Hotel
        2. Hilton's Computerized System
    D. Public and Banquet Space Control
        1. The Function Book
        2. Function Book Control
    E. Guest Room Booking Control
        1. Guest Room Control Book
        2. Holds, Options, Confirmations

Sales within the Hotel Framework

To be effective a hotel and every department in it must be organized. Lines of communication and authority must be clearly drawn, showing how jobs relate to each other. Every employee should know his or her responsibilities, authority, and accountability.

Three conditions must be met in planning an organizational structure. First, each employee should have only one boss. In management circles this principle is called *unity of command.* There are few things more frustrating for an employee than having two or three bosses giving conflicting orders. Similarly, if employees do not know who is accountable to them, the effectiveness of the management process is likely to be seriously hampered.

A second principle is *delegation. Make authority commensurate with responsibility.* When delegating responsibility, management must also delegate the authority to get the job done. A sales manager who is given the responsibility of increasing sales volume must also be given the authority within the sales department and within the total organization to secure those sales.

A final consideration in planning a hotel's organizational structure is *span of control.* This refers to the maximum number of employees that a supervisor can effectively manage. There is no universally accepted figure; it varies with the type of job performed. For example, repetitive jobs may require only one supervisor for every twenty to twenty-five workers, while jobs requiring originality and organizational abilities may call for a more limited span of control. Sales supervision is an example of the latter. Because the job of salesperson is complex, the sales manager will probably have a maximum of seven to ten employees working under him or her.

Another aspect of organization must be discussed: *line* and *staff.* The functions of line and staff departments are distinctly different. Line departments are concerned with day-to-day operations. They are often spoken of as the part of the organization that gets things done—in a hotel, the food and beverage, front office, and housekeeping departments.

Staff departments are essentially advisory. They support the line with information and assistance but technically have no authority over line departments. Sales is a staff department, counseling and advising line departments. Figure 7.1 shows the relationship between line and staff.

Sales is presented as a pure staff department in this chart. While the adviser role traditionally has separated sales from the line, in actual practice this is often not the case. Hotels catering to the meeting and convention market have found that sales must be given more say in the day-to-day line operations. What is promised

Fig. 7.1 Typical convention hotel organization chart.

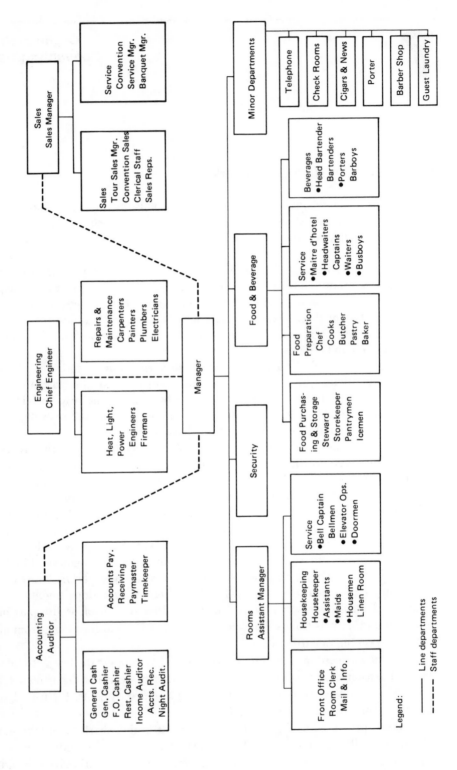

Legend:

——— Line departments

- - - - Staff departments

to convention groups must be delivered. If the sales department doesn't have the authority to carry out its commitments, problems are certain to arise. For this reason, many hotels are now giving the sales department functional authority over the front office, catering, and housekeeping in tasks related to the servicing of conventions.

Organization for efficient sales operation begins with top management itself. The sales structure's position of influence within the hotel is often predicated on upper management's commitment to sales. There are different schools of thought on just where the sales manager fits into the organizational chart. That decision must be made by the general manager, and he or she can make it only after setting marketing objectives and determining how to achieve them.

Marketing Objectives

There is no room for false pride in setting marketing objectives. The very first step, as we have said, is to cast a cold and analytical eye upon your property. Examine its geographic location, age, and physical condition—all the positive and negative qualities that make up your hotel, as was discussed in chapter 2, "Analyzing Your Property."

After an honest self-appraisal, you should set reasonable, reachable targets. It is important to be realistic because the sales effort is expensive and emotionally exhausting, if done sincerely, and the price is too high to be wasted.

The objective of convention sales is primarily to fill rooms. One of the attractions of convention business is that it fills many rooms at a time. Another is that such business can often be controlled to fill those rooms at the most advantageous times, such as during the off-season or slow periods.

In many kinds of hotels, it is imperative to set target times for convention bookings. While it is true that most hotels will take bookings whenever they can get them, this is only because of a lack of control and the inability to pick and choose the business and still fill the house.

Group business can fill the house at times when the usual business will be unable to do so. Thus it makes sense to expend a major effort for this kind of business. It is worth a great deal to a northern beach resort property to fill up in times besides the summer season. Likewise, a southern beach resort is eager for bookings in the spring or summer or fall. And a ski lodge looks for business during the mild months. Why should it look for convention business when the snow is on the slopes and the skiers are flocking in at high seasonal rates?

It is when the principal attraction of the hotel is impotent that the convention is most attractive. So a marketing objective of making a seasonal hotel into a year-round one just about has to turn to the meetings field and its large groups.

Even hotels without severe seasonal limitations develop "holes" in their occupancy charts. Mid-August is often a soft period, even in summer resorts. And for commercial hotels, the latter part of the week is certainly not as good as Monday through Thursday.

This objective—to level out the occupancy peaks and valleys, and to do it by going after convention business—is a decision that must be made by the hotel's top management. Once that policy is made, the proper structure must be formulated to go after such business efficiently. Then provisions must be made to service the business properly.

Sales Structure

Management must structure the sales department in such a manner as to encourage it to go after group business, and yet control it so that such business is handled profitably.

There is an amazing amount of disagreement within the hotel industry about the amount of authority the sales manager should enjoy. One would think that top management would always be in total support of sales, but it just isn't so. Many hotel sales managers are terribly lacking in authority. It would seem that such hotels establish sales staffs because they know it is a proper step, but then fail to make a complete commitment.

A sales staff that is improperly structured, without clearly defined lines of authority, lacks the muscle to carry out its assignment. Such staff alignment speaks eloquently about mangement's degree of conviction that sales effort is the way to full occupancy. This kind of management gladly accepts convention business under optimum conditions but does not back sales efforts sufficiently to get more than occasional business. The lion's share of the lucrative convention market goes to those hotels that go after it was enthusiasm and all the might they can muster.

What should management do so its sales staff can function efficiently? Ronald Hughes, former general manager of the Palmer House in Chicago, says:

> We have a responsibility to our salesmen and saleswomen that they become more involved in the day to day hotel operations, not only for the training benefit, but even more important so that their input and suggestions are built into the operation. The hotel that is market-oriented is a giant step ahead of its competition. To develop

this marketing concept the senior salesman and, especially the Sales Director, must be involved when we are doing our long range budgeting, our short range forecasting, and many of the other basic planning functions.[1]

Management must make it clear that the sales effort has a high priority and that the sales manager has been delegated sufficient authority. To avoid conflicting instructions and battles over priorities, the sales manager must be second only to top management in authority. He or she must report directly to the general manager. In some hotels, the sales manager may report to the resident manager instead. But it is imperative that department heads realize the vital position occupied by the sales executive.

Perhaps it is the custom nature of each meeting that leads us to espouse this cause. Many things can, and do, go wrong at conventions. When they do, action must be prompt—there is no time for departmental bickering.

To function well a sales manager must have full authority over the banquet department, the convention services staff, advertising and sales promotion, a supporting clerical staff and, of course, the sales staff itself. If this seems self-evident to you, it may come as a surprise to hear that this is a very controversial subject in the hotel field. However, we believe it is impossible to mount an effective sales campaign without clearly defined lines of authority.

Let's look at the problems involved. The sales manager must control the vital *function book*, the calendar record of all bookings in the hotel. This will be discussed fully later in this chapter, but assume for now that all booking control is centered in the function book. A sales manager cannot commit the house to a convention if he or she cannot control all the meeting and banquet rooms. It becomes painfully obvious that hotels which farm out their restaurant and catering business to concessionaires are at an acute disadvantage when going after convention business. If the banquet manager functions independently of the sales manager, clashes cannot be avoided.

Similarly, the functions of advertising, sales promotion, and publicity are all tools of marketing. The sales promotion plan must be under the authority of the sales manager because he should control his tools. He must be sure promotion is directed where the sales targets are, and that the deployment of precious advertising dollars is in keeping with his objectives. Things won't work out too well if the ad program goes after tourist business when the marketing plan calls for going after convention business.

---

1. Ronald L. Hughes, "Management's Responsibility to the Sales Staff," *HSMA World*.

Job Title:	Convention Sales Manager
Department:	Marketing
Reports To:	Director of Sales
Basic Functions:	Reviews with Director of Sales the marketing strategy that will obtain maximum occupancy levels and average rate. Responsible for all convention group business related to the market segments within the Western territory as they relate to annual revenue projection.

Consults daily with the Director of Sales concerning the Western territory and how it relates to the marketing success of the hotel through effective merchandising, prospecting, solicitation, and booking of business.

Scope: Sales manager will be the primary person for the booking of long term convention group business with long term being more than six months out.

Work Performed: Initiate prospecting and solicitation of new accounts in the Western territory; manage current accounts to maximize room nights from the account in relation to the hotel marketing plan; responsible for administrative efforts necessary to perform the aforementioned.

1. Quotas for this position are:

Room nights per month:	1200
Soft spot percentage:	20
Phone calls per week:	
Trace:	20
Prospecting:	25
Personal calls per week:	10
New accounts per week:	10

Individual to supply weekly, monthly and annual reports supporting productivity standards.

2. Probe for customer needs: rooms, suites, desired dates, day of week pattern, program agenda, food & beverage requirements, and degree of flexibility in each of the aforementioned areas.

3. When available obtain information on the groups past history, i.e.: previous rooms picked-up, arrival/departure pattern, and double occupancy percentage.

4. Review availability of customer's REQUIRED DATES AND ANY ALTERNATE DATES which should be offered. The dates presented to the customer should satisfy the customer's needs while allowing the hotel to maximize occupancy and average rate.

5. Negotiate with the customer: day/day of the week pattern, day by day room block, group rates (within guidelines as set by DOS), comps, and function space.

6. Tentatively block rooms and function space in accordance to office policy.

7. Confirm in writing, according to office standards via short term contract or long term contract and function room outlined all aspects of the meeting. Tract to insure they received the signed contract.

8. Alert all necessary departments of pending tentative: i.e., front office and credit.

9. Upon receiving the signed contract, process definite booking ticket, definite function room outline, and credit application.

10. Oversee, manage, and tract the way in which reservations are to be made, the pick-up of the group block, adherence to the cut-off date, and any subsequent adjustment to the room block (positive or negative).

11. To periodically contact the customer while in-house to be certain all is in order and going well. To handle any last minute needs as they arise.

12. Conduct an exit interview with the customer to determine their level of satisfaction and ask for additional business.

13. Send letter of appreciation to customer. (Letter should include actual room night consumption and the letter should be tailored to previous exit interview discussions.)

14. Individual is to attend extra curricular activities, meetings, and accept any responsibilities or projects as directed by the Director of Sales.

Supervision Exercised:	Supervise and share one secretary with another individual.
Supervision Received:	Primary supervision from the Director of Sales. Initial training, and re-training as needed, also received from the Director of Sales. Receives direction from the Director of Sales in regards to room merchandising.
Responsibility & Authority:	Upon the satisfactory completing rooms merchandising and operational training, the individual will have the authority to make decisions and confirm directly to the client; dates, room blocks, and rates.
Minimum Requirements:	Bachelor of Arts or Science degree—preferable business, hotel or restaurant administration. Individual must also be professional in appearance and approach.
Experience: *Sales Competencies:*	Minimum of two years experience in hotel sales.

1. Ability to negotiate.
2. Accounts strategizing.
3. Ability to prospect.
4. Ability to judge profitability of new business.
5. Knowledge of product.
6. Knowledge of competition.
7. Ability to make presentations.
8. Ability to organize and plan.
9. Ability to utilize selling skills.
10. Ability to overcome objections.
11. Ability to problem solve and make decisions.
12. Ability to write effectively.

Negotiations between the sales staff and potential clients generally result in promises made. Such promises must be kept. The difference between a successful convention property with many repeat bookings and a less successful one usually reflects on the determination to live up to commitments. The sales manager must have the authority to live up to those promises.

However, it is important to have built-in controls on the sales manager. There is a fear in some hotel quarters that without controls salespeople would give away the house. It is management's prerogative to limit this authority in certain areas or to set certain factors as inviolable. Rate structure and inclusion of "extras" at no cost could be predetermined.

Good sales managers know just how far they can go to get business. In the hotel field, this may not be a constant. A hotel may make additional concessions if a group schedules at a particularly slow spot on the calendar. But even then, the bottom figure must be worked out in advance. If a sales manager gets business only by making excessive concessions, management should review whether it has the right person in a very responsible position.

What is outlined here is really a conventional sales structure, with no pun intended. It applies to situations in most fields. In the hotel field, where we are dealing not with a manufactured product but with a series of custom productions, a pyramid structure with a single entity on top having full authority is needed. The general manager or resident manager must deal with all the divisions of innkeeping. When he or she delegates authority to a sales executive, that person must have whatever it takes to get the job done.

Sales and Marketing Staff

We have said that the sales staff should be headed by one person. After the overall marketing plan has been formulated and accepted by top management, it is the responsibility of that person to execute the plan. We'll call him, or her, the *sales manager,* but he could have a title like sales director or vice-president/sales. This depends on the size of the staff needed and the use of titles in other departments. In smaller hotels sales direction, marketing, selling, and even servicing may all be done by one person.

Positions within Sales

The sales staff is the first contact many people have with a hotel. The travel agent, the corporate planner, and the association meeting planner first establish contact through this office. Thus their first impressions are formed by the warmth, personality, and public conduct of the sales staff.

There is a wide variety of positions within the sales department. Following is a brief description of the job classifications. (Each of these jobs will be covered in much greater detail later in this chapter and throughout the book.)

It is important to remember that sales is a *team effort*. While each individual on the sales staff is given a certain responsibility, his or her efforts must be coordinated with those of the other members of the sales team.

As we have said, the head of the sales department is called the *director of sales*. His, or her, job is to coordinate and direct the efforts of the sales staff. All sales promotion programs must be channeled through him for approval. He works closely with the general manager to determine target markets and the budget appropriations for each market.

The *tour and travel sales manager* is responsible for developing group and charter business for the hotel. He, or she, works closely with travel agents, tour wholesalers, tour operators, and transportation companies. He is generally the person instrumental in putting together tour packages, so must have expertise in pricing and promotion of group packages. The job as it relates to convention sales is in putting together incentive group packages.

The *convention sales manager* is responsible for soliciting convention trade for the hotel. It is his or her job to identify and contact these associations, corporations, and fraternal organizations that could use the hotel for their convention. A convention sales manager may have to work a prospective convention for three to five years before securing the business. Convention sales are generally made through personal visits, so the convention sales manager must build a relationship of confidence with the prospective client. (fig. 7.2)

The *convention service manager* works hand in hand with the convention sales manager. His or her job is to coordinate and service the convention. The convention service manager takes over after the sale has been made and begins to work out the fine details with the convention group. Any problems that arise during the convention will be directed through him. He must work closely with all departments, coordinating the efforts of food and beverage departments, the front office, and the banquet setup crew. In addition, it is his job to see that things run smoothly in the exhibit area.

Another member of the hotel sales staff is the *hotel representative*. This person spends a great deal of time outside the hotel making calls, either cold calls or prescheduled ones, to prospective sources of business. The representative may spend one-third to half of his or her time on the road in an effort to drum up business—convention, tour, or individual—for the hotel. It is also his job to contact former guests regularly, through personal visits, direct mail, or telephone calls in an effort to generate repeat sales.

Sales staffs may also have an *advertising sales manager*. This person's job is to coordinate all promotion materials and establish public relations for the hotel. He or she makes the final decision on advertising media for the resort—radio and television, magazines, newspaper, billboard, or direct mail.

There is much competition for convention sites. Marketing efforts should be supported by advertising and promotion that are carefully planned and executed. You need media advertising, direct mail, and good sales aid material if you are after convention business. The hotel that has its own advertising department for general work should make special efforts to develop material and advertising dealing solely with the convention market. In smaller properties, the sales manager may be his own advertising manager.

In some cases, such efforts may be supplemented by an advertising agency. A properly selected and properly employed agency adds skilled specialists to the work force of the advertising department. Even smaller hotels can afford an arrangement with smaller ad agencies. It is difficult to work without one, in fact. Advertising agencies are not a substitute for your own sales efforts, but they have the skill and the resources to back up the sales department with the required promotional material.

A final, very important part of the sales department is the *clerical staff*. The key to successful sales is careful and detailed records, intelligent use of this data, and diligent follow-up. This calls for a conscientious clerical staff. The clerical staff provides support at the home base and is a vital key to repeat sales.

It would be penny-wise and pound-foolish to foot the considerable expense of fielding a sales staff only to skimp on the support at home. The period of sales effort before signing a convention can be very long, so your salespeople have to stay in sight. With sales calls costing about one hundred dollars or more these days, a follow-up system of letters and phone calls by a well-trained clerical staff is essential. These people will also maintain careful, detailed records of your prospects' convention activities, personnel changes, and other data that may help win the sale.

All of these positions may be found in any property. In smaller establishments the marketing, selling, and servicing may all fall to one person. But whatever the size or type of resort, and regardless of the number of people on the sales staff and their positions, it is necessary that a well-planned and properly implemented marketing strategy be established.

Differences between Large and Small Properties

Small hotels often may not have clearly designated sales staffs of any kind, but it is important that someone be given the assignment of going after business, even if it is on a part-time basis. The resident manager himself may decide that he will be out on sales calls a half-day a week. Whatever it is, should be a planned effort, with a clearly designated amount of time allotted to it.

In larger hotels a specialist sales staff is assigned to the task. If the sales staff does all kinds of selling, such as travel agent contact, make sure that it also receives training in convention sales. Whenever possible, it works best to have full-time sales specialists for convention sales. In the largest organizations, the degree of specialization is carried still further, with salespeople assigned to segments of the market. One sales staffer may go after association business, while another goes after corporate meetings business and still another concentrates on incentive programs.

Obviously, this type of concentration is practical only for chain operations. It is not essential to successful selling to break down the task so finely, but this should tell you that each segment of the market has its own appeals. To save time and money, many hotel and chain operations break the market into geographic areas. This permits the establishment of sales offices in such strong contact areas as Washington, New York, or Chicago.

Hotel chains use *corporate sales staffs,* as well as personnel assigned to specific properties. The corporate staff hunts for business for any hotel in the chain. There are certain advantages to this. A customer who experiences good service and a successful meeting in one hotel of the chain might be induced to stay within the chain for the next meeting. Even when convention organizers have to move the event around the country to increase attendance, they may be sold staying within the chain.

It is also easier for a meeting planner who is scheduling ten similar meetings in as many parts of the country to deal with one salesperson and book all of them at once. Still another advantage comes into play when a meeting planner cannot get a free date at one hotel. The chain may be able to offer another hotel on that date, whereas the independent loses out when firm dates cannot be met.

The chain operation is most efficient in the convention field and its role is expected to grow.

Independent Hotel Representatives

Many hotels feel they cannot adequately cover all the market bases with an in-house sales staff. They may turn to hotel representatives to increase their sales coverage. These representatives may be either part of the hotel's sales staff or, as is more commonly the case, *independent hotel representatives*.

What the Hotel Representative Does

As the title implies, this person represents the hotel. He or she is a specialist, serving as a long arm of the hotel's sales department. Because hotels have different needs, the services provided by such firms vary widely. In some cases, the representative may be hired simply as a field salesperson, soliciting clients who are impractical for the hotel's in-house staff to reach. Other hotels may use the larger representation companies more extensively. Services provided by these firms include consulting, market analysis, advertising, and public relations, in addition to field sales.

Many one-property hotel organizations find it to their advantage to use hotel sales representatives. The attraction to the hotel is that it is represented in the field by a number of salespersons. Thus it resembles the position of a member of a chain; the satisfied customer of the representative is likely to sign on for another of the representative's hotels. In addition, the representative may have convention contacts that the hotel doesn't. Some of these firms have achieved a considerable following in the field.

As is the case with almost any sales setup, there are pros and cons to sales representation. While your own staff is more limited in number and geographic coverage, it can benefit only from sales made for *your* property. This tends to make your own staff sell harder and to be more knowledgeable about and committed to your hotel.

Because of economics, independent representatives usually represent more than one property. This causes many hotels to balk at the notion of being represented by such firms. Quite logically, they question having a competitor represented by the same firm. Hotel representatives answer this criticism by saying that they represent properties of different sizes and market emphasis, not similar properties seeking the same clients.

Should a hotel use an independent hotel representative? If you can afford to field your own staff and it performs satisfactorily, that's fine. If you can afford only the most limited sales efforts, a representative may offer another dimension. What counts is the amount of sales generated.

How to Choose a Hotel Representative

Choosing an independent hotel representative should not be taken lightly. If you were hiring an executive to work in-house, you would most certainly want to interview the person. A hotel should take the same precautions before retaining a hotel representative, familiarizing itself thoroughly with the firm.

Similarly, it is important to acquaint the representative with the operation of the hotel. Personal visits to the property should be encouraged and a tour provided by management. The representative should be given organization charts; operating manuals; charges for meeting rooms, guest rooms, and other facilities; and a statement spelling out in detail the hotel's sales policy.

In choosing an independent sales representative the following questions should be considered:

1. Does the firm represent competing properties?
2. How many hotels does it represent? Has it extended itself so much that it will not be able to meet your needs?
3. Does the representative have a service attitude? Do you want him, or her, to be an extension of your service staff? Is he willing to become part of your team?
4. Can he deliver supporting services you need and advise you on brochures and other printed materials?
5. Does he specialize in the market you are seeking? Does he have knowledge of the group and convention business?
6. Does the firm have offices in the cities that are likely to be your major market areas?
7. Is the representative's staff knowledgeable about your type of operation? Does his staff have a hotel background?

There are many independent hotel representatives, with varying degrees of expertise. Generally, a firm specializes in a particular market, although it overlaps to other sources of business. If your target market is the convention trade, it is, of course, important to be selective in your choice, although few firms actually specialize in the convention field. The majority of the association and trade convention groups are headquartered in Washington, Chicago, and New York. If your representative has an office in one of these locations, your chances of reaching the convention market are greatly increased.

If a hotel is not sure whether a representative is really needed, it would be wise to consult similar-sized properties using the representative. Quiz them on their problems. Discuss yours with them. Obviously, if you are not convinced that you need an independent hotel representative and you do not have faith in his or her abilities, effectiveness is likely to fall short.

Hotel representatives are generally hired on a contract basis. They are usually paid a fee and a set percentage for the volume of business they directly book for the hotel. Clear guidelines should be established. A representative should not be allowed to promote the house, giving it away at bargain prices so that he might receive his commission.

How to Work with a Hotel Representative

Communication is vitally important in achieving maximum benefits from an outside firm. Sonesta Corporation, owner of a number of large hotels worldwide, has devised a plan to reduce paperwork and minimize duplication of effort between its sales department and its independent representatives.

Copies of all promotional and advertising materials are sent to the representatives by the individual hotels via the national sales office. This eliminates duplication and serves as a check, ensuring that only accurate information is sent. A one-report policy has been adopted to reduce paperwork. Rather than sending daily updates on room availability, Sonesta sends only one report a week to the representative's office. Any close-outs or dramatic changes are telephoned.

The plan has been mutually beneficial. Representatives say they are freed from the barrage of paperwork, giving them more time to make calls. Sonesta reports a reduction in costs and the time-consuming activities characteristic of working with hotel representatives.

Banquet Department

Quite frequently the hotel's organizational structure determines how easy it is for communication to flow. In general, the less complicated the organizational lines, the easier the communication process. The effectiveness of an organization might be measured by how unhindered information can flow. In keeping with this, we believe the banquet department belongs under the jurisdiction of the sales manager. Communication problems are sure to arise unless the sales manager completely coordinates banquet sales and food functions at conventions.

An example of a potential problem is illustrated in figure 7.3, a partial organizational chart showing only the sales department and the food service department. It shows a conflict that is characteristic of a poor organizational structure. Note that the banquet department is not under the sales department but reports to the food service manager. When a client requests banquet space, the banquet manager will book one of the hotel's function rooms. This flow seems effective enough on

Fig. 7.3 Partial organization chart showing the possible conflict when the banquet manager does not report to the sales manager.

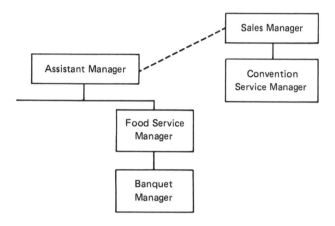

the surface, but the sales department also often needs function rooms when a convention group is booked.

The communication flow, according to the chart, should go from the banquet manager to the food service manager to the assistant manager to the sales department. If the communication channels are properly observed, situations presenting a conflict between the banquet and sales departments would be minimal.

The problem occurs when the communication breaks down. Remember, the more complicated the organizational structure, the more difficult the communication process. Suppose the banquet department booked a function room and the sales department unknowingly scheduled the same room for a training seminar. If no other rooms were available, the hotel would be placed in an embarrassing position and likely would lose business.

Such problems can be avoided if the organizational structure is properly constructed. Ideally, the banquet department should report to the convention service department (fig. 7.1). Trouble follows only when the directions of the two department heads do not coincide, and it works out better when one has the designated authority.

Control of all function space must be overseen by one person—the sales manager. This eliminates confusion and communication problems. It all has to do with the hotel's priorities and marketing plan. Someone must decide who gets the ballroom on a certain night—the convention awards dinner or a local wedding party. The decision must be made with an eye toward the overall scheme of things, and this falls within the responsibility of the sales executive.

While it should be under sales for administrative purposes, the banquet depart-

132

ment should be a self-contained unit able to handle all assignments from a simple workshop lunch to a gala banquet. It is hard enough to find a good sales manager with expertise in convention sales without expecting him or her to be expert in food and beverage, too. The banquet manager should be an expert in that area.

When management finds it necessary or desirable to farm out the banquet department or the restaurants to a concessionaire, a genuine conflict of interest can occur. This can be even worse than when the banquet manager is not under the wing of the sales manager because the concessionaire is not a part of the hotel organization. The contract under which the concession is operated must deal with this problem most clearly. If management equivocates because it does not wish to jeopardize the concession, it will find that it is sorely hampered in its convention sales efforts. And the food and beverage functions are too important to convention service to risk that.

Convention Services

The position of *convention service manager* is a most interesting and important one. This section will serve only as an introduction to the servicing process; Part II deals in detail with every aspect of the convention service manager's job.

When the convention is in the planning stage and in the house, there is a need for one person to coordinate the entire operation. The convention service manager serves as the on-the-scene contact between the convention organizer and the hotel. He or she is the one who sees that all provisions of the contract are carried out. He must be prepared to cope with requests—and emergencies—that come up as the convention nears and during the event itself. A resourceful convention service manager is a prized asset to any hotel. (fig. 7.4)

Just as many hotels find that they cannot field a full-time sales staff, many also do not have a full-time convention service manager. In many smaller properties, the sales manager also serves as convention service manager. In many hotels, the latter job is regarded as a stepping-stone to a position in the sales department.

This position is a very crucial one and must never be downgraded. The convention service manager must have sufficient stature and authority to cope with the unexpected. He must be able to commandeer enough labor to handle emergencies. These may be true crises or merely urgent last-minute requests that must be honored. It is not the time to argue authorization. It is the time for action, and house policy must have clearly defined the position of the convention service manager and the extent of his or her authority. This person could make or break many events by acting or failing to act promptly and effectively.

The convention service manager should report directly to the sales manager. As the sales manager's right arm, the convention service manager handles the function book and controls it in the sales manager's absence. This booking record also gives him an indication of his need for labor. This personnel support may be full-time, part-time, or a combination of the two, depending upon the size and volume of business. Labor union contracts must be honored, and any special requirements should be explained to the convention organizer. Certainly the customer should understand the labor regulations fully to avoid problems during the convention. No one benefits from labor problems during setup period.

Sales Records and Filing Systems

The next chapter deals with the techniques used in soliciting convention business, but before starting a sales promotion program, a hotel should institute a system of sales records and files in the sales department. Large properties generally have a separate sales office, while smaller hotels may have to combine the sales operations under another department or even work sales out of the general manager's office. Every hotel, regardless of size, should have some kind of sales department from which all promotional efforts are directed.

The effectiveness of the sales promotion is determined to a great extent by the department's operating procedures and sales records. Vast amounts of client information must be documented and filed, and the files must be accurate and up-to-date if they are to be meaningful. Similarly, forms and records are valuable only if the information they contain is accessible. If you cannot locate the needed information quickly, the system isn't much good.

C. Dewitt Coffman has said that the "maintenance of accurate and up-to-date file systems is the single, most important mechanical operation of any sales department. Without minutely accurate file records, the sales department is without ammunition."[2]

Three Methods of Filing

The filing method varies with the hotel. Some prefer one method over another, and some use more than one method. But Mr. Coffman says there are three general

2. C. Dewitt Coffman, *Marketing for a Full House* (Ithaca, New York: Cornell University School of Hotel Administration). Reprinted with permission of the School of Hotel Administration at Cornell University.

methods of filing.[3] The first is a straight *alphabetical filing* by the title of the organization, firm, or association, and by the name of the contact person. This method tends to be the easiest.

The second method is to file by the *key word of the title*. This has its advantages when the exact name of the organization is not known. For instance, The Association of Petroleum and Oil Products would be filed under the word *petroleum*. An account could end up under two, three, or four key words. A variation of this method is the three-level way of classification. Examples of this are: Trade-Manufacturing-Shoes; Trade-Manufacturing-Air Conditioners; Trade-Retail-Clothes; Educational-Teachers-High School; Government-Municipal-Fireman; Government-Municipal-Police.

The third method is *numerical*. The files carry an assigned number and a corresponding set of file cards is kept by the number and name. Although it is not as widely used, this system is effective in larger file systems.

Elements of the Filing System

Having considered the three methods of filing, let's take a look at the three most common elements of a convention sales file: the master card, the letter folder, and the tickler file. As each is explained and illustrated, keep in mind that systems vary slightly from hotel to hotel. A simpler system usually tends to be superior to a complicated setup.

The Master Card

Most hotels establish a data bank of prospects. Most often, this is done with a *master card* file (fig. 7.5). Each card carries a quick summary of all you need to know for sales effort—names, titles, addresses, phone numbers, month or months in which the group meets, size of the group, where it has met in the past, what time of year, who makes the initial and final decisions, and other pertinent comments.

With the amount of data to be recorded, most use five-by-eight-inch cards. Filing cabinets are available from commercial stationers.

Use color-coded identification clips on the top edge of the cards to draw attention to particular cards for a special reason, such as *geographic location* if you'd like to go after groups in a certain area. The *month of meetings* is worth color-coding for the times when you have gaping holes in the calendar. *Follow-up* clips remind you to get back to those you've contacted. *Cycles* can be keyed to remind

3. Ibid.

Jan.	Feb.	Mar.	April	May	June	July	Aug.	Sept.	Oct.	Nov.	Dec.	1 to 100	100 to 250	250 to 350	350 to 500	Over 500

Convention Group *NATIONAL LIVESTOCK DEALERS ASSO.   N-02197*

Main Contact *DAVID PRITCHARD*   Title *ASSO. MANAGER*

Address   Phone
City
Other Contacts

How is Decision Made   When

Date	City	Hotel	Attend	No. of Hotel Rms.
				Exhibits
				Functions

you which associations are due back in your area. *Size* is another characteristic worth coding, as you may find the greatest success for your hotel in going after meetings of a certain size. (Smaller meetings generally have shorter lead times and there may be times when you will want to fill some holes in *this* year's calendar.)

The same information should be stored for every corporate account you can research. Use a master company card listing basic data such as location, type of business, address, phone number, and key corporate personnel and titles. Use a trailer card for each division, and put it behind the master card. A sales department may have different kinds of meetings, controlled by different people, and at different locations and times than the training department, or even the sales department of another product group. Use the master card for personnel on the overall corporate level, such as the president or a full-time company-wide meeting planner; use the trailer cards for division personnel, such as the sales manager or the advertising manager. A company like General Electric may have a number of trailer cards.

If you have to start from scratch, you'll need a lot of source material and clerical help. If you start with a hotel's records, the first task is to update what you have.

Obsolete data is not much help. Out of this master record—this data bank—you can develop a master list that will be the basis for an effective sales promotion.

The Letter Folder

The *letter folder* is a standard-sized file folder containing all correspondence and related material and serving as the basic group business record (fig. 7.6). Files are started at the first contact, and everything subsequent relating to the group is recorded. Included in the file might be tear sheets from trade papers, past convention programs, and convention bureau bulletins. The correspondence in the file also tells the story of all previous efforts to secure the group and includes information about servicing the group.

The folders are usually filed alphabetically, and the files include past, present, and prospective groups. They too may be color-coded. The file folder should indicate the manner in which the master card is filed. If done this way, the master card could be classified by category, enabling the letter folder to serve as a cross-reference to the master card.

Whenever a file is removed, a guide card should be left in the file drawer in place of the file. This card shows the name of the group, its file number, the date of removal, and the initials of the person requesting the file. This enables the sales staff to know a file's whereabouts.

The Tickler File

One great aid to effective follow-up is a *tickler file,* also called the *tracer file, bring-up file,* or simply *follow-up file.* These come in various forms, but the cards are always filed by month and date. Some are card files with monthly dividers and card separators marked 1 through 30 or 31 (fig. 7.7). The same system is available in an accordion file with multi-pockets. And there are systems designed to fit within a letter-sized file cabinet.

They work this way: You make contact with a prospect who indicates that no meeting plans will be worked on until October. But you may want to contact that person before then—perhaps in September. A card or note or the copy of some correspondence thus should be placed in the pocket marked September 15.

Your secretary, or you yourself if you don't have such help, must remember to remove everything in the pocket of each date of each month. If you diligently place material in the tickler file but fail to retrieve it on the indicated date, the system obviously won't work. Relying on memory doesn't work either. The tickler file, used properly, works very well, costs little, and takes very little time to implement.

A variation of the tickler file uses colored tabs on the tops of the cards in the

138

Fig. 7.6 The letter folder serves as the basic group business record, containing information about a group in a standard-sized file folder.

	ABBEY HOTEL		
Attendance 900 - 1000	**CONVENTION INFORMATION**	Name of Group NATIONAL LIVESTOCK DEALERS ASSO.	
Usual Month of Meeting JAN		N-02197	

	Previous Meeting Sites			Follow Up Dates		
Year	City and State	Month	Dates	Month	Day	Year
1980	DENVER, COLORADO	JAN				
1981	LAS VEGAS, NEV.	JAN				
1982	MIAMI, FLORIDA	JAN				
1983	BOSTON, MASS.	JAN				
1984	CHICAGO, ILL.	JAN				
1985	DALLAS, TEXAS	JAN				
1986	LAS VEGAS, NEV.	JAN				
1987	PORTLAND, OREGON	JAN				
1988						
1989						
1990						
1991						
1992						
1993						
1994						
1995						
1996						
1997						
1998						
1999						
2000						
2001						

Fig. 7.7 Tickler file. Dates on the three-by-five-inch follow-up card pulled from the file show when the card was "brought up"; the initials are those of the salesperson who reviewed the convention group's file. (From C. Dewitt Coffman, *Marketing for a Full House*, Ithaca, New York: Cornell University School of Hotel Administration. Reprinted with permission).

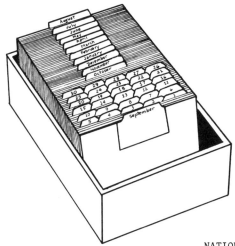

NATIONAL LIVESTOCK DEALERS ASSN.   N-02197
                                                PA

Trace:

DATE	INL.	DATE	INL.
Jan. 12	M.A.		
June 15	M.A.		

file. Each color represents something, perhaps the groups that meet in November or on weekends. The tab system works well to categorize prospects and to encourage you to make additional cold calls each week on suitable prospects.

All records should be updated when a booking has been made. Outdated carbon copies should be removed from the follow-up file. This will avoid an automatic follow-up letter being sent to an association. The same procedure should be taken, of course, if the association has made a booking with another hotel.

Examples of Filing Systems

To give you an idea of how hotels actually incorporate their filing systems, we will examine the systems of the Aladdin Hotel in Las Vegas and the Las Vegas Hilton Hotel.

Aladdin Hotel

The Aladdin's system basically consists of four files: the master file, contact file, key word file, and geographic file.

Master File   The master file is a letter-sized folder, with the association's name printed on the tab, filed alphabetically. It is the major file kept for an organization and includes the association's name, address, phone number, name of the contact person, and information about the association. The tentative group booking is kept in this folder, as well as the definite group booking and any change order or cancellation. All letters and follow-up material are kept in the file.

On the back of the folder is a trace date (follow-up date) keyed to a corresponding trace card filed in the manner discussed earlier. This trace date is crossed off when that date arrives and the file is pulled, and when warranted a new date is written for the next follow-up.

Associated with the master file is the master card, a three-by-five-inch card including only the association's name, address, and phone number, filed alphabetically.

Contact File   The contact file includes three-by-five-inch cards filed alphabetically by the name of the contact person. This and the association's name are the only information in this file. It serves as a cross-reference to the master file and is helpful in associating a name with an association if not readily known.

Key Word File   The key word file contains only the association's name on a three-by-five-inch card, filed under a key word. This file too serves as a cross-reference to the master file.

Geographic File   The geographic file is a cross-reference file consisting of only the name of the association. The card is filed according to one of four areas in which the association or contact person is located: Nevada, Chicago, Washington, D.C., or California. Not only does this file serve as a cross-reference, but it also is a type of "good will." When a salesperson is traveling to one of these four areas, he pulls the names of these associations located there so he can call on them and spread good will.

Hilton's Computerized System

The Las Vegas Hilton is one of many large hotels and a few small ones that use electronic data processing to organize their convention files. The computer stores the names of organizations and associations and pertinent data about the groups.

The Hilton filing system is based on what are called *national files,* consisting of the names of and vital information about all associations. Once a year the sales-people in the Hilton corporation's national sales offices—in Atlanta, Chicago, Detroit, Los Angeles, New York City, Washington, D.C., and San Francisco, with headquarters in Beverly Hills—are required to contact as many of these accounts as possible.

After doing so, the salesperson feeds information into the computer about an organization's next open date, the area it plans to meet, for how long, etc. The salesperson then notifies the Hilton hotels in that area so they can contact the association. The information about the association will be printed out on the hotels' computers.

The Hilton's tracing system is predicated on these leads. Once the hotel receives the information from the national sales offices, it goes into its own system, which consists of one filing method. A large folder type of file is prepared for each firm the Hilton might be working with and it is filed alphabetically according to the title. All information about the group is contained in this file. No other cross-reference files exist, such as the key word (although there is one in the computer system) or contact name. The Hilton corporation never uses contact files as the contact person is continually changing.

The Hilton does use three-by-five-inch trace cards to facilitate follow-up. The cards are filed in the manner discussed earlier.

If a salesperson wants information about a particular account, he or she gets in touch with a national sales office, which punches out the information in its computer. The information, in turn, is printed out on the computer of the hotel that requested it.

When a cancellation occurs or there is a gap in group sales, the computer can be called upon to sift through thousands of cards. In a matter of minutes, the hotel can have a list of groups holding meetings on the open date. Such information would be impossible to collect by hand.

Public and Banquet Space Control

In selling public and banquet space to convention groups, a salesperson must be sure, of course, that the assigned space will be available. There could probably be no greater catastrophe than for two groups to show up at the same time to use the same room for a banquet. Control of function space is essential. The hotel's *function book* shows at a glance which function rooms are occupied and vacant on any day.

Fig. 7.8 Function book reservation sheet. The sales or catering manager must fill out this form and submit it to the one person responsible for monitoring the hotel's function space. Use of a form similar to this prevents the possible of a double booking.

U.S. Grant HOTEL

FUNCTION BOOK RESERVATION SHEET

Group Name _____   Comments _____

Contact _____   _____

Address _____   _____

Phone _____   _____

Dates In House _____

A G E N D A

DAY/DATE	TIME	FUNCTION	SET-UP	# OF PEOPLE	ROOM NAME

Meeting Space Charges:

Sales Rep _____

Date _____

Option Date _____

Date Entered _____

Entered By _____

The Function Book

You cannot plan functions efficiently and without mishap without a function book. There should be only *one,* so there can be no mismatching of entries and no double bookings. You need to have one carefully kept record of all proposed and contracted events.

The most common type of function book has a number of vertical columns, each calling for some essential data. Reading across the page, the column headings might be: (1) organization or person; (2) authorized person(s), with title, address, and phone number; (3) type of function; (4) time required for the event; (5) total time required, including setup, breakdown, and cleanup; (6) number in attendance; (7) type of setup; (8) rates; (9) booked by whom; (10) contract status; and (11) remarks (fig. 7.9).

Reading down, there should be one section for each meeting or function room, with about ten lines for each room. At least six lines are needed to cover each time period—breakfast, morning meeting, luncheon, afternoon meeting, cocktail party, dinner function, or night function. Include several extra lines, because changes seem to be inevitable and these lines are handy for clarity. Here is a case where neatness does indeed count.

A page is needed for every day of the year. Common rules for recording in the function book are: (1) record all bookings in pencil, (2) the name of the meeting group should be recorded exactly as it appears on the file so future referencing is easy, (3) the starting and ending times for each function should be recorded as there may be an opportunity to book another piece of business.

It is most important that salespersons booking a group a year or two in advance provide a tentative program as soon as possible. Never to discuss the assigning of space with a client who can view the function book. The customer may see open spaces and feel that the hotel does not want to give him or her space, when actually it is committed to another group.

Function Book Control

One person should control the function book. It should be the convention sales manager, or with a large staff, the senior sales executive. Because sales personnel travel a great deal, the executive may designate the convention service manager as the one to handle the book. In the case of a chain operation, each establishment maintains its own function book.

The sales staff or representatives may be supplied with a simplified version of the function book indicating confirmed dates and those being held until some specified date. This is used merely to indicate to the salespeople which dates are available for additional bookings.

144

The *single person control* of the function book is essential. Convention space cannot be sold efficiently without controlling the function book. It would seem amateurish to tolerate an arrangement in which the convention sales manager and the banquet manager vie for control of function space, yet it happens. Great difficulties are encountered when control is not centralized and clearly outlined. (fig. 7.8)

Guest Room Booking Control

The control of guest rooms is separate from the control of function rooms. A *guest room control book,* rather than a function book, is used to monitor sleeping room allotments. The more convention business a hotel does, of course, the more need there is for long-range control.

We will use the accompanying hypothetical case to explain the booking and control forms needed for convention sales. Sample reports from several different hotels are illustrated in Figures 7.10 through 7.13.

The Booking Process   Case Study

Through a corporate lead the sales manager of the Fairmont Hotel has learned that the International Marble Association plans to convene in San Francisco. Although the convention is two years away, he knows that now is the time to make contact. He calls the meeting planner and asks him about the dates desired and the association's requirements. From this conversation the sales manager prepares a *call report* (see fig. 7.10) recording the information received in the interview.

The call report is placed in the association's file folder with instructions to send the group a convention brochure. A tickler date is specified for follow-up in three months, when the meeting planner has suggested he will begin serious site selection.

The next time the two parties talk, the meeting planner is exploring dates. If the sales manager has dates open that appeal to the meeting planner, he may offer the group a *tentative booking*. If the group is seeking a large room block and is likely to bring a lot of revenue into the hotel, the sales manager is going to be more inclined to hold space for the meeting planner. Figure 7.11 shows the tentative booking sheet that would be filled out at this stage.

Caution must be used in issuing tentative booking forms. The hotel doesn't want to lose out on other bookings while protecting a tentative that cannot possibly "go definite."

Along with the tentative booking, the sales manager often will supply a proposal letter that includes complete information about the Fairmont and a schedule of the hotel's rate structure.

The meeting planner then returns to his board of directors for a review of the hotels under consideration and a final decision on the site. Assuming the Fairmont receives the nod, the sales manager confirms the booking and fills out a *definite booking sheet* (fig. 7.12). This form has the same detailed information as the tentative form. The definite sheet, like the tentative one, is placed in the association's file folder.

Two other forms commonly used in the convention booking process deserve brief mention, the *convention change sheet* and the *lost business report* (fig. 7.13). If a tentative or definite booking is changed or must be canceled, these forms are used, giving the reason and outlining suggested action.

Fig. 7.10 Call report of Red Lions Inns. A file copy, a trace copy and a copy for the general manager are prepared.

RED LION INNS. **CALL REPORT**

FIRST CALL _____
REPEAT CALL _____
FILE NO. _____

COMPANY / ORGANIZATION: _____

STREET ADDRESS _____

CITY _____ STATE _____ ZIP _____

CONTACT: _____ PHONE: _____

DOES YOUR COMPANY HAVE MEETINGS? ☐ NO ☐ YES HOW OFTEN? _____

SIZE _____ CONTACT _____

WHEN IS YOUR NEXT MEETING? _____ WHERE _____

DO YOU NEED GUEST ROOMS? ☐ NO ☐ YES HOW MANY _____

WHO MAKES THE RESERVATIONS? _____

DO YOU NEED OUT OF TOWN RESERVATIONS? ☐ NO ☐ YES WHERE? _____

DO YOU HAVE SUCH THINGS AS:

- CHRISTMAS PARTIES _____
- AWARDS BANQUETS _____
- OTHER _____

ARE YOU OR ANYONE ELSE IN YOUR COMPANY AFFILIATED WITH AN ASSOCIATION? _____ ASSOCIATION NAME

CONTACT _____ STREET ADDRESS _____

PHONE _____ CITY _____ STATE _____ ZIP _____

COMMENTS: _____

NOTE: ANY ADDITIONAL COMMENTS MAY BE MADE ON REVERSE

SALESPERSON _____ DATE _____

FORM NO. 001-S47 (4/86)

SALES PERSON

Fig. 7.11 Tentative convention booking form. (By permission of the Opryland Hotel).

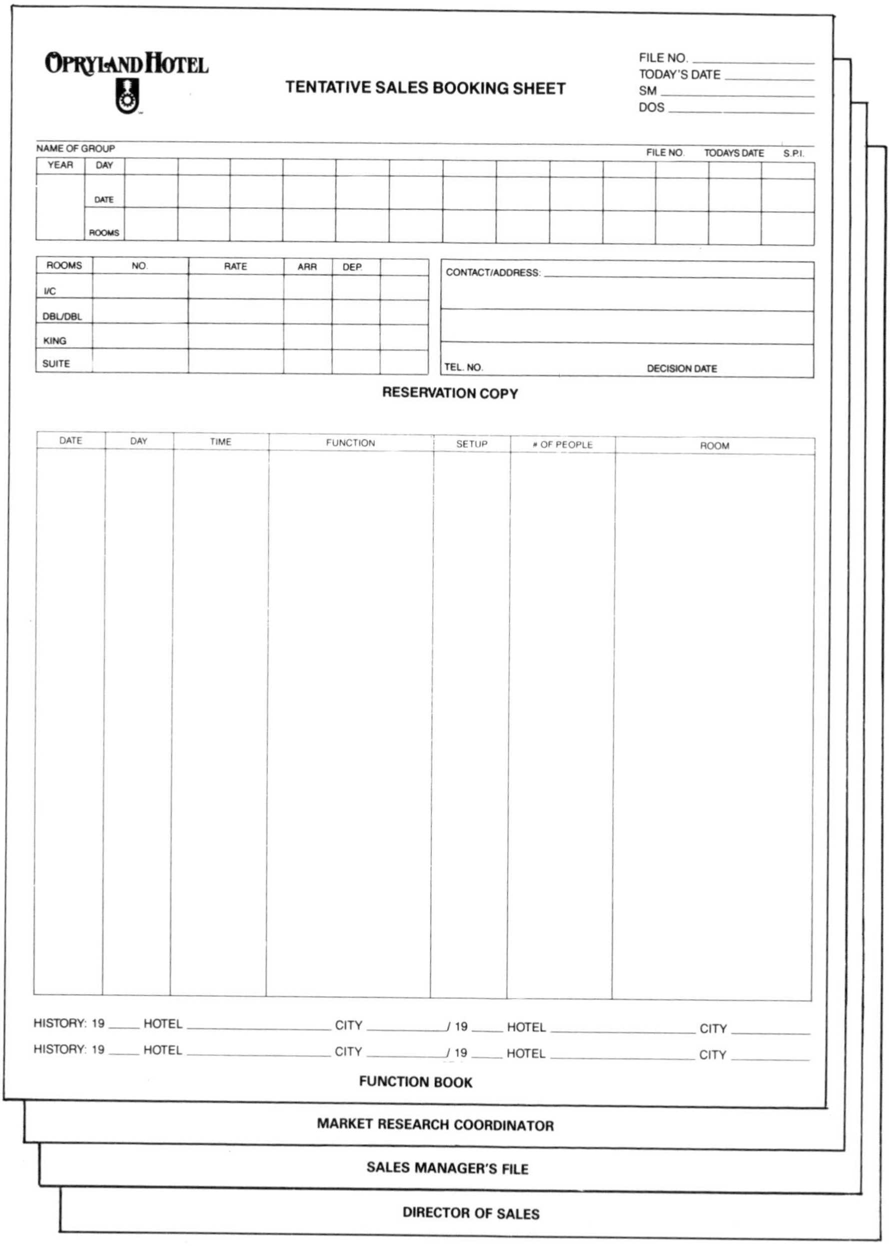

OPRYLAND HOTEL

TENTATIVE SALES BOOKING SHEET

FILE NO. ______
TODAY'S DATE ______
SM ______
DOS ______

NAME OF GROUP | FILE NO. | TODAYS DATE | S.P.I.

YEAR	DAY												
	DATE												
	ROOMS												

ROOMS	NO.	RATE	ARR	DEP	
I/C					
DBL/DBL					
KING					
SUITE					

CONTACT/ADDRESS: ______

TEL. NO. DECISION DATE

RESERVATION COPY

DATE	DAY	TIME	FUNCTION	SETUP	# OF PEOPLE	ROOM

HISTORY: 19 ____ HOTEL ______ CITY ______/ 19 ____ HOTEL ______ CITY ______

HISTORY: 19 ____ HOTEL ______ CITY ______/ 19 ____ HOTEL ______ CITY ______

FUNCTION BOOK

MARKET RESEARCH COORDINATOR

SALES MANAGER'S FILE

DIRECTOR OF SALES

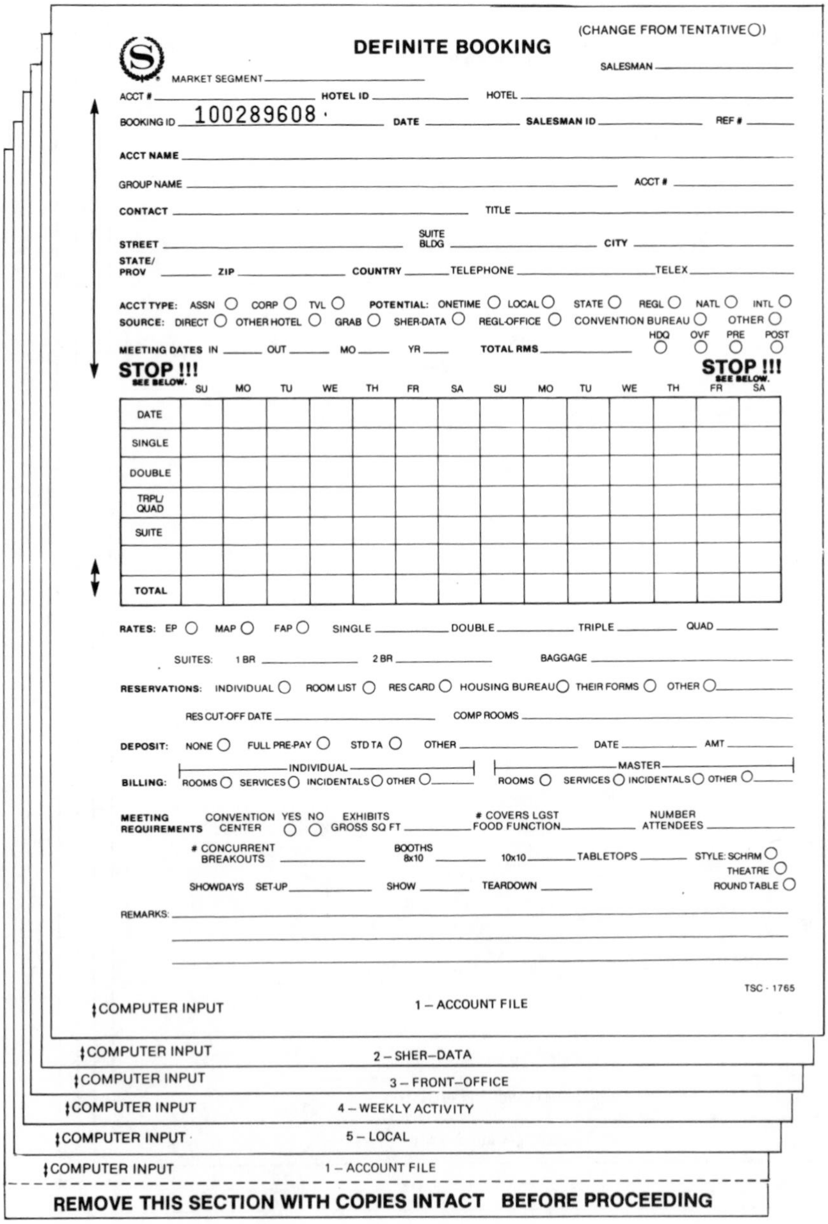

(CHANGE FROM TENTATIVE ○)

DEFINITE BOOKING

MARKET SEGMENT ____ SALESMAN ____

ACCT # ____ HOTEL ID ____ HOTEL ____

BOOKING ID 100289608 DATE ____ SALESMAN ID ____ REF # ____

ACCT NAME ____

GROUP NAME ____ ACCT # ____

CONTACT ____ TITLE ____

STREET ____ SUITE BLDG ____ CITY ____

STATE/PROV ____ ZIP ____ COUNTRY ____ TELEPHONE ____ TELEX ____

ACCT TYPE: ASSN ○ CORP ○ TVL ○ POTENTIAL: ONETIME ○ LOCAL ○ STATE ○ REGL ○ NATL ○ INTL ○

SOURCE: DIRECT ○ OTHER HOTEL ○ GRAB ○ SHER-DATA ○ REGL-OFFICE ○ CONVENTION BUREAU ○ OTHER ○

MEETING DATES IN ____ OUT ____ MO ____ YR ____ TOTAL RMS ____ HDQ ○ OVF ○ PRE ○ POST ○

STOP !!! SEE BELOW. STOP !!! SEE BELOW.

	SU	MO	TU	WE	TH	FR	SA	SU	MO	TU	WE	TH	FR	SA
DATE														
SINGLE														
DOUBLE														
TRPL/QUAD														
SUITE														
TOTAL														

RATES: EP ○ MAP ○ FAP ○ SINGLE ____ DOUBLE ____ TRIPLE ____ QUAD ____

SUITES: 1 BR ____ 2 BR ____ BAGGAGE ____

RESERVATIONS: INDIVIDUAL ○ ROOM LIST ○ RES CARD ○ HOUSING BUREAU ○ THEIR FORMS ○ OTHER ○ ____

RES CUT-OFF DATE ____ COMP ROOMS ____

DEPOSIT: NONE ○ FULL PRE-PAY ○ STD TA ○ OTHER ____ DATE ____ AMT ____

BILLING: INDIVIDUAL: ROOMS ○ SERVICES ○ INCIDENTALS ○ OTHER ○ ____ MASTER: ROOMS ○ SERVICES ○ INCIDENTALS ○ OTHER ○ ____

MEETING REQUIREMENTS CONVENTION CENTER YES ○ NO ○ EXHIBITS GROSS SQ FT ____ # COVERS LGST FOOD FUNCTION ____ NUMBER ATTENDEES ____

CONCURRENT BREAKOUTS ____ BOOTHS 8x10 ____ 10x10 ____ TABLETOPS ____ STYLE: SCHRM ○ THEATRE ○ ROUND TABLE ○

SHOWDAYS SET-UP ____ SHOW ____ TEARDOWN ____

REMARKS: ____

TSC - 1765

COMPUTER INPUT 1 – ACCOUNT FILE

COMPUTER INPUT 2 – SHER–DATA

COMPUTER INPUT 3 – FRONT–OFFICE

COMPUTER INPUT 4 – WEEKLY ACTIVITY

COMPUTER INPUT 5 – LOCAL

COMPUTER INPUT 1 – ACCOUNT FILE

REMOVE THIS SECTION WITH COPIES INTACT BEFORE PROCEEDING

Fig. 7.12 Definite convention booking form. (By permission of the Sheraton Hotels. Processed when a contract is returned signed and business is considered definite. Distributed to Reservations Account file, Sheraton data file, and Weekly Report. Must be approved by Director of Sales.)

149

Fig. 7.13 Change sheet and lost business report, used when a booking is changed or cancelled. (By permission of the Fairmont Hotel and Loews Hotels)

Hotel and Tower,
San Francisco

CONVENTION BOOKING FORM

Definite _____ Tentative _____

Group _____

Contact _____ Title _____

Address _____ Phone _____

City _____

Local _____

Attendance _____ Past Attendance _____

Rooms Promised _____ Past Room Pickup _____

Main Arrival Date _____ Early Arrival Date _____

Main Departure Date _____ Late Departure Date _____

Room Block Held Until _____

Decision Will Be Made: _____

Rates _____

DAY	DATE	ROOMS
Sun		
Mon		
Tue		
Wed		
Thu		
Fri		
Sat		
TOTAL ROOM DAYS		

Booked By _____ Date _____

FORM 224

LOEWS HOTELS

CANCELLATION FORM

HOTEL _____

Group: _____ ☐ Tentative   ☐ Definite

Dates: _____ Total Room Nights: _____

Group Contact: _____

Group Address: _____

Other dates being held (for tentatives) _____

Reason why cancelled _____

Release of Function Space:
   ☐ Yes   ☐ No   Any Comments:

Where are they going? _____

Are there other meetings for which we can be considered? If so, which ones:

_____

_____

What factors would help us get them back for the future?

1.

2.

3.

4.

5.

When should we recontact?

Cancelled by: _____ Date: _____

Booked by (if other than above): _____

FILE

BOOK ADMINISTRATOR

NEW YORK OFFICE

CREDIT MANAGER

RESERVATIONS

CONVENTION SERVICE

CATERING DEPARTMENT

Guest Room Control Book

Every hotel catering to group business should have a guest room control book listing groups holding tentative or definite dates. In some hotels this book is referred to as the *rooms control bible*. Whatever the title, it should list the number of rooms committed to each group. Remember, this book is separate from the function book, which controls public and banquet space; the guest room control book is used only to control sleeping room commitments.

This book is used by the sales department to keep up on the number of rooms it can sell. A proper market mix of group, tour and travel, and individual guest business is desirable for all hotels. Hotels stipulate a maximum *group allotment*, the number of rooms available for sale to groups. The allotment is established by agreement between the general manager and sales director. Special care must be taken, of course, to make sure the sales staff doesn't exceed this allotment. The guest room control book shows at a glance which dates are heavily booked and which are open.

The book's format consists of monthly report sheets with space for the group's name and guest room commitment day by day (fig. 7.14). Such forecast sheets are dated and bound in book form, providing projections several years ahead.

All entries in the guest room control book should be written in pencil. Often definite bookings are listed on the upper half of the page, and tentative bookings on the lower half. This technique indicates the negotiating period of convention sales.

Holds, Options, Confirmations

In the normal sequence of events a convention organizer inquires about the availability of the house on certain dates. Requirements are discussed, and perhaps no obstacles are seen to booking the event. Perhaps board approval is needed or, in the case of a corporate meeting, that of a superior. The meeting planner asks for an *option* on the space. A *hold* is placed on the rooms and an *option date* given. What does this all mean?

The hotel has agreed to hold the space pending final confirmation by the client. This agreement may be verbal or by letter. It is very important to limit the length of such a hold by designating the option date, the date by which the client must either release the space or confirm the order. If the period is too long, the hotel has severely limited its freedom to seek another customer. It should be long enough to enable the client to secure the necessary approval, but not so long that the space is tied up while the client is free to shop for a better deal.

Reputable hotel people will not confirm orders by other parties for the space during the hold period. It does make sense, however, for the sales staffer to contact

152

CONVENTION

| HOTEL | STEWART HOUSE | | | | | | | | | | |
| MONTH | July | YEAR | 1989 | | | | | | | | |

				DAY OF WEEK	M	T	W	T	F	S	S
GROUP	FILE #	SM	PP	DECIS. DATE	1	2	3	4	5	6	7
Anderson Publishing Co.	S 1561	190 Rooms		1/88							
Vartanian Tool and Die	L 1235	50 Rooms		4/88							
Pritchard Dental Supply	S 1991	210 Rooms		9/87							
						1	2	3	4	5	6	7

Fig. 7.14 Sheet from a guest room control book.

FORECAST

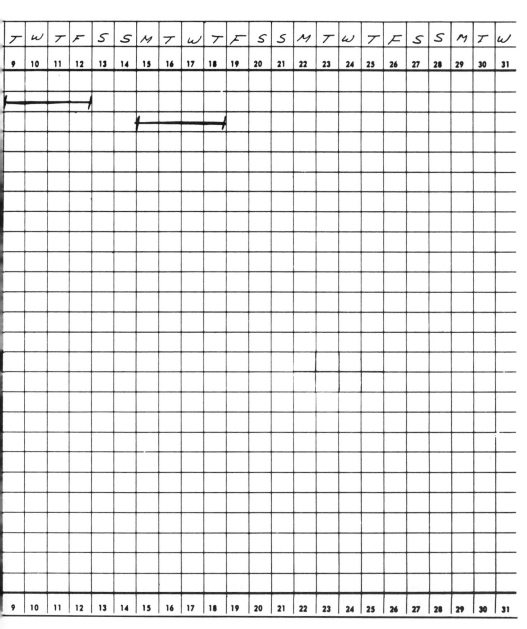

T	W	T	F	S	S	M	T	W	T	F	S	S	M	T	W	T	F	S	S	M	T	W
9	10	11	12	13	14	15	16	17	18	19	20	21	22	23	24	25	26	27	28	29	30	31

the first client, the one with the hold, to ascertain the prospects for confirmation. The client may be unable to confirm or release the rooms because the board that is to decide the matter has not yet met. But it is not uncommon for such a phone call to act as a catalyst to get things moving.

If the client-hotel relationship is very good, the meeting planner may admit that the odds are not favorable for confirmation and the space may be released. Or the hold may be continued. In that case, the second client may be given an option and told about the prior option and its option date. This would put the second party in a position to take the priority option or to book if the first group released, the space on the option date.

When a tentative booking is confirmed—and this may be done by telephone— it is important to sign a contract or letter of agreement. Then the dates are penciled into the guest room control book or the function book. The flow of tentative bookings, holds, and confirmations in and out of the control books makes it *absolutely essential* that there be only *one* copy of each.

It is a good practice at this point to establish a file folder for the event, even though you already have a file folder for the organization. Some hotels file these folders chronologically, but because the function book already lists all events in such order, you may be more comfortable filing alphabetically. It doesn't matter so long as there is some chronological system to remind the hotel of pending events and a single folder containing *all* material relevant to the event.

Study Questions

1. Define the terms *unity of command, delegation, span of control,* and *line and staff.* Discuss the position of the sales department within the total hotel organization and relate your discussion to these terms.

2. What role do marketing objectives play in determining the overall sales structure? Sketch job descriptions for each position within the sales department. Differentiate between the sales structures of large and small properties.

3. What is an independent hotel representative? What considerations are involved in choosing one?

4. Discuss the problems that are likely to develop when the banquet department does not report to the sales manager.

5. Evaluate the following statement by C. Dewitt Coffman from his book *Marketing for a Full House*: " . . .maintenance of accurate and up-to-date file systems is the single most important mechanical operation of any sales department. Without minutely accurate file records, the sales department is without ammunition."

6. What is a tickler file?

7. Compare the filing systems of the Aladdin Hotel and the Las Vegas Hilton.

8. Distinguish between the function book and the guest room control book by tracing the booking process with a hypothetical convention group. When does a tentative booking go definite?

Outline

I. Advertising Techniques

    A. Collateral Material
        1. The Convention Brochure
        2. Preparing a Brochure
    B. Media Promotion
        1. Magazine Advertising
        2. Preparing an Ad
    C. Direct Mail
        1. Planning a Direct Mail Campaign
        2. How Many Mailings?
        3. The Sales Letter
    D. Using an Advertising Agency
    E. Exchange Trade Advertising

II. Selling Techniques

    A. Personal Sales Calls
        1. Promotion Respondents
        2. Past Customers
    B. Tip Sheets
    C. The Cold Call
    D. Sales Blitz
    E. Telephone Usage
        1. Screen Prospects by Phone
        2. Telephone Techniques
    F. Follow-up
    G. Cross-Selling
    H. Internal Sales Promotion
        1. Printed Promotion
        2. Employee Promotion

It is a fact of life that we all have to accomplish our assignments within the confines of a budget. It is a rare job, indeed, that enjoys limitless funds. But support in the form of clerical help, a fair promotional budget, and good organization can put you well on the road to an effective campaign to get convention business.

In the first chapter we suggested that a hotel develop a market plan before stepping out to solicit convention sales. A five-point plan was presented. Using the hypothetical Rolling Green Resort as an example, we analyzed our property, identified our markets, and set the sales promotion budget. Step number 5 of that market plan was reaching the target market, and it is this step that we'll discuss in this chapter.

Convention sales techniques can be broken down conveniently into two types—advertising techniques and selling techniques. We'll discuss them separately.

Advertising Techniques

There are a number of media available to a hotel sales manager to use in an advertising campaign, including

1. newspapers
2. consumer and trade magazines*
3. television
4. outdoor advertising
5. radio
6. direct mail*
7. collateral material*
8. travel guides

However, all of these are not equally effective in reaching the meeting planner. The convention market differs from individual guest trade, and the method used to reach the meeting planner is not the same as that used to capture the individual guest. The individual guest can be defined and located quite easily by studying demographic and geographic data. Newspaper advertising, billboards, and travel guides have traditionally been very effective in reaching this traveler.

These media, however, have not proved equally beneficial in securing the convention market. Reaching the meeting planner requires different forms of advertising. We have discussed the groups that hold meetings and the types of meetings they hold. Now the question facing the sales manager is, which media are the most effective in reaching the convention market?

It is our opinion that only those media marked with an asterisk (*) on the list—consumer and trade magazines, direct mail, and collateral material—are truly effective in reaching the meeting planner. Certainly there are many times when advertising will overlap more than one target market. The association executive may read your hotel ad in the newspaper or see the hotel's billboard ad on the way to the office, but these are not the best media from which to get the maximum value.

Further, once you have studied the convention market, you must have some idea about the kind of convention business you should seek. It is not very effective to take the shotgun approach and say that you'll take any business you can get. Sure, you will, but you may not get any that way. You may be well equipped to handle a variety of meetings and should by no means limit yourself severely. But do be realistic in appraising your property and devote your precious time to going after the kind of business you stand a fair chance of selling—and making a profit from in the final analysis.

When you have selected the segment of the market you plan to zero in on, prepare for the solicitation. You will need intelligently created collateral material, properly designed magazine ads, and effective direct mail pieces.

Collateral Material

Collateral may be a new word to many readers, but the term is frequently used in advertising circles. Collateral sales material is *accompanying material,* used along with direct mail, magazine, and other graphic promotion. Included in this category is a vast array of promotional devices: tent cards, matchbooks, menus, postcards, convention brochures, and rack brochures, to name just a few.

The greatest distinction between collateral material and other advertising is the directness of collateral pieces. Newspaper advertising takes a shotgun approach, while collateral material is more specific, and is often directed right to the decision maker.

Actually, the term collateral, meaning accompanying, may be misleading in convention sales. For most hotels the collateral material, especially the *convention brochure,* is the most important promotional tool used.

The Convention Brochure

Start with the assumption that your prospect has never seen or even heard of your hotel, and certainly has never been informed of its convention capability. Imagine yourself as a meeting organizer looking for a suitable hotel for your next event. The information you would want should be presented clearly and concisely in a con-

Fig. 8.1 Material from convention planning kit that goes to meeting planners. (By permission of the Hotel Utah in Salt Lake City).

vention facility brochure or brochures. A common complaint from meeting planners is the lack of good, accurate descriptive material from hotels.

A brochure will give a planner enough basic data on which to begin some preliminary planning. It should give more *meetings* data than the ordinary tourist, or rack, brochure. The larger meeting rooms should be diagramed, if possible, or at least described adequately. "Large" is not a very accurate phrase. How many people will the grand ballroom accommodate? In what sort of setup? Auditorium-style seating offers greater capacity than seating at round tables. A good brochure will give enough information so that you can devote your personal letters to other things.

The best brochures show scaled outlines—blueprints—of all major rooms. If you want to show each room in some attractive rendition, fine. But also include a simple diagram showing size, exits, columns, windows, primary entrances, and even electrical outlets. Such brochures will be kept for future reference. Brochures are too expensive to produce not to design them carefully for utility and reference.

We have heard some hotel people sneeringly refer to requests for literature as coming from "literature hounds." It is indeed difficult to tell whether the customer who requests the literature is hot or cold, but it is certainly better for your brochure to be filled with many others than to be missing completely.

Every now and then the need for a meeting arises on very short notice. There is no time then for the customer to start research on a hotel. He or she may choose to repeat at some known place, or you may get a chance at the business. Preliminary research from hotel brochures is often used to narrow down the field of contestants. A well-designed, informative brochure costs no more to produce than a bad one.

The brochure need not be so utilitarian that it fails to present your property in a good light, of course. A facility is not chosen merely for its ability to house the event. The beauty of the structure and surroundings, the convenience of the location, and the expertise of the staff are all important. But such data should not be included in the brochure at the expense of basic facilities information. You could include in your presentation kits the usual hotel brochures dealing with the tourist attractions of the property.

Leave some material with the customer that will review the salient points of your presentation; it will help the customer when he or she discusses your property with others involved in the selection of a site. Design your material to enable your contact to present your case completely and favorably. Good brochures will work for you in sales presentations, mailings, and trade shows, and through intermediaries such as convention bureaus, airlines, and convention specialists.

Preparing a Brochure

One of the primary sources for ideas for preparing a convention brochure is, of course, existing pieces. Begin collecting brochures. There are some excellent ones in the field. Start a reference file of brochures you admire for one reason or another. They'll give you many ideas you may want to incorporate into your own brochure.

The convention brochure may be prepared in a number of ways. It can be the fold-out type or loose-leaf pages in an attractive cover folder or a bound presentation of several pages. Whatever type you decide upon, certain information should be included. Following is a checklist you might use in preparing your next convention brochure.

☐ Name
☐ Address
☐ Telephone Number
☐ Area—Location Map
☐ City
☐ Climate
☐ Special hotel attractions
☐ Cooperating hotels nearby
☐ References from past conventions
☐ Arrival/Departure Guest Information
☐ Church Services
☐ Accommodations—Descriptions and Floor Plans
☐ Recreation and Activities
☐ Room Service
☐ Theme Party Arrangements
☐ Shipping and Receiving Procedures
☐ Checklists and Time-Table Planning Guides for Meeting Planner
☐ Guest rooms (room block policy, reservations, rates, registration)
☐ Public dining rooms (names and capacity)
☐ Meeting rooms (names, capacity for types of functions)
☐ Exhibit space (dimensions, scaled drawings, floor load, ceiling height)
☐ Audiovisual equipment available
☐ Banquet and beverage arrangements
☐ Billing procedures
☐ Spouse entertainment
☐ Gratuities
☐ Dress
☐ Emergency First Aid Procedures
☐ Signs and Notices Policy
☐ Transportation (tours, parking facilities, distance to airport)
☐ Convention service personnel (setup service)
☐ Special services and facilities (photographic service)

Media Promotion

Much that has been discussed in previous chapters about ways of reaching prospects is worth repeating. Advertising in specialized magazines will help you to ferret out sales prospects. These convention publications have national circulation among frequent meeting planners. The campaign you can mount will depend a great deal on your budget.

If you have determined that you have had better success with certain kinds of meetings from particular industries, you may wish to try ad campaigns in media concentrating on such readership. Certain newspapers such as the *Wall Street Journal* and magazines such as *Fortune* and *Time* have been used at one time or another by hotels to get convention business. Television and radio spots have also been used. But, by and large, the major efforts have been made in the specialized meetings publications that we discussed in chapters 4 and 5.

Magazine Advertising

Magazine advertising offers several advantages. First, ads can be printed in color and photographs reproduced with good quality. Second, many magazines have a long reading life. Back issues of such magazines as *National Geographic* are kept and reread, giving their ads a longer life. Third, and most important, magazine advertising gives the hotel the opportunity to key its convention sales efforts on a select group of readers.

There are several important guidelines that we feel will make your magazine ads more effective.

First, use color. If you feel the cost of a full-color print is too high, consider using a single color. Blue or red will set your advertisement off from all the black-and-white ads, and one color can be done with little extra expense.

Also, put together a continuous ad program. Single hit-and-miss ads are not effective. Most agencies advise running an ad at least every other month throughout the year.

Don't skip in and out of one magazine. As we have mentioned, there are about six leading trade publications in the meetings market, and most meeting planners subscribe to all of them. Stay with one of the best and don't try to place ads in every magazine.

The positioning of your ad is very important. Key on the top right-hand position of the page. Studies have shown that this is where the reader's eye is drawn. Try to get a place in the editorial section of the magazine, and specify that you want your ad to appear alone on a page, and not surrounded by competing properties. This will probably cost more, but it is well worth the added expense.

Preparing an Ad

No one ad is going to appeal to everyone. What appeals to one decision maker may turn another off. Does that mean that there is no sense in trying to put together an appealing ad? Obviously, the answer is no. You, probably with the aid of an advertising agency, will try to put together an advertising campaign that will get a response from at least a majority of meeting planners.

Thumb through magazines. Examine the ads that really appeal to you, ads that get your attention. You probably will find that they consist of the following four distinct elements:

1. headline
2. illustration, either art or photograph
3. definite body copy
4. logo or signature

The *headline* gets the reader's attention and entices him or her to read on. It may be a question, a provocative statement, the company name, one word, or a complete sentence.

All of the descriptive words in the dictionary cannot describe the majestic setting of your hotel as well as a picture can. Often the *illustration* is the most important part of the ad. It may be a photograph or art work. It may be large, occupying a prominent position, or it may be assigned a secondary role to the copy. Regardless of the illustration's position, it should tie into the overall message of the ad.

One of the most common mistakes in preparing ad, and brochure, illustrations is the absence of people in the hotel guest room or public space. Nothing looks so sterile as a room that does not have some people to portray action.

The *copy* should be specific and to the point. Use plenty of white space and large or bold type for easy readability. The text should include your name, address, and phone number. It should tell the reader what makes your hotel different and why he or she should choose it over another property. Ideally, the copy should call for a specific action on the part of the reader.

The copy, as all facets of sales, should be honest. Don't promise what you can't deliver. Something may look good in print, but if it isn't representative of your hotel, the client will be disappointed. Keep the copy simple. Use short sentences and words that are easy to comprehend.

The *logo* is your signature, a means of ready identification. It may take a number of forms, but it should be distinctly yours. It should be used in all media efforts. It generally appears toward the bottom of the ad.

Figure 8.2 shows two ads. Note in both examples the attention-getting, clever headlines, the supporting illustrations and copy, and the distinctive logo.

Direct Mail

A popular tool in the promotion person's kit is direct mail. It can be used to screen prospects, to follow up advertising leads, and to make a printed sales presentation in detail and volume that would be too costly to duplicate in space advertising. Direct mail preselects the client and reaches him or her personally and privately. No other media can do this as effectively.

Unfortunately, the cost of direct mail efforts has increased over the years, especially with the rapidly increasing postage rates. However, an efficient program can be produced at almost any budget level.

Planning a Direct Mail Campaign

Direct mail pieces frequently end up in the waste basket. This generally happens because the campaign was not well thought out. Direct mail advertising cannot be done haphazardly. As with every element of convention sales and servicing, a direct mail campaign must be planned in advance and monitored for effectiveness.

Direct mail is only one part of a hotel's total advertising effort. Mail pieces should blend with other media advertising. Similarly, the direct mail campaign must be integrated into the hotel's overall sales objectives. Who are you trying to reach? If the objective is to increase the convention market share by 10 percent, then direct mail literature should be directed at meeting executives, not travel agents.

Before sending any mailings decide on a *follow-up* method. Ideally, your direct mail efforts will give you a list of "hot" leads of follow up. (Direct mailings make your sales calls more productive because the prospects have been prescreened and many of the basic data have already been presented.) Questionnaires such as those in figure 8.3 are often included in direct mail pieces. These lay the groundwork for the personal call and perhaps the closing sale. Plan who will handle the responses and how. The list of new leads generated through direct mail will be wasted if these prospects are not attended to promptly.

A direct mail campaign is only as good as the mailing list used. If your hotel does not have one, start one immediately. Begin by compiling a list of people who have met in your hotel in the past. Keep in mind that we are a most mobile busi-

Fig. 8.2 Convention advertisements. Note the headlines, illustrations, copy, and logo. (By permission of the Sheraton Corporation and Beaver Creek Resort.)

Suppose you wanted to stay at one of the most exclusive hotels in Chicago, but you didn't want to stay in Chicago.

No problem, we're happy to say. Because you'd most likely be staying with us. At the Sheraton Oak Brook.

The plush country atmosphere only seems a whole world away from the exciting pulse of Chicago. (Yet it's really just 25 minutes from Rush Street. And only a short drive to either Midway or O'Hare Airport.) Here's where you'll make yourself at home. In rooms you won't just stay in. But live in. In elegance. And it doesn't stop there. The Raintree Dining Room offers the gourmet a sumptuous repast. At night, we'll entertain you with star attractions at the fabulous Redhead Lounge. And when night turns to day, get a fresh start at the Chukker Coffee Shop.

Our meeting facilities are vast. At the Sheraton Oak Brook, we've put business and pleasure in their place. Our's.

Shopping is great, too. A leisurely stroll instantly brings you to fine stores of international renown.

So when you come to Chicago, be our guest at the Sheraton Oak Brook. We're close to everything. Yet nothing comes close to us.

Sheraton-Oak Brook Motor Hotel
SHERATON HOTELS AND MOTOR INNS, A WORLDWIDE SERVICE OF ITT
1401 WEST 22ND STREET, OAK BROOK, ILLINOIS   312/325-8555

"Beaver Creek is the first resort in Colorado with meetings facilities planned in. Not tacked on."
– *Wayne Stetson,*
Staff Vice President, National Association of Homebuilders.

Most resort communities in the Colorado Rockies grew up around skiing, and added meeting facilities later, to fill hotel rooms when the snow melts. But Beaver Creek is different. It was planned as a year-round resort from the beginning. And its conference and convention facilities were an integral part of that planning.

"I would choose Beaver Creek primarily because of its centralized layout and variety of spacious meeting rooms. Even a large and tightly scheduled conference could be easily handled."

The Village Hall, in the center of Beaver Creek, will have over 30,000 square feet of meeting and banquet space. The building will have nine different rooms, capable of accommodating groups from 10 to 1,500. There will be more meeting and banquet rooms in the adjacent lodges and hotels, and complete audio-visual capability in all the conference areas. Five hundred forty-five luxurious guest rooms, as well as one hundred and six condominium units will be available for conference delegates by late 1982.

Beaver Creek's recreational amenities will be as complete as any resort's, anywhere. There will be an 18 hole Robert Trent Jones, Jr. golf course in the valley and three more championship courses within a ten minute drive. The resort will have an equestrian center. Swimming. Hiking. Tennis. Even white water rafting nearby, as well as the atmosphere of famous European spas, with thermal baths, exercise facilities, and instruction to introduce people to activities they have not experienced before. In the Village there will be elegant shops and boutiques, and a selection of superior restaurants convenient to a pedestrian mall.

Beaver Creek is located in a quiet valley surrounded by more than a million acres of national forest, so it will be a great place to get work accomplished. Yet it's easy to get to. The valley is just two hours from Denver by interstate highway, and half an hour from Denver's Stapleton International Airport by scheduled commuter airline.

Meeting planners are already booking conferences for Beaver Creek's first season, starting in Spring, 1982. If you're thinking about a Rocky Mountain location for a future meeting, maybe you should find out what impressed them about Beaver Creek.

For more information, contact Michael J. Hughes, Director of Sales and Marketing, Beaver Creek Resort Company, 410 17th St., Suite #530, Denver, CO 80202. Phone (303) 623-6800. **Beaver Creek** A member of The Krisam Group.

Fig. 8.3 Sample questionnaires included in direct mail pieces (By permission of the Mount Airy Lodge and Loews Anatole Hotel.

mount airy lodge

Mount Pocono, Pennsylvania 18344
Telephone: 717-839-8811

FREE DIRECT LINES
New York City: 212-966-7210
212-226-0841
Philadelphia Area: 215-561-5650

DIRECT TOLL FREE NUMBERS
From Eastern Pa. (Area Codes 215 & 717)
1-800-532-8271
From N.Y., N.J., Md., Del.
1-800-233-8116

GROUP & CONVENTION FORM

In order that we may up date our files and supply you with accurate information, we would appreciate your completing this form and returning it in the self addressed envelope. Thank you.

1. Name of Organization:_____

    Your Name:_____Phone Number_____

    Address:_____City:_____State:____Zip:_____

2. Are you planning any function? ( ) yes   ( )no

3. Would you be interested in Mount Airy Lodge? ( ) yes ( ) no

4. If yes, for what function: ( ) Convention   ( ) Seminar

                              ( ) Incentive Program   ( ) Social Outing

                              ( ) Board Meeting   ( ) Conference

Month:_____Days of Week:_____Year:_____Any Specific Dates:_____

Number of Persons:_____Number of Rooms:_____

5. Have you ever held a function in the Poconos? ( ) yes ( ) no

6. Are there any reasons why you cannot hold a function in the Poconos?

    ( ) yes   ( ) no If yes, please state reason_____

7. Do you have a copy of our full color 24 page convention brochure?

    ( ) yes ( ) no If no, would you like one? ( ) yes ( ) no

8. What do you look for in a convention site?_____

    _____

9. What convention publications do you read?_____

    _____

10. If you can supply any additional information regarding your

    requirements, it would be greatly appreciated:_____

    _____

    _____

LOEWS ANATOLE
HOTEL

1. Company Name: _____

2. Address: _____

3. Phone Number: _____

4. ( ) Association ( ) Corporation ( ) Other: _____

5. Preferred meeting month of your convention: _____

6. Pattern (circle days of meeting plus arrival day): S M T W TH F S

7. Number of guest rooms required: _____

8. Convention for   1985   City _____ Hdq Hotel _____

9. Convention for   1986   City _____ Hdq Hotel _____

    Plans for   1987   City _____ Hdq Hotel _____

    Plans for   1988   City _____ Hdq Hotel _____

    Plans for   1989   City _____ Hdq Hotel _____

    Plans for   1990   City _____ Hdq Hotel _____

10. What is your first open year? _____

11. Meeting space required: ( ) Hotel ( ) Convention Center ( ) Both

12. Exhibits? Gross Sq. Feet _____ 8x10's_____ 10x10 _____

13. May we solicit you for future business: ( ) Yes ( ) No

14. Do you ( ) A. Rotate to certain cities -- or --
            B. Make site selections based on
                ( ) decision of board of directors
                ( ) membership invitation
                ( ) vote

15. Whom in your company should we contact regarding the following:

    Group Meetings   Name:_____ Title_____

    Conventions   Name:_____ Title_____

    Individual   Name:_____ Title_____
    Travel

16. Would you like to be included on our mailing list for special rate
    package information? ( ) Yes ( ) No

17. Is there another Loews Hotel we could contact on your behalf?
    ( )LOEWS MONTE CARLO, Monaco   ( )LOEWS L'ENFANT PLAZA
    ( )LOEWS LA NAPOULE HOTEL & CASINO, France   Washington, DC
    ( )LOEWS WESTBURY, Toronto, Canada   ( )LOEWS GLENPOINTE,
    ( )LOEWS LE CONCORDE, Quebec City, Canada   Teaneck, NJ
    ( )LOEWS HARBOR COVE, Paradise Island, Nassau ( )THE REGENCY, New York, NY
    ( )LOEWS VENTANA CANYON RESORT, Tucson, AZ ( )LOEWS GEORGIO, Denver, CO

    Comments/Requests:_____
    _____
    _____

ness society and lists must be updated frequently. Expect many returns and changes of names and addresses after each mailing; remember to budget for the postage due on returning pieces.

As we have discussed, there are several directories and a number of publications that supply the names, addresses, and phone numbers of most association, corporation, incentive, fraternal, and other meeting planners. It is also possible to rent names from the circulation lists of suitable magazines.

It is a good policy to develop two lists: a general one of all the prospects you feel reasonably sure are relevant and a preferred list of screened prospects and past customers. You probably will mail more frequently to the second list than to the first.

Convention bureau notices from past years also can be a source of prospects for your mailing list. Major city-wide conventions are channeled through the bureau. Groups that have met in years past may hold many smaller meetings that you might be able to attract. The convention bureau list might also show that some groups have a repeat pattern for the city. These groups should be given a high priority in the sales campaign.

How Many Mailings?

A number of mailings is needed with most forms of direct mail advertising to achieve the best results. A one-time mailing is not too effective unless it is a birthday or holiday greeting or an answer to an inquiry. We believe that a series of mailings is more fruitful.

When using more than one mailing, the frequency, as well as the content of the message, is important. There is no hard and fast rule, but the maximum interval between mailings is considered to be about two months.

Obviously, multiple mailings must never be the same. The first letter must be an attention-getter. Its content must be appealing and must retain the reader's interest. Future mailings should be built around the theme presented in the first one, but the information and point of the letters should be different. In some cases, you may want to build on each letter sent. The point of your message may be the same, but the content should be stated differently and creatively or the reader's interest is sure to wane.

It is effective to use well-written personal letters, with convention brochures as enclosures. Seemingly personal, individually typed letters can be done at reasonable cost using local letter shop services or automatic typewriters like the IBM Memory. If you want to create more ambitious direct mail programs, it is advisable to use your advertising agency or local creative services to produce the

Fig. 8.4   Direct mail do's and don't's. (From *Contemporary Hotel Advertising*, p. 35. Reprinted with permission by the Hotel Sales Marketing Association).

Some Important Do's and Don'ts about Hotel Direct Mail

Do

- keep in mind that direct mail is a pin-point medium—most effective when used on specific markets with identifiable characteristics.
- fashion, compile, or acquire mailing lists with the utmost care. It is the single most important element of the mailing.
- keep lists up-to-date. Remember lists deteriorate at a rate of 20% or more a year. "Dead" names cost you money.
- insist on quality production and careful attention to details on your mailings. The impression your reader gets from your mailing is the impression he gets of your hotel. Make sure that first impression says "I care."
- spell names right. A person's name is his most important possession.
- personalize wherever possible and use your reader's most important possession to advantage. Direct mail is the only medium in which you can.
- follow up inquiries fast. Results decline in direct proportion to time. And be sure information requested is furnished.
- make your copy interesting and persuasive, of course. But most of all make it sincere and believable. Promise only what you can deliver—and *deliver what you promise*.
- tell the reader exactly what you want him to do. Ask for the business.
- be consistent. Repeat your important sales points often.

Don't

- try to say too many things in one mailing. Make one important point clearly and completely in any one mailing.
- forget to plan and prepare for follow up of leads that may be developed. Make sure literature and manpower is available in sufficient numbers.
- determine the timing or size of mailing by the amount of folders available.
- go after stale names. Any name inactive for three or more years is of questionable value.
- quit after one or two mailings. Good salesmanship and good advertising require patience.
- tire of a good theme or program before your readers do. They pay a little less attention to your promotion than you do. Only *results* can tell you when a good idea is wearing thin.
- make it hard for your readers to reach you. See that your address and phone number appear on every major element of your mailings.
- mail duplicate pieces to the same person. They not only cost money for printing and postage but create an impression of management carelessness and disinterest.
- try to "do it yourself." Direct mail is a complex medium. A qualified consultant helps you two ways—by maximizing results and minimizing production and postage costs.

mailing pieces. But don't underestimate the strength and penetration power of personal letters addressed to a person by name. Of course, the high cost of postage and the cost of the brochures and mailing pieces make it advisable to polish your techniques.

The Sales Letter

Most direct mail programs incorporate a gimmick or gift into the mailing (fig. 8.5). Such gimmicks are important, as they often serve as an attention-getter, but the meat of the mailing is the *sales letter*.

The functions of a sales letter are to convince and to sell. Time does not permit a salesperson to make personal calls on every prospect, so the message must be communicated through the written word.

Effective letter writing is a skill that can be developed. Write in the client's language. Avoid use of hotel terms that will confuse or mislead. Someone once said, "You must write not so that you can be understood, but so that you cannot possibly be misundersood." Don't give the sales copy second billing in direct mail pieces. Be specific, and make your correspondence meaningful and convincing. Following are a few fundamental techniques to use in effective letter writing:

1. Use the correct titles of hotel personnel, as well as the person with whom you are dealing.
2. Be informative but brief. Stick to the facts and avoid vagueness.
3. Be yourself; write like you speak. Write as if the client were sitting with you in the office.
4. Emphasize key points by underlining them or by using bold-faced lettering.
5. Most important, *always ask for the business*. Find out who makes the decisions and when.

Using an Advertising Agency

Many convention hotels have found it advantageous to use advertising agencies, but frequently there is misunderstanding on how an advertising agency is paid. Advertising agencies are paid by the medium, not by the hotel. This may seem strange, but it is the case. Such media as newspapers, television, radio, magazines, and trade publications generally give a standard 15 percent reduction to advertising agencies. This does not mean a hotel can prepare its own ads and knock 15 percent off the bill. Commissions are paid by the media only to bona fide advertising agencies. While this policy may seem questionable on the surface, the media justify paying the commission because of the business the agencies bring in.

Fig. 8.5 Direct mailings sometimes include novelties or gifts. A series of three novelty mailings, *left,* announced to meeting planners the new Registry Hotel at the Minneapolis/St. Paul airport. The objects—a rubber sandwich, a rubber baseball and glove, and a balsa wood airplane—were keyed to fliers stressing the hotel's proximity to the airport and a sports center. The campaign won a first-place award in the Hotel Sales Management Association's annual advertising contest. *Right,* a series of three office reference books and a library holder were sent by the Sheraton-Chicago Hotel to prime group business prospects. Enclosures included a letter and a reply card, as well as a brochure with one mailing. (By permission of Bob Stein of Gardner, Stein, and Frank, Inc., Chicago, Ill.).

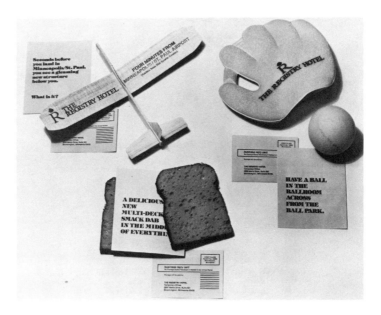

172

 meet at *"The Lago"*

where setting and service make the difference

Date

(Name)
(Address)

We'll not make any "bones" about it, Mr. _____.

. . . we want your 1964 Meeting here at The Lago Mar. You can't find a more compatible setting, nor more helpful service anywhere. And from these, successful meetings spring.

But we know that choosing a site is a "chancy" business at best. Kind of like "rolling dice". There are hundreds of attractive hotels in scores of desirable locations available to you. They all sound good. But if they don't deliver - it's your chips that are cashed in.

There is a way to take the gamble out of this decision . . . Lago Mar, of course. In the next few months, I hope to convince you of this fact.

In the meantime, perhaps the dice will remind you not to "gamble" with the possible success of your coming meeting. Select your site with careful deliberation.

When you do you will "Meet at the Mar".

                    Cordially,

                    Sidney Banks
                    Title

P.S. Care to have details? Call collect (Phone number) - or
      return the enclosed card.

Lago Mar FORT LAUDERDALE, FLORIDA 33316 • 305 523-6511

meet at *"The Lago"*

where setting and service make the difference

Date

(Name)
(Address)

Dear _____ :

If you think that's a sailfish hook . . . you're right!

And if you haven't had the thrill of setting a hook like this into one of
those saltwater acrobats - you've something to really look forward to.

Spectacular sport fishing is just one of the reasons Ft. Lauderdale is such
a popular year-round sportsman's paradise. Duffers have a half dozen of
Florida's finest courses nearby - (our guests are welcome to play them all).
Two Teniko tennis courts - two swimming pools and 800 feet of private
oceanfront bathing are available on the premises.

For the less strenuously inclined, Ft. Lauderdale offers the finest flat and
dog racing in the country; Jai Alai; sightseeing in the Everglades; and The
New York Yankees.

But, if you're the type that prefers the sport of beating last years' <u>sales
quota</u> - you'll find a Ft. Lauderdale Sales Meeting the perfect warm-up.
While offering all the activities and attractions of South Florida, it is
removed from the busy Miami area and its many distractions. It provides
the privacy you need for your conferences while in easy reach from anywhere
in the U.S. Nearby Broward International Airport is served directly by five
major airlines - and Miami by just about all others.

No matter how far flung your sales staff - you can get them to and from Ft.
Lauderdale quickly - and get your story across while they are here.

                         Cordially,

                         Sidney Banks
                         Title

P.S. Care to have costs and reserve tentative dates? Call Collect
      (phone number) or return the enclosed card.

Lago Mar FORT LAUDERDALE, FLORIDA 33316 • 305 523-6511

It is extremely important when a hotel uses an advertising agency that both agree on the direction of the advertising campaign. Naturally, a hotel is more familiar with its strengths than the agency. In order for the agency to really sell your property, it must be continually informed of any changes planned.

What services can you expect from an agency? The advertising agent should help the hotel prepare professional ads and printed pieces. He, or she, should suggest ideas for new copy. He should study the hotel's present market objectives and advise the hotel on new prospects. And he should review the effectives of the advertising and counsel the hotel on ways to improve.

Exchange Trade Advertising

Exchange trade advertising is an arrangement in which the hotel exchanges its services (rooms, food, beverage) for advertising (magazine, radio, television, outdoor, newspaper). Such arrangements are also referred to as *reciprocal advertising* and *trade-out advertising*. This type of advertising agreement can be very worthwhile so long as the hotel fully understands the procedure.

Whether you are paying cash or exchanging services, your hotel's advertising efforts must be directed at your target markets. If you are trying to build group meeting business, a trade exchange with a billboard specialist would not be the wisest use of your money. (It is important to realize that such advertising is not free; there is a cost to the hotel, and it must be budgeted, just as cash payment advertising is.)

As with all types of advertising, you get what you pay for. There is a tendency for hotels to look on trade-outs as bargain business and not to set the high standards typical of cash payment promotion. This is foolhardly. You should insist on the same quality, with ads that are large enough and run frequently enough to produce results.

Bob Stein, author of *Marketing in Action for Hotels/Motels/Restaurants* and senior vice-president of an advertising agency, has several recommendations for hotels that might be negotiating exchange trade agreements.

1. Consider variations on the "one-for-one" arrangement, especially when the publication or station approaches you. You could receive $1.50 or $2.00 of advertising for every dollar of hotel facilities, especially if food and/or beverage are included in the arrangement. When such is the case, point out that food and beverage represent an out-of-pocket cost to you, whereas available publication space or radio and T.V. time ordinarily do not.
2. Consider these limitations, all of which mean money in your pocket: For com-

mercial hotels and motels, (a) rooms only, and then only during periods when you don't expect to be at capacity, or (b) food only, rather than food and beverage. For A.P. (American Plan) or M.A.P. Modified American Plan) resorts, the room portion only.

3. Bring your advertising agency into the picture and require the publication to pay the customary 15 percent commission. Your ad agency will undoubtedly handle the placement of the advertising, and if it receives the commission, you will not be required to pay it.

4. Include as a condition of your reciprocal deal that your facilities are limited to the use of certain individuals (publisher, station manager, key executives, employees), and secure in advance a list of those persons.[1]

Exchange trade advertising offers some real advantages to a convention hotel and its possibilities should be investigated. It will mean increased record keeping, but it also affords an opportunity to build excellent relationships with media firms. A friend in the media can be a real asset when it comes to editorials and publicity on your hotel. And the hotel is in a position to extend extra courtesies to the medium's important clients. In the final analysis, exchange trade advertising can be mutually beneficial if a fair arrangement is negotiated.

Selling Techniques

If advertising is often the means of getting the client's attention, then personal confrontation is usually needed to close the sale. We'll now discuss the tools that the sales staff uses to make the sale, including personal sales calls, telephone usage, tip sheets, and internal selling.

Personal Sales Calls

The most effective tool in convention sales, or any other kind of sales, is the personal sales call. It offers you the opportunity to present your case in a detailed manner, to answer questions immediately, and to read the reaction of the prospect so you can gain a better understanding and take immediate remedial action, if necessary. The interaction between vendor and prospect is essential. A rapport may be established that may pave the way to completing the deal.

There is a problem with sales calls, however. They are getting more and more expensive. Studies estimate that such business visits cost some one hundred to one hundred fifty dollars each. In the convention business, where prospects may be

---

1. Reprinted courtesy of *Lodging Hospitality Magazine,* a Penton/IPC publication.

176

Fig. 8.7 A sales tool used by many convention salespersons is the audio-visual projector that breaks down into a handy attache case. The salesperson might use the projector when making personal sales calls. The projector here is used by the Sahara Hotel in Las Vegas. An audiovisual cassette, when inserted in the machine, gives the customer a presentation of the hotel's convention facilities.

located throughout wide areas, the cost is probably even more. We do not suggest that such calls should be eliminated or even reduced. But the cost does indicate the need to increase the productivity of such calls and to use all of the advertising techniques discussed earlier to lay the foundation on which the personal call can close the deal.

Suppose you are newly assigned to a hotel sales staff. You are understandably eager to make personal calls that you just know will result in bookings. Where do you start? Given limitations of time and money, what sort of system will prevent wasted effort? You start by exercising some judgment about the relative promise offered by prospects.

Promotion Respondents

As we said, you should reply promptly to those people who respond to your hotel's promotional efforts. Such a reaction to your ad or direct mail piece indicates interest, at the very least. With no knowledge about dates of any possible events, groups sizes, and so on, you just have to follow up personally to get enough data on which to base an intelligent presentation. If you have such a lead, contact the prospect at once. Whether this is by letter or phone depends on how many such leads are available to you and the details supplied with the leads.

Some ads bring in little more than a name, title, company, and address. Some publications have reader inquiry cards that supply such data, and sometimes a bit more. If you get a sizable group of such prospects, you might choose to screen them further by sending letters with your convention brochures enclosed.

Some hotels build in a way for the groups to respond anew for additional information, perhaps with an enclosed reply card or an invitation to write or call. A phone call and/or a personal call seems in order if you receive such a show of further interest. If you do not get any reply of any kind after a predetermined period of time continue the follow-up. Techniques for follow-up will be discussed later in this chapter.

The use of a coupon in an ad or a return postcard in a direct mail piece permits you to request details that can help you screen the prospect further and to indicate the degree of urgency.

The most desired reaction from an ad or letter is a personal phone call or letter from the prospect. If such a response doesn't move that person to the top of your *must see* list, you would do well to consider some other way to earn your living. Geographic considerations may prevent the personal sales call immediately, or at all, but you must follow up as soon as possible.

Such leads represent people who have *recently* indicated a degree of interest. That calls for prompt action, because such leads are perishable. If they responded to your material, they very likely may have responded to others as well.

Past customers

Satisfied customers are great prospects, but it is amazing how many sales staffs fail to follow up such people in time to get more business. Meeting planners who have had successful events at your hotel have confidence in your staff and property. Their personal experience bolsters the suggestion that they use the place again for another successful event. In cases where an event is moved around the country, you are limited, but don't take old cycles too much for granted. They are only to guide you; they are not absolute. And there are other meetings besides the annual convention that your customer can book.

Go back to every past customer, even the ones who had bad experiences. Time is a good healer and some very good customer-vendor relationships started with a difficult situation. Don't write that company or association off. You may be able to point out why the present setup will prevent a recurrence of what happened before. The sales call may start off difficult, but a show of interest on your part will help melt the frost. Besides, there is an old adage that says selling starts when the prospect says "no."

Besides being excellent prospects for more bookings satisfied customers are prime sources for new sales leads. Many business people are not all reluctant to recommend your facility to others. This applies to executives within their own company as well as those in other organizations. If all went well in your relationship with them, they may be pleased to recommend you. And don't be too timid to ask. Such recommendations are a great help not only in locating other prospects but in selling them, too.

Tip Sheets

Sales lead services are often referred to as *tip sheets*. Usually stemming from a trade publication, tip sheets offer information about frequent convention and meeting planners. All of the names on the report will not be high-priority prospects for you, of course. They must be scanned to eliminate those that do not fit your marketing plan and those whose specifications indicate that they are not likely prospects. The groups may be too big. They may be looking for dates you cannot supply because of your season or prior commitments. They may be users of resort properties or airport hotels or downtown ones. Don't bother with those that are looking for some kind of property other than yours; concentrate on those that use your kind.

It is important to realize that other hotels are receiving the same tip sheet. After the initial screening, you should take quick action.

Probably the most widely used tip sheet service is *Databank,* put out by *Successful Meetings* (fig. 8.8). *Databank* uses a computer to research thousands of corporations and associations. Facts recorded include where the group has met in the past, its future and tentative plans, how many doubles and suites it commonly uses, how many banquet covers, who makes the decisions and when, what exhibit space is needed, and what type of facilities are sought. The computer matches the hotel's requirements with the association's meeting needs, so the hotel receives tip sheets only on those groups that would be viable pieces of business.

179

Fig. 8.8 Sample "tip sheet." (By permission of *Successful Meetings*).

SM DATABANK
Division of **SM**/SUCCESSFUL MEETINGS

TOULA DePRINCE
research director

10/26/   FILE NO. BUGYP00021
CONFIDENTIAL REPORT

GYP   ANNUAL MTG
H R   **SAMPLE REPORT**
201
WAS

SCOPE: INTERNATIONAL EXHIBITS: 50 BOOTHS FREQUENCY: EVERY YR. NO. MTGS: 1

SITE DECISION: 2 YRS IN ADVANCE BY EXEC DIR IN FALL
PREFERRED AREA: METRO OR RESORT
MEETING ROOMS: 16 NEEDED LARGEST FOR 200
FOOD FUNCTIONS: 3 HELD LARGEST FOR 900
SLEEPING ROOMS: 40 SINGLES, 400 DOUBLES, 60 SUITES, FOR 900 FOR 6 NIGHTS
  (SUN-THU)
SPORTS: TENNIS, GOLF
PRE/POST CONV: MONTEGO BAY
NO. TRNG/EDUC SEMINARS: 6

                          ** HISTORY **
DATES   SITE   HEADQUARTERS   ATTENDANCE

82 FEB 26-MAR 3   SAN FRANCISCO, CA   SHTN-PALACE   400
83 MAR 10-15   MIAMI BEACH, FL   DEAUVILLE   400
84 MAR 10-14   LOS ANGELES, CA   INTERNATIONAL   500
85 MAR 9-12   WASHINGTON, DC   MAYFLOWER   750
86 MAR 22-25   NEW ORLEANS, LA   JUNG   750
87 MAR 6-9   LAS VEGAS, NV   INTERNATIONAL   1,000
88 MAR 5-8   ATLANTA, GA   HYATT REGENCY   1,000
89 MAR 17-20 (T)   LAS VEGAS, NV   MGM GRAND   1,000
90 MAR
  IS CONSIDERING: LONDON ENGLAND, DUBLIN IRELAND, NEW YORK CITY NY, FL, UT
91 MAR
  IS CONSIDERING: SAN FRANCISCO CA, SD   1,000
92 MAR
  IS CONSIDERING: HOUSTON TX   1,000
93 MAR
  IS CONSIDERING: FL   1,000
94 MAR
  IS CONSIDERING: CA   1,000
95 MAR
  IS CONSIDERING: DALLAS TX   1,000

1422 CHESTNUT STREET, PHILADELPHIA, PA. 19102 (215/563-0680)

The Cold Call

Once you decide that a prospect is indeed a valid one, you must make contact and try to sell it. Sales calls in which you initiate the contact without any degree of interest indicate by the prospects are called *cold calls*. The anticipated percentage of success in these cases is understandably lower than when you are dealing with past customers or recommendations. It is often a problem just getting in to see the right person.

You can increase the efficiency of such efforts if you precede your visit with some sort of preliminary campaign. You might send your convention facilities brochure to the contact person, along with a personal letter. Follow up with another letter if you hear nothing within a few weeks. Then call for an appointment. If you fail to get an appointment, try again.

Don't completely rule out calling without an appointment. This is not the most desirable effort, of course, except when you are already in the area for another appointment. Sometimes it works, but even if you cannot get an appointment, you stand to lose little. It is a good practice to cross-index your prospect list geographically. It increases the number of sales calls you'll make on a trip because you can mix cold calls with your appointments.

Be careful that your telephone effort for an appointment doesn't turn into a detailed telephone "visit." It is better to be there in person. Stress that you have material that must be shown, such as an audiovisual presentation.

Sales Blitz

The *sales blitz* is hitting a given area with great concentration for a brief period. Often done in coordination with a convention bureau and other hotels from your locale, the blitz is a favorite tool of new hotel properties. Several hotel colleges also have participated in blitz programs, providing sales-oriented students to a hotel for three or four days during the Christmas and Easter breaks.

It might involve setting up a hospitality suite and making a presentation in the city you are blitzing. Invitations go out to prospects; a special program and attraction, such as a famous personality who might serve as a magnet, are arranged. Contacts made during the hospitality hours may be followed up in the next day or two. In the case of a soon-to-open property, the manpower needed may be recruited from other areas of the staff. The manager, the banquet manager, the convention service manager, and local service companies that stand to benefit from such bookings may all be part of the blitz team. Representation from auto rental companies, audiovisual service organizations, and/or decorator companies helps build the feeling that there are lots of interested people and potential.

When you screen prospects and contact them, keep in mind that many executives will attend if they are told that your group will be in town for a minimum period of time and that there is no telling when such an opportunity might be repeated. Local political figures such as the mayor might be induced to participate.

A successful sales blitz experience was told by Howard Feiertag, former sales director of American Motor Inns. (Generally, blitz programs are conducted by chain operations.) Staff members from various departments of the hotel participated. Such an approach, it was felt, might build morale within the organization by making the staff members feel that they were a part of the management team.

Questionnaires were developed, a briefing meeting was held in which sales kits were handed out and interviewing techniques were discussed, assignments were made, and the blitz teams sent out. The results of the one-day blitz were ninety-one leads, two definite bookings, and a noticeable increase in employee morale.

Telephone Usage

Because sales prospects are scattered all over the country, and because personal calls cost so much, the telephone is a vital tool in convention sales. But it should not be a substitute for as many personal visits as you can manage. Telephone calls do increase customer contact, screen prospects to make personal sales calls more effective, and offer immediate contact in urgent situations.

Firms that make many long-distance calls use an arrangement offered by the telephone company to maximize long-distance time and rate efficiency. This is called *Wide Area Telecommunications Service,* or simply the WATS line. An organization contracts with the telephone company for a minimum number of hours of long-distance service into one or more areas or zones; unlimited service is also available. The user can also buy any or all of the zones radiating out from its area to others, until it has coast-to-coast coverage.

The caller using a WATS line dials numbers directly, with no operator assistance, and is billed only for the exact time used for the call. No minimum call time is required. This encourages station-to-station usage because if the party is out of the office, the call to the prospect's secretary lasts only a few moments and costs little.

There is a minimum amount of time that you must buy for each zone you order. Telephone company representatives will help you decide which bands you need, and frequently advise against ordering certain bands. For proper guidance by a telephone representative, collect past long-distance bills. If you suspect that volume into a particular area might not be too heavy, straight station-to-station calls may be the most economical. The phone company will send a training specialist to instruct your staff in the most efficient and economical use of the telephone.

Screen Prospects by Phone

Telephone contact is excellent for screening prospects after a lead has been picked up from a tip sheet or as a recommendation from a customer. A superior sales presentation requires some knowledge of the prospect's needs. After learning more about the situation in the screening process, you might even choose not to pursue the prospect. You may find that because of its size or time of event, the prospect does not fit your profile of the desirable customer.

If you can't penetrate to the meeting planner, the assistant or secretary may be able to furnish additional information that will enable you to be more effective when you do get to the decision maker.

Screening by phone will help you plan sales trips with greater expectations of scoring. You appear on the scene better prepared and more knowledgeable. Your proposals come off better. You will find that you will make a maximum number of effective calls per trip if you prescreen prospects.

Telephone Techniques

Selling by phone is not trouble-free. It is easier for a sales prospect to be abrupt when not face-to-face. When actually faced with someone in a customer-vendor relationship, most people are at least courteous and usually are reluctant to be curt. But it is easy to dismiss a voice on an impersonal electronic instrument.

How do you combat that? A cheerful manner and voice help. Knowing the name of the person you want to talk to is another vital step. Eliminating the *hems* and *haws* in your delivery and being organized in your approach are extremely important. Ask a few questions that should be easy to answer, just to get the ball rolling. And a good, basic rule is to phrase questions so that they cannot be answered with a simple "no." You must get some basic knowledge about the group before you can sell it intelligently. When do they hold their meetings? How long are they? How many people? How far in advance do they decide on the site? Who makes the decisions?

It helps to offer something of value to the meeting planner. It can help break the ice to explain your need to verify the contact's name, title, and address so you can send him or her the item offered. It may be a meetings checklist that is an attraction only to meeting planners. That checklists for any kind of meeting are popular has been shown by the great reader response to such offerings in trade magazines and by the amount of such literature carried away from trade shows. You can make up a checklist that will help you screen the kind of customers you want.

Such a giveaway item may help you to set up a personal meeting or make a follow-up letter seem most natural. If possible, it is best to deliver the item in person so you have a door opener. It costs little and can be personalized for your hotel.

Using such a device, a phone call can save you from wasting time by learning perhaps that Mr. Jones no longer has the meetings responsibility and that you should see Mr. Smith.

Don't ignore assistants and secretaries. You may have trouble penetrating to your prospect when you call, but you can glean a great deal of information from assistants and secretaries. Today's assistant is tomorrow's manager. And secretaries can make it easier or tougher to get in to see the boss. If you win them over, you may find that your phone calls get through. A secretary may tip you off that her boss always comes in before 8 A.M. because things are quiet and he likes to get a jump on things. A personal visit before the office gets going may make it easy to establish the desired rapport.

The phone is a business tool, and a great one. Learn to use it well. Give information quickly and smoothly. Beware of just small talk. Direct the conversation. You cannot know what is happening at the other end of the line, so be brief, informative, and get right to the point. Figure 8.9 is a checklist that might be distributed to everyone on the sales staff who takes or places sales calls.

Follow-up

Every contact should be followed up. When you phone, you are looking for information and an appointment. If you get the appointment and it isn't far off, you have little time for a follow-up. If there is time, a friendly note confirming the date is good. You might enclose hotel brochures. If you don't have the date, you need to send all the information in an individually typed letter. It may be a form but not form-printed; it should be typed. Then follow that letter with a phone call. The tickler file we discussed in chapter 7 is a great aid to effective follow-up.

The follow-up is a vital sales tactic. It maintains customer contact and tells the prospect you care about his business. It says that you are well organized and will take care of matters. After all, if you don't keep on top of things before the con-

Fig. 8.9 Telephone technique check-list.

Telephone Technique Checklist

- ☐ Have an outline to speak from, but do not "can" your talk.
- ☐ Identify yourself.
- ☐ Have pencil and paper handy.
- ☐ Be courteous and agreeable.
- ☐ Speak slowly and clearly.
- ☐ Get to the point—be brief but not abrupt.
- ☐ Put your personality into the call.
- ☐ Take the lead in the conversation, but be a good listener when the prospect voices his or her views.
- ☐ Get full information from the prospect.
- ☐ Try to get the prospect to visit the hotel.
- ☐ Ask for an order and try to get a commitment.

---

tract is signed, what will it be like after the meeting is committed? Follow-up keeps you in the prospect's mind should something break. A meeting may be planned that did not exist at the time of original contact; the salesperson who is right in there may be the one to come away with the business.

It is equally important to follow up after the sale. Not only will this help you maintain good relationships with clients, but you also will have a chance to guide them and possiby to discern where trouble spots are likely to develop. Keep in touch. It will be greatly appreciated by the client and will enable you to serve him or her better and your employer more efficiently.

Cross-Selling

Chain organizations have a distinct advantage over independents with the use of inter-hotel cross-selling. Cross-selling materials include

1. *individual rack, corporate, and convention brochures* bearing the names of all properties in the chain
2. *placemats* identifying the chain's hotels on a map
3. *matchbooks* containing individual hotel names and phone numbers on the outside and a listing of other hotels on the inside
4. *company ads* that carry the entire chain listing

Cross-selling is an integral part of a corporate sales strategy. Clients identify size with success. When the meeting planner knows that the hotel he, or she, has chosen is part of a network of hotels, he associates prestige with the property. Another advantage of cross-selling is that the company gets the most out of its advertising dollar.

Of course, this method of promotion is effective only when the convention is satisfied with the service, guest rooms, catering facilities, and the handling of meeting room arrangements. If the client is sold on one property he or she may be sold on the chain. On the other hand, should one hotel fail to deliver all that was promised, the convention may never again consider any hotel within the chain.

Internal Sales Promotion

A major area that should never be overlooked is promotion of in-house services to the convention delegate. Up to this point, we have considered only the methods of attracting the convention group to the hotel—the external selling. The other form of promotion, *internal* selling, is persuading the delegate to use the hotel's facilities and services once he or she is in the hotel.

In chapter 3 a pie graph of a study done by the International Association of Convention and Visitor Bureaus (fig. 3.5) showed that the average convention delegate spends more dollars in outside restaurants than restaurants inside the hotel. This should not be. Hotels need to offer enough variety to keep the delegate in the house and to prevent him from being lured to a competitor across the street.

You can do this with two types of internal promotion, *printed* promotion and *employee* promotion.

Printed Promotion

Every delegate must be made aware of all the services and facilities available in the hotel. Signs, service directories, in-house promotion packets, and tent cards are just a few of the methods commonly used to promote the use of the hotel's facilities. This practice of promoting other profit centers in the hotel is often called *crisscross advertising*.

The most popular form of printed promotion, and perhaps the most important source of internal sales, is the *guest room directory*. This directory, which has promotional material on all the hotel's services in a single packet, is placed in the guest's room. Included in the directory might be postcards, do-not-disturb cards, restaurant menus, liquor prices, and valet cards. The phone numbers of the hotel's restaurants, laundry, room service, shops, and reservations desk should also be included.

Guest room directories have taken three forms: (1) a listing placed under glass on a table or wall in the room; (2) loose-leaf pieces placed in an attractive folder; or (3) printed and bound booklets. Regardless of the style used, it is extremely important that consistent colors and type styles be used to give the pieces a unified look. The directory should be coordinated to add to the attractiveness of the guest room.

There are a number of places other than the sleeping rooms where printed material might be used. Two excellent places to post restaurant information are inside and just outside the elevator. Directional and informational signs strategically placed in the lobby may be used to inform the customer. And front-desk personnel may distribute promotion packets at registration time.

Employee Promotion

CONVENTION DELEGATE: "What's going on in the Copa Room tonight?"
BELL CAPTAIN: "Some singer or comedian or something."
CONVENTION DELEGATE: "Male or female?"
BELL CAPTAIN: "I really don't know. I haven't even been in there and don't have the time to find out for you."

This dialogue is typical of many hotels. Convention hotels must get across to their employees the importance of the convention delegate. Room clerks, waiters and waitresses, bellmen, parking attendants, and all other employees having guest contact need to be trained in personal selling.

When your front desk clerk is checking in the delegate, does he or she suggest that the guest try the hotel's restaurants? Does your bellman ask for suits that need to be pressed? When the Plaza Hotel in New York City was owned by Sonesta Corporation, each bellman had his own reservation cards, with his name printed as the return addressee, and he asked if the guest would like him to make a return reservation. Telephone operators would suggest breakfast with the wake-up call, and room service waiters would recommend the closed-circuit movies on television.

Unless a delegate is advised, many of the hotel's services and facilities may go unused. If the delegate uses similar ones outside the hotel, your property is losing revenue. Adopt the philosophy that "everybody sells." It will increase revenues and, at the same time, improve guest relations.

Study Questions

1. Techniques for convention sales are broken down into two types—advertising techniques and selling techniques. List the advertising media available to a hotel and comment on the effectiveness of each in reaching the convention market.

2. Define collateral advertising material and discuss its importance as a promotional tool.

3. What four elements are present in a well-prepared magazine ad?

4. Poorly planned direct mail campaigns can be costly and even damaging. Outline the steps to take in organizing an effective direct mail promotion, commenting on the number of mailings and the importance of the sales letter.

5. What is exchange trade advertising? A tip sheet? A sales blitz? Cross-selling?

6. What services can a hotel expect from its advertising agency?

7. Distinguish between external and internal selling.

Outline

I. Letter of Agreement

    A. Names of Organization and Hotel
    B. Official Dates
    C. Number and Kinds of Rooms
    D. *Rates*
    E. Arrival Pattern
    F. Public Space
    G. Complimentary and Reduced Rate Rooms
    H. Prior Visits
    I. Working Space
    J. Registration Control
    K. Exhibit Space
    L. Food Functions
    M. Coffee Breaks
    N. Liquor
    O. Audiovisual Equipment
    P. Union Regulations
    Q. Master Account
    S. Cancellation
    T. Penalty Clause
    U. Proposal Letters

II. The Convention Liaison Council

III. Model Letter of Agreement

9

Many details have to be discussed when an association or corporate meeting planner indicates a willingness to consider a hotel for a particular event. A proposal is generally made by the hotel setting forth prices and terms. This proposal is later turned into a *letter of agreement.*

The word *contract* frightens many people—people who readily enter into an agreement made formal by a letter. Most business people would not dream of drawing up a contract without legal counsel, but will sign a letter that lists the terms of an agreement. For all practical purposes, a letter of agreement and a contract function pretty much the same way, the difference being semantics and perhaps legal form.

Letters of agreement are usually written by either of the two parties and signed by persons in authority of both parties.

Letter of Agreement

A letter of agreement should include, in simple language, all arrangements that have been negotiated and agreed to. This protects the client and the hotel, but it also does something else of extreme importance. By itemizing all matters to be covered, it is essentially a clearly stated checklist of what is expected of either party. This is vital because most misunderstandings reflect a lack of communication and a lack of experience and expertise by either the hotel executive or the client or both.

The letter of agreement should cover each point clearly in a separate paragraph. Each step of the way should be documented. If the hotel's initial proposal is so detailed, it may serve as a letter of agreement, but this is not the usual case.

Nothing should be left to verbal agreement. The parties that negotiated the deal may no longer be employed by the hotel or the client when the convention actually takes place. In any case, memory is decidedly fallible. Everything should be included *in writing.* This will eliminate many misunderstandings when the time comes to settle up the accounts, and even prevent malfunctions during the meeting itself.

It is also sound practice, whenever the information is available, to call a hotel that had previously been used as a convention site by the group. This is the kind of cooperation that, we are happy to say, is commonplace among good hotel executives. You can find out in advance where possible pitfalls lie. This information is also helpful intelligence data to use during the negotiations. Certain concessions are commonplace. Such inter-hotel conversations will keep you abreast of current practices and trends throughout the hotel industry. (fig. 9.1)

Fig. 9.1 Inquiry questionnaire. It is sound practice to track the historical performance of meeting groups. A questionnaire such as illustrated here requests a post-convention critique from hotels used by the meeting group in the past. This information is extremely valuable in negotiations because it gives the hotel an early feeling for whether the group can meet its commitments.

AN ATLAS HOTEL

Post Office Box 80098
San Diego, California 92138
(619) 232-3121

Dear Colleague:

The U.S. Grant Hotel is working with:

We understand this group met with you. At your convenience we would sincerely appreciate receiving the following information:

1.

Date								
Original Room Block								
Actually Used								

Meeting Requirements (Program if available):

2.

	Persons	Set-up
General Session	_____	_____
Breakouts	_____	_____

Catered Functions:

3.

	No. of Functions	Persons
Breakfast	_____	_____
Lunch	_____	_____
Dinner	_____	_____
Receptions	_____	_____

4. Comments: _____

_____

Thank you in advance for your cooperation. We will be happy to reciprocate at any time.
Sincerely,

_____
Signature

Some discretion should be exercised not to make inquiries from a hotel—or a hotel within a chain—that is in a position to make a last-minute bid to book the business. But with some care, past sites of the group could be valuable sources of helpful data.

In any case, certain information must be recorded and points negotiated and recorded, leading to a proposal and the final letter of agreement. We will list all that should be covered in the letter and include at the end of the chapter a recommended letter that is used by many in the industry. It is worth repeating that a soundly written letter of agreement helps both parties execute a successful meeting and prevents misunderstanding by stating what is to be done, by whom, and at what price. Nothing is part of the agreement that is not included in the letter.

Names of Organization and Hotel

Name both parties to the agreement. Both the organization and the hotel should be clearly indicated, along with the intent to select the hotel as the site for the meeting. The meeting should be identified by name or any other designation.

Official Dates

It sounds basic, but make sure the exact dates of the event are listed. They are often referred to as the *official dates.* It is wise to indicate the dates for moving in and moving out as well.

Not only the date, but also the hour of beginning and ending should be specified. This protects the hotel against a meeting tying up a room beyond the cut-off time. You don't want a breakfast ending too late to set up the room for a luncheon or training session later in the day.

Number and Kinds of Rooms

Specify the number of guest rooms to be held, spelling out the number of suites, single, double, and twin rooms. Sometimes a client will want the location of the rooms specified, as in the case of a multi-building structure. If you agree to it, specify the number of rooms in Building A and the number in Building B.

Also include reservation *cut-off requirements.* For example, a paragraph something like this might be used: "A cut-off date of thirty days prior to the opening of the convention is established. At this time any of your room commitment unused will be released to the general public. After the cut-off date we will continue to accept your group's reservations on a space-available basis."

Rates

Specify clearly the rates for each type of accommodation. If a range is agreed to, list rates from the lowest to the highest. If a flat rate is negotiated, state it clearly. If rooms are to be priced differently in different sections of the hotel, it may be wise to list such rates separately. And when listing rates for suites, be sure to note that the suite includes a parlor and a number of guest rooms, such as a parlor and one bedroom or a parlor and two bedrooms. (See the glossary of convention and meetings terms in the back of the book.)

Arrival Pattern

It is important for you to know when the guests will arrive. If 400 rooms are being held, it is unlikely that all 400 room occupants will arrive on the same day. A flow chart should be indicated, and you should state that you will hold so many rooms for arrival on one day, so many for the next day, and so on.

The agreement might call for 100 rooms for arrival on Monday, January 10, 200 rooms for arrival on Tuesday, January 11, and the remaining 100 rooms on Wednesday, January 12. It is wise, too, to indicate the breakdown of the rooms into singles, doubles, twins, and suites.

You may find arrival dates easier to secure than check-out dates, but these too are of great importance to you.

Public Space

The experienced convention planner will want you to hold all your public rooms until he or she has firmed up the program and the resultant traffic flow pattern. If the event is far in the future and if it will not occupy the entire hotel, this is very difficult for you to do so. You need public space to sell other meetings. Keep in mind that while the eye-catching events are the big ones, most meetings do not fill the hotel; usually there are several in the house at once.

This is a point to be negotiated, but it is reasonable to hold all rooms that might possibly be used for the event. A date must be set by which the program will be completed to the point that unused public space can be released. If you agree to hold rooms without setting an option or release date, you may find yourself unable to use them for other meetings or banquets.

Complimentary and Reduced Rate Rooms

It is commonplace in the convention industry for hotels to supply some rooms free. This varies a great deal. A hotel may be more generous if the meeting is scheduled during an off-time of the week or season. A more successful hotel may be tougher when it comes to concessions. A very common rule of thumb is one complimentary guest room for every fifty rooms booked. If charges are to be made for meeting rooms, specify the rooms and the rates. Such charges are usually made in the event that few guest rooms are used.

A hotel and a client may also agree to a number of reduced rate rooms. This is often done for staff members, speakers, and performers. This is subject to negotiation, of course, and should not be taken for granted.

A contract clause on complimentary rooms might read:

> We will be pleased to offer one complimentary guestroom for every fifty (50) room nights utilized or one (1) bedroom suite for every one hundred (100) room nights utilized. The complimentary commitment will be provided on a cummulative basis for the length of the meeting. The Hotel offers a choice of accounting procedures for complimentary rooms. A bottom line dollar credit on the Master Account will value each unit at the daily average guestroom rate generated by the group, or, guestrooms/suites can be pre-complimented prior to arrival.

Prior Visits

A hotel often will not charge for guest rooms used by the meeting organizer and his or her staff during visits to the hotel before the event to make preliminary arrangements. This is often done on a *space-available* basis. It isn't unwise to set a numerical limit.

Working Space

Offices, press rooms, and similar working space should be discussed. If a charge is to be made for them, specify the rates. If no charge is to be made, specify this, but also spell out the maximum number of rooms to be used. Many meeting planners insist upon indicating the location of such rooms to make sure that the locations are convenient to the meeting sessions.

Registration Control

In the case of association conventions, hotels usually agree to clear all requests for accommodation from people of that particular industry with the convention organizer. You need to do this in order to credit the association with the total number of rooms used in conjunction with the convention. All such rooms should be applied against the guaranteed number of rooms. In addition, a convention organizer often wants to control the use of suites as hospitality centers or even as setups which circumvent the exhibit itself and its booth space and decorating costs.

Exhibit Space

If a charge is to be made for the exhibit hall, say so clearly and state what is to be included in the charge. Items to be considered are hours the exhibit is to be open, electricity, air conditioning or heat, carpeting, and the number of tables and chairs. Some hotels charge on the basis of the number of booths sold by the association. List what the hotel is to furnish and what must be contracted for with a show decorator.

Food Functions

Specify how much notice you require for guarantees on food functions. Forty-eight hours' advance notice is the most common. If you need more time, and you may over weekends, negotiate it and include it in your letter of agreement. Menus have to be priced and approved. Most hotels will agree to set tables for a percentage above the number guaranteed in order to accommodate additional guests. Many set for an additional 10 percent; others hold it to 5 percent; and still others base the percent on the number of persons to be served. For example, a paragraph such as this might be used.

A 48-hour guarantee is required on all meal functions. Your catering manager must be notified of the exact number of attendees for whom you wish to guarantee payment.

For functions scheduled on Sunday or Monday, the guarantee must be received by noon on the preceeding Friday. The hotel will set up as follows:

20–100 persons set	5% over guarantee
101–1000 persons set	3% over guarantee
1001 and over	1% over guarantee

In the event a guarantee is not received, the original estimated attendance count will be prepared and billed.

Coffee Breaks

It is amazing how many arguments stem from coffee break arrangements. Many meeting organizers think of coffee in terms of coffee shop standards. Spell out the costs and labor required for all coffee breaks. Include prices for cakes, soft drinks, and juice, too.

Liquor

Spell out the hotel's policy on liquor service. If you charge by the bottle, an arrangement should be made for inventory control, and the credit given for unopened bottles after the convention. It is important to list the person authorized to tally the inventory and issue the credit, both for the hotel and the client.

Audiovisual Equipment

Some hotels supply audiovisual equipment from their own inventories; others use local dealers. In either case, it is important to show the rate structure for equipment and services, or to indicate that it is the convention staff's responsibility to make its own arrangements. You may prefer to supply the names of local service companies that deal directly with and bill to the client. Some hotels will accept the local dealer's bills and rebill the convention.

Union Regulations

Convention organizers are accustomed to union help and regulations, but you should list the basic workday, rates, and overtime charges. You should also state any out-of-the-ordinary union requirements in your labor contract. Making your client aware of them eliminates much aggravation later on.

Many astute meeting planners will not sign confirmations or agreements without first checking out union conditions. The hotel has a responsibility to alert the meeting planner to the possibility of local labor contracts terminating before the meeting, any likely labor rate increases, or possible labor disputes.

Master Account

The meeting planner will have a master billing account. He or she must furnish the hotel with a list of people authorized to sign for charges that are to be placed in the master account. The client must also indicate which charges the convention organization will pick up for such people as speakers and performers. The client may choose to pay room rate only and let the individuals pay all incidental charges. In the case of a corporate meeting, this arrangement may have to be clarified for each attendee. Make it clear that the master account will have to be verified and initialed before the client leaves after the meeting.

Method of Payment

Specify how you are to be paid. If you want a deposit, say so and give the date that it is due. Also negotiate any additional sum to be paid, as well as the final payment.

Most convention organizers prefer to go over the master account before they leave the hotel, but some hotels cannot have it ready that quickly. But most hotels do insist that the master account be approved by the client before leaving, while

Fig. 9.2 Hotel negotiation policies and practices. Source: Policies and Procedures of the Hotel Sales Office. Hotel Sales Marketing Association. Used with permission.

The Hotel Sales Marketing Association recently surveyed over 1,000 lodging properties to determine common sales office practices. One section of this comprehensive study provided valuable data on the current negotiations policies and practices of hotels on the key issues of contracts, group deposits, reservations, complimentary guest rooms, and meal guarantees. The highlights of their report follow:

* Contracts

Ninety percent of the respondents require a signed contract for function space and guestrooms.

* Reduction/cancellation of guestroom blocks

Approximately 40 percent of the respondents levy no penalties in the event of a reduction or cancellation of a room block—regardless of the timing of these actions. When a penalty is levied, most respondents to the survey calculated the penalty on the basis of one night's revenue per room held.

* Group deposits

Twenty-nine percent of the respondents require a deposit from all group bookings. Forty-seven percent may require a deposit, depending on the client. Twenty-four percent do not require a group deposit at all. When a deposit is required, most calculate the amount based on one night's revenue per room held.

* Credit

Fifty-four percent of the respondents require that a conference group file a formal credit application prior to arrival. Sixteen percent have no such requirement. Thirty percent responded "sometimes."

* Individual reservations/deposits

Nearly half of the respondents require that an individual deposit accompany an individual reservation. Sixteen percent do not require individual deposits. Thirty-seven percent sometimes require individual deposits.

* Complimentary Guestrooms

Though the most often employed guideline for determining the number of complimentary guestrooms to be granted to a conference is one per 50 rooms occupied, 20 percent of the respondents grant one complimentary guestroom per 25 rooms occupied.

* Meal Guarantees

Sixty-six percent always require 48 hours notice from groups for a meal guarantee and over two-thirds of the respondents permit no leeway if the number falls below the guaranteed meal count.

all matters are fresh in the mind and the staff is available for consultation. It is a common practice to leave some portion of the account unpaid, should there be some items that require negotiations or that aren't ready for final accounting.

Cancellation

Many conventions are planned a number of years in advance, so occasions do arise that call for a cancellation of the event. Most hotel people include a cancellation date, with the provision that the event itself is canceled and not that another meeting site is selected. Obviously, the contract would be meaningless if the client could continue to shop for another site and cancel whenever a better opportunity presented itself.

A release clause also might be included in the agreement. There should be a provision for cases when either party might be forced to cancel because of circumstances beyond its control. For example, the hotel should not be held responsible for nonperformance in the event of a strike, lockout, fire, or failure of heat, light, and power. It also might be specified that a hotel can substitute a different room of similar size without penalty. (fig. 9.3)

Penalty Clause

What happens when either party fails to live up to an agreement? The most common examples of this are the failure of a hotel to hold rooms as promised and the failure of the meeting organization to book the number of rooms being held. What can either party do?

There is recourse in the courts when a contract is defaulted, but is this practical? Can a hotel sue a convention organizer or an association? The problems are many. Damages must be proved. This can be done if guest rooms go unoccupied for the convention period. But in a tight community like the convention business, this may prove to be a hollow victory, giving the hotel a bad image that could result in lost business in the future. The hotel is faced with a dilemma.

Meeting planners ask similar questions. What can they do when the hotel fails to live up to the agreement? What recourse do they have when members are "walked" to other hotels and have to scramble for last-minute accommodations? What can they do about facilities promised but not available?

There have been suggestions that a specific penalty clause be included in the

Fig. 9.3 Sample cancellation policies of four hotels. (Used with permission of Loews Anatole Hotel, Opryland Hotel, South Seas Plantation Resort and Hotel del Coronado Legal Department, Timothy R. Binder, General Counsel.)

Loews Anatole Hotel Cancellation Policy

In the event that you have to cancel your meeting within _____ of the actual date, you will be asked to pay a cancellation fee of half of the anticipated room revenue. This fee will be used to recuperate loss of revenue which cannot be replaced. In the event we are able to resell all or part of your block, an adjustment will be made.

In the event of a national emergency or an act of God, where you had no control over the circumstances, the above paragraph is null and void. If you are able to rebook this meeting or one with similar requirements within one year of the cancellation date, we will be pleased to apply the cancellation fee to this meeting.

Any controversy or claim arising out of, or relating to cancellation of this contract or the breach thereof, shall be settled by arbitration in accordance with the rules of the American Arbitration Association, and judgment upon the award rendered by the Arbitrator(s) may be entered in any Court having jurisdiction thereof.

South Seas Plantation Cancellation Policy

Cancellation Notice Received	Cancellation Charge
0–60 days prior to scheduled arrival date	Full payment on rooms for the duration of the dates agreed upon
60–90 days prior to scheduled arrival date	75% of the above
90–120 days prior to schedule arrival date	50% of the above
120–180 days prior to scheduled arrival date	Forfeit deposit

NOTE: Same Cancellation Policy applies in the event the agreed upon length of days is reduced.

It is further provided there shall be no right of termination on your part for the sole purpose of holding the same meeting in another city of facility. Neither does South Seas Plantation have the right to cancel your room block if another larger group requests the same space and dates.

Opryland Hotel Cancellation Policy

In the event that it becomes necessary for you to cancel your conference with us, we would be in a difficult position to try to resell your room nights and would, no doubt, result in additional lost revenue for our Hotel. We will, however, attempt to resell the room nights that were reserved for you and would only assess a cancellation fee for those room nights not resold over the initially agreed upon dates. This fee would be based upon the unsold room nights multiplied by your established group rate for that period.

Hotel Del Coronado Cancellation Policy

In the unfortunate event that the Group must cancel this meeting because of extraordinary and unforeseeable circumstances, the Group agrees (1) to pay one night's rent for the number of rooms confirmed if the cancellation occurs within one year of the scheduled dates, the night paid for being the night the largest number of rooms had been confirmed, and (2) to pay the rent for the entire number of rooms confirmed if the cancellation occurs less than three months prior to the scheduled dates of the meeting.

letter of agreement. Such clauses call for specified payments or action by both sides. The hotel agrees, for example, to arrange and pay for accommodations at other hotels if it overbooks. The meeting organization agrees to pay for any rooms held under the agreement if the hotel proves "no-shows" and that the rooms remained vacant that night.

The difficulty lies in getting hotels and clients to include such clauses in their letters of agreement. To some extent, such arrangements are already present in corporate meeting situations when the company *guarantees* the number of guest rooms. When the company doesn't meet the guarantee, it pays for the rooms anyway. This is easier in corporate meeting planning because the organization has greater control over the employees' actions. When the vice-president/sales orders employees to attend the annual sales meeting, the only absentees are those who are sick or those who missed a plane.

The association has a more difficult time because it does not control its members. Attendance is at the member's option. The organizer makes an attendance projection that is a combination of experience, judgment, guesswork, and prayer, based on such considerations as past attendance at conventions, attractiveness of the site, and members' activity in the society. Given an unusual year or a spell of bad weather that washes out several planes, a real no-show problem presents itself. Associations try to cooperate by guaranteeing a minimum, but they are afraid that few rooms over the minimum will be held for very long.

An optional paragraph might be included in a letter of agreement—we say *optional* because not every organization will agree to its inclusion. The stark reality of the situation is that little can be done without such a contractual agreement. Even then, the chances of collecting damages are slim. A penalty clause offers a moral stand on which to present a bill. Without it, most hotels choose to chalk the matter up as a bad experience.

Roger Smith, former regional director of sales for Westin Hotels, says about the use of penalty clauses in contracts:

> Twenty years ago there were maybe five hotels in the United States that could handle some association meetings. As competition gets bigger and broader, the need for a contract is going to be greater, because people are more enticed to pull out of a commitment they made five years ago because there's another city that's more spectacular.
>
> What bothers me most about contracts is that they always seem to be one-sided. They're not bilateral; they're unilateral. A contract is no good unless it has a built-in penalty, and most contracts don't. What happens if the hotel does not meet what it says it will? What happens if the association does not?
>
> We successfully sued a state or regional, I'm not sure which, in the Pacific

Northwest. But to sue successfully, you must show a loss. If someone cancels a meeting three years in advance, you have to wait until the three years are up to show a loss.[1]

If doing business by contract and/or letter of agreement seems complex and detailed, meeting planning indeed is. Think of the letter as a checklist or order form. Arranging for a convention requires more than ordering a certain number of guest rooms. Your letter of agreement shows you, the hotelier, what the client expects, and it shows the client his or her responsibility. It works out well when thought and time are given to each detail. The first letter may be the hardest to write; when you get it polished, save it as a sample.

It will help you if you list details in such a manner that they can be transposed directly onto function setup sheets. That makes the meeting easier to service and errors less likely to occur. Do keep in mind that some details just cannot be supplied when the letter of agreement is signed, so provision may have to be made to add a supplementary agreement later on.

Proposal Letters

Before offering a letter of agreement, many hotels send the meeting planner a proposal letter. All groups that have been issued tentative dates and are being actively solicited should receive a complete letter of proposal. This letter should spell out exactly what the customer will receive at the hotel. Figure 9.5 shows a sample proposal letter used by the Arizona Biltmore.

Proposal letters usually follow a standard format, including much of the same information as the letter of agreement, but they are usually not as detailed. Major areas are often capitalized and/or underlined, for example:

Dates: Arrival—Sunday, January 1, at 11:00 A.M.
Departure—Wednesday, January 4, at 1:00 P.M.

Convention brochures, fact sheets, complimentary letters from past groups, and other promotional materials might be enclosed. The conclusion to your proposal letter should always ask the prospective customer to take action—to do business with you. Finally, whenever a proposal is sent, a trace date should be established for follow-up.

1. "What You Need to Know to Work Effectively with Hotels," *Association Management*. Used with permission of *Association Management* magazine.

Should the group accept the proposal, indicating it has chosen your hotel, a letter of agreement should be sent, along with a note of thanks. It is customary for this letter to be sent in duplicate, and to request that it be countersigned by a responsible person from the association and returned. As we explained, this constitutes a legal contract whereby both parties have agreed to the terms and arrangements. An alternative to the duplicate-copy method might be a letter from the meeting planner stating that the letter of agreement is correct and accepted.

Appendix D is the proposal letter used by Caesars Palace in Las Vegas. The reader should compare this letter with that of the Arizona Biltmore.

The Convention Liaison Council

The best customers are the ones who really know their business. And they like to do business with vendors who know theirs. It is amazing how rapidly and steadily the convention business grew, with very little done to expand areas of knowledge and expertise. Fortunately, leaders of four associations met in 1949 to come to grips with the situation. This group—including both vendors and buyers—formed a council to establish a set of commonly accepted trade standards.

The Convention Liaison Council, as it is now known, adopted four basic objectives that are worth noting. They are

1. to bring about a sympathetic understanding and acceptance among these organizations of the responsibility of each to the other
2. to create a sound and consistent basis for handling convention procedures and practices through a program of study and education
3. to conduct educational and other activities of mutual interest to the participating organizations
4. to acquaint the public with the fact that conventions are essential to industry and to the economy of the community and nation

The four original organizations were the American Hotel and Motel Association, the American Society of Association Executives, the Hotel Sales Marketing Association, and the International Association of Convention and Visitor Bureaus.

Other organizations joined from 1956 to 1988. A complete list of the sponsoring organizations of the Convention Liaison Council is found in Appendix A.

The first Convention Liaison Council manual was published in 1961 as part of the council's educational program. It had a most interesting format and is worth hunting for. The manual presented detailed responsibilities of each of the three

Fig. 9.5 Sample proposal letter, sent before offering a letter of agreement. (By permission of the Arizona Biltmore).

Temperature: 85 degrees

The Arizona Biltmore

John H. Sienold
Vice President
Marketing and Sales

Re: Mother's of America

Dear Mrs. Kingsbury:

Certainly enjoyed our telephone conversation on Tuesday...and needless to say, we are gratified at the prospect of serving your association in March of 19__.

We could very comfortably accommodate you for arrival Thursday, March 24 with departure Sunday, March 27, 19__. We could accept some early arrivals on Wednesday, March 23. However, it would be limited to 20 guest rooms. Therefore, the block of rooms we could make available to you looks something like this:

MARCH, 19__

DAY	Wednesday	Thursday	Friday	Saturday	Sunday
DATE	23	24	25	26	27
ROOMS	20	80	80	80	0

Although we have not yet established our convention rates for the calendar year of 19__, currently out "group" European Plan during March are $90 single and $96 double occupancy. Full American Plan (includes room, breakfast/lunch/dinner) is currently available at $120 single and $140 double occupancy. I've enclosed several discriptive brochures along with a most comprehensive "fact" sheet. ' $ you can see, we do make available Arizona's most complete resort property! We are the only hotel in Phoenix that has its own 18-hole championship course, horseback riding, stables and complete tennis center. Also, please keep in mind that we are a "5 Star Hotel", one of only nine in the entire country. We've maintained this accolade for the past 15 years (as long as the award has been in existence).

If the arrangements that I outlines are agreeable, please drop me a note and I will protect some space for you on a tentative basis so that the space does not disappear to another meeting planner. Thank you again, and please let me know about your travel arrangements so that I can set aside the necessary time to personally acquaint you with the Biltmore.

Cordially yours,

John J. Jamison
Convention Sales Manager

JJJ/cp
encl.

Phoenix, Arizona 85002
Telephone (602) 955-6600
A Tolley Industries Company

groups involved in a convention—the sponsoring organization, the hotel, and the convention bureau—and showed how they were interrelated. It also contained useful checklists and forms.

The manual was revised and enlarged in 1972, 1980 and 1985. The new editions eliminated the tripartite division, and were addressed to the convention official to guide him or her as the principal executive of a convention. But the theory of the tripartite relationship continues throughout this most useful guide. The letter of agreement in figure 9.6 is from this manual.

Model Letter of Agreement

This letter of agreement was prepared after more than two years of work by representatives of the customer groups through the American Society of Association Executives and the sellers through the Hotel Sales Management Association and the American Hotel and Motel Association. The document clearly spells out all pertinent details. It may be used in total, or paragraphs covering the specific needs of the buyer and seller may be extracted.

The conditions contained in this document should be read and studied to determine its acceptability for your property. Used conscientiously, it can be of great assistance in strengthening the relationship between the hotel and the meeting planner. It is a suggested format and should be adapted to meet individual needs. The important thing is to reach agreement on each service area and execute a written agreement. Note that the council refers to an *association,* but the form is applicable to corporate meetings as well.

The letter is to be written on the letterhead of either the facility or the organization.

Study Questions

1. Distinguish between a letter of agreement and a proposal letter.

2. What is meant by the master account?

3. How extensively are penalty clauses used?

4. What is the Convention Liaison Council? Who are its members? Discuss its contributions to the convention field.

5. Review the sample contract endorsed by the Convention Liaison Council. In what ways would the contract be different for an association convention than for a corporate meeting?

Fig. 9.5 Model letter of agreement worked out by hotel and association representatives. (Reprinted with permission from the *Convention Liaison Manual*, published by the Convention Liaison Council.)

21. Letters of agreement

The agreement format between buyer and seller presented here has been worked out and agreed upon by American Society of Association Executives and representatives of the hotel industry. It is published in this Manual as a model you may wish to follow in whole or in part or adapt should you feel the necessity of a Letter of Agreement.

However, it is recommended that any organization using all or a portion of this model in its negotiations seek the advice of its counsel to be sure wording fits the organization's existing range of policies.

Suggested Letter of Agreement for Convention or Meeting to be Written on Association or Facility Letterhead

Note that this is only a suggested format. It should be adapted by the association or facility to meet its needs. The important requirement is to reach agreement on each service area and execute a written agreement of that. This suggested agreement is not prepared for convention center use; the booking of these convention facilities requires a quite different approach.

Dear Sir:

This will confirm the arrangements made by _____ and _____
(hotel representatives)   (assn. representatives)
concerning the _____ forth-
(organization or group)
coming meeting/convention.

The _____ hereafter referred to as the "Association" and _____ Hotel/Motel hereafter referred to as the "Facility" agree that:

1. The association hereby engages the facility and its staff for a meeting/convention and the facility agrees to furnish same on the following terms: (By mutual agreement in writing, these rates, as well as the rates set forth in paragraph 1(f) hereof may be revised or otherwise changed.)

(a) Scheduled dates & days of meeting/convention from_____to_____.

(b) Start exhibit setup _____ A.M./P.M.
_____.   hour
date

(c) The rates to be charged by the facility for sleeping rooms are as follows:

Single Room from $_____ to $_____ or Flat Rate _____
Double Room from $_____ to $_____ or Flat Rate _____
Twin Room from $_____ to $_____ or Flat Rate _____
Suites from $_____ to $_____ or Flat Rate _____

Other from $_____ to $_____ or Flat Rate _____

(d) The association presently estimates the number of rooms required to be as follows:

No. of Single _____ minimum and _____ maximum

No. of Double _____ minimum and _____ maximum

No. of Suites _____ minimum and _____ maximum

No. of Other (specified) ____ minimum and ____ maximum (See suggested Penalty Clause Terminology—Appendix A)

Note: If room is from X to Y dollars (paragraph c) then specify at **each rate.**

It is anticipated that_____of those attending
(number)
may wish to have an earlier check-in. The dates for early check-in are_____, in which case the facility will provide rooms therefor at convention rates specified. The same rates will apply for____days following the convention/meeting.

The facility guarantees it will provide at least the maximum number of rooms set forth in paragraph (d) and the association agrees to provide occupancy for the minimum number of rooms specified.

The association agrees to keep the facility informed periodically of registrations received in advance so that more exact estimates can be made as to the room requirements. It is agreed that periodic changes in the above estimates (d) may be made from time to time prior to the meeting/convention, but in no case shall the minimum or maximum number set forth in this agreement be changed except by written agreement. The association and facility shall agree in advance on a mutually satisfactory review schedule of convention developments and specify when and how rooms may be released by either party. (Review dates and times should be specified in this letter of agreement.) After the agreed upon cutoff date(s) the association and facility will be held responsible to meet the final agreement.

Facility agrees to refer all requests for suites (if all are held) and/or public rooms to association for approval before assignment if the applicant is identified with the association or industry it serves.

The association shall/shall not request room deposits of convention delegates.

The facility agrees to provide the association with a final occupancy report showing number of rooms occupied each day of the convention period. (See Appendix B)

(e) It may also be incorporated in this contract an agreement by the facility to improve, remodel, or create certain rooms or areas or add services prior to the event covered by this contract. The specifics of the changes in the facility should be spelled out in this contract and failure to meet the requirements by a specified date would be cause for cancellation of the agreement by the association without penalty. Reasonable and adequate notification to the association should be required of any remodeling which would result in a change in the number of suites or public space available.

(f) Anticipated meeting room requirements:

Room Reserved	From Date & Hour to Date & Hour
_____	_____
_____	_____

Type of Function Anticipated	Rental charge, if any
_____	_____
_____	_____

A tentative schedule of meeting rooms required will be submitted to the facility at least _____ months in advance of the meeting/convention. A firm and detailed schedule of meeting rooms required will be furnished the facility not later than _____ months before the meeting/convention. Unless otherwise specified in this agreement, public space as outlined above shall be reserved for the association unless released in writing. (If total facility is being booked the language should state "All public space shall be reserved for the association without charge (or with charges as specified) for use at the discretion of the association. If the association is utilizing only a part of the facility, the above room schedule should be completed.)

(g) Anticipated exhibit space required. The facility agrees to reserve _____ rooms for use as exhibit space. Cost for space shall be _____ (if any).

Services to be provided in exhibit hall by facility include _____

(here specify such items as cleaning, extra lighting, carpeting, advance storage, security, number of microphones available, audio-visual equipment available, operator rates, power supply, or other items agreed upon.)

The facility warrants that the following union regulations prevail in the exhibit hall and will promptly notify the association of any change. Current conditions are: (outline union requirements in exposition hall) _____

_____

_____

_____

(**h**) Special equipment needs of the association: Description and rates:

_____

_____

(**i**) A guarantee of the number of persons attending each food or beverage function will be given to the facility at least_____ hours in advance of the function. The facility agrees to set for_____ % over the guarantee. The above food functions (package) shall be provided at a per person cost of $_____. Beverage/liquor by drink and/or bottle shall be provided at a cost of $_____. Such prices are subject to review up to six months prior to the event.

If a meal function is to be added to the package, the price applied shall be the same as that included in the above package for a like meal.

(**j**) The following complimentary accommodations will be furnished by the facility to the association. Description of rooms and suites, dates of availability and numbers:

_____

(**k**) The facility will give the association notice of any construction or remodeling to be performed in the facility which might interfere with the event. In such event, facility must provide equal alternate space within the facility under contract.

2. The facility and association agree that the following procedure shall be followed with regard to gratuities _____

_____

(**Note**—specific individuals, amount or percent and procedure may be spelled out.)

3. It is agreed by the parties that the foregoing sets forth the essential features of the agreement between the parties and that **specific details** as to registration, rooming of persons attending, handling of

material, special services, collection of tickets, accounting, master account charges, promotion publicity and other matters will be worked out in writing to the satisfaction of both parties prior to or during the meeting/convention and generally following the procedures set forth in the **Convention Liaison Manual** published by the Convention Liaison Committee, 1101 16th Street, N.W., Washington, D.C.

4. This agreement will bind both the association and the facility and except as above provided in paragraph 1(e), may be canceled by either party only upon the giving of written notice at least_____(years) (months) (days) prior to the dates of the meeting/convention or no later than_____(specific date). It is further provided that there shall be no right of termination for the sole purpose of holding the same meeting/convention in some other city or facility.

5. The facility and the association **each** agree to carry adequate liability and other insurance protecting itself against any claims arising from any activities conducted in the facility during the meeting/convention.

6. The performance of this agreement by either party is subject to acts of God, war, government regulation, disaster, strikes, civil disorder, curtailment of transportation facilities, or other emergency making it inadvisable, illegal or impossible to provide the facilities or to hold the meeting/convention. It is provided that this agreement may be terminated for any one or more of such reasons by written notice from one party to the other.

Yours very truly,

_____(Association)
By_____Chief Elected
Officer (title)
_____Chief Paid
Executive (title)

Accepted:

_____(Hotel)(Motel
By_____General Manager
_____Sales Manager

For associations using more than one facility, a similar contract should be executed with each property.

Note: Appendix A may be added to cover overbooking situation. Appendix B is a suggested reporting form for use by the facility. ⟶

APPENDIX A

Penalty Clause Terminology (may be inserted in paragraph 1d)

In the event the facility does not provide the maximum number of rooms specified in this contract and rooms are needed by the association, the facility shall at its own expense secure comparable nearby accommodations and provide at its expense transportation to and from such rooms. This shall apply to each day during which maximum rooms are not provided and delegates must be housed elsewhere.

If the minimum number of rooms finally agreed upon are not occupied by the association, it shall upon audited proof that the rooms were not occupied and were held available for association occupancy, reimburse the facility at the agreed upon single occupancy rate for each room for each date not occupied. (American Plan arrangements will not include food in reimbursement arrangement.)

APPENDIX B

Hotel Report Form

Following the convention or meeting the facility should be instructed to furnish the association all data with respect to its use of the facility. It is suggested that the facility agree to furnish the information at the signing of the contract. This information is important for the planning for the next convention or meeting and will give valuable information for negotiating future contracts or agreements.

Post Convention Report

ASSOCIATION NAME_____

HOTEL NAME_____

CONVENTION DATES_____   Single_____
                                    Room Rates in Effect: Double_____
ROOMS BLOCKED_____   Other_____

1. List for each convention day room occupancy by type.

TYPE	DATES			
Single				
Doubles				
Extra Occupants				
Parlors				
Comps.				
Average Rate				
Room Revenue				

II. List for each convention day number of—

	DATES			
Arrivals				
Cancellations				
No-Shows				
Check Outs				

III. Complete the following for each meal function.

FUNCTION (meal or reception & Date)	GUARANTEE	PLATE COUNT	TICKETS COLLECTED (if any)

IV. List room service revenue, for association hospitality suites.

REVENUE $	DATE

V. List the following exhibit detail.
• Number of booths_____
• Net square feet_____
• Comments_____

_____

Completed By_____

Title_____

Bibliography   Part 1

The Art of Hotel Advertising
Hotel Sales & Marketing Association
1400 K Street, N.W., Suite 810
Washington, D.C. 20005

Automatic Hotel/Motel Sales Functions:
A How-To Manual on Computerizing the Sales Office
by Charles L. Eudy
The Foundation of the Hotel Sales & Marketing Association
1400 K Street, N.W., Suite 810
Washington, D.C. 20005

The Basics of Hotel Sales & Marketing
Hotel Sales & Marketing Association
Office of Education & Training
333 N. Gladstone Avenue
Margate, NJ 08402

Front Office Selling Tips
by David C. Dorf, CHSE
Hotel Sales & Marketing Association
1400 K Street, N.W., Suite 810
Washington, D.C. 20005

The Group Market: What It Is and How To Sell It
by Dr. Margaret Shaw
The Foundation of the Hotel Sales & Marketing Association
1400 K Street, N.W., Suite 810
Washington, D.C. 20005

Hospitality for Sale
by C. DeWitt Coffman, CHSE
The Educational Institute of the American Hotel & Motel Association
1407 S. Harrison Road
East Lansing, MI 48823

How To Do It All . . . On Time: A Time Management Workbook
by William T. Brooks
Hotel Sales & Marketing Association
1400 K Street N.W., Suite 810
Washington, D.C. 20005

Improve Your Marketing Techniques: A Guide for Hotel Managers and Caterers
by Prof. J.R. Sumner
Northwood Books
93-99 Goswell Road
London ECIV 7QA England

The Management of Hotel Sales & Marketing
Hotel Sales & Marketing Association
Office of Education and Training
333 N. Gladstone Avenue
Margate, NJ 08402

Marketing For a Full House
by C. DeWitt Coffman, CHSE
The School of Hotel Administration
Statler Hall
Cornell University
Ithaca, NY 14853

Marketing Hotels into the 90s
by Melvyn Greene
American Edition:
AVI Publishing Company
P.O. Box 831
Westport, CT 06881

Marketing in the Hospitality Industry
by Dr. Ronald A. Nykiel
CBI/Van Nostrand Reinhold Co.
115 Fifth Avenue
New York, NY 10003

Marketing Your Hotel Through Direct Mail
The Foundation of the Hotel Sales & Marketing Association
Office of Education & Training
333 N. Gladstone Avenue
Margate, NJ 08402

Policies and Procedures of the Hotel Sales Office
by Leo M. Renaghan and Teresa Mywrang
The Foundation of the Hotel Sales & Marketing Association
1400 K Street N.W., Suite 810
Washington, D.C. 20005

Situation Analysis Workbook
The Foundation of the Hotel Sales & Marketing Association & The Educational
Institute of the American Hotel & Motel Association
Hotel Sales & Marketing Association
1400 K Street N.W., Suite 810
Washington, D.C. 20005

Strategic Hotel/Motel Marketing
by David A. Troy, CHSE
The Educational Institute of the American Hotel & Motel Association
1407 South Harrison Road
East Lansing, MI 48823

Strategic Marketing Planning in the Hospitality Industry
Edited by Robert L. Blomstrom
The Educational Institute of the American Hotel & Motel Association
1407 South Harrison Road
East Lansing, MI 48823

Part 2

Convention Services

Introduction

Selling a convention on the worth of your facility is only half the job; now you must deliver what has been promised. Mel Hosansky, editor of *Successful Meetings* magazine, claims that hotel salespeople are not selling guest rooms, recreational facilities, or complex audiovisual equipment. He says hotels are "really selling reassurance," reassurance that whatever problems may arise during a group's stay, the hotel will be able to handle them.[1] To a great extent, the meeting planner's job depends on how well the hotel does its job.

Asked what he considered most essential to the success of serious business meetings, one meeting planner expressed himself to *Resort Management* magazine as follows:

> I have given considerable thought to your questions about those aspects of a facility that are really appreciated, as opposed to those that cause annoyances. While my comments may border on oversimplification, I believe them.
>
> A room is a room, and food is food, and a golf course is a golf course . . . and so, in my opinion, it gets down to service.
>
> What makes a meeting something to be remembered? It is the limousine driver who chats with you enroute to the hotel; it is the gal at the registration desk, or guy, who is really glad we are here. It is the bellhop who carries your bag to the room with a smile; it is the maid who is always kind of walking up and down the hall like your mother did when you were a youngster. It is the waitress in the dining room who makes you feel as if you are the only person she has to wait on all day, and the fellow who helps with the meeting room and is always ready to realign chairs, bring in new equipment, set up projectors, etc. It is the gal or guy at checkout time who says "Come back" (and you know the invitation is meant).
>
> All of these people have one thing in common . . . they share a way of life that is stimulating, exciting and rewarding. Their responsibility is more than just "a place to work" or "it's a job." I'm not sure how you cultivate this kind of rapport in this type of facility, but few places have it to offer.[2]

---

1. Reprinted by permission of *Meetings & Conventions* magazine. Copyright ©. Ziff-Davis Publishing Co.
2. Jack C. Knight, "What Do Conference Planners Really Want?" *Resort Management.*

Outline

10 The Service Function

Only the Beginning

Securing a convention is only the beginning. We should be much more concerned with how a convention goes out of a hotel than with how it comes in. Delegates are well traveled today, and their wants are no more unreasonable when they are convention delegates than when they are individual guests.

Hard work and many dollars are invested in advertising and promotional material in an effort to recruit group business. Yet, a pleased and satisfied delegate is the best and most economical advertising medium. He has friends with whom he cannot help but share his travel experiences. And if your hotel has made a favorable impression, the delegate is certain to stay with you on return visits.

Nothing attracts another piece of group business more than a satisfied convention. Thus, it is crucial that all promises made in the selling process be fulfilled. In addition, an indelible impression will be made when the hotel provides some little unexpected service that is above and beyond the preconvention promises.

Service Is the Key

Often the service follow-through is regarded as an afterthought to the heavy emphasis placed on selling a convention. But failure in the essential service phase is costly. Corporate meeting planners evaluate the success of their conventions on the extent to which hotels' commitments were kept. Lack of communication, poorly trained and indifferent employees, failure to heed details, and rude responses to requests are all detriments that may be instrumental in losing future meeting business.

How might the hotel better service the convention group? Most important is a well-trained and courteous staff with a service attitude. The hotel industry is essentially a people business and hotel staff members must be made aware of the importance of convention delegates. They should be trained to understand that nothing short of top performance is expected.

Furthermore, one person should be designated to direct the convention staff and serve as a liaison between hotel personnel and the convention chairperson. This individual's primary responsibilities is to coordinate the convention group's activities and see that all events function smoothly.

Hotels can build good will in other ways—by making arrangements with labor if exhibits are used, obtaining any official permissions that are required by local government departments, such as police or fire, and assisting with transportation needs. Also, help convention delegates schedule their time and keep them informed about the facilities available in the hotel. Book special entertainment, arrange guided tours to points of interest, and provide the highest quality food and beverage service possible. In short, do not give convention delegates a reason for leaving your hotel.

Regardless of how smoothly the program is planned, snags and slipups inevitably spring up at the last minute. If the hotel helps meeting planners solve these problems, future business is nearly always assured. It may be necessary to shuffle meeting rooms around, help find a last-minute substitute speaker or prepare a special entree for the wife of the chairman of the board. The attitude with which the hotel accepts these common occurrences will, to a great extent, determine the scene of next year's convention. If the hotel can lick these crises, the parting handshake may well be accompanied with the salute, "I'll see you next year."

Who Services?

One of the frequently discussed issues in convention management is the extent to which the hotel salesperson should be involved in the servicing process.

Some hotels say that a salesperson is just that, a salesperson, and that he or she shouldn't become involved in servicing the client. They claim that the service function is a specialty, distinct from selling, and that there is a more efficient use of staff and a higher rebooking percentage when salespeople spend 100 percent of their time selling. Others hold that the convention salesperson should handle the sales and servicing completely. They suggest that the sales representative should follow up all hotel visits, write up the actual bookings, and coordinate the servicing of the group during its stay at the hotel.

Resort Management, a leading lodging and foodservice publication, asked a number of hotel operators how they handled sales and servicing. Following are the comments of three managers on the methods in which they handle this controversial issue.

TAMARRON RESORT
William H. Sageser
Manager, Hotel Operations

The Tamarron is a resort owned by Golf Hosts International located in the Rocky Mountains about thirty miles from Durango, Colorado. Its accommodations include 368 guest rooms and 7,000 square feet of meeting space.

I find that both direct sales and service selling have very valid points. However, I feel that the points in service selling far exceed those in direct sales. As you pointed out, the advantages of direct sales do give the opportunity to the sales staff to concentrate their total effort in booking business, and do not tie them up in the laborious task of accumulating the multitude of details that it always takes to conduct a successful conference. But, when you have a sales department whose only responsibility is getting meetings on the books, they seem to lose contact with the other departments and see their responsibilities as only that of putting business on the books.

I am a strong believer in service selling with modifications. I believe there is a definite need for a conference coordinator to assist in the many details that are involved in successful conferences. However, conference coordinators should never eliminate any of the responsibilities of the sales person who actually sells the group.

I think the sales person who is instrumental in booking business has got to be kept involved from beginning to end. By doing this, it builds confidence in the association executive for the hotel, makes the sales person more aware of the strong and weak points of his people, and consequently, makes him a much better sales person in booking other groups and puts him in an excellent position to rebook meetings. It also helps the sales person tremendously in building his own reputation with the meeting planners because they understand the promises and assurances that he made when the booking was made, and they see that he is always available and visible during the conference to see that these promises are carried out.

KINGSMILL
Jack C. Knight
Managing Director

The Kingsmill Resort is a part of a large development program undertaken by Anheuser-Busch, Inc., just outside of Williamsburg, Virginia. It houses a large convention center and has more meeting square footage than either of the other two properties discussed.

There is so much more to this question concerning service selling vs. direct sales than meets the eye, that I can only classify the subject as "an explosive issue."

The subject is not just "How is the salesman best employed?" or "How can management keep his salesman happy?" or "How to reduce sales costs," but, perhaps, should be defined a "Complete client satisfaction insures rebooking without sales costs." Meeting planners are not sheep, but they need a shepherd to turn to at all times.

Let us, therefore, trace sales procedures, starting with a given company name only, coupled with a reasonable belief that this company could possibly hold meetings.

Sales Step 1:   Having been given a cold lead by the sales manager, a sales telephonist is employed to determine the company's meeting plan profile. The information she sets out to obtain is broadly as follows:

A. meeting frequency
B. time(s) of the year
C. length of meeting—arrival date and departure date

D. number of attendees
E. type of property preferred and why
F. type of meeting
G. purchase center and responsible individual
H. any other attendant information which will help the account executive

Sales Step 2: Having qualified the prospect, the information obtained is then turned over in a written report to the area account executive who then telephones for an appointment, or, if feasible, arranges for the conference planner to participate in a house visit. Sales literature is normally not passed until personal face-to-face contact is made with the potential client.

Sales Step 3: When the verbal sale is made, the client is then turned over to the property's conference coordinator. He or she is responsible for documenting all of the client's needs, preparing the sales contract or letter of agreement, and following through every step of the way to the end of the meeting.

While the conference coordinator has the full responsibility for the smooth running of the client's meeting, and for informing, by conference specification sheet, the various department heads concerned, the conference coordinator will, where practical, introduce the client and sit in on discussions with the various department heads (such as food and beverage director, front desk supervisor, conference setup manager, etc.). The client receives a copy of the internal conference specification plan in order that he or she may check that all arrangements have been made in accordance with his or her instructions. The points to be learned by this process are:

A. The "salesman" does not waste his or her time soliciting prospects who would not be suitable for the particular property.
B. The "salesman" can devote 100% of his or her time "selling" the live prospects who have already been qualified.
C. After the verbal sale has been made, the client is assured that there is a responsible person who will look after his or her needs, and who will always be available on the spot, and is, therefore, not "out of town"; "will call later," etc.
D. Management can reduce the number of salesmen needed because the salesman spends 100% of his time selling to live prospects not 30% of his time on checking internally, 30% making introductions to department heads, and other time setting up meeting rooms.
E. Service promises, concerning actual meeting room availability, function areas and times, audiovisual equipment availability, etc., are kept because the con-groups who will be in the house at the same time. How often, in poorly coordinated properties, is a client anguished when he finds a particular meeting room, a function site, or a particular piece of equipment promised by the salesman is not available because it has been committed elsewhere.
F. Furthermore, and equally important, a strong conference coordinator will control the flow of traffic into a main dining room by staggering the times groups break from cocktail parties, banquets, and recreational activities. Such planning minimizes the burdens on the chef, the head bartender, setup men, and above all, it provides the client with the type of service he anticipates receiving.

In other words, efficient service throughout the length of the meeting and attention to small detail is of paramount importance, and when given, assures that a client will automatically rebook additional meetings at that particular facility.

JUG END
Angus MacDonald
President, General Manager

The Jug End in the Berkshires is a 180-room resort in Massachusetts with about 6,000 square feet in its largest meeting room. It, like the Tamarron, is a mountain resort with winter skiing and summer golf facilities.

> In many cases, the servicing of group business depends on the size of the house. If the property has 50 rooms or less, many times the owner/manager can sell and service the property himself (or with the help of his wife) . . . but, when the property is larger than that, I like to see specialists handling the servicing.
>
> Let the salesmen do the selling . . . get the business "in the house." The reputation of the hotel (and the food and service) is mostly dependent on in-house servicing. On larger groups, the salesman should be on hand to welcome them, and then, the servicing should be handled by others, preferably on the food staff, since the food staff is so made up that, should one member be unavailable, the whole service operation does not fall apart. I have seen sad situations develop where details have not been properly attended to by the salesmen, and such lack of attention or mishandling reflects poorly on the whole hotel operation.
>
> Should the group planner prefer to deal with the owner/principal of the hotel, we don't object. We will do everything he wants to make him feel at ease. The big thing is not to have a meeting planner come in and feel uneasy . . . be fearful that the meeting might "bomb out," and so jeopardize his own future in his company. It is also important to let meeting planners know that you recognize their authority and attendant responsibilities, and to assure them that you are not going to let them down.
>
> In our property, I always make it a point to meet the head of each group. He has done a great deal of planning for the meeting, has spent thousand of dollars in organizing the meeting, considerable money on transportation, etc., plus what he will spend at our hotel. Consequently, I feel that the head of the hotel has an obligation to the convention group to let them know that the entire staff, from the top right down to the bottom, is interested in making their meeting a success.[1]

Judging from this discussion, there seems to be basically three approaches to the question, "Who services?"

William Sageser of the Tamarron says the sales manager should sell, arrange, and work the meeting from beginning to end. He feels that the salesperson who does not get involved in servicing may be concerned only with putting business on the books, thus perhaps making hasty promises that are impossible to keep.

1. "Group Sales and Service," *Resort Management.*

Opposed to this view is Jack Knight of the Kingsmill, who suggests that once the sale is made, the salesman should step aside and turn the meeting planner over to the in-house conference coordinator. This coordinator then documents the client's needs, draws up the letter of agreement, and follows through to the end of the meeting.

A third, middle-of-the-road, approach is practiced at Jug End. In this case, says Angus MacDonald, the salesperson generally meets the group as it arrives but then steps out of the picture until the function is nearly completed. During the closing day of the convention, the salesperson is likely to re-enter and attempt to sell upcoming meetings.

Which approach should you practice? The conclusion we have drawn from our experience is that "the best approach is the one that works." Certainly no one procedure can be tagged as the best for all situations. However, if the size of the hotel can justify an in-house convention service manager, we tend to cast our support toward separation of sales and service.

The Convention Service Manager

Throughout the remainder of the text, we have taken the position that the servicing responsibility is handled by the convention service manager. Such a practice assures the association or corporate executive that whatever his or her requirements—reservations, banquet, meeting room setup—there is one individual with complete authority and responsibility for his or her meeting.

The title "convention service manager," as evidenced by the Kingsmill and Tamarron discussions, is not universally accepted. Hotels have given the person in charge of convention service various titles, including conference coordinator, convention coordinator, convention manager, service coordinator, and, in many smaller properties, banquet or catering manager. (Chapter 14 offers a thorough discussion of the role of the banquet manager as practiced in most small properties.)

Regardless of the title, the position carries a lot of prestige and a hefty amount of responsibility. If any one person can make or break a conference, it is the convention service manager. The convention service manager has been referred to as "the person who makes things happen." He, or she, is the meeting planner's contact person, and so should be readily available to handle all of the convening group's on-the-spot needs. Quite simply, he or she is the single communication link between the meeting planner and the hotel.

Ideally, the convention service manager has the authority to get the job done and to get it done fast. The meeting planner is able to rest much easier when he has the assurance that his liaison has the authority to fulfill his needs within each department of the hotel.

Leroy Smith, association executive of the National Automobile Association, has suggested that the convention service department should report directly to the hotel's general manager, not to the director of sales.[2] He suggests that an organizational structure such as that in figure 10.1 gives the convention service manager line control over the functions of the front desk, housekeeping, banquet, and food and beverage departments as they relate to convention servicing.

The working hours of the person in charge of service are often very long. Bill Tobin told us when he was convention service manager at Caesars Palace in Las Vegas, "I want to give the meeting planner the impression I never go home." One hour before every function, he checked out the facilities with the group's coordinator. This is a commendable policy, but when there are several groups within the house, one having a late cocktail party and another planning an early-bird breakfast, the convention service manager may find little time to himself. Cutting still further into time off are the preconvention and post-convention meetings often scheduled for weekends.

But in addition to the normal salary paid by the hotel, the convention service manager may receive compensation for long hours in the form of gifts and tips from the meeting planner. Association and corporate executives have been known to be extremely generous in saying thanks for a job well done. Further remuneration is sometimes received from the hotel. The Sheraton Waikiki, recognizing the importance of its convention service manager, has given him a suite within the hotel.

How does one become a convention service manager? While there is no standard rule, most have advanced through either the banquet or front office department, where they were exposed to the problems frequently encountered in group business. Then some sponsor, observing the employee's performance and service attitude, placed him or her over this important department. Often the next step up the corporate rung is to convention sales. The hotel convention salesperson who has had experience in group servicing knows what can be promised and what can be delivered, and thus is a most valued employee.

The Transition

Another frequently debated subject in convention management is, "How and when should a meeting planner be turned over to the individual within the hotel who will have charge of coordinating his conference?"

2. Speech at a Hotel Sales Marketing Association meeting in Las Vegas.

224

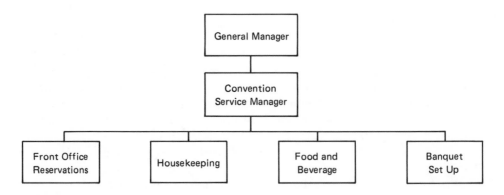

It is difficult to divorce the salesperson entirely from the service function. The salesperson who simply dismisses a client after the sale, assuming that the convention service manger will shoulder the burden, will probably not get a rebooking.

The transition must be handled smoothly. The client should be handled with kid gloves from the salesperson to the convention service manager. Frequently the client has dealt exclusively with the salesperson for two or three years and has complete trust in the sales staff. The salesperson's exit can be traumatic if the planner has not been reassured of the service manager's competence.

We recommend that once the sale is made, the salesperson step aside and turn the meeting planner over to the service people. We don't believe, however, that the client should be abandoned by the salesperson. We suggest that the salesperson greet the planner, if possible, when the meeting comes to the hotel and reassure him that he is in good hands. Further, the salesperson should keep in touch and reenter as the meeting closes to suggest a rebooking.

A customer who is sold a new car by a lot salesman is certainly likely to return to the same salesman for his next new car if every time he brought his car in for an oil change or tune-up, the salesman remembered and greeted him. It's the same way with conventions and hotel salespeople.

Importance of Communication

Let's consider a fictional situation. The Cannon Corporation, a large torpedo manufacturer headquartered in the East, has scheduled a convention in a Seattle hotel. The Cannon meeting planner has informed the convention service manager of a

Fig. 10.2 Communication is extremely important in servicing conventions. Information centers are frequently set up to keep delegates posted on the convention schedule. And many hotels assign pocket pagers to meeting planners for communication with the hotel's sales staff. (Courtesy of Paul Emmerich)

heavy 4:00 P.M. check-in on Sunday. The convention service manager included the following instructions to the front desk and the hotel's restaurants:

Attention: Lanny Kingsbury—Front Desk Check-in
As this is a major check-in day for Cannon Corp., I recommended you make plans to staff the desk to handle the overlead during the peak around 4:00 P.M. Traffic should be heavy with 600 delegates arriving on two charter flights.

Attention: Marney Vartanian—Public Feeding Facilities
I would recommend full staffing by 5:00 P.M. due to the heavy arrival. Food and beverage functions are nonexistent during Sunday evening so delegate traffic will be particularly heavy in all restaurants.

The hotel has made plans to handle the overloads, according to the instructions. At one o'clock Sunday in Seattle—4:00 P.M. eastern time—600 delegates arrive at the hotel. The delegates, anxious to get settled, face long lines and a mini-mum hotel staff. *Someone forgot to communicate* the time change between the east and west coasts. To compound the problem, the delegation has arrived at the peak of the previous day's check-out. The Cannon Corporation is ready to fire its prod-uct in the hotel's lobby.

Who is to blame? The meeting planner is outraged. He charges, "We have supplied you with a big piece of business and immediately you blow it." The hotel counters, "We were ready for you. We didn't deliberately try to give you a bad time. You told us four o'clock, we were ready at four o'clock."

Whether the fault lies with the meeting planner or the convention service manager, the hotel's image is damaged, perhaps beyond repair.

The convention service manager should not be satisfied with just selling rooms and food. He, or she, is also in the business of providing service. This means he should be a problem solver for the client, not a problem maker. A hotel should re-quest full and detailed information so it can better serve the group. Likewise, the hotel should communicate accurate data to the client. The clearer the communica-tion in the beginning, the less likely there will be disappointments later.

An Overview

Thus far, we've talked about the importance of service, the role of the convention service manager, and his or her position in the hotel's organizational structure. In Part II we will cover in detail every facet of this person's job and how he or she works with other departments within the hotel. To give the reader a clear picture of where we are heading, we will present an overview of the convention service manager's role, step-by-step.

Step No. 1 Once a group is booked, the convention service manager reviews all correspondence to find out what information has been documented and what in-formation is still required. Many times he, or she, will review files from two or three years before the date of the convention.

Step No. 2 The booking is listed in the function book, and contact is made with the meeting planner through a letter of introduction (fig. 10.3). This letter specifies that the association will be dealing with him while in the hotel. At this point, the salesperson goes behind the scenes and the convention service manager begins to get answers to the three basics: reservations, program, and billing. If at any time he feels he is losing a group, he will immediately turn them back over to the salesperson.

Step No. 3   Tracing—using follow-up letters, telephone calls, and personal contact with the association executive—is initiated to build a relationship of trust and cooperation between the two parties. Correspondence is made as clear as possible, but with lots of detail.

Step No. 4   Details of the program are formulated in a *personal interview* with the association executive at least six months before the event. Reservation requests are also mailed to the delegates at about this time (chapter 11) in an effort to determine the number of guest rooms.

Step No. 5   A monthly preconvention meeting is held with all department heads to review upcoming groups (chapter 12). All *convention specification sheets* are gone over and discussed in detail.

Step No. 6   Two or three days before the conference opens, a preconvention meeting is held with the front office manager (chapter 12), the supervisor in charge of room setup (chapter 13), the catering manager (chapter 14), and the association executive. The entire program is reviewed, the menus are reaffirmed, and the meeting setups are verified.

Step No. 7   During the convention, the service manager is on hand as much as possible. He will be at each meeting location one hour ahead of time to view the setup. He will check the audio-visual equipment (chapter 15), exhibit setups, and security (chapters 16 and 17).

Step No. 8   A post-convention meeting (chapter 18) is scheduled at the completion of the event. Here all charges to the master account for billing are verified and initialed a second time by the association executive. The post-convention meeting is a review of the event by those persons in attendance at the preconvention meeting. At this time, as we said, the salesperson steps in and tries to sell the group on a repeat convention. When the convention service department does its job, a rebooking percentage of 70 percent is not uncommon.

Fig. 10.3 Letter of introduction sent by the convention service manager to the meeting planner.

Newport Beach

December 26, 19__

Ms. Sue Bachar
Coordinator
ATLAS AMBASSADOR TOURS
25 West 43rd Street
New York, NY 10036

Dear Ms. Bachar:

I was delighted to hear from Heidi Neal that Atlas Ambassador Tours will
be holding its conference at Le Meridien Newport Beach on April 12-22, 19__.

As Conference Services Manager, I will be responsible for coordinating the
menus, meeting room set ups, audio visual needs and sleeping room
accommodations for your upcoming conference.

I would like to verify that your method of reservations will be rooming
list. I have enclosed copies of our rooming list form for your use.
Please be sure to include accurate arrival and departure dates, as
well as correct billing information.

To insure the success of your meeting, I will call to request the
meeting room set ups, audio visual needs, coffee break schedules and
menu selections at least 20 days prior to your group's arrival. Final
guarantee numbers for all meal functions must be received by us three (3)
working days in advance. A guarantee cannot be lowered after this time.

Should you be sending materials to the hotel for your conference, please
use the following address and information on all labels:

         ATTENTION: Noreen Crawford   HOLD FOR ARRIVAL:
         Le Meridien Newport Beach   Atlas Ambassador Tours
         4500 MacArthur Blvd.   Ms. Sue Bachar
         Newport Beach, CA 92660   April 12-22, 19__

Due to limited storage space at the hotel, we cannot accept materials
that arrive prior to three (3) days before your conference.

I am looking forward to working with you toward a most successful meeting,
and hope that this information will be helpful in finalizing your arrangements.
Please feel free to contact me should you have any questions.

Sincerely,

LE MERIDIEN NEWPORT BEACH
Noreen Crawford, CONFERENCE SERVICES MANAGER

4500 MacArthur Blvd., Newport Beach, California 92660-2010
(714) 476-2001 Telex: 3719355-853459 Telecopier: (714) 476-0153
Groupe Air France

229

Fig. 10.4 Convention service checklist Detailed checklists serve as planning guides and often prevent the overlooking of important items in staging a successful convention. Numerous checklists exist for helping the meeting planner avoid oversights, but few are available specifically for the convention service manager. This is the format used by the New York Penta Hotel, and is the best checklist we have seen in the industry.

New York Penta Hotel

7th Avenue & 33rd Street, New York, NY 10001
Telephone: (212) 736-5000   Telex: 220932

CONVENTION SERVICE CHECK-LIST

NAME OF GROUP: _____

DATES OF MEETING: _____

MEETING PLANNER: _____

MASTER ACCOUNT ADDRESS: _____

_____

_____

TELEPHONE NUMBER: _____

SALES MANAGER: _____

BANQUET MANAGER: _____

TWELVE (12) MONTHS AWAY FROM MEETING DUE DATE: _____

COMPLETION DATE

1. Sales Manager to turn event file over to Convention Service with a copy of the signed contract, a copy of the approved booking notice, a copy of the approved definite room block, a copy of the credit form (if credit has not been determined, trace three days and follow-up), and a past history on pick-up for the last two (2) years.   _____

2. Review Master File.   _____

3. Verify definite program, confirm diary space, meeting room rental, exhibit rental, set-up charges, and date all space hold to be released (if it is applicable).   _____

4. Confirm room commitments with Front Office and GRC for accuracy, based on past history, block VIP Suites. Determine when room rate will be established, and trace if not already established.   _____

5. Determine if all exhibit information is complete in contract and remind account of need for floor plans to be approved, exhibitor's contract to be approved, hold harmless clause signed, insurance certificate for $250,000.00.   _____

6. Initial contact and letter of introduction – obtain other
    key meeting personnel and names.   _____

    a) Request most recent convention history.   _____

    b) Review credit procedures and billing address.   _____

    c) Review reservation procedures, when mailing will go out,
        clarify need for approval of reservation form if they act
        as housing bureau.   _____

    d) Inquire about need for hospitality suites, who will use
        them, their name and address, and previous suite number
        if annual.   _____

    e) Ask about public relations opportunities, famous people,
        unusual events, and newsworthy issues.   _____

    f) Inquire if account is tax exempt, ask for N.Y.S.
        Exemption Form.   _____

7. Discuss their needs and requirements for outside security
    per Corporate Policy.   _____

8. Send New York Penta meeting planner fact book.   _____

9. Send New York Penta Convention Kit.   _____

10. Order reservation cards (if the sales person has already
    done so, obtain a copy of this form).   _____

SIX (6) MONTHS AWAY FROM MEETING DUE DATE: _____

1. Contact public relations for coordination of publicity. Place
    director of Public Relations in contact with the meeting planner.
    (If this is applicable.)   _____

2. Accentuate need for the accounts to provide detailed instructions
    at an early date so that proper service may be administered.   _____

3. Explain convention resume procedures.   _____

4. Reconfirm staff and VIP housing requirements and double check
    suites blocked.   _____

5. Determine audio visual needs. Discuss how extensive set-ups
    are. Sell in-house audio visual company.   _____

6. Discuss registration personnel and procedures. New York Penta
    needs to maintain integrity of our property. All signs must be
    professionally printed, no signs allowed on walls. No signs
    allowed in the main lobby, except by management approval.   _____

7. Coordinate contact with banquet representative, give name, telephone number, have banquet representative call account.   _____

8. Review account's needs in regard to office equipment, i.e., typewriters, telephones, need for decorations or decorators, florist.   _____

9. Request name of drayage company. Review needs of union labor. This is a union house.   _____

10. Inquire into anticipated companion programs, anticipate bus tours. Coordinate information regarding bus tour loadings and unloadings.   _____

11. Request finalized meeting and exhibit floor plans for approval.   _____

12. Review final meeting schedule and check diary.   _____

THREE (3) MONTHS AWAY FROM MEETING DUE DATE: _____

1. Reconfirm required suites and staff requirements with guest and Front Office.   _____

2. Review billing arrangements, identify all master accounts and authorized signatures.   _____

3. Remind client of cut-off date for rooms.   _____

4. If rooms do not materialize, a rental may have to be implemented (if there is not a rental or sliding scale in the contract) by the Sales person.   _____

5. Request official printed program. Compare published program to space requirements in regard to time, set-up times, coffee services, etc.   _____

SIX (6) WEEKS AWAY FROM MEETING DUE DATE: _____

1. Process letter for VIP's.   _____

2. Verify attendance at all functions, establish rental based on contractual agreement and establish master account and billing instructions along with authorized signatures.   _____

3. Secure deposit if required, due 30 days prior to arrival date, unless we have devised a payment schedule.   _____

4. Review file on the departmental basis to alert key people of
    heavy or unusual requirements.   _____

5. Review microphone requirements.   _____

6. Review lighting requirements, and any production set-up needs.   _____

7. Review room block against pick-up and cut-off date with the
    Convention Service Manager.   _____

8. Review complimentary rooms. If pick-up is below what the client
    anticipated, and is causing a comp room assignment problem,
    confer with Sales Manager and Convention Service Manager to
    explore best means of satisfying the customer.

9. Request complete set-up information.   _____

10. Review room registration, check-in arrangements.   _____

11. Review special housekeeping arrangements, if applicable.   _____

12. Obtain a copy of authorized signatures for the master account.   _____

13. Review cash advance needs.   _____

14. Review safe deposit needs.   _____

15. Review shipping arrangements of materials.   _____

THREE (3) WEEKS AWAY FROM MEETING DUE DATE: _____

1. Forward resume and check with Catering on menu progress.   _____

2. Distribute resume to hotel departments and include
    affiliated activities.
                                                                      _____

3. Establish date and time for a pre-convention meeting,
    process in-house memo.   _____

4. Inquire if client wishes to guarantee rooms not picked up.   _____

TWO (2) WEEKS AWAY FROM MEETING DUE DATE: _____

1. Order limousine if applicable.   _____

2. Re-check program with diary for possible quick meeting room
    turn-over and enter proper times for all events.   _____

3. Review complimentary room arrangements.   _____

4. Request posting instructions.   _____

FORTY-EIGHT (48) HOURS AWAY FROM MEETING DUE DATE: _____

1. Check hospitality and complimentary orders and VIP reservations. _____

DURING MEETING DUE DATES: _____

1. Check setting of meeting rooms (a.m., afternoon and p.m.). _____

2. Public Space Mgr. or Asst. to complete event checklist for
    each function room. _____

3. Assist with restaurant reservations for VIP's. _____

4. Review shipping arrangements for post convention materials. _____

5. Review complimentary room arrangements. _____

6. Compare room pick-up to complimentary list, make necessary
    adjustments. _____

7. Set-up post convention meeting. _____

8. Verify booth and exhibit hall by walk through with customer. _____

9. Determine exhibit rental charge if determined by booth. _____

10. Determine repeat booking potential and advise Sales Manager. _____

11. Review master account with account credit department at a
    predetermined meeting. This should be completed each day. _____

IMMEDIATELY AFTER MEETING DUE DATE: _____

1. Call account and send thank you letter. _____

2. Complete report of convention and profit and loss
    statement and distribute. _____

3. Determine report on abnormal circumstances in the post convention
    memo. _____

4. Post-Convention report to include under "comments" section an
    objective evaluation of the hotel's performance. _____

5. Turn file over to Convention Service Manager for review. _____

ONE (1) MONTH AFTER MEETING DUE DATE: _____

1. Breakdown work file and return appropriate correspondence to
    master file. _____

Study Questions

1. Assess the quotation of the meeting planner in the introduction to Part II. Do you agree?

2. Do you think that sales department personnel should become involved with group servicing? Refer to the approaches used by the Tamarron Resort, the Kingsmill and the Jug End.

3. Where does the convention service manager fit into the hotel organizational structure? Thoroughly discuss the job of the convention service manager, identifying how he or she works with other departments in performing the service function.

4. What is meant by the *transition?*

5. Define *tracing.*

Outline

I. Reservation Systems

    A. Postal Reply Cards
    B. Rooming Lists
    C. City Housing Bureau
    D. Toll-Free 800 Reservations

II. Room Assignment

    A. Priorities
    B. Rate Structures
    C. Rooms Reserved
    D. Arrival/Departure Pattern
    E. Release and Confirmation Dates
    F. Complimentary Arrangements
    G. Other Hotels
    H. Historical Performance

III. No-Shows/Overbooking

IV. Check-in—Check-out

    A. Check-in Procedure
    B. Check-out Procedure

V. The Computer Influence

    A. Reservations
    B. Registration and Room Assignment
    C. Check-out and Billing

The letter of agreement has been signed and countersigned. The dates are firm. The room block is specified in the contract. At this point, many departments and organizations become involved as the service process branches out into different areas.

One such area is the assigning of guest rooms through the front desk. Through cooperation between the convention's housing staff and your own front office and reservation departments, this area plays a strong supportive role in the success of a convention.

Reservation Systems

Guest room reservation information is sent to the group's membership three to six months before the event. There are three reservation systems that are primarily used today.

Postal Reply Cards

The usual agreement calls for the meeting planner to mail reservation forms to his or her membership along with other material. These self-addressed postal reply cards are printed by the hotel and sent in bulk to the convention group's headquarters. A cover letter from the hotel is enclosed with the reply cards.

From its mailing list the convention headquarters then sends the cards to the members. Figure 11.1 shows the return reservation cards used by two hotels. In each case, the convention delegate is to return the card directly to the hotel's reservation department.

It is important for the hotel to use a clear reservation system. This is vital for internal use, for coordination with a housing bureau, and for confirmation to guests. If you have to develop a form or revise one that has given you trouble, look at our samples or start from scratch, keeping the following factors in mind:

I. Clarity.
    A. Be concise.
    B. Allow enough space for hand printing. Ask guests to print or type. Design for standard typewriter spacing whenever possible.
    C. Use a paper stock that will take pencil or pen.
    D. Use multi-part form, either containing carbons or requiring none. Number and/or color code each part. Clearly label for proper distribution.
    E. Use standard-sized forms for easy handling and storage.

238

Fig. 11.1 Sample reservation reply cards that are sent by convention delegates directly to the hotel. (By permission of the Orlando Marriott and Harrah's Hotel)

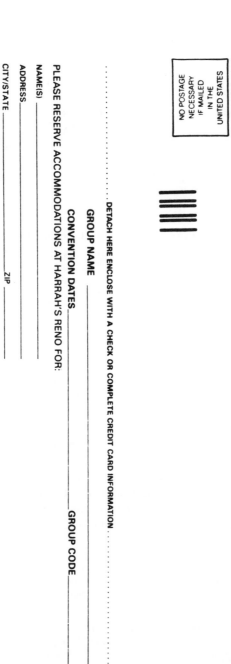

THE ORLANDO MARRIOTT WELCOMES

ARRIVAL DATE: _____ DEPARTURE DATE: _____

ARRIVAL TIME: _____ FLIGHT NO.: _____

NUMBER OF ROOMS: _____ NUMBER IN PARTY: _____

ADULTS: _____ CHILDREN & AGES: _____

SPECIAL REQUEST: _____

NAME: _____

ADDRESS: _____

CITY: _____ STATE: _____ ZIP: _____

TELE. #: _____

For those who wish to arrive early and/or extend their stay, the above mentioned special group rates will apply to three nights before and/or after the dates indicated above - rooms subject to availability.

THIS IS A RESERVATION REQUEST AND MUST BE ACCOMPANIED BY ONE(1) NIGHTS ROOM DEPOSIT. A WRITTEN CONFIRMATION WILL BE SENT TO YOU AFTER RECEIPT OF DEPOSIT. ALL REQUESTS MUST BE RECEIVED BY _____. AFTER SUCH DATE, THEY WILL BE ACCEPTED ON A SPACE AVAILABLE BASIS.

DAILY ROOM RATES   SINGLE: $ _____   DOUBLE: $ _____

SUITE: $ _____

CHILDREN STAYING IN THE SAME ROOM WITH THEIR PARENTS NO EXTRA CHARGE

ALL RATES ARE SUBJECT TO 8% STATE TAX

MAXIMUM NUMBER OF PEOPLE IN ROOM - FIVE (5)

RESERVATIONS ARE TENTATIVELY HELD PENDING RECEIPT OF DEPOSIT OR AMERICAN EXPRESS OR DINERS CLUB CARD NUMBER _____ EXPIRE DATE: _____

Special request for location, connecting room, etc., will be noted but cannot be guaranteed. Suites are space available at rates above and will be confirmed by RESERVATIONS MANAGER.

CHECK IN: 4:00 PM AFTER   CHECK OUT: 11:00 AM

Baggage **must** be checked with the Bell Captain if departure time is later than 11:00 A.M.

II.   Get and give enough information.
    A. Get the information you need.
       1. Arrival and departure dates.
       2. Arrival and departure times.
       3. Rate requests (unless flat rates are part of agreement).
       4. Kind(s) of room(s) requested.
       5. Number in the party.
    B. Give enough information.
       1. Eliminate need to find and refer to other material.
       2. Indicate how long room will be held.
       3. Indicate if and how the room may be held past that time (guarantee or deposit).
       4. Indicate if deposit is required of all reservations.
       5. Use self-addressed forms or specify where reservation is to be sent.
III. Keep it simple.
    A. Use terms in common usage. Indicate number of bedrooms in suites.
    B. Don't ask for unnecessary data.
    C. Test new forms before printing.

The reservation card policy of the Chicago Hilton reads as follows:

> The Chicago Hilton and Towers will supply your organization, at no charge, a reasonable amount of self addressed reservation cards imprinted with the name of your association and the dates of your convention.
> In the event that your company or association plans to use its own housing form or you intend to use the Chicago Convention and Tourism Bureau for housing, the Chicago Hilton and Towers must approve the copy in writing prior to its being printed in its final form and sent to your members or the Bureau to ensure that all information listed on the form pertaining to the Chicago Hilton and Towers is correct and complete, thus eliminating any discrepancies in room rate when your members receive their confirmations.

Note the hotel must approve the copy of the reservation card if the group plans to use its own housing form. This policy assures the hotel that all required information is communicated to attendees and minimizes the possibility of misunderstanding.

Rooming Lists

Although reservation reply cards are the most common method, they are not necessarily the most desired. Many hotels prefer to get a consolidated rooming list from the meeting planner rather than receiving individual reservation cards from the members.

When rooming lists are used, the reservation reply cards are not returned to the hotel, but to the housing staff at the association's headquarters. The meeting planner prepares the rooming list from the reply cards received and sends it to the hotel prior to the cutoff date.

It is extremely important that the front office knows whether a group's reservations are coming individually or through a list. It is standard operating procedure that the trace file on any group for which a rooming list is expected be brought up in sufficient time to remind the customer that the list is expected.

Rooming lists are most commonly used by corporate accounts and incentive travel groups where attendance is almost always mandatory or at least highly predictable. The convention service manager should encourage the use of rooming lists, when possible, because it reduces the load on the reservation department.

Figure 11.2 is a rooming list used by the Hershey Lodge and Convention Center. When the hotel receives the list, the front office merely assigns from the block of rooms committed to the group and makes preparations for preregistering the guests.

City Housing Bureau

When several hotels are used, the convention is commonly called *city-wide* and the reservations are handled by a city housing bureau. We will illustrate this more complicated reservation system with the hypothetical National Popcorn Association case study.

Tally Sheets

Whether a housing bureau, reservation reply cards, or rooming lists supplied by the association are used, a breakdown of the precise types of rooms needed must be made and kept current. This tally sheet (fig. 11.6) gives the hotel a clear picture of each day's convention reservations and group movements and provides an arrival and departure flow study for each group.

The hotel's reservation department sends out confirmations from the tally sheet (fig. 11.7). If a housing bureau is handling reservations, a confirmation form by the hotel is a must. Confirmations should be made in any case, but it is particularly crucial when a number of hotels are pressed into use.

Fig. 11.2 Sample rooming list supplied to the hotel by the meeting planner. (By permission of Hershey Lodge and Convention Center).

THE

HERSHEY
LODGE & CONVENTION CENTER

ROOMING LIST

Group Name: _____

Date: _____

Group Number: _____

(For Lodge use only)

Send to attention of:

_____

Convention Coordinator

To guarantee your room block, this list must be received 30 days prior to arrival.

ARRIVAL DATE	DEP. DATE	ROOM TYPE	NAME (Last Name First)	SHARING WITH Please also list sharer's data on next line.	NUMBER OF PEOPLE OCCUPYING RM.	NUMBER OF CHILDREN	COMMENTS

Toll-Free 800 Reservations

The use of 800 numbers by convention delegates is becoming an increasing problem in convention reservations. Rather than using the reservation forms supplied by housing bureaus or association headquarters, convention delegates are having secretaries reserve rooms through the hotel's toll-free service. This presents a problem when the secretary does not say that the reservation is being made for a convention. The hotel and meeting planner agreed to reserve a specific block of rooms, but the commitment is now overestimated. The hotel may be stuck with unfilled guest rooms and the association will not get credit for the number of complimentary rooms to which it is entitled.

There are few solutions to this growing problem, but it might be helpful in the case of a large group for the hotel to make a special mailing of reservation reply cards to the association's membership. Another alternative might be for the hotel to take out an advertisement with a tear-out reservation form in the most popular periodical of the convention group.

National Popcorn Association   Case Study

The NPA has an active membership of 3,550 delegates. The association executive and the site selection committee have narrowed down their selection for the upcoming annual convention to Chicago, Miami, and Las Vegas. It will be necesary for such a large group to use a number of hotels, so the planners have been in touch with the convention bureaus of each city.

The NPA staff makes personal visits to each site and picks hotels. It then prepares a list of the desired hotels in each city and asks the convention bureaus to request room commitments and bids from each property.

The bid sheet used by the Las Vegas Convention and Visitors Authority is shown in figure 11.3. Upon receiving it,

the hotel sales department checks room availability for the dates designated. It then specifies the number of singles, doubles, and suites the hotel has available and gives a price range for each. Note that the hotel stipulates a cutoff date by which time the NPA must send a written acceptance of the hotel's offer. The completed form is then mailed back to the convention bureau. The bureau forwards or personally presents the proposal sheets to the association's site selection committee for analysis and a decision.

On the basis of price, location, and service, the NPA chooses Las Vegas as the site for the convention. It also selects a headquarters hotel and, designates four others as overflow hotels.

Approximately eight months before the

convention the NPA association executive requests assistance from the Las Vegas Housing Bureau in setting up a reservation system. The association, in conjunction with the housing bureau, prepares a reservation form (fig. 11.4) to be sent to each member, who in turn completes it, writes out a deposit check, and returns them to the housing bureau. The members each indicated their first, second, third, and fourth preferences in hotels, and they have also specified the type of room desired. The housing bureau sorts through the forms and approves reservations on a first-come, first-served basis. As each reservation is approved, the form is returned to the sender specifying which hotel he or she is to stay in during the convention. If none of the choices is available, the form is returned to the member with a note of explanation and a request for new choices.

As each batch of new reservations is approved, it is sent to the respective hotel and processed there by the reservation department. A weekly housing report (fig. 11.5) prepared by the housing bureau is sent to the hotels and to the association indicating the reservation status of the hotels' room blocks. This report is extremely important to the hotel. If the room block is not filling up as expected, the hotel will probably contact the association and ask for an update on its room commitment. Although the housing bureau specifies a thirty-day cutoff, if only half of the 3,550 rooms committed are reserved, the five hotels might have difficulty in booking the remaining guest rooms.

Room Assignment

Priorities

It is important that the convention planner supply a list of VIPs to the hotel. It is necessary to codify certain types of guests and the accommodations indicated for them. Association officials such as officers, board members, and staff get special treatment. This is certainly important when you have accommodations in different buildings of the hotel. Exhibitors, speakers, and entertainers may also come in for special treatment.

It is important to block rooms so that oceanfront rooms and suites in resort hotels and the "best rooms available" in commercial properties are assigned to VIPs without question, regardless of the occupancy of the house. It is often the responsibility of the convention service manager to see that these reservations are in order. He or she should set up a procedure to check the day before arrival on what type of accommodations are blocked for VIPs and also on the day of arrival to make sure that these accommodations are delivered. In addition, the service manager might find out the VIPs' arrival times.

Fig. 11.3 Sample bid sheet filled out by hotel and returned to city convention bureau. The bureau then forwards it to the convening association's site selection committee. (Courtesy of the Las Vegas Convention and Visitors Authority).

LAS VEGAS CONVENTION BUREAU
CONVENTION CENTER - PARADISE ROAD
P.O. BOX 14006
LAS VEGAS, NEVADA 89114

Date: May 15, 19__

FROM: Chantal Puepke, Convention Sales

SUBJECT: <u>REQUEST FOR ROOM COMMITMENT</u>

THE _____National Popcorn Association_____ HAS REQUESTED US TO OBTAIN TENTATIVE / FIRM ROOM COMMITMENTS FOR THEIR CONVENTION IN LAS VEGAS, NEVADA. FOR MEETING DATES OF __Oct. 18, 19__ THROUGH __Oct. 21, 19__ . THE _____Abbey Hotel_____ AGREES TO RESERVE THE FOLLOWING NUMBER OF SLEEPING ROOMS AT THE RATES SHOWN BELOW: PROVIDING A WRITTEN ACCEPTANCE BY THE CONVENING ORGANIZATION IS RECEIVED BY THE HOTEL OR MOTEL PRIOR TO __Sept. 15, 19__ .
DATE

NUMBER OF:

SINGLES __100__ RATE __$24—28__

DOUBLES __475__ RATE __$28—32__

TWINS _____ RATE _____

SUITES __25__ RATE __$75—118__

GRAND TOTAL ROOMS __600__

ROOM DEPOSIT (IS) (NOT) REQUIRED. (IF REQUIRED, STATE AMOUNT) $50.00

SIGNED BY:

Chantal Puepke   _Abbey Hotel_
NAME   HOTEL OR MOTEL

Sales Manager   _May 20_
TITLE   DATE

* * * * *

PUBLIC SPACE AVAILABLE __yes__   __negotiable__
                                                    RATE OR GRATIS

PUBLIC SPACE DESCRIBED ON ATTACHMENT (NOTE TO HOTEL: IF APPLICABLE PLEASE ENCLOSE BROCHURE)

RESERVATIONS FOR PUBLIC SPACE TO BE REQUESTED AND CONFIRMED BY LETTER.

* * * * *

NOTE: TO BE COMPLETED IN TRIPLICATE. MAIL TWO (2) COPIES TO THE LAS VEGAS CONVENTION BUREAU. HOTEL OR MOTEL TO RETAIN ONE (1) COPY.

Fig. 11.4 Typical reservation reply form used when a city housing bureau handles hotel assignment. The delegate fills out the form and returns it to the housing bureau. (Courtesy of the Las Vegas Convention and Visitors Authority).

APPLICATION FOR HOTEL ACCOMMODATIONS

MAIL COLORED COPY TO:
NPA Housing Bureau
Las Vegas Convention/Tourist Authority
P.O. Box 14006
Las Vegas, Nevada 89114

October 19-21, 19
Las Vegas Convention Center
Industry Day
October 18th

Send Confirmation to:

Company Name _____

Attention _____

Street Address or P.O. Box _____

City _____ State _____ Zip Code _____

Hotel Preference:

1. _____ 3. _____

2. _____ 4. _____

Please Reserve The Following Accommodations: (See reverse side for Rates and Map Locations)

.... Singles(s) for .... persons(s)   Rate Preferred $ .... per room

.... Double(s) for .... person(s)   Rate Preferred $ .... per room

.... Parlor Suite(s) with .... Bedroom(s) for person(s)   Rate Preferred $ .... per suite

REMARKS: ....
....

If Rate Requested Not Available, Next Higher will be Assigned.

List each type of room, its occupants and their arrivals and departures.

Type of Room	Names of Occupants	Arrival & Departure Dates & Hours
1.		
2.		
3.		
4.		
5.		
6.		

Please Attach List of Additional Names, if necessary.

CONFIRMATION OF THE ABOVE REQUEST WILL BE SENT BY THE HOTEL.
PLEASE MAKE ALL RESERVATION CHANGES DIRECTLY THROUGH THE CONFIRMING HOTEL.

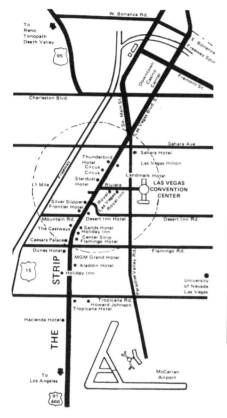

LAS VEGAS HOTEL RATES

NPA INDUSTRY DAY—OCT. 18TH—Hotel A
NPA SHOW—OCT. 19, 20, 21 —CONVENTION CENTER

ROOM BLOCK	HOTEL	KING	DOUBLE/ DOUBLE	PARLOR SUITES†	
				1 BEDROOM	2 BEDROOM
(1500)	A Headquarters	$30-42 $47-50	$30-42 $47-50	$88-110 $114-145 (Hospitality Suites Available)	$121-155 $168-197
(1000)	B*	$36	$36	$90 (Hospitality Suites Available)	$125
(600)	C*	$24-28	$28	$75-90 (Hospitality Suites Available)	$103-118
(250)	D**	$32-38	$32-38	$90-110 (Hospitality Suites Available)	$150
(200)	E*	$20 Single or Double Occupancy			

*One night room deposit required with reservation.

**$50 deposit required with reservation.

†Rates for special Hospitality Suites on request.

All rates subject to 6% Clark County Room Tax.

248

LAS VEGAS CONVENTION/VISITORS AUTHORITY

CONVENTION CENTER
PARADISE ROAD · P O. BOX 14006
LAS VEGAS, NEVADA 89114
TELEPHONE · AREA CODE 702 · 735 · 2323

May 2, 19__

NATIONAL POPCORN ASSOCIATION

HOUSING REPORT
OCTOBER 19-21, 19__

HOTELS	COMMITTED		ASSIGNED		BALANCE	
	ROOMS	SUITES	ROOMS	SUITES	ROOMS	SUITES
A	1400	70	1110	70	290	
B	200		86		114	
C	1000	11	386	11	614	
D	300		29		271	
E	400	3	167	3	233	
VIP'S	200				200	
Totals---	3500	84	1778	84		

Copies of above sent to hotel sales officers, room reservation managers
    and association directors.

Should there be any discrepancies, please contact this office immediately.

The handling of deposit checks by the housing bureau can be avoided if the NPA collects the deposits itself and pays each hotel its respective amount. This procedure is almost the only method some groups use and it is definitely preferred by the hotel.

Once NPA reservations start coming in, the hotels start convention reservation records and master accounts for the group. Usually a rooming list (fig. 11.2) is developed and each delegate is assigned a room and sub-account under the master. If, and when, checks are received by the hotel, a credit is added to the sub-account.

Fig. 11.6 Sample tally sheet giving the hotel a summary of convention reservations and group movements. (Reprinted with permission from the *Convention Liaison Manual*, published by the Convention Liaison Council.

HOUSING COUNT TALLY

Name of Organization or Convention _____

Convention Official _____

Address _____ Tel. No. _____

Convention Dates: _____

Number of Rooms Allotted: _____

Breakdown:

Singles _____

Doubles _____

Twins _____

Suites _____

Total _____

Arrival and Departure	Day Date	Arr.	Dep.	Arr.	Dep.	Arr.	Dep.	Arr.	Dep.	Arr.	Dep.	Arr.	Dep.	Arr.	Dep.	TOTAL ROOMS USED
Singles																
Doubles																
Twins																
Suites																
Parlors																
Complimentary																
Makeup Suites																
Total Res. per Day			X		X		X		X		X		X		X	
Total Dep. per Day	X		X		X		X		X		X		X			X

It is the policy of some hotels to have the sales office see that VIPs get the proper attention. The feeling is that the salesperson's self-preservation is determined by his or her impression on the association's decision makers, and the decision makers are usually found on the priority list.

The VIP list should also be coded to include the possible supply of fruit, liquor, and/or flowers. The allocation of suites is also important, especially if the hotel has a limited number. Discuss this with the convention planner. Some associations have a rule that non-exhibitors cannot maintain hospitality suites.

Take care to hold a small number of rooms in a prime area of the hotel for late priority listings; they inevitably appear late in the game.

Rate Structures

One of the preliminary decisions to be made in booking a convention is what rates to charge for delegates' rooms. Because most large-scale conventions are planned

250

Fig. 11.7 Reservation confirmation form sent out by housing bureau. The guest, the hotel, and the housing bureau retain copies. (Courtesy of the Las Vegas Convention and Visitors Authority).

Name_____ Pr._____

_____

Address _____ (Convention)

_____

Type Room _____ Rate $_____ to $_____

Time of _____ A.M.

Arrival: _____ P.M. Date_____ Departing Date _____

Confirmed by_____ Hotel

Signature _____

    Title _____ Date_____

ATTEN: HOTEL MGR. 1. Signature and date to appear legibly on all copies. 2. Separate by holding top and bottom of paper and snap off at perforation. 3. (a) Mail Guest Copy to applicant. (b) Retain two hotel copies. (c) Return Blue & Pink copies to:

HOUSING BUREAU, CONVENTION CENTER, PARADISE ROAD, LAS VEGAS, NEVADA.

GUESTS: **PLEASE NOTIFY YOUR HOTEL OF LATE ARRIVALS AND ANY OTHER CHANGES OR CANCELLATIONS. SEND A COPY** to the Housing Bureau, Las Vegas Convention/ Visitors Authority, P.O. Box 14006, Las Vegas, Nev. 89114.

     PRESENT THIS CONFIRMATION WHEN YOU CHECK INTO YOUR HOTEL.
GUEST COPY   **THANK YOU**

HOTEL COPY

PRESENT THIS CONFIRMATION

HOUSING BUREAU COPY

well in advance, the hotel will not commit itself to any firm rates. This policy is usually made clear during initial negotiations. It is also included in the final contract, worded in small print something like this: "All rates subject to change . . ." This protects the hotel in case of price changes in the future.

Naturally the rates will vary between hotels and even within the hotel itself. Rates are often determined according to (1) season—busy or slow, (2) size of group, (3) length of stay, (4) type of room, (5) number of persons in the room, and (6) the known attendance and difficulty with the group's past conventions. Of course, the interpretation of these factors is up to the individual.

Many hotels work within the limits of certain rate scales determined by management. The main ones are

1. *Rack rates.* All rates remain as posted, with no discount or favors. This is generally preferred by the hotels for easy bookkeeping.
2. *Run-of-the-house rates.* All similar rooms except suites are priced at the average between minimum and maximum rates, despite level or location. Some guests pay more than the normal price for a room; some pay less. This is also called a *flat-rate arrangement.*
3. *Discounted rates.* This type, also called *spread rates,* is used primarily when the result will bring preferred return business, encourage current business, or attract business from the hotel's competition for preferred groups.

Small groups tend toward use of flat rates, while large conventions find spread or discount rates more to their liking. Rack rates are seldom used for conventions unless the group is small or the hotel is running a high occupancy.

The discount ranges up to thirty percent of the rack rate. Naturally, the hotel's objective is to insure that it gets the business, but at the highest possible rate. Questions often asked about the group in determining the amount of discount are

1. How much can it be expected to spend? Will it have cocktail parties? Banquets? Requests for meeting and exhibit space?
2. What are the opportunities for future business with the group?
3. Is the group willing to put down a firm financial hold on the rooms?

Regardless of the rate decided upon, it is important to make the rate arrangements clear. If there is a range of rates, the reservation form should indicate the range and serve notice that rooms in the next higher category will be supplied if those at the requested rate are no longer available. Even if the contract calls for rack rates, it is best to indicate those on the reservation form. Figure 11.8 shows examples of group reservation cards depicting run-of-the-house and spread rates.

Rooms Reserved

You must know both the number and kinds of rooms to be held. Most agreements with convention planners call for a guarantee of a total *number* of rooms to be used. This may be fine at the negotiating table, but as the event approaches you need to know how many of these are singles, doubles, twins, or suites. Don't forget that there is much confusion about suite designation. Some hotels go so far as to indicate suites as having "one bedroom for two people" or "two bedrooms for four people." In addition, people confuse twins and doubles. This can be clarified by indicating "one bed for two people" or "two beds for two people."

Arrival/Departure Pattern

In assigning rooms you need an overall pattern that will indicate when people will arrive and depart. The convention planner may have some idea from previous years, but you will have to finalize detailed patterns when you get the reservations from the guests. Even for corporate meetings, where the meeting planner has greater control, attendees frequently arrive a day or two early because of transportation difficulties, personal travel plans, or the attraction of local tourist or recreational facilities.

Be especially careful if you designate the availability of a *specific* suite. That extra-special VIP suite may be earmarked for the chairman of the board, who may very well decide to test your golf course and arrive a day or two before the meeting or stay in it several days after the event. Impress upon your client that you must have advance notice of such plans to make sure the room is available and that there is no conflict with another group.

You also need to plot the arrival pattern so you can govern your staff's assignments. You need enough desk clerks and bellmen on hand for a big influx of guests at a particular time. This is a special problem for European hotels because most large planes arrive from the United States in the early morning but check-out time for departing guests is not until noon or so.

Release and Confirmation Dates

Many conventions are booked very far in advance. The number of rooms blocked out is an estimate, based on past conventions. This makes communication between hotel and planner extremely important.

The letter of agreement, as we said in chapter 9, should indicate a date by which the organization will either confirm or release the rooms. Reservations received after the cutoff date, usually about thirty days, are accepted on a space-available basis only. In all cases, the reservations should be confirmed individually, with a copy sent to the meeting planner.

The hotel and association should re-examine the room commitment on several intermediate dates and readjust the number if necessary. Mutual reassurance will reduce the chances of double booking by delegates and overbooking by hotels.

The convention planner must keep an ear to the ground for early signals that might affect meeting attendance. These could include an unusual circumstance like a fiftieth anniversary of the association, an unusually good or bad year, the selection of a prime resort site, or an unusual increase in the number of members

Fig. 11.8 Group reservation cards showing run-of-the-house rates, *left*, and spread rates, *right*. (Adapted with permission from Jerome J. Vallen, *Check In—Check Out*, published by Wm. C. Brown Company Publishers)

National Popcorn Assn. May 4-8	National Popcorn Assn. May 4-8
ABBEY HOTEL RESERVATION DEPARTMENT	**ABBEY HOTEL RESERVATION DEPARTMENT**

Left card:

National Popcorn Assn.
May 4-8

**ABBEY HOTEL
RESERVATION DEPARTMENT**

Please make the following reservations quoted on European Plan.

Reservations must be received by the Abbey no later than April 15.

☐ Guest Rooms—Single $30

☐ Guest Rooms—Double $34

☐ Suites: Petite $44
       Deluxe $56

Will Arrive _____ Time _____

Will Depart _____ Time _____

Name _____

Address _____

City _____

State _____ Zip _____

Reservations will not be held after 6 p.m. unless otherwise requested.

Right card:

National Popcorn Assn.
May 4-8

**ABBEY HOTEL
RESERVATION DEPARTMENT**

Please make the following reservations quoted on European Plan.

Reservations must be received by the Abbey no later than April 15.

☐ Guest Rooms— $28 $30 $32 $34
       Single

☐ Guest Rooms— $32 $34 $36 $38
       Double
       (Please circle rate choice)

☐ Suites: Petite $44
       Deluxe $56

Will Arrive _____ Time _____

Will Depart _____ Time _____

Name _____

Address _____

City _____

State _____ Zip _____

Reservations will not be held after 6 p.m. unless otherwise requested.

recruited that year. The smart planner will communicate his, or her, apprehensions and revelations to his hotel counterpart so that all his people may be housed conveniently.

You should not bury your head in the sand and go blithely about your business if you don't receive periodic communiques from your client. D-Day will come and you may face a milling mob around the registration desk or a multitude of unfilled rooms. You cannot afford just to wait hopefully if you don't hear from your client. Keep constant tabs on the reservations being received and interpret how the flow affects the total number of rooms being held.

Constant communication between both parties leads comfortably to the day when the organization executive confirms or releases the number of rooms held. (This is doubly important to resort properties that have little or no business off the street, especially during off-season periods.)

The planner and hotel person who keep in touch constantly and adjust room allotments along the way seem to continue to do business together. They execute meetings together without the shock of housing problems at the outset of the event.

Complimentary Arrangements

Most hotels offer concessions to group business. It is common, as we have said, to extend one complimentary guest room for every 50 rooms used, or one suite for every 100 guest rooms.

A rooming list supplied by the meeting planner should specify who will occupy these rooms. It is the planner's responsibility to spell out the extent of the complimentary arrangements to the guest, with a copy for the hotel. Avoid all those heated arguments at the cashier's window by planning ahead.

The meeting planner should tell his or her people, especially if complimentary rooms are used by speakers and program members, what they must pay for themselves and what should be applied to the master account. In the case of the convention staff, perhaps the entire bill is to be placed on the master account. It is easiest to use complimentary rooms for staff, but it doesn't matter so long as everyone knows what is expected of him or her.

Additional concessions are sometimes granted. Some hotels provide a complimentary cocktail party upon arrival, free travel to and from the airport, and free meeting space. There is no general guideline. A hotel must use sound judgment and integrity.

Other Hotels

As we explained earlier in this chapter, sometimes a number of hotels are to be used for a large convention. In such instances, a competitor becomes a friend. It is nice to have a nearby hotel bail you out with a number of rooms when you may have overbooked. It is just as nice to receive guests from the other hotel when you have a number of rooms available—and to have the favors returned on other occasions. It pays to work together.

Similarly, you may be unable to supply a function room for the convention or for a local customer's banquet. Show your customer that you are interested in his welfare even when you are full by helping him to book his event at another hotel. The other hotel may appreciate the recommendation and reciprocate; your customer appreciates the help and the fact that you didn't turn your back on him when you didn't need the business. Always look to the future. The key to success in the hotel business is a good reputation for expertise and *caring*.

A variation may involve only the use of hotel facilities such as golf courses or tennis courts. An inter-hotel billing arrangement must be worked out so that your guests may just sign the tabs. Transportation also must be worked out in the case of multi-hotel involvements, which may bring local bus companies into the act.

Historical Performance

Whenever possible, find out where the group met in previous years. It may be best to do this after the contract is signed in order to maintain business security. Don't hesitate at that point to call the sales managers of the hotels used in the past. They will gladly cooperate because they will want to call you sometime for the same reason.

The historical pattern of a convention tells you a great deal. It can inform you early that this group seldom meets its commitments, or that it always does. You may learn that more attendees show up each year than are expected, or that early departures are common. You may find out that the no-show situation is an ever present problem.

If nothing else, these calls will give you insight into the meeting planners and let you know whether you are dealing with well-organized pros who can be relied on to control their conventions or planners who lack expertise or experience.

If you do learn that a convention generally fails to fill its quota, don't duck the issue. Call the convention executive and indicate that you know they had problems in previous years and ask him or her to reconsider the number of rooms to be held. Don't just release rooms without telling him because he may have good reason to believe it will not reoccur. He may have taken corrective steps, or something may have happened in his industry that will stimulate attendance. At the very least, you may hasten the room release date and get a more realistic appraisal.

There are a number of industry publications (such as *World Convention Dates*) that provide lists of the past and future meeting sites of the majority of corporate and association groups in the United States. Also members of the International Association of Convention and Visitor Bureaus exchange their experiences with conventions in order to better understand their customers.

Westin uses three interrelated procedures in an effort to assess the accuracy of a convention's commitment by observing its past performance.

First, a standard letter of inquiry is sent, along with a questionnaire, to the last two hotels in which the group met. The letter states that the group has booked with a Westin property and asks the hotels to make a post-convention critique of the group. The critiques then are matched with the requirements that have been requested. If there is an indication that the group has exaggerated its needs, the hotel goes back to the customer to clarify the discrepancy.

Westin's second procedure is to question a meeting planner who books a year or more in advance about his schedule of upcoming meetings. Through the use of the tickler system, the hotel brings up the file two weeks before the group's next meeting and two weeks after it.

On the first date, the hotel wishes the meeting planner the best in his scheduled meeting and advises him of an evaluation questionnaire to be sent in four weeks. The planner obviously is impressed with the hotel's meticulous approach to detail, and the hotel can be alerted to any changes or trends that might alter the number of guest rooms or function space it is holding for the group.

The third technique used by Westin might be called "preparticipation." When convention groups with complicated programs or unusual requirements are booked, the hotel salesperson and the convention service manager might request to be admitted as observers to the group's next meeting. By observing the meeting process and requirements, the convention service manager is better able to service the group at its forthcoming convention in his or her hotel. And, again, the client is reassured that he or she is in good hands.[1]

When the convention planner and the hotel executive have mutual confidence in each other, they can work things out so that all delegates are housed and no one gets hurt by variations in expectations.

No-Shows/Overbooking

The bugaboos of the hotel convention business are those interwoven horrors, the *no-show* and *overbooking*. Instead of pointing the finger of blame at each other, hotel personnel and hotel users must work together to cope with these annoyances.

No-shows too often result from delegates making multiple reservations because they fear they won't get a room at their first-choice hotel. Overbookings stem from hotel's experiences with no-shows and their fear for that perishable commodity, tonights' room bookings. (fig. 11.9)

There are no simple answers to the problems. All hotels specify a release date, but many medical and other professional societies are not accustomed to making advance commitments and have a hard time living with a thirty-day cutoff. The Hotel Sales Marketing Association strongly recommends the use of deposits as

1. "Pre-Meeting Planning and Servicing," *HSMA World.*

Below we have printed the overbooking policy of the famous Greenbrier, a five star resort hotel in White Sulphur Springs, West Virginia.

The Greenbrier, as a firm policy, will not overbook. It does not condone the policy and will exercise every effort to see that the rooms contracted for will be available. There are circumstances, however, when individuals, due to illness or other reasons, will refuse to vacate a room on the date promised. This can result in the Hotel not being able to have that room available to honor a reservation with a deposit. Should that happen, The Greenbrier will be responsible for lodging and transportation costs to the nearest available substitute accommodations in the vicinity of The Greenbrier. Meals, sports facilities and all other services at The Greenbrier will be available at regular guest rates. Immediately upon a room becoming available, the individuals will be notified and transportation (if required) provided back to The Greenbrier. If the individual chooses not to move to The Greenbrier, no further obligation exists on the part of The Greenbrier and transient fees will be charged at The Greenbrier, subject to availability of services.

To make the "no overbooking policy" work, The Greenbrier adheres to the following deposit policy.

DEPOSIT:

All requests by individuals for reservations must be accompanied by a $100.00 deposit for each room. Cancellation, failure to "show", late arrival or early departure will cause forfeiture of deposit, unless written cancellations or changes in dates are made 15 days in advance of scheduled arrival date. Checks should be made payable to The Greenbrier. The deposit will be returned to the individual if a written cancellation is received by The Greenbrier 15 days prior to the arrival date.

Reservations will be filled in the order in which they are received and must be received no later than 45 days prior to the date of the meeting.

---

a solution to no-shows. But others say that even with the thirty-day cutoff and the deposit, the problem of overbooking still might arise because of the guest who decides to stay over another day; this is called *under-departure*. The hotel may have set aside a block of 250 rooms, have received deposits for each room, and so it would seem, should not have any problem accommodating the group. However, twenty vacationers decide that because of the nice weather they will stay another day. Here the overbooking problem arises.

Another solution offered is the use of guaranteed reservations. A guaranteed reservation is a room being held without deposit, but for which payment is guaranteed. In case of a no-show, billing takes place in the usual manner. But many hotels cite difficulties in collecting such payments. It seems there is an education problem. Often the term *guaranteed reservation* is misinterpreted, with the guest not understanding that he is agreeing to guarantee payment.

Most city and airport hotels get a certain amount of walk-in business after five o'clock to fill in no-show vacancies. But resort properties don't have this reserve factor, so there is an increasing trend for these properties to insist on deposits. This is appealing, but a hotel that is going to take deposits must also consider the necessary control, the record keeping, and the possibility of refunds.

No-show history is a good reason for you to contact hotels previously used by the association. In return, it is a smart meeting planner who checks among his or her peers for the hotel's overbooking pattern. Wise planners also inform their members of the practice of hotels to hold reservations only until a certain hour, such as 5 P.M. They urge their members to arrive earlier than that or to guarantee or reply to make sure they get their rooms.

It is the official policy of some hotels to overbook. They use a numerical factor determined by their general performance records, not the record of a particular convention. These hotels accept the difficulties that arise when they have to walk customers to other hotels as a necessity of avoiding empty rooms. This policy reflects on a management that is only too aware that you can't rent yesterday's room. It also reflects on the failure of many guests to appear, despite confirmed reservations. The situation must improve through mutual performance and confidence.

It takes diplomacy at the registration desk when people arrive late in the evening, after their reservations have been released and their rooms are no longer available. Apologies should be extended, along with an explanation of the cutoff hour and the need for it. The clerk should make some effort to arrange for other accommodations. A phone call to a nearby hotel might bring results, and at least indicate to the guest that you are concerned. It is essential that some efforts be made to secure other housing when you are overbooked. Many hotels pay the guests' cab fares to the substitute hotels.

Many of the problems that come up can be handled if both key people in the convention—the convention executive and the hotelier—are honest with one another and communicate regularly.

Check-in—Check-out

A hotel should determine in advance when the heaviest influx of delegates can be expected so it can staff accordingly at the front desk. It would be foolhardy to step off on the wrong foot in the beginning. A delegate who is forced to wait in long lines becomes disgruntled and is a likely complainer throughout the stay.

Check-in Procedure

Arrival lines can be noticeably shortened if a distinction is made between guests with and without reservations. By the process of preregistration, rooms are assigned in advance according to the rooming list provided by the group or developed by the reservation clerk based on reservation requests. If the group arrives together, the group representative merely signs and the keys are given to him in envelopes labeled with the guests' names and their assigned rooms. If the group members are expected to arrive individually, the registration cards are started for them and the keys again put in envelopes marked with their names. All the guest then does is sign for the key and go on his way.

Preregistration of all guests is being done more frequently now. Special receiving desks, and even special lobbies, are being used by some hotels that service large amounts of group business. These arrangements minimize lobby confusion, long lines, and slow check-in procedures.

Whether individual or group check-in is used, the convention service manager should ask that the meeting planner be present at check-in time. Some properties set up a table in the lobby area from which the planner can greet and assist delegates. This helps prevent conferees from continually asking room service, bell captains, or the front desk about meeting programs and locations.

Check-out Procedure

A poor check-out procedure can destroy an otherwise perfectly organized convention. The group may have had a smooth meeting for three or four days, with excellent food and beverage service, but when the delegate arrives at the cashier's window to checkout, he or she is greeted by a long line, or worse, a sharp remark from the cashier. That delegate is very likely to leave the hotel with a bad taste, and three or four days of good meetings are out of the window. Group check-out procedure may be one of the little elements of a convention, but it really counts, particularly if it is not handled expeditiously.

When the company is picking up the rooming tab, let the guest merely drop off the key. Figure 11.10 illustrates the express check-out system provided at the Boca Raton.

Check-out is another area where the hotel must be flexible when dealing with convention customers. Hotels frequently establish check-out times at noon or 1:00 P.M. If the wrap-up meeting is a luncheon that breaks about this time, late check-out service should be provided so members can give full attention to the conference climax. This helpful attitude is certain to leave a lasting impression with the meeting planner.

But if guest arrival patterns prohibit late check-out, guests should be told to sign out before the luncheon session. Their bills should be ready so that the entire group can be processed quickly and their baggage checked in a convenient storage place until departure time.

260

Boca Raton HOTEL and CLUB — EXPRESS CHECK OUT

We want you to stay. But if go you must, just fill out this Express Check-Out form. Give it to the room clerk on the day you leave. We'll speed you on your way. Just fill in the card and sign your name and we will send the bill to you.

(Come back and visit again real soon)

EXPRESS CHECK OUT: Please check out room number _____

on (day) _____ , (date) _____ , (hour) _____ , and mail statement to:

_____
NAME   (please print)

_____
ADDRESS

_____
CITY   STATE   ZIP

The following credit cards are acceptable for identification purposes only. The Boca Raton Hotel and Club will bill you: American Express, Diners, Carte Blanche, Air Travel Card.

Card No. _____   _____
                                     (signature)

The Computer Influence

One of the most important trends for the lodging and foodservice industry, and for industry in general, is the increased use of computers and data processing systems. While an in-depth discussion of computers is beyond the scope of this text, we will briefly consider the types of system available and their relevance for servicing group business.

Our industry is one of the last major business segments to use the computer. Being last has not necessarily been a detriment, as we have been able to benefit from the learning experiencs of other industries. In the early seventies several good computer systems and equipment for hotels began to appear. Larger hotels and hotel chains with the capital sufficient to make the large initial investment were the first to take the step into computerization. Now the mini-computer, a low-cost in-house system, has made it possible for smaller properties to benefit. Today there are a number of hotels with either front-desk or back-office systems in operation.

Two distinct data processing systems are now being used: off-line and on-line. The off-line system is less desirable because it does not provide the instantaneous results that an on-line systems does. Processing is done in batches with off-line systems, which makes the information provided less timely. Further, off-line computers are often used on a time-sharing arrangement, with the computer located outside the hotel and access shared by other businesses at scheduled times.

An on-line system, on the other hand, is incorporated into the hotel, using a relatively low-cost mini-computer. The advantage is immediate processing, with more relevant, up-to-date information for decision making. The recent introduction of the in-house mini-computer has had an influence on all departments of the hotel. Each phase in the servicing of group business, from the initial reservation to check-out and billing, has been streamlined by the computer.

Reservations

When the reservation department receives a postal reply card (fig. 11.1) from a convention delegate, all the information about the guest is typed into the computer and stored on a magnetic disk file. The magnetic disk is much like a 33 1/3-rpm record. Once the information is imprinted, there is no need to duplicate the data. The same information is used for confirmation and deposit receipt notices, preregistration, and check-out and billing procedures.

The computer is tied into an electronic printer. At the end of the day, the printer will automatically type out confirmation slips, eliminating a time-consuming manual step. And the computer is programmed to call up the number of rooms reserved to date by any convention. This eliminates the onerous task of keeping a tally sheet (fig. 11.6) on each convention.

Registration and Room Assignment

The computer has proved to be a time-saver in other areas, scoring significant reductions in preparation of rooming lists and room assignments. Delegates are listed alphabetically within each convention group and assigned rooms according to the type of accommodation and rate range requested. When delegates arrive, they are given preprinted registration cards, again prepared by the computer, which they inspect and sign if all is in order. This method of preregistering saves much time and labor at check-in (fig. 11.11).

Fig. 11.11 Sample registration form, rooming list, and check-out listing prepared by computer. (Courtesy of NCR Systemedia Marketing, Dayton, Ohio).

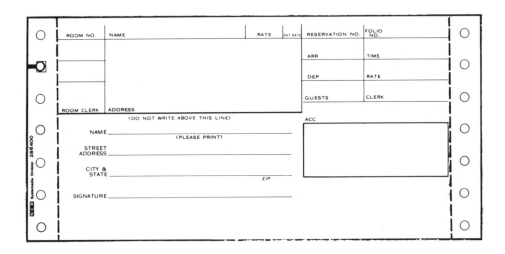

Check-out and Billing

Throughout the delegate's stay, charges are posted to an electronic folio. When the guest is ready to check out, he or she is given a running account of the transactions. Computer systems also have the capacity to maintain master accounts for the association staff and to separate all charges by specific service location.

The applications of the computer to the front-desk operation are but a small part of the benefits that are obtained from such a system. Management information, such as marketing information, and the control features are probably the biggest advantages of an in-house computer. Nevertheless, the computer does free front-desk personnel from laborious bookkeeping and paper shuffling, allowing them to provide convention delegates with prompt, personalized service that ensures their return.

Study Questions

1. Describe in detail the three reservation systems used in handling group bookings.

2. Trace the procedures used in servicing a city-wide convention. Make reference to the various forms used by the housing bureau including the bid sheet, the housing report, the reservation and confirmation forms, and the tally sheet.

3. Distinguish between rack rates, run-of-the-house rates, and spread rates.

4. Identify the three procedures used by Westin in assessing the accuracy of a convention's commitment.

5. What is the relationship between no-shows, under-departures, and overbooking?

6. Assess the present-day application of the computer in servicing convention business and project its likely role in the future.

Outline

I. Preconvention Meeting

    A. Westin's "Operation Excell"
    B. Key Personnel Roster

II. The Specification Sheet

III. The Function Sheet

IV. Themes

V. The Communication "Pipeline"

12

After the letter of agreement has been signed by both parties and the reservation reply cards sent, the event must be planned in great detail. Some conventions are planned a number of years in advance; others, a year or two. Some member of the organization's staff will be the primary coordinator for the group. It may be the executive secretary for a small or medium-sized association or a convention coordinator for a larger organization. It could also be a professional convention coordinator who is paid a fee by the association to run the event.

For the hotel, logistics are controlled by the convention service manager. As we discussed, the convention service manager is a most vital person on the hotel staff. He or she is the liaison person with the client and the control person within the hotel. It is not an exaggeration to consider the convention service manager as the key to the success or failure of an event. He or she is responsible for seeing that the event is properly planned and for taking quick, positive action should things go wrong during the event.

In many small hotels, the catering manager may serve as the convention service manager. It is not unusual in such a case for the catering manager also to be active in soliciting banquet business. If this is the case, communication with the sales department and use of the function book must be diligently controlled. This is doubly true when many promises are verbal, and not documented in correspondence or the letter of agreement.

Preconvention Meeting

A smart hotel sales executive will arrange for a pre-event meeting to introduce the hotel's convention service personnel and the organization's people. Such preconvention meetings are essential and go a long way toward eliminating much of the trouble that often appears during conventions. From that meeting on, it should be the service manager, not the sales contact, who deals with both the client and the hotel staff. If a hotel wants to do much in the way of convention business, it must develop both good salespeople, ranging far and wide, and good convention service people, functioning in the house. In larger convention facilities, a convention service manager would have an assistant and possibly other specialists.

Westin's "Operation Excell"

Hotels should make it a firm practice to bring the entire convention staff together for an unhurried preconvention session with the association executive. This get-together gives both parties an opportunity to review the convention agenda item by item to make sure that everyone fully understands what is to take place and to finalize any last-minute details.

Westin's Larry Stephan, director of sales at the Detroit Plaza, uses a program called "Operation Excell" to facilitate the servicing of convention groups.[1] The program consists of two parts: The first is the preconvention meeting a day or two before the arrival of the association's main delegation. At this time, the meeting planner and his or her staff meet with the convention service manager and the hotel's department heads who are involved in the direct servicing of the group. Information is exchanged and the upcoming program is thoroughly reviewed.

The second stage of "Operation Excell" is the post-convention meeting. The same people meet for an after-the-fact review of the conference. Chapter 18 offers an in-depth discussion of the post-convention meeting.

This procedure is not put into operation at every convention, nor is it always necessary for all department heads to be present. Major conventions and smaller ones with complicated requirements, however, will be preceded by such a meeting. The convention program determines which department heads will be notified.

A small ceremony takes place at the end of the preconvention meeting. The meeting planner and his key personnel are given VIP pins, which serve two functions: They give distinction to the meeting planner and let him, or her, know that the hotel is aware of his position and the importance of the meeting, and they help the hotel staff single out members who are in charge should there be any last-minute changes or requests.

This concept, which works well for Larry Stephan, has application for any size of property, whether resort, commercial hotel, or motel. The following is a step-by-step review of the Operation Excell checklist.

---

1. A preconvention date and time is agreed upon by the hotel and the association executive. A reminder is sent out to all departments involved, with a notation that all department heads are to be there ten minutes before the meeting begins. This is to give the convention service manager a chance to prepare the staff for any unusual characteristics or demands of the convention group. All the normal procedures used in setting up meeting rooms should be applied in planning an Operation Excell meeting. Taking care of details such as the proper seating setup, the right-sized meeting room, and comfortable chairs gives the client the impression that the hotel will service his or her meeting as well as it runs its own. Coffee, soft drinks, and sweet rolls should be provided so there is an atmosphere of informality. To instill confidence that the hotel knows how to

1. "Pre-Meeting Planning and Servicing," *HSMA World*.

service meetings, the convention service manager should check the room an hour ahead of time for those little things such as lighting, clean ashtrays, pads and pencils, and air conditioning that make for a pleasant, attractive meeting setup.

2. An inventory of nameplates of all department heads should be maintained so that the client may relate in the meeting to the key people on the hotel's staff. VIP identification pins are presented to the meeting planner and his or her staff

3. The meeting format gives department heads a chance to ask questions about matters that relate directly to their roles in servicing the group. The convention service manager then goes over the program event by event. If there are areas of misunderstanding or changes are needed, the client has an opportunity to inject input. A secretary should be on hand to take note of these changes. These last-minute changes are then typed up immediately after the meeting and distributed to all concerned.

4. A specification sheet, which covers the entire convention program and is the hotel's in-house communication medium, should be distributed not only to those at the Operation Excell meeting but also to every department in the hotel. Each department needs to be kept informed so it can forecast staffing needs. For example, if no luncheons or dinners are scheduled on a particular day, the people in charge of staffing the hotel's coffee shop and restaurants should be alerted to the possibility of an extra-heavy volume. Likewise, if a late evening activity is scheduled outside the hotel, security personnel should be informed to take extra precautions.

As we said, Westin's Operation Excell has application for any convention property. It is so important to get off to a proper start. A well-organized preconvention procedure such as this one will eliminate many of those unforeseen crises and could well mean the difference between a successful convention and one that is plagued with disorganization.

Key Personnel Roster

Meeting planners often request the names of specialists and department heads so they have logical contacts should trouble arise. Many convention service managers prefer instead to have all requests channeled through them. The wisest course lies somewhere between the two positions.

If the convention service manager will *always* be on the scene and available to the meeting planner, it is possible for him or her to receive every request. But if this is not feasible, an assistant should be designated to act in such instances. And if this too is not practical, department heads should be trained to inform the convention service manager of all requests. In the case of future events, these contacts can be coordinated. But on the scene during the convention, a meeting planner will often refuse to wait until the manager can be located before taking action in what he terms a crisis.

Minita Westcott, past president of both the Chicago Trade Association Executives Forum and the American Trade Associations Executives, suggested:

> One person on the hotel staff should be assigned to the convention for the duration of the meeting. This person should be readily available to handle all on-the-spot needs. It makes for a smoother meeting all the way around if the executive of the association can meet and get acquainted with all top members of the hotel staff with whom this executive and his staff will have to work.[2]

In summary, we feel it a positive action to furnish a roster of key hotel personnel to the client (fig. 12.1), along with the request that all action be taken through the convention service manager, *whenever possible.*

The Specification Sheet

The convention service manager is responsible for writing a detailed schedule for each convention. The title for this schedule varies from hotel to hotel. It is known as the master prospectus, the resume, the bible, the summary, or the specification sheet. We will use the latter term.

The *specification sheet* is not to be confused with the *function sheet,* which is explained next. The specification sheet gives the hotel staff a comprehensive overview of the entire program, from preconvention to post-convention, whereas the function sheet details only a single event.

Although they are titled differently, all convention hotels use similarly constructed specification sheets when servicing groups that meet for more than one day. Specification sheets set forth activities hour by hour and day by day, covering meetings, meals, sports activities, coffee breaks, cocktails, reservation procedures, billing, women's programs, exhibit instructions, special events, and anything else that needs the hotel staff's attention. It is undoubtedly the single most important element of the convention servicing process, providing the tool for planning and communication among hotel departments.

The specification sheet is prepared by the convention service manager in conjunction with the meeting planner. Much of the information is extracted from correspondence with the convention group and needs only to be put in the required

2. *HSMA Sales Manual.*

Fig. 12.1 Hotel key personnel roster. The meeting planner should have a principal contact on the hotel staff at all times during the day. (Reprinted with permission from the *Convention Liaison Manual*, published by the Convention Liaison Council.

HOTEL PERSONNEL

HOTEL STAFF PRINCIPAL CONTACT FOR OVER-ALL SERVICE DURING THE CONVENTION OF _____

Period	Hours	Name	Title	Phone Extension
Early morning	_____ a.m. to _____ a.m.			
Daytime	_____ a.m. to _____ p.m.			
Evening	_____ p.m. to _____ p.m.			
Saturdays	_____ to _____			
Sundays	_____ to _____			
Holidays	_____ to _____			

HOTEL KEY STAFF BY DEPARTMENTS

Check marks (✔) on the hotel staff list given below indicate the departmental key personnel with whom the organization will come in contact during the servicing of this convention.

Check (✔)	Department	Name	Title	Phone Extension

format. The sheet is distributed to all people involved in servicing the convention at least a week before the group arrives.

The length of the specification sheet varies, of course, with the size, number of days, and details required in each convention. We have known some specification sheets to be more than forty pages long; however, most run eight to twelve pages for a three-day session.

The importance of putting everything in writing cannot be overstated. The more detailed the better. "Nobody told me" is heard far too often in hotels. Putting everything in writing lessens the chance of hearing it.

We feel the best way to really grasp the working of a specification sheet is to see one illustrated. Figure 12.2 is a specification sheet written for a fictitious convention group, the Architectural Draftsmen International.

Fig. 12.2 Sample group specification sheet detailing a fictitious convention. Many hotels use legal-sized paper for the form. At the left is a list of the people and departments that will receive the sheet.

General Manager
Food/Bev. Dir.
Comptroller
Front Office
Showroom
Exec. Chef
Beverage Mngr. (2)
Coffee Shop
Room Service
Group Billing
Hotel Manager
Asst. Hotel Mngrs. (2)
Food Checker
Reservations
Publicity
Security
Housekeeping
Head Houseman
Head Banquet Waiter
Sales (2)
Food & Bev. Control
Linen Control
Doorman
Benihana Manager
Stage & Sound (2)
Public Porters
Steward
Catering Director
Group Services (4)
Uniform Room
Purchasing

```
*  *  *  *  *  *  *  *  *  *  *
   GROUP SPECIFICATION SHEET
*  *  *  *  *  *  *  *  *  *  *
```

SUBJECT: Architectural Draftsmen International

DATES: February 16-20, 19__

CONTACT: Jay Bryan
                             Master Draftsman
                             206 Clark - Suite 307
                             Lakeview, Michigan 48850

HOTEL SALESPERSON: Lanny Kingsbury, National Sales Mngr.

ARRIVAL/DEPARTURE
  PATTERN: 300 rooms have been committed to
ROOM RES. MANAGER   this group. Most are arriving late
ASSISTANT MANAGERS   Sunday, February 16 and departing
FRONT DESK   Thursday, February 20, 19__.
HOTEL CASHIER   Arriving individually - preregister.

                             RATES - European Plan
                             $35.00 Single or Double occupancy,
                             plus 6% County room tax,
                             net, non-commissionable.

                             SUITE RATES - One Bedroom
                             $ 50.00 - Petite Suite
                             $ 85.00 - Deluxe Suite
                             $100.00 - Royal Suite

LOCATION: DESERT VIEW, FOUNTAIN VIEW, POOLSIDE
                             HEXAGON, CENTRAL TOWER

COMPLIMENTARY
  ACCOMMODATIONS: A King Bedroom (North Tower) for
                             Marney Vartanian, Associate
                             Convention Manager
                             ARR: February 15, 19__
                             DEP: February 20, 19__

                             Additional complimentary units to be
                             assigned based upon 1 complimentary
                             unit for every 50 rooms actually
                             occupied. (Names forthcoming)

HOSPITALITY
  REQUEST FOR: Ms. Marney Vartanian
                             Dewars Scotch w/setups
                             ARR: February 15, 19__

RESERVATION
  ACCEPTANCE   This group utilized our return
  PROCEDURE   reservation cards.

MASTER ACCOUNT: All Group functions should be billed
                             To the master account. Ms. Marney
                             Vartanian will be the authorized
                             signer.

INDIVIDUAL
  ACCOUNT: Rooms, tax, and incidentals to be
                             paid by the individuals.

```
*  *  *  *  *  *  *  *
  SCHEDULED FUNCTIONS
*  *  *  *  *  *  *  *
```

Saturday, February 15, 19__

3:00 P.M.	ADI/HOTEL STAFF PRECONVENTION MEETING	Board Room
	15 Persons	
Attn: Houseman	"U" shape.	
Attn: Banquet Wtr.	Complimentary coffee, soft drinks, sweet rolls	

Sunday, February 16, 19__

6:00 - 8:00 P.M. — ARCHITECTURAL DRAFTSMEN INTERNATIONAL COCKTAIL RECEPTION — Sec. F

Approximately 30 persons. All are convention officials and board members.

Attn: Houseman — Cabaret style.

Attn: Banquet Wtr., Bar Manager — Call brand liquor to include: Beefeater, Johnny Walker Black, Dewars, Smirnoff, Jack Daniels Black, Old Grand Dad, CC, Bristol Cream Sherry @ $26.00 ++, $28.00 ++ and $30.00 ++. Two bottles Chablis and Pinot Noir @ $7.00 per bottle ++. Beer @ $1.00 ++.

Attn: Banquet Wtr., Exec. Chef — Following hors d'oeuvres; 5 orders Polynesian Pu-Pus @ $7.50 ++, 5 orders Selection #3 @ $6.75 ++, 10 orders Selection #4 @ $6.75 ++, 10 orders hot seafood @ $8.50 ++, 10 orders cold seafood @ $8.50 ++, and one shrimp bowl @ $100.00 ++. Hors d'oeuvre table to be decorated with two gold candelabra and 6 silver chafing dishes, white tapers. Cold hors d'oeuvres to be passed by waiters.

Attn: Accounting — Bill to Texas Instruments - Exhibits Master Account.

Sunday, February 16, 19__

3:00 - 6:00 P.M. — REGISTRATION — Foyer

Attn: Houseman — 6' draped tables rear of registration desk. 2 house phones. 1 directory board. Ice water stand. Bb/c/e. (blackboard/chalk/eraser)

Monday, February 17, 19__

   9:00 A.M. - NOON   GENERAL BUSINESS SESSION   Sec F
                            500 Persons

   Attn: Houseman   Theatre style with stage 12' x 40' x 24"
                            twenty feet out from kitchen wall. Projection
                            platform will be required against kitchen wall
                            for rear screen projection. Size to be
                            determined. Head table for 8 on stage.
                            American Flag stage right. 1 35-mm Carousel
                            slide projector. 1 Lantern slide projector.
                            1 electric pointer. 2 center aisle mikes.
                            Central dimmer to be located at projection
                            platform. 1 projectionist.

   9:30 A.M. - NOON   EXHIBIT HALL SETUP   Exhibit Hall

   Attn: Hall Supervisor   20 - 8' x 10' exhibit booths to be set
                            up by Scott Stubbs Service Company.

   12:15 P.M.   LUNCHEON   Sec B
                              500 Persons

   Attn: Houseman   Rounds of 10 with raised head table on 32"
                              dais for 12 centered in south wall.

                            Lighted table podium mike center of head table.

   Attn: Banquet Wtr.,   Tickets to be collected except at the head
         Exec. Chef   table. Linen will probably be alternated on
                            this function. This to be advised.

   Attn: Banquet Wtr.,   Serve our Group Luncheon Menu #7 with tomato
         Exec. Chef   juice appetizer @ $6.10 ++.

   Attn: Accounting   Bill to ADI Master Account

Thursday, February 20, 19__

   3:00 - 5:00 P.M.   ADI/HOTEL STAFF POST-CONVENTION MEETING   Board Room
                            Same setup as on Saturday.

Note on the left-hand side of the first page the individuals and departments that receive this information. Also note on this page the complimentary accommodations, the arrival and departure schedules, the reservation procedure, and the billing to both the master and individual accounts.

The next two pages of the sheet give you an indication of the detail required in the specification sheet. Every scheduled event is documented, with thorough instructions about room setup and food and beverage arrangements. Note that the specification sheet opens with a preconvention setup and closes with a post-convention meeting.

While reading through the sheet, keep in mind the importance of the meticulous recording required in the preparation of this statement; we will refer back to it in the ensuing chapters.

The Function Sheet

When the program is finalized, each function should receive individual attention. This is done by means of the function sheet. Such attention to details translates into service efficiency.

Two function sheets are presented for your review. Figure 12.3 is the form used for our architectural draftsmen convention.

The function sheet for the cocktail party gives the reader an understanding of how the function sheet and specification sheet are related. You might think of the specification sheet as a camera taking an overall panoramic picture of the convention and the function sheet as zooming in to take a close-up view.

The function sheet, like the specification sheet, has been tagged with a variety of names: event form, worksheet, banquet sheet, etc. Function sheets too vary from hotel to hotel in the amount of detail required. The individual function forms are generally prepared from the specification sheets and are the work form for the hourly employees. For example, figure 12.3 is prepared from the specification sheet by the food and beverage manager and is the form from which the bartender, housemen, and cooks will work in servicing this event.

Figure 12.4 is the function sheet endorsed by the Convention Liaison Council. This form is more detailed than the architectural draftsmen convention, with all information clearly noted for each event. Meeting room setup control is strongly emphasized in this form. Date, time, room, and hotel (should more than one location be used) are designated for the meeting.

It may be a general session or a small committee meeting. Document it. The basic seating layout, decorations, visual aids, and any special services required should be listed on the function sheet. Copies of each function sheet, like the specification sheet, should be distributed to hotel department heads at least a week prior to the event.

It is absolutely essential that *each program segment* have its own function sheet. Only in this manner can you be assured that all details will be handled. Document the head table, platform, basic seating layout, and all the basic arrangements. But also have a checklist for small but needed items like water and glasses, ashtrays, pads and pencils, audiovisual equipment, sound systems, floral arrangements, etc.

You may find that many well-organized association and corporate meeting planners make their own checklists of what is needed. Such customers are a delight. Make sure to get copies of their lists, but you still should make your own function sheets, incorporating their itemized requests.

Fig. 12.3 Function sheet (Banquet Event Order). This form is used to detail each convention function on the specification sheet.

FUNCTION ORDER - FOOD AND BEVERAGE

EVENT DATE February 16, 19-	DAY Sunday	ORDER NO 126
ORGANIZATION Architectural Draftsman International		FILE NO N-614

POST AS
Architectural Draftsman International Cocktail Reception

BILLING ADDRESS
Bill to Master Account Texas Instruments, 120AK, Lakeview, MI 48851

CONTACT Deanne Pritchard	ON SITE CONTACT Robert Olson	BUS PHONE NO 363-1906	RES PHONE NO

EXPECTED 30	GUARANTEED 30	SET UP 33	BOOKED BY Amber S.	DATE TYPED 2/1

TIME	SETUP REQUIREMENTS	LOCATION	TIME	MENU	LOCATION

6:00 PM - 8:00 PM Cocktail   Sec. F

Cabaret Style Set-Up
Draped Cocktail Rounds with ashtrays, no chairs

5 orders Polynesion Pu-Pus @ $7.50++,
5 orders selection #3 @ $6.75++,
10 orders selection #4 @ $6.75++,
10 orders hot seafood @ $8.50++,
10 orders cold seafood @ $8.50++,
1 shrimp bowl @ $100.00++

Hors d'oeuvre table to be decorated with two gold candlabra and 6 silver chafing dishes. White tapers.
Cold hors d'oeuvres to be passed by waiters

Food @ $6.75 +T+T
Seafood @ $8.50 +T+T
Shrimp bowl @ $100.00 +T+T

HOTEL TO ORDER

X Decorations
3 Tropical Florals
Charge to Master
___Entertainment

REFRESHMENT BREAK

AUDIO VISUAL

Time: Location:

SPECIAL NOTES

BEVERAGE REQUIREMENTS

RECEPTION:
Call Brand Liquor to include: Beefeater, Johnny Walker Black, Dewars, Smirnoff, Jack Daniels Black, Old Grand Dad, CC, Bristol Cream Sherry @ $26.00 ++, $28.00 ++ and $30.00 ++. Two bottles Chablis & Pinot Noir @ $7.00 ++ per bottle. Beer @ $1.00 ++.

SUMMARY OF CHARGES

FOOD: See Menu
BEVERAGE: See Beverage Requirements
RENT:
LABOR:
PARKING:
DEPOSIT RECEIVED:
METHOD OF PAYMENT:
BALANCE DUE DATE:

WINE SELECTION:

TIME.   LOCATION

WE NEED YOUR ASSISTANCE IN MAKING YOUR BANQUET A SUCCESS. PLEASE CONFIRM YOUR ATTENDANCE AT LEAST 3 BUSINESS DAYS IN ADVANCE. IF WE ARE NOT CONTACTED WITHIN THE SPECIFIED TIME, YOUR EXPECTED ATTENDANCE WILL SERVE AS YOUR GUARANTEE. THIS WILL BE CONSIDERED YOUR MINIMUM GUARANTEE. WE WILL ADD THE CUSTOMARY 17% SERVICE CHARGE AND SALES TAX. FOR GROUPS SERVED UNDER 25 THERE WILL BE A $50 LABOR CHARGE. I HAVE READ AND I UNDERSTAND THE REVERSE SIDE OF THIS DOCUMENT.
IF IN AGREEMENT, PLEASE SIGN ONE COPY AND RETURN X _____

MER-189

A master schedule should be made. This will assist you in determining the number of pieces of anything needed anywhere at any particular time. You have specified on a number of function sheets that a Carousel slide projector is needed, but the master schedule would indicate how many such projectors are needed at the same time.

Fig. 12.4 Function setup form endorsed by the Convention Liaison Council. Reprinted with permission from the *Convention Liaison Manual*, published by the Convention Liaison Council.

(ORGANIZATION NAME)

FUNCTION _____

Date: _____ Time: _____ Hotel: _____ Room: _____

Total Expected Attendance: _____ Organization Representative(s): _____

No. of Men _____ Hotel Representative(s): _____

No. of Women _____ Other Participants: _____

ARRANGEMENTS WHICH MUST BE MADE BY HOTEL

CHECK LIST OF ITEMS HOTEL TO PROVIDE	CHECK LIST OF PROPERTIES HOTEL SHOULD PROVIDE FOR MEETING ROOM SETUP
Canapes _____	**Dais:** Flowers ☐ **Visual Aids:** Blackboard-chalk-eraser ☐ **Other:**
Flowers _____	Lighted Lectern ☐ Easel ☐ Ashtrays ☐
	Microphone ☐ Motion Picture Screen ☐ Ice Water ☐
	Spotlight ☐ Motion Picture Projector ☐ Glasses ☐
Liquor _____	☐ Pointer ☐ Carpet ☐
	☐ Slide Projector ☐ Portable Mike ☐
Menus _____	☐ Sound Slide ☐
	☐ Vu-Graph ☐
	☐ ☐
	☐ ☐

	LAYOUT STYLE	DIAGRAM OF LAYOUT
Music _____	Platform for dais ☐	
Page Service _____	Dais set for ____ ☐	
Photographer _____	Schoolroom ☐	
Telephone _____	U-Shape ☐	
Transportation _____	Conference Table ☐	
	Individual Tables ☐	
Other _____	Lounge ☐	
	☐	
	☐	

DIRECTORY LISTING IN LOBBY TO BE:

Many hotel people feel that such details are truly the responsibility of the convention staff. However, it is the hotel staff that will be called upon under crisis conditions to rectify any oversights. You could prevent such difficulties by being well organized, by creating such accurate checks yourself and suggesting them to the client that those last-minute panics are avoided.

If the convention planner is inexperienced and fails to anticipate his needs correctly, he may say that you gave him insufficient notice. You may end up as the victim. Given a choice between blaming you and accepting the blame himself, he may find it all too easy to blame you.

Not only is it important to plan defensively, but your suggestions and organization also will establish your reputation. Clients will retain the memory that meetings at your place always run smoothly. That memory is the one you want to leave with clients.

276

Fig. 12.5 Theme parties are frequently used by meeting planners to stimulate interest and involvement. Hotels that stock or have ready access to theme decorations are a step ahead of those that don't. (Courtesy of Paul Emmerlich).

Themes

Every meeting planner tries to do something different at each event. Most conventions have a high percentage of people who repeatedly attend, so the planners want to do something different. A cocktail party just seems so ordinary.

Many pros among convention planners disguise that same old cocktail party by introducing a different party theme each year. Through decorations and perhaps dress or advertising specialities, the standard cocktail party is freshened and achieves a different flavor. Most convention planners love theme setups, but many cannot afford a one-time use of a theme, or they lack the imagination or staff to develop one. The hotel that develops a library of themes for its clients' use may be the one to enjoy more bookings.

Look for help from many quarters. Convention bureaus and tourist offices may be a source of material for a theme party. A Hawaiian luau one year can be a Mexican fiesta the next year. Airlines can supply posters and decorations. When a hotel helps a client develop such a theme, manufactured pieces such as signs and art work can be stored for future use at reduced cost. In some cases, all that may be required of the convention service manager is the ability to suggest a source for such items. A supplier of low-cost plastic "straw hats" makes it easy to execute a Gay Nineties theme.

Clients respond to such suggestions. More, and bigger and better, parties result; everyone benefits. Left to their own devices, too many meeting planners come up with the same dull meetings. Hotel people should be the pros, the ones to supply the expertise, the material, or, at the very least, the suggestions.

You can be the catalyst for better and more exciting events. Everyone will remember that great party at your hotel. Remember to take or obtain photographs of good theme parties in your hotel, regardless of who suggested or created them. File them so that later you can stimulate a client's thinking. They work well in sales presentations, too. Successful hotels will develop theme packages or at least work with suppliers who will.

The Communication Pipeline

Securing program, billing and reservation information from the meeting planner is one of the most important tasks of the convention service manager. It has been said that "the job of servicing meetings is 95% communication and 5% service." Letters, telephone calls and personal on-site visits are normally used to get this "pipeline" of information flowing. One excellent tool to initiate the communication process is to send a Resume Questionnaire (Fig. 12.6) to the meeting planner. This form consolidates a list of important questions and reduces the frequent telephone calls and exchanges of correspondence on individual items.

Study Questions

1. What is the purpose of the preconventional meeting? Who should attend?

2. Describe Westin's "Operation Excell." Outline the four stages of this program.

3. Distinguish between the specification sheet and the function sheet. What information does each contain?

4. Some convention service managers prefer not to give the meeting planner a key personnel roster. What do you think their logic is in refusing such a request?

278

New York Penta Hotel

7th Avenue & 33rd Street, New York, NY 10001
Telephone: (212) 736-5000   Telex: 220932

RESUME GUIDELINES

1. EVENT TO BE POSTED AS FOLLOWS: _____

    _____

2. OFFICIAL OFFICERS:

    <u>NAME</u>   <u>TITLE</u>

    _____
    _____
    _____
    _____
    _____

3. AUTHORIZED SIGNATURES:

    <u>NAME</u>   <u>SIGNATURES</u>   <u>TITLE</u>

    _____
    _____
    _____
    _____
    _____

4. MASTER BILLING ADDRESS, TELEPHONE NUMBER AND TO WHOM'S ATTENTION IT SHOULD
    BE LISTED. (Upon approval of the hotel's Credit Manager)

                    _____
                    _____
                    _____
                    _____
                    _____
                    _____

5. NEW YORK STATE TAX EXEMPT: _____ YES _____ NO

    (If your organization is tax exempt, please forward a copy of the
    certificate to the Convention Service Department.)

6. CONVENTION HEADQUARTERS HOTEL: _____

    OTHER HOTELS USED: _____
                       _____
                       _____

-2-

7. EXPECTED CONVENTION REGISTRATION: _____ADVANCE _____ON-SITE

8. WILL THERE BE A NECESSITY FOR HOTEL SAFETY DEPOSIT BOXES FOR THE CONVENTION
    OFFICERS? _____ YES _____ NO
    (If yes): HOW MANY? _____ AND WHAT NAMES SHOULD BE LISTED UNDER:

    _____

    _____

    _____

    _____

9. MONEY EXCHANGE: Will there be a necessity for the officers to exchange large
                     bills during the conference? _____ YES _____ NO
                     (If yes, in what denominations?)

                     PENNIES _____   NICKLES _____   DIMES _____   QUARTERS _____

                     $1 BILLS _____ $5 BILLS _____ $10 BILLS _____ $20 BILLS ____

                     OTHER _____

10. RESERVATIONS: _____ Hotel Form   _____ Own Form   _____ Housing Bureau

                     _____ Rooming List   _____ Phone In

11. ARRIVALS: Will most of your attendees be arriving by:

                     _____ Automobile   _____ Train   _____ Commercial Airline

                     _____ Chartered Bus

                     Note: For bus arrivals, please have the persons(s) and/or
                     organization contact our Reservation Manager directly.

12. HOSPITALITY SUITES: Please have the companies who will be sponsoring
                          Hospitality Suites contact our Room Service Manager
                          directly for their food and beverage needs. Also,
                          our Reservation Manager and Credit Manager should be
                          contacted to expedite their reservation and billing
                          needs.

13. BUS DEPARTURES: Have you contracted buses for tours, trips, etc.
                     _____ YES   _____ NO
                     If yes, please advise us of your schedule in the program
                     and set-up instructions. (All buses are to depart from
                     the hotel's side entrance on 33rd Street.)

14. CELEBRITIES: Will any of your speakers attract media attention?
                     _____ YES   _____ NO

                     If yes, please list their names and speaking date/times below:

                     _____

                     _____

                     _____

                     _____

                     _____

                     _____

-3-

15. SECURITY SPEECH: Do you require our Security Department to give a
                         short speech on security tips on New York City and
                         the hotel?

                         _____ YES   _____ NO

                         If yes, it will be conducted at your first General
                         Session.

16. OFFICERS, SPEAKERS AND V.I.P. RESERVATIONS:

            NAME: _____   Double - 1 Bed

         ADDRESS: _____   Twin - 2 Single Beds

                  _____

    TELEPHONE #: _____

    ARRIVAL DATE: _____   ESTIMATED TIME: _____

    DEPARTURE DATE: _____   ESTIMATED TIME: _____

    ROOM TYPE: _____ SINGLE _____ DOUBLE _____ TWIN

               _____ 1 BEDROOM SUITE _____ 2 BEDROOM SUITE

               (Sharing With: _____)

               Arrival: _____ Departure: _____

    BILLING INSTRUCTIONS: _____ Pays own room, tax and incidental charges

                           _____ Room and tax to the Master Account

                           _____ Room, tax and incidentals to the Master Account

    SPECIAL REQUIREMENTS: _____

****

            NAME: _____   Double - 1 Bed

         ADDRESS: _____   Twin - 2 Single Beds

                  _____

    TELEPHONE #: _____

    ARRIVAL DATE: _____   ESTIMATED TIME: _____

    DEPARTURE DATE: _____   ESTIMATED TIME: _____

    ROOM TYPE: _____ SINGLE _____ DOUBLE _____ TWIN

               _____ 1 BEDROOM SUITE _____ 2 BEDROOM SUITE

               (Sharing With: _____)

               Arrival: _____ Departure: _____

    BILLING INSTRUCTIONS: _____ Pays own room, tax and incidental charges

                           _____ Room and tax to the Master Account

                           _____ Room, tax and incidentals to the Master Account

    SPECIAL REQUIREMENTS: _____

****

-4-

NAME: _____   Double - 1 Bed
ADDRESS: _____   Twin - 2 Single Beds
         _____

TELEPHONE #: _____
ARRIVAL DATE: _____ ESTIMATED TIME: _____
DEPARTURE DATE: _____ ESTIMATED TIME: _____
ROOM TYPE: _____ SINGLE _____ DOUBLE _____ TWIN
           _____ 1 BEDROOM SUITE _____ 2 BEDROOM SUITE
           (Sharing With: _____)
           Arrival: _____ Departure: _____
BILLING INSTRUCTIONS: _____ Pays own room, tax and incidental charges
                        _____ Room and tax to the Master Account
                        _____ Room, tax and incidentals to the Master Account

SPECIAL REQUIREMENTS: _____
****

17. REGISTRATION: (Speakers-Exhibitors-Registrants)
    DAY   DATE   TIME   LOCATION(S)
    _____
    _____
    _____
    _____
    _____

18. ADMISSION: _____
    _____

19. EXHIBITS: DAY/DATE   TIME   LOCATION(S)
    Dryage Set-up: _____
    _____
    Exhibitors Set-up: _____
    _____
    Show Opens: _____
    _____
    Exhibitors Dismantle: _____
    _____
    Dryage Dismantle: _____
    _____

20. NUMBER OF EXHIBITORS: _____ TYPE OF BOOTHS: _____
    * Forward the exhibitors contract to the Convention Service Department.

-5-

21. HOTEL HOLD HARMLESS CLAUSE: Please sign and return.

22. CONTRACTORS: (Contact, address and telephone number)

DRYAGE CONTRACTOR   SECURITY CONTRACTOR

_____   _____
_____   _____
_____   _____
_____   _____
_____   _____

AUDIO VISUAL CONTRACTOR   TYPEWRITER CONTRACTOR

_____   _____
_____   _____
_____   _____
_____   _____
_____   _____

NOTE: For your convenience, arrangements may be made for contractors
         through the Convention Service Department.

COPY MACHINE/OFFICE EQUIPMENT CONTRACTOR   SIGN CONTRACTOR

_____   _____
_____   _____
_____   _____
_____   _____
_____   _____

SOUND AND/OR LIGHTING COMPANY   OTHER CONTRACTORS

_____   _____
_____   _____
_____   _____
_____   _____
_____   _____

23. CONVENTION BUREAU PERSONNEL USED: _____ YES   _____ NO

_____
_____
_____
_____

24. ROOM SERVICE/RESTAURANTS/BARS: (L-Light, M-Moderate, H-Heavy)

	BREAKFAST			LUNCH			DINNER			COCKTAILS		
Room Service	L	M	H	L	M	H	L	M	H	L	M	H
Restaurants	L	M	H	L	M	H	L	M	H	L	M	H
Bars	L	M	H	L	M	H	L	M	H	L	M	H

-6-

25. TELEPHONE INSTRUCTIONS:

    Will there be a need for outgoing calls?   _____ YES   _____ NO

    If yes: _____ LOCAL   _____ LONG DISTANCE _____ BOTH

    The special code word for all outgoing calls will be: _____

26. CHECKROOM FACILITIES:

    The hotel does have a Main Checkroom loctated in the rear Lobby. Will
    you require a second checkroom? _____ YES   _____ NO (If yes, our
    Checkroom Manager will contact you directly for charges incurred.)

27. PACKAGE ROOM:

    Will you be shipping boxes to the hotel Package Room? _____ YES _____ NO

    If yes, approximately how many? _____Basic Size: _____Basic Weight:_____

28. PROGRAM AND SET-UP INSTRUCTIONS:

    Attached, please find an example of the format followed for the Convention
    Service resume. We suggest this format for simpler communications and
    easy understanding. For more detailed set-ups, we suggesst attaching
    a diagram.

    This information will be included in the hotel's convention resume,
    which is distributed to all departments in the hotel.

NAME OF ORGANIZATION: _____

Page _____

PROGRAM AND SET-UP INSTRUCTIONS

DAY/DATE	FUNCTION	LOCATION	TIME	SET-UP INSTRUCTIONS

NAME OF ORGANIZATION: _____

PROGRAM AND SET-UP INSTRUCTIONS

DAY/DATE	FUNCTION	LOCATION	TIME	SET-UP INSTRUCTIONS
Monday, 12/13/83	Registration	Georgian Foyer	8am-5pm	3 - 6' x 30" tables with 2 chairs each 2 easels, a corkboard, a wastepaper basket
	General Session	Georgian Ballroom	9am-5pm	Theater style for 200pp facing a head table for 6pp on a 1' high platform. Provide a table lectern. Audio: Provide a lectern mike. Audio Visual: Provide a carrousel projector with remote control with long cord and screen.
	Coffee Service	Georgian Foyer	10:30am-11am	Please discuss with the Banquet Manager.
	Luncheon	Gold Ballroom	12N-1pm	Please discuss with the Banquet Manager.
	Coffee Service	Georgian Foyer	3pm-3:30pm	Please discuss with the Banquet Manager.
Tuesday, 12/14/83	Registration	Georgian Foyer	8am-5pm	Set-up: Same as the previous day.
	General Session	Georgian Ballroom	9am-5pm	Set-up: Same as the previous day.
	Coffee Service	Georgian Foyer	10:30am-11am	Please discuss with the Banquet Manager.
	Luncheon	Gold Ballroom	12N-1pm	Please discuss with the Banquet Manager.
	Coffee Service	Georgian Foyer	3pm-3:30pm	Please discuss with the Banquet Manager.

Outline

I. Function Rooms

    A. Types of Function Rooms
    B. Meeting Room Plans
    C. Room Assignments
    D. Function Room Size and Layout
    E. Timetable for Set-up and Break-down
    F. Function Room Charges
    G. Release Dates
    H. Use of Meeting Rooms by Others
    I. Employee Procedure Manuals

II. Meeting Setups

    A. Scaled Drawings
    B. Function Room Furniture
        1. Chairs and Tables
        2. Platforms
        3. Lecterns
    C. Basic Meeting Setups
    D. Setups with Tables
        1. Schoolroom Style
        2. U Shape
        3. Horseshoe
        4. Hollow Square and Hollow Circular
        5. Variations
        6. Board of Directors
        7. Round Tables
        8. Circular Buffet Table
    E. Setup Time
    F. Breakdown of Function Rooms
    G. Rules of Thumb

Any hotel can supply guest rooms. A convention hotel is one that has function rooms and the staff to handle such events.

Function Rooms

When the hotel sales representative originally solicited the convention, he or she presented the client with information about the hotel's meeting rooms. Most larger convention hotels have a number of suitable meeting rooms, and often more than are needed for an event. In the case of a smaller meeting, the hotel needs to obtain the release of unneeded meeting rooms as early as possible to enable its staff to sell another event.

Often a convention planner will request that all the convention facilities be held for his or her event, at least until the program is roughed out and it is obvious what facilities are needed. This is rarely possible. Unless the convention is large and virtually sells out the house, the hotel management cannot lock up a precious commodity like meeting rooms for any longer than absolutely necessary.

It is urgent, therefore, for you to get together with the meeting planner to place a hold on the rooms thought to be needed and to urge that planning be done to determine realistically the needs of the event. There is no pressure if you have no other meetings scheduled for those dates, but most sizable hotels handle a number of smaller meetings simultaneously.

Types of Function Rooms

Before assigning rooms, the convention service manager must be aware of what the hotel has to offer. A common mistake is to assume you have only those rooms specifically designated as function rooms. Actually, all public space may be function area depending on the group and its needs.

Some of the most common function rooms depicted in the hotel's convention brochure are

1. exhibit halls
2. ballrooms for banquets
3. conference rooms for meetings

Unless meeting planners are advised otherwise, these are the rooms with which they work as they lay out their schedules. Unknown to them, perhaps, is the possible use of the foyer, the parking lot, and swimming pool areas for cocktail parties; the upper-floor suites equipped with conference tables for small, intimate meetings; and the garden area behind the hotel for an evening party. The possibilities are limited only by the imagination of the convention service manager. The unusual is often what makes a hotel unique, so it is important to keep in mind that all public areas may be used as function space.

A relatively new concept in the use of meeting space is the *break-out room*. For example, a large teaching session might divide into smaller groups of four or five to involve the conferees and to provide feedback for the instructors.

The trend toward break-out configurations as a method of training is becoming increasingly popular. To accommodate these setups many hotels are making suites available near the main conference room; others have provided rooms that can be subdivided with movable, sound-proof air walls.

Meeting Room Plans

If the hotel's convention brochure does not present the meeting rooms in complete detail, it will be necessary to prepare other material. Meeting planners will probably ask for scaled drawings of each room showing such details as exits, electrical outlets, and any obstructions. We suggested when we discussed convention hotel brochures in chapter 8 that such material be included. If the brochure is sufficiently detailed, it might serve. Usually, however, the brochure doesn't have all the data needed. Now you need a virtual blueprint (fig. 13.1).

Meeting planners also need to know the capacity of the rooms under a variety of setups, and they should be guided by the convention service manager in deciding what would be the best kind of function for each room. (Later in this chapter we will discuss the setups commonly used.)

Convention planners must be made aware of the kinds of rooms available to them. Much of this probably was part of the sales presentation, but the convention service manager may be dealing with a different person than the sales representative did.

Room Assignments

The convention service manager is the person most qualified to assign rooms for specific events. Of course, this should be done in close communication with the meeting planner. The service manager knows the hotel and its facilities; the meeting planner knows the event and its characteristics. (fig. 13.2)

Fig. 13.1   Detailed meeting room plans (By permission of the Dunes Hotel, Las Vegas).

CARAVAN EXHIBIT HALL

School Room Style Seating	Approx.	450
Theatre Style Seating	Approx.	800
Banquet Style Seating	Approx.	650

MONACO ROOM

School Room Style Seating	Approx.	250
Theatre Style Seating	Approx.	500
Banquet Style Seating	Approx.	300

Fluorescent Ceiling Lights
220/110 Outlets
Exit Lights
Electric Floor Outlets
Recessed Ceiling Lights
Wall Bracket Light Outlets
Telephone
Air Wall Room Dividers
Ceiling Speakers
Plumbing Outlets
Duplex Recp't. Outlets
Portable Transformers Available
Ample Stage Lighting
Rheostat Lighting
Movable Spotlights in Ceiling
for Displays
Closed Circuit T-V Facilities Beside
Telephone Jacks

Ceiling Height of Caravan Exhibit Hall — 13 Ft.

Ceiling Height of Monaco Room — 12 Ft.

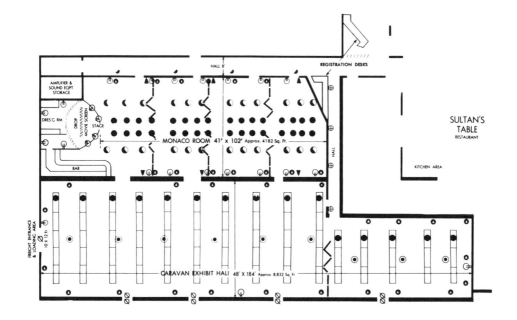

Fig. 13.2 An overall facility schematic is a helpful sales tool. Using a plan as illustrated here the salesperson can help the meeting planner visualize the attendees' flow from guestrooms to function rooms. (Courtesy SunBurst Resort Hotel and Conference Center)

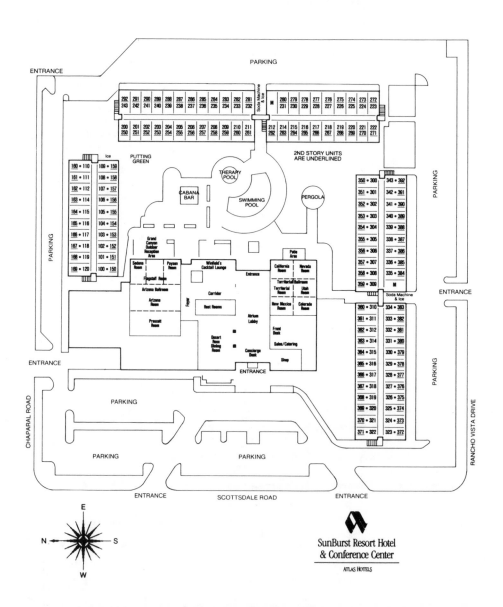

In assigning a room, its size, its capacity under a specific layout, the type of event, and the presentation style should be considered. These fundamental requirements probably were hashed out during the sales presentations, but other factors must be considered too.

Consider the room's location within the hotel in regard to traffic in corridors, elevators, escalators, parking arrangements, and coat check rooms. Don't forget to find out what will be going on in the room next door. A rock band next door to a speech could be disastrous. A seemingly ordinary meeting can become quite noisy merely by adding a sound film.

All program segments must be definitely allocated to specific locations about sixty days before the event, at the latest.

You should get a list from the client of all the people on his or her staff who are authorized to move an event to a different location, should the need arise. Just before the event, and especially during it, it is absolutely essential to know the channels of authority within the convention staff. Time may be too short and the need for action too great to let you double-check any instructions. Cancellations of sessions, changes in timetables, and the like may be made at the last minute.

Such a list should be in writing, of course. And the degree of authority should be specified. What can these staff members order? Changes in layout or location can be costly in terms of time and labor.

The list you get from the convention organizer should be similar to the list of your department heads that you give to the organizer. The key people of *both* the hotel and convention group staffs should attend the preconvention meetings. Let them get acquainted before the pressure begins. Discuss possible changes. This is the time to indicate what the hotel staff will need in the way of time and labor to bring about such program alterations.

Because association conventions must cope with optional attendance at both the convention and individual programs, it is often necessary to move workshops and meetings from one room to another to accommodate smaller or larger groups. Airing such possibilities in advance allows your staff and the client's staff to understand such conditions and to react more quickly and constructively in crisis situations.

Function Room Size and Layout

Many factors come into play when discussing meeting room size. First and foremost, of course, is the number expected to attend. Then you must consider the room setup desired and the number and type of audiovisual equipment needed. Additional space may be required for clothes racks, props, or tables to distribute literature. And you must allow more space if coffee service is scheduled.

The basic layout indicates the style of seating. It is wasteful of labor to set each room to utmost capacity, but you obviously must provide enough seating. This is the time to examine the kind of sessions that will go on just before and just after this specific program to make sure the setup is the same or enough time is allotted to make the change. Hotels are frequently able to put similiar meetings back to back and thus keep manpower and equipment change-over time to a minimum.

The meeting planner will also have to confer with you about the style and size of the head table. Pads, pencils, folders, and printed material may all be placed on chairs or tables. And water glasses and pitchers may be put at a number of tables or stations, if tables are not used. Don't forget ashtrays. And some meetings call for name signs.

Each session has its own requirements. Attention to details is the key to convention service.

Timetable for Setup and Breakdown

Most hotel brochures do an adequate job of presenting the basic contours of each meeting room. Few, however, tell the convention organizer how much time is required for room setup and breakdown. The result may be a program that is designed much too tightly to permit good service. And too often the hotel bears the stigma of failing to perform well, give good service, or show much expertise. The planner might lay out the program more realistically if he or she had some idea of the time needed to perform these services.

Too often the sales representative is only too willing to take on any task, under any conditions, for fear of losing the business. The truth is that many meeting planners would gladly loosen up their timetables if they knew what was involved. The planners are interested in these problems because they want their shows to run smoothly and on time.

Many hotel brochures are designed to show how a room is used in a variety of ways. The hotel prefers to present the rooms as versatile and to play down any limitations. But there is a great need to communicate to help fit the program into the rooms.

Function Room Charges

How do you determine what to charge for meeting space? Is there a set formula?

Brochures list rates for guest rooms but rarely for meeting rooms. The latter situation is most flexible; it depends on the meeting group, the time, and the space required. If the group uses enough guest rooms, there is usually no charge for meeting rooms. In the case of food functions, the cost per person also covers the use of the room. (fig. 13.3)

In cases where a group feels that guest room rates are too high, the hotel may reduce the rates and charge extra for the exhibit space instead. The group then passes this cost along to the exhibitors.

There may very well be circumstances in which the hotel management prefers to charge for a function room. You should consider having a listed price for each room; after all, it looks great when you waive the fee. When you do charge for a function room, a list of charges should be available. You might outline a sliding scale arrangement, tying the meeting room fees to the number of guest rooms used for the convention.

There seems to be a trend today to charge for space. We think that a hotel that handles a number of small meetings would be wise to consider a fee, particularly if the group plans to meet in one room, hold a food function in another, and conduct break-out meetings in another three to five rooms.

In such situations room charges should be stipulated if the guest room commitment is not enough to cover the labor costs of setting up, servicing, cleaning, and tearing down. After all, a hotel is in business to make a profit.

You might also want to charge for meeting rooms when companies participating in a trade show take the opportunity to hold dealer or sales meetings. The people attending may already be registered for the trade show, and the requirements of the trade show would place great strain on the allocation of meeting rooms. Of course, if the food functions of such additional meetings mount up, it may justify not charging for use of the room. But a room charge may be justified if the food function is only a coffee break.

In final analysis, there is no hard and fast rule on charging for meeting space. A hotel needs to look at the food, at the room, at all the profit areas to determine its rate structure.

Release Dates

When a convention buys out the house, a request to hold all rooms seems reasonable. But a release date still should be set in the letter of agreement. At some early date when a rough program is available, the room assignments can be tentatively made. At this point, *some* function rooms can be released if there seem to be more than enough. The convention in the house should have a priority for meeting rooms,

Fig. 13.3 Guide to function space charges.

The Sheraton Waikiki provides meeting planners with the following function space pricing policy. Note the charges increase if sleeping rooms slip from the original room block commitment. Meeting room rental at this 1900 room property total approximately $250,000 per year.

SHERATON FUNCTION SPACE CHARGES:

The Sheraton Waikiki charges for function space under the following circumstances:
1. All Exhibits
2. All function rooms that are held on a 24-hour block
3. We charge for function space for groups that have meetings only and are holding no sleeping rooms at the Sheraton Waikiki Hotel.
4. We charge for function space when unusual or costly set-ups are required.
5. We charge for function space when the sleeping rooms decrease proportionately from the original commitment.

FUNCTION SPACE VS. SLEEPING ROOM CONSUMPTION
(PROPORTIONATE SLIDING SCALE)

Percent of Decrease From Original Block	Amount of Meeting Room Charges
Up to 40% decrease	No charge
41%–60% decrease	50% charge for meeting rooms as listed on "meeting room charge sheet"
61%–80% decrease	75% charge for meeting rooms as listed on "meeting room charge sheet"
81%–100% decrease	100% charge for meeting rooms as listed on "meeting room charge sheet"

*In addition to the above "sliding scale," . . . the hotel will also take into consideration your definite food and beverage events when determining your meeting room charges.

but you may get other calls. Here again it becomes obvious why there is a need to have just one function book, under one person's control.

At a somewhat later date, when a detailed program is worked out, try to get unneeded rooms released. There is an understandable tendency for meeting planners to try to hold onto every room indefinitely, to have a reserve of meeting rooms for some occasion that may come up. But that practice can inhibit your other sales efforts.

Use of Meeting Rooms by Others

Some organizations ask, or demand, that all requests by other groups for meeting facilities in the hotel at the time of their event be cleared with them. In many cases, their concern is understandable. They are trying to control the entire environment of their event and they don't want rival or competitive organizations meeting at the same time under the same roof. This is especially true of corporate meetings, where apprehensions of industrial security cannot be dismissed lightly.

The hotel must be careful about this. Imagine an IBM research seminar in the house at the same time as Control Data or Honeywell meetings! When a competitive organization appears on the scene, the usually easygoing meeting planner gets quite uptight. And you may find yourself needing strict security systems for a relatively easy, small seminar.

And should you be concerned about only the exact dates of the meeting, or must you worry too about the days immediately before and after the event?

Small properties use such situations to sell themselves. Certainly in the off-season the small resort can claim with some justification that walk-in business from competitive personnel is highly unlikely. If you can handle only one average-sized group at a time, why not turn this limitation into a positive sales asset? The meeting organizer is assured of receiving all your facility and attention and need not worry about traffic patterns and unwanted guests.

There is another instance in which the convention organizer may want to veto a meeting held in the hotel during his or her dates. Many marketing companies hold dealer meetings at trade shows. Most association executives have no objections, and many feel that it adds importance to their event. But many have strong ideas about timing such meetings to make sure that they do not pull delegates away from the main sessions or events that the program offers at the time.

It is safe to say that you can expect convention managers to be interested in who and what is scheduled in the hotel during *their* time.

Employee Procedure Manuals

The convention service manager, as we have said, is the in-house coordinator of the convention. He, or she, works with virtually every department in the hotel. His authority in dealing with these departments is to a great extent determined by his character and the respect he has earned from those with whom he works. In most hotels, the convention service manager does not have direct line authority over rooms or food and beverage departments. This often necessitates that he use tact and discretion in getting the job done; in many cases he is more of a diplomat than a manager.

However, he does have line authority within his own department and must function as manager there. Serving under him are three to ten housemen who set up the function rooms. Each of these men should be trained in the various types of meeting setups. Our experience shows that this is best accomplished with the use of procedure manuals.

A procedure manual should not be confused with a job description. A procedure manual tells the employee how to do the job, whereas a job description is prepared primarily for management and states the job's responsibility and authority. Ideally, a procedure manual should include illustrations or drawings. For example, setup illustrations similar to those used in this chapter should be included. The manual also should include a step-by-step outline of the houseman's job.

The procedure manual will have the same importance for employees in the convention service department as the master recipe card does for a cook. Successful restaurants are largely successful because of consistency; the same should be true for convention servicing. A procedure manual will help assure that setups will not be done in a slightly different way each day. It is often difficult for employees to recall each procedure in a setup and all the supplies that are required. The manual eliminates exclusion of certain steps, as well as serving as a valuable training tool for new employees. Manuals might also include rules and regulations that apply to the setup houseman.

Efforts should be made to personalize the manual. It should be published in a small booklet form that can easily fit into a shirt pocket for quick reference.

No such manual is permanent. On the contrary, new tables, chairs, and operating techniques will necessitate updating. Hopefully, the employees themselves may suggest ways to perform certain aspects of the job better.

Meeting Setups

The physical arrangement of chairs and tables plays an important role in meetings. Convention planners know that the atmosphere of a meeting can be enhanced or destroyed by the size of the room and the manner in which it is arranged. Thus it is essential that you have an orderly presentation for each of your facility's meeting rooms, giving its dimensions and its capacities under a variety of layout designs.

Scaled Drawings

You should have accurately scaled drawings of each function room for your own use and for distribution to customers. Begin with a single sheet listing each room's basic dimensions, ceiling height, permanent stage, if any, and capacity under the most popular meeting layouts (fig. 13.4). Add to this a scaled drawing of each room (fig. 13.1). Include the doors, windows, pillars, elevators, electrical outlets, and any obstructions.

These drawings should be accurate enough to be used to designate meeting or exhibit layouts. They should be part of your convention facilities brochure, but you should also have a supply of individual sheets to offer to meeting organizers for their use.

If you indicate capacity on the drawings, keep in mind that different setups accommodate widely differing numbers of people. Some properties have simplified room arrangement planning by the use of a magnetic planning board. The setup for a particular room is worked out in advance by using scaled metallic pieces to represent various sizes of furniture. The meeting planner using such a technique is able to get a better feel for the setup suggested by the convention service manager.

Function Room Furniture

Hotel function rooms get heavy use. Often a number of functions are scheduled on one day for a single room, with only an hour or two between events. These events are often quite different, and housemen must work quickly to set up a variety of functions—business meetings, lectures, training sessions, fashion shows, banquets. The only flexibility the room can provide is through the use of air walls or folding division doors. The major measure of change must be provided by the equipment and setup.

Function room furniture is the term coined for the equipment used in meeting and banquet rooms. Jacob Felsenstein of King Arthur Incorporated, a leading supplier of such furniture to the hotel industry, has suggested four general features to look for in function room furniture.

Fig. 13.4 Meeting room capacities and dimensions at the Westin Hotel Renaissance Center Detroit (used with permission).

Specifications:

	THEATER	SCHOOL ROOM	CONFERENCE	"U" SHAPED	RECEPTION	DINING	DINNER DANCE	WIDTH	LENGTH	TOTAL SQUARE FEET	CEILING HEIGHT	MAXIMUM WIDTH ENTRANCE	MAXIMUM HEIGHT ENTRANCE
❶ RENAISSANCE BALLROOM	2,700	1,250			3,500	2,270	1,970	202'	136'	25,500	20'	16'	7'
❷ COLUMBUS	1,180	570			1,600	1,050	800	93'	136'	12,656	20'	16'	7'
❸ CABOT	514	318			700	500	340	53'	122'	6,422	20'	16'	7'
❹ CARTIER	514	318			700	500	340	53'	122'	6,422	20'	16'	7'
❺ RENAISSANCE FOYER					2,000	(700)				15,000			
❻ MICHELANGELO	94	46	30	28	100	80		27'	36'	972	10'	6'	6'8"
❼ MONET	50	28	22	24	60	50		20'	30'	596	10'	6'	6'8"
❽ da VINCI	50	28	22	24	60	50		20'	30'	596	10'	6'	6'8"
❾ RAPHAEL	28	12	12	16	35	30		20'	15'	305	10'	6'	6'8"
❿ RENOIR	50	28	22	24	60	50		20'	30'	596	10'	6'	6'8"
⓫ GRECO	94	46	30	28	100	80		27'	36'	972	10'	6'	6'8"

Floor load capacity in all function space, 100 lbs. per square foot.

All seating capacities will have to be diminished when extensive A/V equipment, head tables, or stages are used.

1. *Strength and durability.* Watch for the weakest link such as mechanical folding devices which are easily broken, or strong components which may depend on a weak hinge or spring. Safety of guests is a foremost consideration. Simple and effective folding devices minimize the possibility of failure by complicated locking devices and human error. Frequency of use means frequency of cleaning. Parts which rest on the floor must be made to withstand and facilitate frequent scrubbings, waxings and vacuuming.
2. *Ease of handling.*   Folding or knock-down equipment should be simple to set up. Equipment which is light in weight may not be the most durable. There are a variety of carriers such as dollies and trucks which are designed to aid in handling.
3. *Ease of storage.*   Equipment should be able to be stacked so that one piece does not mar the next, and in a manner which prevents vulnerable parts from protruding. In choosing dollies or trucks, check to see that they are designed to handle the particular piece of equipment in your particular setting.
4. *Flexibility.*   It may be advisable to buy a piece of function-room furniture which serves two or more purposes in order to avoid extra handling or storage. Examples: a Knockdown Cabaret Table allows for different-sized tops to be used interchangeably with the same column and base, enabling it to fill many different needs; one Dual Height Folding Platform serves two different levels, many different purposes, can save up to 50% on initial outlay and an additional 50% on handling costs and storage space.[1]

Chairs and Tables

Meeting furniture can vary a great deal, but there are certain types and sizes that are used most frequently. We use these basic types when we present layouts and schematics for setups. Your capacity figures should be based on such equipment, and will vary when you use other than the standard. Most variations are used in small meeting setups such as board room facsimiles; we have relaxed during many such meetings in posh swivel armchairs.

Most chairs used for meetings are eighteen inches wide by eighteen inches deep by seventeen inches high. Stacking armchairs (not the deluxe type mentioned in the previous paragraph) are slightly larger, such as twenty by twenty by seventeen. Most folding chair units are smaller and not as comfortable, and generally are used for last-minute overflow accommodations. Smart meeting planners want their attendees to be comfortable and relaxed so they can concentrate on the program.

Rigid chairs are recommended for food functions. They are more comfortable than folding chairs, which are smaller and lower.

The standard height for tables is thirty inches; the standard depth, either thirty

1. Jacob Felsenstein, *Guide to Function-Room Furniture* (Pennsauken, N.J.: King Arthur Incorporated.)

or eighteen inches. When people are to be seated opposite each other, the thirty-inch table is required. When people sit on only one side of the table, as we shall discuss in *schoolroom* setups, the eighteen-inch depth is sufficient and saves much space. There is a growing use of fifteen-inch tables to save even more space. The thirty-inch-deep rectangular table, however, is used most frequently for head tables, even when people are seated on only a single side. This deeper table is also used for display tables, exhibit stands, and other purposes. It is most versatile and comes in lengths of four, six, and eight feet so that a variety of total lengths may be achieved easily.

Round tables are used for many food functions and also for some kinds of meeting sessions. They most often are four, five, or six feet in diameter. Comfortable seating calls for a five-foot round table for eight to ten people, a six-foot table for ten to twelve people. The four-foot round table will handle four to six people and is also used at cocktail parties and similar setups.

An almost infinite number of variations can be made by using half-round tables, available in five and seven and one-half feet, and quarter-round, available in two and one-half and four feet. The more imaginative serpentine tables are commonly used for buffets. You are restricted only by your imagination in developing unique buffet arrangements.

Tablecloths, mitered on the corners, are used on tables because most banquet and meeting room tables are damaged and unsightly from continual breakdown and storage. Several companies have begun to market folding tables that are attractive and not easily damaged, and they can be used without tablecloths, saving on laundry and labor costs. Such tables, however, are expensive and fail to provide the warmth and color of tablecloths.

Head tables, as well as display and buffet tables, require special drapery. Traditionally, pins and tacks have been used to attach floor-length linens for such setups. But a new technique is being used by many hotels. Velcro, a product with looped nylon fibers, can be purchased in strips one-half inch wide. The velcro adheres to both the drapery and the table, making a fast attachment when pressed.

"Snap-drape" skirting is also available. Plastic clips are fitted along the top edge of platforms and tables, and grippers sewn into the upper pleat of the skirting are snapped into place quickly. Snap-drape skirting is made of permanent-crease polyester and fiberglass, making it easy to clean and wrinkle-free.

Platforms

Folding platforms are used in many ways; they elevate head tables for banquets and speakers. They come in different sizes, with different names: platform, stage, dais, podium, or rostrum. You must construct them to size. Check local safety regulations carefully. The usual heights are six, eight, twelve, and sixteen inches, plus a thirty-two-inch *high riser*. Lengths may be four, six, or eight feet, or any combination of these. Widths vary from four to six feet. If you maintain adequate stocks, a variety of combinations can be created.

If the platforms are old and unsightly, put pleated skirting around the bottom and perhaps carpeting on top.

Lecterns

Some lecterns are placed on tables and called, logically enough, *table lecterns*. *Floor lecterns* sit on the floor. It is important to stock the kind with permanent light fixtures that have enough connecting wire to reach wall outlets.

Many a room becomes difficult to set up because the wall outlets are on the same circuits as the overhead lights and are controlled by a common switch. There are frequent occasions to dim house lights for effect or for greater visibility of audiovisual presentations. Make sure the lectern's light unit is connected to a wall outlet that will not be cut off with the overhead lights. It is wise to check each setup carefully after all is ready for the meeting; smart meeting planners will double-check such items themselves.

Permanent stages allow you to develop more sophisticated lecterns with full audiovisual controls. Such units don't lend themselves to the temporary setups of most meeting rooms, but they are received most enthusiastically by program members. You should consider these units whenever a permanent installation is possible. A must item that is most versatile for temporary setups is a portable lectern with a built-in sound system that plugs into a normal electrical outlet.

Basic Meeting Setups

A number of basic seating arrangements have evolved. Be sure that your customer is using the terminology correctly. Layout or schematic sheets will help in this area.

Auditorium Style

One of the most common seating arrangements calls for chairs to be set up in rows facing the speaker, stage, or head table. This is called *auditorium* or *theater style* (fig. 13.5). It can be used in both very large meeting rooms and relatively small ones.

When arranging chairs in auditorium style, set up two chairs first to indicate

Fig. 13.5 Variations of the auditorium style seating arrangement (Reprinted with permission from *Function Room Set-Up Manual* by Gerhard M. Peter, published by Hotel Sales Management Association).

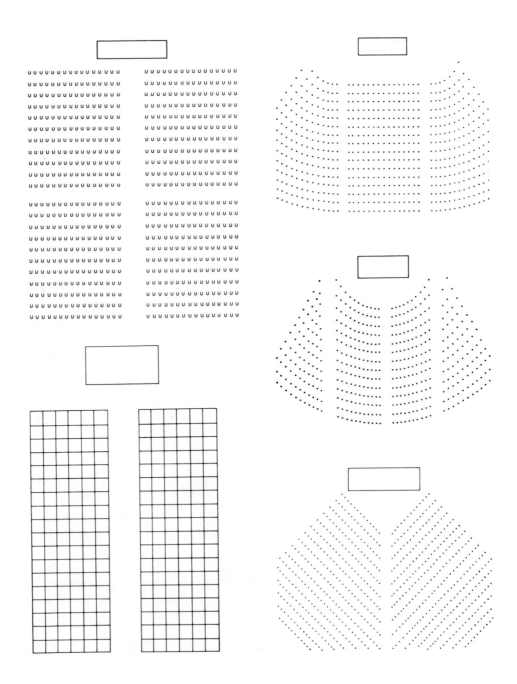

the position of the aisle. At least two inches must be left between chairs side by side; this is called the *space*. The *distance* is the dimension from a chair to the one in front of it. Minimum distance should be thirty-three inches from chair center to center.

When chairs have been positioned to indicate the aisles, the bulk of the chairs can be placed. When you can specify carpeting, get it in one-square-foot patterns. This is most popular with hotel people because it helps to align setups. If there is no carpeting, the lines in hardwood floors might guide you.

Aisle sizes and numbers are regulated by local fire departments. If you have any doubts, get the specifications from the fire department. Most regulations call for aisles to be six feet wide if 400 or more people are involved. Smaller groups can be accommodated with aisles of four or five feet. Double aisles are preferred if the meeting format calls for questions from the floor or anything else that will result in much back-and-forth movement of people or the passing of objects such as microphones.

The first row of chairs should be about six feet from the front edge of the head table or platform. The most popular auditorium style uses a center aisle. In larger halls, fire departments may require aisles across the front and back of the room and an additional horizontal aisle halfway down. It pays to check and keep a written record of local fire regulations.

Keep in mind the number of chairs in a row. It is extremely uncomfortable for an attendee to have to make his or her way across fifteen people to find a seat in the middle of the row.

There are variations of the straight auditorium style setup. They require more room than the straight style, so some floor space is wasted. One is *auditorium style, semicircular, center aisle* (fig. 13.5). You need at least twelve feet from the head table or platform to the front row of chairs. Set up the first row, then set two additional aisles. Set the outside chair where you want it. Use a piece of string, tied loosely between the two end chairs of the curved row. Line up the rest of the rows measured from the first one.

Another version is called *auditorium, V shape* (fig. 13.5). Set it up the same way, but the side sections form an angle to the center aisle.

You can vary any of the auditorium setups with a solid *center block* of chairs instead of a center aisle (fig. 13.5). Allow for four-foot aisles on either side of the center block.

Space and distance vary from the norm when armchairs with writing arms are used (fig. 13.5). Because of the bigger dimensions of these chairs, use three-inch spacing and thirty-five inch distance from chair center to center. The most common arrangement of these tablet chairs is the basic auditorium style, but they can be used in any of the other variations as well.

When tables are set up on a dais, regardless of the seating arrangement on the rest of the floor, make double sure that the head tables are draped down to the floor. Place water and ashtrays at the lectern and on the head table. Use one ashtray and one water carafe for every two people seated on the stage.

Setups with Tables

Schoolroom Style

A favorite setup for both large and small groups is the *schoolroom style* (figs. 13.6 and 13.7). Use the eighteen-inch-deep rectangular tables and allow for a center aisle. The recommended distance from table center to table center is forty-two inches, but allow several inches more whenever possible. Figure on about twenty-four inches of table space for each person.

The thirty-inch-deep tables are wasteful in schoolroom setups because people are seated on only one side. But sometimes you do have to use them, especially if a great deal of paperwork is to be done. In such cases, allow fifty-four inches from center of table to center of table. The length of each row depends on the room size and attendance.

The table should be draped. Place pads and pencils at each setting, plus water pitchers for every sixteen persons. Either put a glass at each setting or provide a tray with ten or twelve glasses for every sixteen persons. Provide one ashtray for evey six persons, or even fewer.

A variation is *schoolroom, perpendicular style* (fig. 13.6). In this arrangement, the rows of tables are perpendicular to the speaker's table. Thirty-inch-deep tables are used because people will be seated on both sides. It is necessary to allow additional room for each person because the seats must be turned somewhat to face the speaker. Allow thirty inches of table space per person instead of twenty-four for the wider table and fifty-four inches from center of table to center of table. Tables should be six feet from the head table, with six-foot aisles on both sides of the room and a four-foot horizontal aisle in the center.

Schoolroom setups may also be V *shape*, off a center aisle (fig. 13.6).

U Shape

Smaller meetings prefer to set up in a more face-to-face arrangement. The U *shape* is popular (fig. 13.8). Use thirty-inch rectangular tables if people will be seated on both sides; use eighteen-inch-deep tables if only the outer sides will be used.

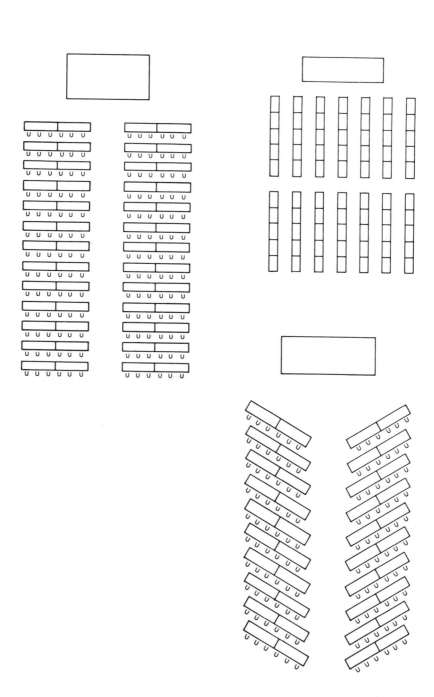

Fig. 13.6 The schoolroom style arrangement, with variations. (Reprinted with permission from *Function Room Set-Up Manual*).

306

The usual per-person table allowance is twenty-four inches, but training and technical groups may need more space for material so often specify thirty-inch tables. Drape the front part of the U all the way to the floor. When the tables are draped, make sure the crease is straight and that it runs continuously along the center of the table.

Horseshoe

The *horseshoe* is just like the U shape except the head table is connected to both legs with serpentine section to soften the corners (fig. 13.9).

Hollow Square and Hollow Circular

The *hollow square* and *hollow circular* arrangements are preferred by meeting planners who want to do away with the head table concept (fig. 13.10). They are

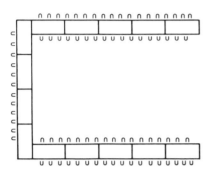

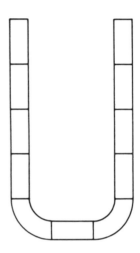

formed like the U shape or the horseshoe except that the open end is filled in. Naturally, chairs are placed only on the outside. The hollow square and the hollow circular are popular for small meetings.

Variations

The *E shape* is a variation of the U shape (fig. 13.11). You need about four feet between the backs of the chairs to facilitate traffic. The *T shape* (fig. 13.11) has a head table thirty inches deep. A single leg extends from the center of the head table for as long as needed. The leg is often set with double tables to make a sixty-inch solid rectangular unit.

Board of Directors

The *board of directors* is a popular arrangement for small meetings. It calls for a single column of double tables making a draped table of sixty inches by as long as necessary (fig. 13.12). Allow twenty-four inches of table space per person. The board of directors arrangement is so popular that many convention hotels have permanent setups with fine wooden tables and deluxe executive-type chairs. Suites equipped with such permanent fixtures are versatile small meeting rooms.

The *board of directors, oval* setup is simply the board setup with a sixty-inch half-round table at each end of the long table (fig. 13.12). Chairs may be set at the curved end.

Fig. 13.10 The hollow square and hollow circular arrangements, for groups that do not want a head table concept. (Reprinted with permission from *Function Room Set-Up Manual*).

Fig. 13.11 The E shape and T shape arrangements are variations preferred by some groups. (Reprinted with permission from *Function Room Set-Up Manual*).

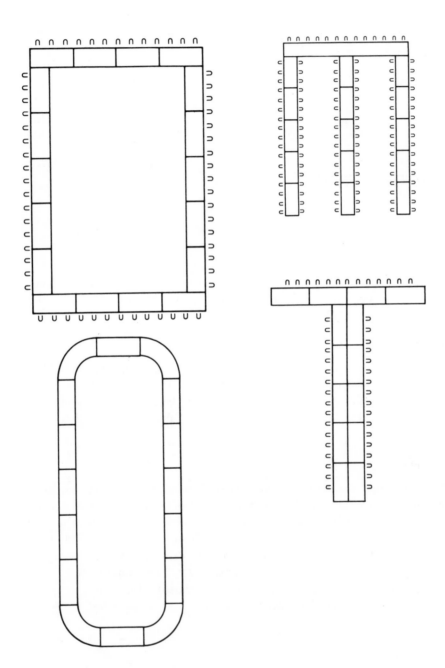

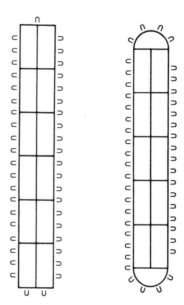

Fig. 13.12 The popular board of directors seating arrangement, and the oval variation. (Reprinted with permission from *Function Room Set-Up Manual*).

Round Tables

Round tables (fig. 13.13 and 13.14) can be used when meetings break up into smaller discussion groups without leaving the room. Round tables are also used most often for food functions.

The most popular is the five-foot table, which seats eight to ten. Use the design in the carpet or lines in the floor to align the tables in neat rows. Allow at least nine feet from center of table to center of table.

Waiters need about twenty-four inches between chairs and walls. Chairs should be placed near the tables and positioned after the waiters have set the tables. The front edge of the chair should just touch the tablecloth. After the function, stacking the chairs immediately facilitates cleanup and breakdown.

Circular Buffet Table

The *circular buffet table,* most useful at food *functions,* is made by using four serpentines and four thirty-inch deep four-footers (fig. 13.15). This makes up a twenty-by-twenty-foot buffet table. A round center table can be used for flowers or a display. Tier arrangements can be made with risers.

310

Fig. 13.13 Round tables can be used for food functions and for meetings that break up into smaller discussion groups. (Reprinted with permission from *Function Room Set-Up Manual*).

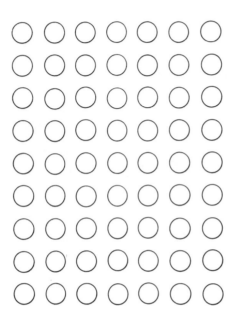

Many variations can be made by using tables of various shapes. You are limited only by imagination, time, and space. If you design one you particularly like, draw a schematic of it. You can show this to a prospective client and use it for future reference.

Setup Time

As we said earlier, it is very important to know exactly how long it takes a crew to set up each room under the many seating arrangements. Many a meeting program has failed because those planning it did not take into account the time it takes to set up and break down. The hotel person who overlooks this basic requirement is surely an amateur. The hotel staff should also make the meeting planner aware of

Fig. 13.15 The circular buffet table arrangement and variations. (Reprinted with permission from *Function Room Set-up Manual*).

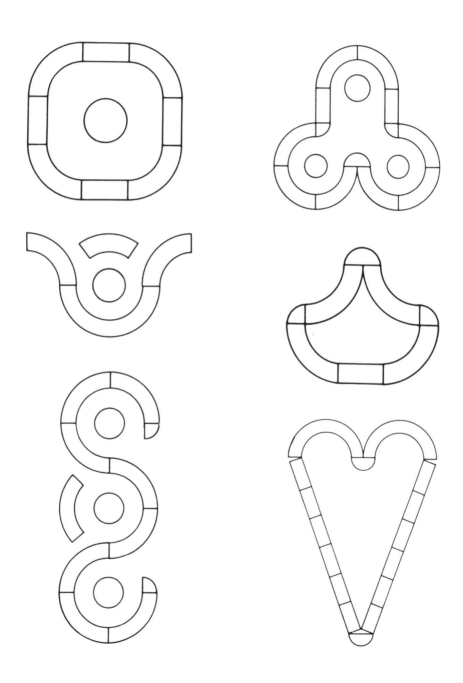

such a timetable so that he or she can take it into consideration when the program is mapped out. We strongly recommend that convention service managers have charts made up indicating such labor requirements.

These charts should list the time it takes to set up each room for maximum capacity under each seating arrangement. They should also give the time it takes to break them down, plus union regulations regarding workday, hours, overtime charges, and any unusual contract characteristics that may affect costs and time. Specify the number of people needed. Time may be saved by using a larger crew but this will cost more, of course. Sometimes a meeting planner might choose such an option.

Breakdown of Function Rooms

After a meeting or party is completed, housemen should break down the room and clean it. The reason for this is obvious. Business could be lost, or a poor impression given, if a prospective customer saw an untidy meeting room while walking through the convention area.

Chairs and tables need to be stacked. Function chairs probably receive more damage than any other furnishings in a hotel. Housemen who display more speed than caution in setup and dismantling should be instructed to avoid such carelessness.

If the meeting room isn't scheduled for immediate use, tables and chairs may need to be stored. Storage is a common headache in convention servicing. Hotels often do not allot adequate and accessible storage space for function room equipment. Space that is too small or is difficult to maneuver in shortens the life of the equipment. Furniture that is "forced" into storage is often damaged.

Some properties keep formal control over the location and storage of their equipment. In large convention hotels where the volume justifies it, a requisition system is used for issuing equipment and supplies. An inventory is taken periodically and all articles are locked up when not in use.

Rules of Thumb

Three rules of thumb are used as general guides to estimate seating capacity in various types of meeting arrangements.

1. *Auditorium style seating*—divide the conferee seating area (square feet) by six.

2. *Schoolroom style seating*—divide conferee seating area (square feet) by eight. (These two methods are useful for a quick, general forecast of seating requirements. Allowance is made for standard chair distance and aisle passage; if wide traffic aisles are desired, add one square foot per person.)

3. *Banquet style seating*—round tables: divide the room area (square feet) by ten; oblong tables: divide the room area (square feet) by ten.

   (The figures used for these banquet setups are for maximum seating. You should add two square feet per person if more space is desired. The type of table service will also influence these figures. Less area might be used for buffet or cafeteria-style seating than for formal dinners.)

Study Questions

1. "All public space may be function area depending on the group and its needs." Assess this statement and list the most common types of function rooms. What are break-out rooms?

2. How would you determine what to charge for meeting space?

3. What is "function room furniture"?

4. Distinguish between a schoolroom setup and an auditorium arrangement. Sketch each of the setups discussed and specify dimensions of each.

5. State the rules of thumb for auditorium, schoolroom, and banquet style seating capacities.

Outline

I. Food Service

    A. Types of Food Functions
    B. Attendance
    C. Function Room
    D. Charges
    E. Staffing

II. Beverage Service

    A. Types of Setups
    B. Pricing Methods
       1. By the Hour
       2. By the Bottle
       3. By the Drink
    C. Hospitality Suites
    D. Brands
    E. Beverage Control
       1. Host Bar Control
       2. Cash Bar Control
       3. Coupon Sales Control
       4. Automated Bars

III. Post-Function Actions

IV. In-House Coordination: Large vs. Small

    A. Role of the Catering Manager
    B. Servicing and Selling
    C. Communication and Cooperation Needed

V. Food and Beverage Service: The Process

14

Food Service

Food and beverage functions play an important part in convention programs. The kinds of functions can vary greatly, from a hospitality suite serving soft drinks and liquor, plus some peanuts and pretzels, to a full-scale banquet. But all food functions are important, and they represent another area where close communication and cooperation are needed.

Many convention planners prefer to complete all negotiations in detail before signing the letter of agreement. Some even want to go so far as to select menus and agree on prices. You can easily understand why a convention planner would prefer this because it makes budget projections so much easier. But with many conventions planned several years in advance, it is not possible for a hotel to make such accurate quotations.

Most hotels will gladly say what they charge for menus currently in use, feeling that this is a sufficient guide for meeting planners. There is obvious danger in pricing a menu so far in advance. Most meeting planners with any experience at all realize that any such agreements may have to be modified because of rising costs. If you examine the dollar values of the past fifty years, you see constant inflation. When the spiral goes up sharply, everyone recognizes the inflation, but in reality, there has a been a steady curve upward over the years.

You must be very careful when you have to make price guarantees for dates several years ahead. Most hotels have adopted a policy of quoting room rates not more than two years in advance and firm menu prices not more than six months before the event.

You cannot avoid such a policy unless you have no need to be competitive and can build in a fat reserve in your quotations. But few of us, if any, have such prerogatives. To be competitive, you figure prices closely and cannot absorb inflationary additions to costs.

You will find some exceptions, but most meeting planners understand such limitations and are concerned about unduly squeezing a hotel. After all, each event is a custom production and the planners are concerned with the quality of what they will receive. If they *are* obliged to set an early price on tickets, they understand that a flexible attitude on the menu can enable them to carry out the meal function while allowing the hotel a fair profit.

All agreements on menus, prices, and terms must be made in writing and signed by both parties. This avoids all sorts of misunderstandings.

Types of Food Functions

Meetings may call for breakfasts, luncheons, dinners, dinners with entertainment and/or dancing, coffee breaks, bars, receptions, buffets, and continuous hospitality setups in suites, meeting rooms, or exhibit halls. Each function should be dealt with separately to make sure of all details. As we stressed in chapter 12, a function sheet (fig. 12.3) should be filled out for each event, listing all the information needed for smooth execution.

Group menus come in a variety of forms and sizes. For convenience, we recommend a small bound booklet such as the one in figure 14.1 containing the Dunes Hotel's convention and group banquet menus. The Dunes booklet gives both sit-down and buffet suggestions for breakfast, lunch, and dinner. Note that each selection is identified by number, which makes for easier communication.

Two other types of food functions held in conjunction with beverage service are coffee breaks and cocktail receptions with hors d'oeuvres. Coffee breaks ideally should be set up in a room adjacent to the meeting room. If this is not possible, the coffee and other items should be carted outside of the meeting room and served when the person in charge of the group gives the signal for the waiters to enter.

The cocktail reception with hors d'oeuvres is often mishandled. This function is supposed to create a carnival atmosphere that will carry over to the dinner. It also gets the dinner guests together so you can start to serve the dinner on schedule. Suggest a one-hour maximum for such events to the meeting planner.

Two basic methods are used in charging for hors d'oeuvres and finger food: by the person per hour and by the bowl or tray. Figure 14.2 shows these two methods as used at the Dunes.

In chapter 12 we discussed the use of theme meetings by many associations. In such cases, meeting planners often request special menus, decorations, costumes, and entertainment to carry out the theme. The focal point of any such function is the menu. Hotels that have theme or ethnic banquet suggestions are a step ahead. Likewise, the property that has a store of props, costumes, or centerpieces has a better chance of landing the party business. In presenting theme menus, be honest about your capabilities and suggest what you do best. It is better to refuse a request than to fail with a theme your staff is unable to handle.

Attendance

The meeting planner initially will estimate attendance at a food function. This is important because it permits you to see the scope of the event. This figure is only for preliminary preparations, however, and must be re-examined later.

317

Fig. 14.1 Group menus used by the Dunes Hotel in Las Vegas. (By permission of the Dunes Hotel).

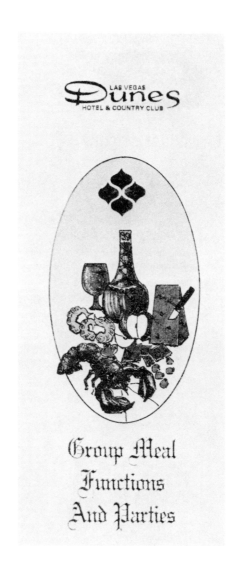

Breakfast Menus

No. 1 — $4.90 per person

Fresh squeezed Orange Juice
Scrambled Eggs · Bacon
Hashed Brown Potatoes
Sweet & Hard Rolls · Toast
Marmelade · Jam · Butter
Coffee

• • • • • •

No. 2 — $5.35 per person

Half Grapefruit Maraschino
Ham Omelette
Marmelade · Butter
Sweet & Hard Rolls
Coffee

• • • • • •

No. 3 — $5.45 per person

Fresh Orange Juice
Scrambled Eggs with Ham & Sausage
Hashed Brown Potatoes
Hard Breakfast Rolls
Small Danish Pastries
Jam · Butter
Coffee

• • • • • •

No. 4 — $6.50 per person
(Buffet Breakfast)

Assorted Juices
(Tomato, Orange, Prune, Grapefruit)
Assorted Compote of Fruits
Fresh Scrambled Eggs
Ham · Sausage · Bacon
Hashed Brown Potatoes
Jam · Marmelade · Butter
Assorted Rolls · Small Danish Pastries
Coffee

• • • • • •

Luncheon Menus

CHOICE OF ONE . . . .

Tomato Juice, Fruit Cocktail
Soup du Jour
Tossed Green Salad
(Oil & Vinegar; or Thousand Island Dressing)

• • • • • •

No. 1 — $7.60 per person

Assorted Sea Food in Patty Shell Newburg
Fresh Garden Green Peas
Ice Cream Cake
Rolls & Butter
Coffee

• • • • • •

No. 2 — $6.50 per person

Chicken A La King on Patty Shell
Garden Green Peas in Butter
Strawberry Ice Cream Cake
Rolls & Butter
Coffee

• • • • •

No. 3 — $6.55 per person

Half Broiled Chicken
Rissolées Potatoes
Buttered String Beans
Frozen Chocolate Eclair
Butter & Rolls
Coffee

• • • • • •

No. 4 — $7.50 per person

Half Chicken Saute a Sec
Mushroom Sauce
Rizotto a l'Italienne
Buttered Green Peas
Profiterolles Au Chocolat
Rolls & Butter
Coffee

Buffet Menus

(Minimum 40 Persons)

No. 10 — $10.25 per person
Chicken Saute A Sec
Stuffed Cabbages
Rice Pilaff
Buttered Peas
Cold Sliced Ham
Cold Sliced Turkey
Sliced Imported Salami
Seafood Salad
Potato Salad
Sliced Tomatoes
Mixed Green Salad
Bowl of Assorted Relishes
Fruit Jello
Domestic Cheese and Crackers
Assorted Layer Cakes
Coffee · Rolls & Butter

* * * * * *

No. 11 — $12.25 per person
Ballotine of Capon Chasseur
Seafood Newburg
Baked Rice
Buttered Peas
Mixed Green Salad
Sliced Tomatoes
Cole Slaw
Potato Salad
Bowl of Assorted Relishes
Stuffed Eggs
Imported Sardines
Cold Sliced Turkey
Cold Sliced Ham
Cold Sliced Tongue
Sliced Imported Salami
Macedoine of Fresh Fruit
Fruit Jello
Assorted Layer Cakes
Domestic Cheese and Crackers
Coffee · French Rolls & Butter

Dinner Menus

CHOICE OF ONE. . . . .
Tomato Juice, Fruit Cocktail
Soup du Jour
Tossed Green Salad
(Oil & Vinegar; or Thousand Island Dressing)

* * * * * *

No. 1 — $9.40 per person
Baked Sugar Cured Ham · Raisin Sauce
Creamed Spinach Au Gratin
(In Individual Dishes)
Parsley Potatoes
French Rolls & Butter
Coffee

* * * * * *

No. 2 — $9.40 per person
Roast Tom Turkey
(Savory Dressing Giblet Sauce)
Broccoli Mornay
Candied Yams
French Rolls & Butter
Coffee

* * * * * *

No. 3 — $11.25 per person
Breast of Cornish Game Hen
Stuffed with Wild Rice Veronique
String Beans Sautés Au Beurre
French Rolls & Butter
Coffee

* * * * * *

No. 4 — $10.75 per person
Breast of Capon on Virginia Ham Eugenie
Corn Fritters
Baby Carrots Aux Fines Herbes
Rolls & Butter
Coffee · Tea · Milk

320

Canapes and Hors d'Oeuvre

No. 1 — $6.50 per person

Hot

Grilled Cocktail Franks - Mustard Sauce
Swedish Savory Meatballs
Knishes
Chinese Egg Rolls
Butterfly Shrimps, Cocktail Sauce

Cold

Canapes
Savory Cheese Spread, Pimento
Cornets of Imported Genoa Salami
Smoked Nova Scotia Salmon
Deviled Eggs with Anchovies

No. 5

Cold Canapes . . Large Tray . . **$68.50**
(Serves approximately 25 persons)
Medium Tray . . **$46.00**
(Serves approximately 15 persons)
Selection: A Variety of Assorted Cold
Canapes Including
Stuffed Eggs Moscovite

. . . .

The convention planner owes it to the facility to keep it informed of the closest possible estimates of attendance at each food event. The planner may not know much more than before, but a time will be set by which a firm guarantee must be given in order to prepare for the event.

All properties doing banquet business face the problem of determining a fair and workable guarantee policy. Naturally, no one policy is applicable for all hotels or all situations. However, the Hotel Sales Marketing Association surveyed a sample of hotels a number of years ago and found that most adhere strictly to their guarantee policies. Those surveyed stressed the importance of fully explaining the guarantee and working with the meeting planner to set a realistic attendance figure.

Most hotels will accept a guarantee only forty-eight hours before a food function. The meeting planner than agrees to pay for the guaranteed number of people whether or not that many appear. If 200 people are guaranteed for luncheon at a per-head charge and only 185 show up, the organization will pay for all 200. It is unfortunate that this has become a touchy situation. It is not uncommon for some compromise to be reached, but the obligation is clear-cut.

What happens when more show up? The experienced meeting planner will ask that places be set for more than the guaranteed number. A safety margin of 10 percent is common, although we know of hotels that will set only an additional 5 percent.

Often the guarantee is included in the function sheet and is signed by both the hotel and a convention representative. Any agreement between the hotel and client is binding. Usually the guarantee is made twenty-four hours in advance and places are set for an extra 10 percent. If the guarantee calls for 200, the hotel sets tables and chairs for 220. If 210 show up, all is in readiness and the bill indicates 210. If 230 show up, the hotel is allowed to substitute ten meals of a quickly prepared item.

Be careful about other circumstances that may affect the timing of the guarantee. The hotel may require a greater lead time before a weekend or holiday because a full staff may not be working then. And kitchen purchases and preparations may not be possible, or only on an overtime basis.

Another guarantee method suggested by meeting planners, but seldom used, is to guarantee only labor. If only 185 of the guaranteed 200 showed up, the association would pay for only the cost of one waiter and not the extra fifteen meals prepared. Obviously a hotel should never consent to this unless the extra meals can be used somewhere else.

There should be some clear understanding, in writing, about who in the organization is authorized to make changes in attendance estimates, guarantees, menus, and prices.

Function Room

The type of function room to be used for a food event depends on the nature of the session, its location in relation to other functions and the hotel traffic flow, and the kind of seating arrangement desired. Pay attention, too, to the decor, lighting, and other decoration requested. And thought must be given to heating and cooling controls.

All these factors must be considered when the convention service manager sits down with his or her counterpart in the convention organization to select a room for the function. Priorities may dictate that the most suitable room go to another event, but any room used for a food function should be able to provide satisfactory results.

A reminder is in order here to note the time it takes to set up the food function room and to clean it up afterwards. It is important to know whether the cleanup noises will disturb the meeting session going on next door. It may not be possible to avoid such proximity, but it shouldn't come about because no one thought about it. The clash of silver and china can be most distracting at a serious meeting and can reflect on the hotel's image.

We remember when the Salvation Army had a meeting scheduled next door to a luncheon for the governor of Hawaii. As the governor was presenting his opening remarks, the Salvation Army opened its meeting in the traditional way with a song, to the resounding beat of the bass drum. Needless to say, the hotel's convention service manager gave greater consideration to a group's program after this incident.

Charges

Most food functions are charged on a per-head basis. Every hotel should devise a head-count procedure to determine the actual number of covers (meals) served. Guesswork has no place in banquet billing. The charges should be agreed to in writing, and the menu selection should be indicated.

Many meeting planners prefer to use coupons or tickets. The delegate at registration time is issued a coupon book with tear-out tickets for each group function. Caution must be used if the meeting planner suggests this system. There are two common methods of ticket collection.

1. *At the door*. A table should be set up, with a representative from the association and one from the hotel there to collect tickets.
2. *At the banquet table*. In this case, the waiter collects the tickets. This can be a touchy area if delegates do not have their tickets. A common delegate response is, "I left the ticket in my room." This is a difficult situation to police; if the hotel is paid for only the tickets collected, the waiter is forced to refuse service. Hotel personnel should be instructed what to do if a conferee shows up without the proper ticket.

Counting the dishes expected to be used in advance is another method of determining the number of covers served. The chef or convention service manager then counts the number of dishes that were not used and subtracts this from the first figure. Still another, and perhaps the best, system is to actually count the people seated. The convention service manager and the meeting planner should both take counts. This should be done immediately after the entree has been served.

Some food functions, such as coffee breaks and hospitality centers, obviously cannot be charged in this way. Whatever the formula is, spell it out clearly. You may charge for coffee by the cup or by the gallon, fruit juice by the gallon, Danish pastry or sweet rolls by the piece or by the tray.

Some canny sales managers will give away hors d'oeuvres, favors, or cigars and cigarettes in such cases if it enables them to close the deal at higher rates for rooms or meals. Psychologically, the practice may make for a better presentation, and economically, it may represent less than the price advantage. In addition, the higher rate will bring in a further dividend should more people attend. The buffet and hors d'oeuvres are fixed costs on your part, while the higher rate for additional guests adds to your profit.

Small food functions are often tagged with additional charges. If the function is not large enough to cover labor and setup costs, hotels frequently add on to the bill. Figure 14.3 is an example of banquet labor and miscellaneous charges.

Staffing

Hotels generally provide more waiters per guest as the price per cover increases. The average is one waiter per twenty guests, but the ratio may go as low as one to twelve if the price and service warrant it. For large parties there should be one captain for every 150 guests.

Premeal briefings should be conducted by the captains for all large banquets. Menus, special service requirements, station assignments, and other pertinent items should be reviewed. The setup and service of the head table should be assigned to the captains. Special attention is paid to silverware, glasses, and proper arrangement of place settings.

Finally, the times for putting the food on the plate and serving must be carefully controlled. It is necessary to adhere closely to scheduled meal times, so extension of cocktail parties should be kept to a minimum.

Beverage Service

More discontent has been voiced over beverage service and charges than over most factors of a convention. Much of this is due to unfamiliarity with pricing policy and the inability of inexperienced meeting planners to estimate the amount of liquor needed.

Fig. 14.3 Hotels frequently add on to the bill if the food function is not large enough to cover labor and setup costs. (By permission of the Las Vegas Hilton).

Banquet Labor and Miscellaneous Charges

I. Food

A. *WAITER LABOR CHARGE* 15.00
   (All functions with less than 20 guests)

B. *OVERTIME CHARGE*
   FOR WAITER 4.50/hour
   Breakfast over 2 hours
   Lunch over 3 hours
   Dinner over 4 hours

C. *SERVICE CHARGE* . . . . 5.00/extra table
   For setting less than 10 covers per table

D. *CARVER (CHEF)* 15.00/hour
   After two hours

E. *HOUSEMEN* 4.50/hour
   4 hours minimum

F. *EARLY SETUP OF BANQUET*
   ROOMS . . . . 4.50/hour per waiter
   Prior to meal functions

G. *PORTER* . . . . 40.00/8 hours
   (If no food functions and meeting room complimentary)

II. Beverage

A. *BARTENDER CHARGE –*
   If less than $150 sales, labor charge . . . 35.00

B. *BAR SUPPLIES – If group supplies liquor*
   Cocktail Napkins
   Stir Sticks 50/person
   Assorted Bar Fruit
   Mix – Sodas 1.25/quart
   Bloody Mary Mix, Orange Juice
   and Sweet & Sour 4.00/quart
   Blenders 5.00/each

C. *EXTRA BARTENDER CHARGE* 7.50/hour
   4 hours minimum

D. *EXTRA BARBOY CHARGE* . . . 37.00/8 hours
   8 hours minimum

Unfortunately, meeting planners or the hosts at hospitality suites usually specify their favorite brands of liquor, and they are familiar with package store prices. Many planners and hosts resent what they consider to be unfair markups on name-brand liquor by the hotel. Some hotels have taken to charging the same prices as local liquor stores; other have a much higher rate—two or three times the cost. This is a management decision. The additional revenue gained by marking up must be weighed against the frequent ill will engendered.

Of all the price policies at a convention, the liquor arrangement brings the loudest and most frequent outcry.

Types of Setups

A number of beverage arrangements are used in catering to private parties. We will discuss the four most common procedures specified by meeting planners.

The first and most typical type of bar is the *host bar,* where the guests are free to drink the beverages and the host pays the bill at the end of the function. Also called an *open bar,* this is most frequently used by corporate meeting planners. This type of bar is stocked to prepare all types of drinks and is manned by a bartender. A purchase amount is almost always guaranteed. If, for example, at least $150 worth of beverage is not consumed, the host will pay for what was consumed, plus an additional amount to cover labor. Figure 14.3 shows typical labor costs for beverage service.

The second most common arrangement is the *cash bar,* also called the *C.O.D. bar* and a *no-host bar.* Each person pays for his or her own drinks. A minimum guarantee is also specified by the hotel in this case.

Coupon sales are used at many private parties. Delegates buy tickets or coupons ahead of time and give them to the bartender when the drinks are served. The coupons may be sold by the hotel management or the host organization. Coupon sales eliminate the use of cash at the bar and the need for a cashier there.

Stanley Stearman, executive vice-president of the National Society of Public Accountants, said of the use of coupons for beverage functions:

> We give everyone two drink tickets along with their banquet ticket. They are actually perforated stubs which are turned into the bartender in return for drinks. Not only does this method limit consumption to two drinks per person, but it also gives me control over my liquor costs. I pay a certain amount for each stub which has been turned in. The only disadvantage to me is that I have to pay full price even if someone redeems his stub for a soft drink.[1]

The South Coast Plaza in Costa Mesa, California, uses still a different method in servicing private parties. The *captain's bar* is a self-service or make-your-own-drink bar, which has been stocked with full bottles of the liquor and mixes needed to make all basic bar drinks. This bar is always hosted. The meeting planner and the convention service manager inventory the bar before and after the party, and the association is charged for how much is consumed. There is no guarantee on this type of setup because there is no bartender labor cost.

Pricing Methods

Liquor charges can be figured by the hour, by the bottle, or by the individual drink. Whichever is used, make sure that someone on the convention staff has been designated to tally up after the affair with a designated member of the hotel staff.

1. Bob Skalnik, "Liquor Control," *Association and Society Manager.* Copyright by Barrington Publications, Inc., 825 S. Barrington Ave., Los Angeles, Calif. 90049.

Meeting planners often ask advice on how much liquor will be needed. The chart in figure 14.4 should prove helpful to you and your customers in making such estimations.

By the Hour

When liquor is priced *by the hour,* a flat rate is charged for each person present during a specified period of time. Sometimes a flat rate is charged for a cocktail party of a specified time period, and additional time is charged on an hourly basis. At other times the rate is given only as an hourly charge. If food is to be served, what kind and how much must be discussed and listed in the agreement.

If your hourly charge is based also on the number in attendance, you will need a way to determine the accuracy of the count. Collecting tickets or invitations at the door is one way to do this.

Extension of the time period and the admission of people who do not have tickets require approval by an authorized person. The head count and the time period should be acknowledged immediately after the event by having the authorized person initial the tally.

By the Bottle

The convention organizer may prefer to pay *by the bottle* consumed. This system calls for charges on all bottles opened, regardless of how much of the contents is consumed. Some hotels permit the host to keep the opened bottles; others do not. Obviously the bartender must be aware of the arrangement, and it must be made part of the work order for the beverage event.

Sometimes the charges for the bartender are part of the per-bottle price. If so, it should be indicated in the work order/agreement; if not, the rates and hours should be.

The by-the-bottle system is very popular for hospitality suites, both with and without bartenders.

Make sure that the liquor supply given is stored securely. Good hotel people assist their guests in arranging this. It is also imperative that both the hotel and the convention organization have people designated to tally and record the number of bottles used and returned for credit.

Food may be served and charged separately. And under certain conditions, there may be a room charge. Much depends on the anticipated volume and the basic agreement under which the event takes place.

Fig. 14.4 Guide to help estimate the amount of liquor and service needed. (Reprinted with permission from *The Schenley Guide to Professional Hosting*, published by Schenley Affiliated Brands Corp.).

Figure 14.4
Reception Drink* and Service Estimator

*Based on all-male attendance and easy access to bars. With 50 percent female attendance, average is 2 1/2-3 per hour; with 100 percent female attendance, average is 2-2 1/2 per hour

Number of guests	½ hour	¾ hour	One hour	1¼ hours	1½ hours	1¾ hours	Two hours
25-55	2	3	3¾	4	4¼	4½	4¾
60-104	2	3	3¾	4	4	4½	4¾
105-225	1¾	2½	3	3½	4	4	4½
230-300	1½	2	2½	2¾	3	3¼	3½
315 & up	1½	2	2½	2¾	3	3¼	3½

RECEPTION SERVICE ESTIMATOR

Number of guests	Number of bartenders	Number of waiters with food	Number of waiters without food
25-100	1	2	1
105-205	2	3	2
215-325	3	3	2
350-475	4	4	3

DRINK ESTIMATOR

Bottle size	Drink size	Number of drinks
4/5 Qt.	1 oz.	25
4/5 Qt.	1¼ oz.	20
4/5 Qt.	1½ oz.	17
Quart	1 oz.	31
Quart	1¼ oz.	25
Quart	1½ oz.	21

By the Drink

Charges can also be made *by the drink* on the basis of the individual drinks served. There should be agreement on the size of drink to be poured, and the bartenders so instructed. These rates include the mandatory use of bartender service.

This arrangement is used by many meeting planners. The chart in figure 14.4 is helpful if estimates are requested, but be sure to point out that these are only *estimates*.

The guests may pay for drinks in cash or with prepaid coupons, or the host may pay for the entire session.

Food charges again are a separate item, and there may be a room charge. Don't forget to give advance notice of gratuities, taxes and a clear schedule of bartender's work regulations.

Hospitality Suites

Many exhibitors sell their wares at the end of the day in hospitality suites and use complimentary beverages as an inducement to draw prospects. Hospitality suites are also hosted by meeting planners as a way to build good will.

Many meeting planners and exhibitors avoid what they consider to be excessive prices charged by the hotel by bringing in liquor purchased outside the hotel. They then order mixers, ice, and glasses from room service. Hotels have varying policies regarding such action. Some hotels have a *corkage* charge to cover the use of liquor that is purchased elsewhere. Some have two sets of prices for the setups— a higher rate if the order is not accompanied by liquor orders; a lower rate if it is. It eliminates many arguments if the policy is clearly spelled out to the meeting planner and the guests.

Union regulations often dictate the circumstances under which a bartender must be employed. Tell your client in advance about such regulations. Explain the hours involved, overtime charges, and the like. Also spell out the circumstances under which no such help is required. The choice under such conditions should be the customer's. Don't forget to include information about gratuities and taxes.

Brands

Most hotels offer a selection of standard brands to the meeting planner. Upon request, special brands may be used. This depends on suitable notice and the agreement of the hotel. When the hotel uses house brands, there should be clear notification. Sometimes there is a different price for house brands than for standard brands; sometimes the prices are the same.

Beverage Control

Formal and rigid procedures for issuing liquor and the use of it should be maintained. The banquet department is generally responsible for issuing the liquor.

Since it is impossible to judge how much or what kind of liquor will be preferred, it is customary to stock 25 percent over what the group is estimated to consume. This policy eliminates shortages, but it must be controlled.

The excess must be returned to the storeroom at the end of the function. Special banquet requisition forms are used for private parties, showing all the bottles issued, consumed, and returned. Immediately after each function all bottles—full, empty, and partially used—should be accounted for.

The Ramada Renaissance Hotel uses the requisition form shown in figure 14.5. The banquet manager uses this form for each function, showing the number of bottles originally issued, any additional issues, and all returns. Each bottle issued is marked with a distinctive means of identification. At the end of the party, the banquet manager totals the requisition by determining the amount of each item consumed and its price and then making the appropriate extensions. This total is transferred to the banquet guest check, which is verified and signed by the meeting planner. A percentage of the check total is usually added to the bill as a gratuity for the staff.

Host Bar Control

Because cash is not taken with host or open bars, they are the easiest to control. Opened bottles of liquor may either be returned to the storeroom for credit or bought by the meeting planner. If the meeting planner takes the opened bottles, this should be noted on the requisition sheet, along with the name of the guest. Some groups buy the cracked bottles but prefer that the hotel hold the bottles in storage for them. Such bottles should be clearly marked.

Cash Bar Control

This arrangement requires the most rigid controls. A bartender should not be allowed to take cash, as he would then be controlling both cash receipts and the issuing of liquor. A less-than-honest bartender could pour smaller than average drinks and pocket the cash on every fourth or fifth drink without being detected.

Cash bars thus necessitate at least two employees, a bartender and a cashier. At the end of the party, cash sales should be equated with the potential sales for the amount of merchandise consumed.

Coupon Sales Control

A cashier is not necessary if the meeting planner issues tickets prior to the event. The bartenders collect tickets for the drinks and turn them over to the banquet

330

Fig. 14.5 Bar requisition form shows number of bottles issued, consumed, and returned. The "budget function" refers to the price quoted to the group. (By permission of the Ramada Renaissance Hotel San Francisco).

RAMADA RENAISSANCE HOTEL SAN FRANCISCO

BANQUET WINE/LIQUOR REQUISITION

NO. 001399

DATE 8-25-87	DAY OF WEEK MONDAY		TIME 6:00 PM
FUNCTION RECEPTION		ROOM FOYER / Renaissance Ballroom	
ORGANIZATION NAME SINGER		BANQUET CHECK # 06272	
BANQUET EVENT ORDER # 02135		TENDERS IN CHARGE Bill / Cheryle	
CLIENT'S ACCOUNT # 12948			
NUMBER OF GUESTS 275			

MANNER OF SALE: ☒ BY DRINK ☐ BY BOTTLE ☐ BY HOUR

TYPE OF BEVERAGE: ☐ PREMIUM ☒ HOUSE ☐ SPECIAL LIST

TYPE OF SALE: ☒ HOSTED ☐ CASH BAR

COST

CODE	DESCRIPTION	ISSUED QUANT.	SIZE	RETD BOTT	USED BOTT	NO. DRINKS	DRINK PRICE	TOTAL	LIQUOR	WINE	MISC	% POT
	HOUSE BOURBON	3		1.7	1.3	43	3⁰⁰	$129.⁰⁰	8.³⁰			6.5%
	HOUSE SCOTCH	3		1.9	1.1							
	HOUSE GIN	4		2.4	1.6							
	HOUSE VODKA	4		1.1	29							
	HOUSE BRANDY	2		1.8	.2							
	HOUSE RUM	2		1.6	.4							
	HOUSE TEQUILA	2		1.3	.7							
	HOUSE WHISKEY	2		1.8	.2							
	HOUSE WHITE WINE	18		2	16							
	HOUSE RED WINE	6		3	3							
	MILLER LITE BEER	24		5	19							
	HEINEKEN BEER											
	PREMIUM BOURBON											
	PREMIUM SCOTCH											
	PREMIUM GIN											
	PREMIUM VODKA											
	PREMIUM BRANDY											
	PREMIUM WHISKEY											
	PREMIUM TEQUILA											
	PREMIUM RUM											
	TOTALS											

ISSUED BY _____ RETURNED BY _____ APPROVED BY _____

RECEIVED BY _____ RECEIVED BY _____

WHITE - FOOD AND BEVERAGE CONTROL   CANARY - BANQUET MAITRE D'   GOLDEN ROD - BEVERAGE MGR.

manager. The manager, in turn, inventories the bar before and after the function and compares the consumption of liquor with the tickets collected.

If tickets are to be sold at the party, a cashier will be needed, and cash banks must be issued. The banquet manager should issue numbered tickets to the cashier and get them back, along with the cash box, when the function is completed. He can then verify the number of tickets issued with the cash receipts.

Automated Bars

Several hotels are making use of metered bar systems. A long-standing complaint of meeting planners is the tendency of bartenders to over-pour in host bar setups. They feel the staff members are encouraged to pour on the heavy side because their tips are figured as a percentage of sales. Another problem area is the counting and storing of opened bottles. Both of these problems are eliminated with automated bars.

Automated bars operate much like soda bars, with individual push buttons for each liquor item—vodka, gin, bourbon, scotch, rye, etc. Quart bottles are placed upside down in the wells and dispensed by a vacuum system. Each bottle has its own dispensing unit and meter. The size of drink is determined by the meeting planner, and the dispensing unit is set accordingly. The meters are checked and recorded before and after the party, with the difference being the amount consumed.

The control feature offered by metered bars is what makes them attractive to both the meeting planner and the hotel. They provide a consistent drink and eliminate over-pouring, but they are not without their limitations. The machine dispenses only the alcohol; mixed or blended drinks still must be prepared by a bartender. And only eight bottles can be filled on most units, limiting the choice of drinks. Some observers also say that metered bars are impersonal, lending a mechanical atmosphere to cocktail parties.

Post-Function Actions

Prompt action must be taken at the end of each food function to eliminate possible billing difficulties and to bring each function segment to a satisfactory close.

If billing is based on attendance, the captain in charge should tally the number of persons served or the number of tickets collected and have the authorized convention person sign an acknowledgment of the total. Make sure that the person signing is the person designated in writing by the convention organization.

If beverages were served, tally the unopened bottles of liquor and/or soft drinks and have the amount acknowledged by signature. Any bottles to be returned for credit must be signed for as well.

Most convention groups use a master billing account for the food functions. If the terms are cash, the money or check should be presented when the tally is certified as correct. If cash is collected by the organization, the hotel should provide a safe place for it or accept it in payment and give a suitable receipt.

A summary of the food function should be added to the file folder for later analysis of the entire convention.

In-House Coordination: Large vs. Small

Throughout Part II we have continually referred to the convention service manager as the person who coordinates the convention. We don't want to give the impression that this one person does it all. As can be seen from the material covered thus far, many departments are involved in servicing a convention.

The extent to which the convention service manager actually becomes involved with these departments is determined primarily by the competence of the department heads. If the reservation manager, the front-office manager, and the catering manager are on top of their jobs, the convention service manager's headaches are minimized. On the other hand, if the reservation manager is new or is inclined to make mistakes, the convention service manager will have to spend more time overseeing the operation of this important area.

Role of the Catering Manager

The in-house coordination in *small properties* is generally not handled the same way as in larger properties; the major difference is the role played by the *catering manager*. In larger properties catering managers are only in charge of food and beverage; seldom do they become involved in sales and seldom are they required to account for more than the food and beverage service. But in small properties, primarily because of economics, their areas of responsibility branch out.

Smaller properties often do not have a sufficient sales volume to justify carrying a person strictly to coordinate conventions. Nevertheless, one person should be given this responsibility. In most smaller properties it is the banquet or catering manager who wears two hats: one as the head of his or her department, the other as the coordinator of group business.

What distinguishes a large property from a small one? Certainly there are no clear lines of division, but our experience has shown that hotels with fewer than 250 guest rooms might well handle servicing somewhat differently than larger ones.

Figure 14.6 is the catering manager's job description adapted from the operating manual of Doubletree, Inc., a small chain headquartered in Phoenix. Doubletree's quality hotels range from 140 to 300 guest rooms, and are typical of many similar-sized properties whose catering managers double as convention service managers.

Servicing and Selling

The division between sales and service is less pronounced in small hotels than in large ones. As we discussed in chapter 10, there is wide variation among hotels in the extent to which the sales department participates in servicing.

In smaller hotels servicing and sales, particularly of food and beverage functions, are more likely to be handled by the same person. Part of the catering manager's job might be to actively solicit and schedule group banquet business. Often the catering manager is given charge of the function book. This is fine so long as the lines of authority, responsibility, and communication are clearly understood.

The problem arises when the left hand does not know what the right hand is doing; when the sales department books a convention that conflicts with the catering department's efforts. The problem is likely to be acute when the two departments are located in different areas of the hotel. In this case, the sales department seldom sees the function book and must rely on the phone or memos to communicate with the catering department. There may even be inter-departmental rivalry for function space, with each department trying to show greater sales and profit from the group business booked than the other.

Communication and Cooperation Needed

Another difference in the servicing procedures of large and small hotels is the increased need for clear communication channels in small properties. When the property has a convention service manager, there is generally good cooperation, with one independent person coordinating the efforts of the other departments. But when the catering manager serves as the coordinator, there seems to be more

Fig. 14.6 Job description of a catering manager used at Doubletree Inns. The catering manager often serves as the convention service manager in small properties. (By permission of Doubletree, Inc.).

Catering Manager's Job Description

1. *Basic Function*:

   To service all phases of group meeting/banquet functions; coordinate these activities on a daily basis; assist clients in program planning and menu selection; solicit local group catering business.

2. *General Responsibility*:

   To maintain the services and reputation of Doubletree and act as a management representative to group clients.

3. *Specific Responsibilities*:

   a. To maintain function book. Coordinate the booking of all meeting space with the Sales Department.

   b. To solicit local food and beverage functions.

   c. To coordinate with all group meeting/banquet planners their specific group requirements with the services and facilities offered.

   d. To confirm all details relative to group functions with meeting/banquet planners.

   e. To distribute to the necessary inter-hotel departments, detailed information relative to group activities.

   f. To supervise and coordinate all phases of catering, hiring and training programs.

   g. To supervise and coordinate daily operation of meeting/banquet setups and service.

   h. To assist in menu planning, preparation and pricing.

   i. To assist in referrals to the Sales Department and in booking group activities.

   j. To set up and maintain catering files.

   k. To be responsive to group requests/needs while in the hotel.

   l. To work toward achieving Annual Plan figures relating to the Catering Department (revenues, labor percentages, average checks, covers, etc.)

   m. To handle all scheduling and coverage for the servicing of catering functions.

4. *Organizational Relationship and Authority*:

   Is directly responsible and accountable to the Food & Beverage Manager. Responsible for coordination with kitchen, catering service personnel and accounting.

autonomy of departments. The catering manager perhaps has not worked in the front of the house and is unfamiliar with the unique problems there. Likewise, the reservation and front office departments lack understanding of the handling of food and beverage.

Such a situation is not necessarily detrimental, so long as each department does its job and there is good inter-departmental communication. The difficulty might arise when the association executive questions the hotel's handling of his membership's registration. If the catering manager is his contact in the hotel, he may find little relief for his problem. Perhaps the catering manager is too busy with the upcoming dinner or has not been schooled in the procedure of registering guests. Or perhaps—and this is a more common problem—he doesn't have the authority to go into the rooms department and straighten out the situation.

This is the meeting planner's nightmare: a contact without the muscle to get the job done.

The autonomy of departments also leads to the lack of specification sheets, which we mentioned in chapter 12 as the backbone of control and communication in convention servicing. Substituting for the specification sheets are memos from the sales department to the rooms department and individual function sheets prepared by the catering manager for all the meeting room and food and beverage set-ups. Memos and function sheets are fine ways of communicating, but a comprehensive schedule of the overall convention program is still needed.

Food and Beverage Service: The Process

To conclude this chapter we will present a step-by-step look at the catering process from the initial booking request to post-function billing.[2]

Initial booking actions:

1. Banquet book: When space is requested, the banquet book should be checked to determine if space is available, taking into consideration the desirability of the business and other factors.
2. Booking slip: When a booking is taken, on either a tentative or definite basis, a booking slip is prepared in two copies; one is retained and one is forwarded to the sales department, advising it of the booking. If guest rooms are involved, booking is not accepted as definite until the reservations department has been contacted and room availability confirmed. The booking slip is also used to advise the sales department of a turndown, a tentative that becomes definite or is canceled, and a cancellation.
3. The function is then entered into the banquet book in pencil.
4. File folder: A file folder is prepared for the function and pertinent data is posted to the front of it.

2. Adapted from *Group Sales Manual* (New York: Hotel Sales Marketing Association.

5. Confirmation: A meeting room confirmation is then mailed, along with sample menus in some cases. The duplicate of the confirmation is put in the file folder.
6. Public relations: If the nature of the function warrants it, the public relations department is notified by memo of the booking, along with any pertinent data.
7. The file folder is filed chronologically according to date of the function. A miscellaneous correspondence file is also maintained for correspondence unrelated to booked functions.
8. All pertinent data secured up to two weeks before the function is posted to both the banquet book and the file folder. Additional information normally not included in the banquet book is included in the file folder.

Function preparations:

9. Two weeks prior: The banquet book and the file folder are checked to determine if all menus and other necessary information have been secured. Any information that is lacking is obtained from the group executive via letter or telephone. Usually, through correspondence exchange and the mailing of sample menus by the banquet department, pertinent information is secured well before the two-week-prior period.
10. Work forms: Once all necessary information has been obtained, work forms are prepared; (the advance period varies according to the extent of preparation necessary). Orders are also placed personally or by telephone for flowers, projection equipment, and any other needs that are provided by outside suppliers.

Post-function actions:

11. Checks: At the conclusion of each food and beverage function, the food captain brings a check bearing the group executive's signature to the banquet department for rechecking and certifying; he then forwards the check to the front office cashier.
12. Outside billing: The banquet department verifies bills presented by outside suppliers, prepares a paid-out voucher in duplicate, and gives one copy to the supplier. The other copy is retained in the file folder.
13. At the conclusion of the function, the party order and allied memos are taken from the menu book and placed in the file folder.
14. The file folder is then reviewed, and all charges incurred by the group are secured from the responsible department heads. Charge vouchers are made out in duplicate. One copy is sent to the front office cashier; the second copy is retained in the file folder.
15. The file folder is then returned to the separate alphabetical file of past functions.

Study Questions

1. Discuss the procedures used in establishing a guarantee for food functions. What are the methods of coupon collection?

2. List the four most common beverage service arrangements and describe the appropriate pricing methods. What is a corkage fee?

3. Formal control procedures are desirable for issuing liquor and use of it. Describe the system used by the Ramada Renaissance Hotel.

4. "The in-house coordination in small properties is generally not handled the same way as in large properties." Expand on this statement, distinguishing the catering manager from the convention service manager.

5. Trace the banquet service function from the initial booking request through post-function billing.

Outline

I. Outside or Inside?

    A. Audiovisual Specialists
    B. In-House Equipment

II. Types of Audiovisual Equipment

    A. Sound Systems
    B. Lecterns
    C. Lighting
    D. Screens
    E. Slide Projectors
    F. Rearview Projection
    G. Motion Picture Projectors
    I. Projector Stands
    J. Spare Parts
    K. Other Presentation Devices

III. Charging for Audiovisual Equipment

IV. Signs and Notices

    A. Hotel Rules
    B. Sign Responsibility
    C. Price Schedule
    D. Locations

V. Union Regulations

It is a rare meeting today that doesn't incorporate an audiovisual presentation somewhere in its program. The more sophisticated users of A-V systems require little help from the hotel staff. They know precisely what equpiment they need and what characteristics are required in the facility. If they don't bring their own gear, they usually contact an A-V service company for logistical support.

The meeting planner who is less knowledgeable about audiovisual systems might very well need support from the hotel staff. So someone on the staff should at least be familiar with, if not expert at, A-V systems to provide such service or to help the planner get it locally. It is not realistic to expect convention sales and service personnel to be expert in every facet of the convention business, but all should be conversant in the terminology and requirements.

Outside or Inside?

Audiovisual Specialists

Most hotel managers prefer to use local A-V service organizations rather than to cope with this area in-house. Outside rental firms are used when

1. the hotel lacks adequate storage space
2. equipment is used so infrequently that investment in a piece cannot be justified
3. the call for certain equipment, such as movie projectors, is so heavy that it is not feasible for a hotel to inventory so many pieces

When an outside firm is used, most convention service managers prefer to order the equipment themselves rather than have the association do it. There are three reasons for this. First, they are assured that the equipment will arrive in plenty of time to set it up. Second, they can determine how large to set the stage, since the screen is often placed on a raised dais. A third, not so admirable, reason is that audiovisual companies often pay commissions to hotels that book them instead of the competition.

An outside company offers the hotel's client a specialist with a full staff and inventory of equipment. An expert staff can be relied upon to maintain the equipment and to handle any on-the-scene malfunctions. Many hotel managers have said that they would install an inventory of such equipment only when the volume of such rental would enable them to hire at least one full-time specialist to manage a small department. That person would assist in planning, setup, operation, and service.

This is sound thinking when the hotel is in an area with good service companies. But in the more remote resort areas, the nearest A-V dealer may be some distance away. If that is the case, last-minute malfunctions or additional needs can constitute a severe problem. Large conventions should contract with A-V service companies that will go anywhere to handle the convention. The fees they charge are usually a small price for the convention organization to pay for a smooth A-V presentation.   .

But it is not practical to call in such organizations for the small meeting. Yet some meetings, particularly training ones, use a great deal of such equipment and need some assistance.

In-House Equipment

If an arrangement with a local A-V service company cannot be made, a hotel may decide to stock at least the basic A-V requirements. Training is available so that current members of the hotel staff can handle and maintain the equipment.

The question might well be asked, "If a hotel is going to have its own equip-, ment, what types and how much of each must be stocked?" Naturally, the type and quantity vary from hotel to hotel. Figure 15.1 shows the audiovisual equipment supplied by two well-known convention hotels. But no one list or rate schedule can be applied to every hotel; a hotel must consider the needs of its clients in offering the proper assortment of A-V equipment.

Successful Meetings magazine asked associations, "Which audiovisual equipment do you use most frequently?" The results of this survey are shown in figure 15.2. Hotels that need to know what type of equipment they should stock might take a cue from this survey. The most popular piece, as could be expected, was the versatile 35-mm slide projector. The overhead projector was ranked second and the 16-mm movie projector, third. We'll discuss each of these pieces, and others, in this chapter.

One generalization we can make from this study is that meeting planners prefer the less complex audiovisual equipment, rather than the more expensive, elaborate equipment such as multi-screen productions or audiovisual cassette setups.

Some hotels are reluctant to bring in local companies on a one-time rental basis for fear that the service may not be up to their own staffs' standards. But if you call on the local company frequently for your clients, you have the muscle to

Fig. 15.1 Comparison of audiovisual equipment supplied by two hotels. (By permission of the Broadmoor Hotel and Stouffer's Waisha Resort).

AUDIO VISUAL

THE WAIOHAI RESORT
AUDIO VISUAL AND VIDEO RENTAL EQUIPMENT

The Waiohai Resort has a wide variety of audio visual equipment available for your use in meetings and conferences. If your requirements should exceed the number of units available at the hotel, we would be happy to assist you in securing them at the prevailing rates.

An audio visual and video specialist is available to work closely with you to determine the types of AV equipment, sound systems, and lighting you will need.

16mm Projectors Eiki MT-1 Sound Projector Auto Threading	$35.00
8mm Sound Projector Fairchild Seventy-07 Projector (cartridge)	25.00
Overhead Projector Beseler VG-314 Projector Bell & Howell 388B Projector with Acetate Roller	35.00 35.00 35.00
Opaque Projector Bessler Vulyte, II Projector	35.00
Slide Projector 35mm Auto-focus AF-3 Ektagraphic Slide Projector with Remote On/Off & Zoom Lens	35.00
Above with ENG Lamps available for purchase (30% Brighter)	
Edna-Light Electric Pointer	20.00
Tape Recorder, Cassette Wollensak #2851 Cassette Recorder AC with Built-in Slide Sync.	30.00
Tape Recorder, Reel-to-Reel Wollensak 6020—2 track—mono	25.00
Slide Dissolve Unit Kodak Dissolve Control EC-K	30.00
Additional Projection Screens 50" x 50" to 70" x 70" Tripod Models	15.00
Video Equipment RCA Slectravision ½" VHS-Format Video Cassette Player with Monitor 19" T.V. Monitor RCA Color Video Camera, Hand-held ¾" U-matic Video Cassette Recorder	 75.00 30.00 100.00 100.00
Sony V-Star Projector, up to 12' Image (A/V Technician Required)	600.00

All prices plus 4.17% sales tax.

poipu beach • kauai, hawaii 96756

CONFERENCE SERVICES

The Broadmoor has earned an enviable reputation for planning and conducting successful conferences of every magnitude.

Skilled technicians and a complete inventory of audio/visual equipment allow The Broadmoor to meet your conference requirements—from the staging of a Broadway show to small group meetings. And The Broadmoor will help locate special items not in inventory.

For more information, contact Sales and Conferences, Extension 5777.

CONFERENCE SERVICES	PER HOUR
TECHNICIAN........................	20.00

AUDIO-VISUAL EQUIPMENT

ITEM	PER DAY
2-Track Sony Tape Recorder..............	15.00
TEAC 3440 Reel to Reel.................	30.00
TEAC 2-Track Reel to Reel..............	25.00
3-Speed Turntable......................	5.00
Dual Turntable.........................	15.00
Black Lites............................	10.00
3-Position Signal Unit..................	2.00
Electric Typewriter (2 Selectrics, 2 IBM)....	10.00
Manual Typewriter......................	5.00
TV Set—Color..........................	25.00
Panasonic ¾" Video Cassette	
Tape Player NV-2110M.................	55.00
JVC ½" VHS Video Cassette Player.........	55.00
Monitor for Video Cassette Player.........	35.00
Wollensak & 3M Cassette Recorder........	15.00
2551-2558	
AVL Dove Unit.........................	50.00
Sony KP-2600 Video Beam Projector......	150.00
3M Overhead Projector 66	
(Transparencies Only).................	17.00
3M Overhead Projector 66 AR............	17.00
Opaque Projector T57..................	17.00
3½" x 4" Lantern Slide Projector..........	17.00
Kodak Carousel—	
35mm, w/4-6" Zoom Lens..............	17.00

ITEM	PER DAY
Kodak Carousel—	
35mm Ektagraphic 850................	17.00
Kodak Carousel—	
35mm Ektagraphic 860................	17.00
8mm Projector.........................	10.00
35mm Movie Projector..................	50.00
Super 8 Projector.......................	10.00
Bell & Howell	
16mm Sound Audio Load 545...........	17.00
Bell & Howell	
16mm Sound.........................	17.00
3M Dissolve Unit......................	15.00
Electrosound Dissolve Unit...............	20.00
Screen 70 x 70.........................	7.50
Screen 8 x 8...........................	12.50
Rear View Screen 9 x 12.................	45.00
Rear View Screen 8 x 8.................	25.00
Screen 10 x 10 with Stand...............	20.00
Screen 12 x 12 with Stand...............	25.00
Screen 20 x 20 Built-in International	
Center...............................	35.00
Screen 9 x 27 RV Built-in Colorado Hall.....	75.00
Theatre Screen 12 x 20..................	25.00
110 Electric Pointer.....................	7.50
Battery Operated Electric Pointer..........	3.00

(Rates subject to change without notice.)

5/85

demand *excellent service,* rather than the business-as-usual kind. After all, the malfunctions generally happen on the weekends or at night. If you can achieve a good working relationship with an alert and eager A-V company, your problems are solved. If not, you had better set up some sort of department of your own.

Equipment used at a convention, then, can come from any of three sources— the *convening organization,* the *hotel,* or an *outside A-V specialist* hired by either

EXTENT OF USE OF
A-V EQUIPMENT

Ranked in Order of Use*	Percentage of All Respondents Who Use Equipment
35mm Slide Projectors	95%
Overhead Projectors	75%
16mm Projectors	79%
Tape Recorders	58%
Chalkboards	60%
Opaque Projectors	38%
Flipcharts	46%
3 1/4 x 4 Projectors	28%
8mm Projectors	23%
Rear Projection	25%
Filmstrip Projectors	25%
Flannelboards	31%
Closed Circuit TV*′	18%
Videotape Recorders**	18%
Programmers**	10%

*While all respondents indicated use of equipment, not all rated equipment on a preference basis.

**These figures must be interpreted in the light of large attendance groups responding to the survey, rather than a totally representative figure for all associations.

the convention organization or the hotel. And equipment can come from any combination of the three.

The first need is to coordinate service. Another is to identify hotel equipment permanently to make it easy to sort out the material afterward. You can use decals or permanent stencil imprints in paint.

Your own equipment will fare better from security and maintenance standpoints if responsibility for it is assigned to specific individuals. These people should receive special training in the care and operation of such material. The dealer from whom the merchandise is purchased should agree to train your personnel; it requires merely some demonstration, not a lengthy course. And technical representatives of A-V equipment manufacturers can be reached through the dealer to provide advice and training assistance. Companies like Eastman Kodak, Bell &

Howell, and the 3M Company have long been aware of hotel needs and are willing to assist in training efforts.

Everyone in convention sales and service should be at home with the kind of equipment needed for most meetings.

Types of Audiovisual Equipment

Sound Systems

A sound system is the kind of A-V system that most hotels own. A supply of microphones, microphone stands, amplifiers, and speakers is the first A-V system purchased by a hotel staff.

Top-quality sound amplifier systems are a must. Speakers should be distributed so that there are no "dead spots" in sound. When sound systems are used with projection equipment, they should be located in the same area as the screen. Studies have shown that people tend to comprehend better when the sound and visuals come from the same direction.

You need a variety of microphones, stands, and long extension cables to handle meeting situations. It may be necessary to supply a mike for every one or two panelists at the head table or speakers at lecterns, and/or to have several microphones on the floor for questions from the audience.

If you join any but a brand new facility, take inventory and have a list ready of what is available for use, in good working order. Call in a consultant on sound systems and find out what constitutes a basic inventory. Discuss this with experienced convention coordinators too.

Any basic inventory should include a variety of microphones. A *lavaliere* mike is popular with speakers because it hooks around the neck with a ribbon or cord, leaving the hands free. It is always properly positioned. This type of mike has a variety of optional positions such as the lapel of a business suit. It is also called a *lapel, neck,* or *pendant* microphone.

Floor stands for microphones are free-standing and adjustable, with a sleeve or collar into which a mike slips easily. A *roving* mike may be equipped with a floor stand, but it also needs a long cable to reach out to different parts of the audience. *Table* mikes have short stands that rest on a table, desk, or lectern. Some meeting planners use *cordless* microphones as roving mikes. These should be tested in each room to make sure the signal doesn't come through neighboring amplifiers.

All cables should be taped to the floor or carpet to avoid accidents in a darkened room. Avoid at all costs cables that run across the dais. Run such connectors along the front of the stage, hiding them in the draped skirting.

Have an attendant available during conventions. It helps to have the person on hand for the larger events and available for troubleshooting at smaller events such as workshops.

All systems should be set up and *tested* before the meeting. And spare microphones should be available; equipment is not indestructible. Find out if the meeting group plans to have someone in charge of volume control and distribution of microphones.

If the hotel uses Muzak or similar background music or a paging system, make sure you can control or eliminate such distractions in each meeting room. This is essential. And many times larger rooms are subdivided by temporary walls and the controls are in only one segment. The meeting planner may not know which subdivision has the controls. Orient the convening organization staff to such control locations.

Many hotels provide one or two microphones free and charge for additional ones. For example, the Disneyland Hotel in Anaheim provides the first two microphones free and charges ten dollars a day for each additional mike.

Lecterns

A *lectern,* as discussed in chapter 13, is a speaker's stand, which holds notes and papers and has suitable illumination. More sophisticated lecterns have controls with which the speaker can manipulate lighting and audiovisual equipment directly.

You should have a good inventory of table lecterns, floor models, and some with self-contained sound systems. It is helpful if the lectern has a flat area that securely holds at least a water glass. This area should be large enough so that writing implements such as pen, pencil, chalk, or an electric pointer can be stored.

Lecterns should be easily accessible. They often must be approached in a relatively darkened room, so the access path must have some illumination. Cables must be taped, like those of microphones or light units. Tripping the guest speaker is not a recommended way to start a session.

Most hotels have their names or logos painted on the lectern faces. Because speakers are commonly televised and photographed, the hotel name can result in much publicity through local and national news media. It is often necessary to show some goodwill gestures to TV people so they will compose the scene large enough to include the hotel logo.

Lighting

Lighting requirements should be handled by a specialist. If the hotel has a permanent stage, a professional service company should equip it for versatile lighting. But most often platforms are temporary and lights must be furnished on stands. If platforms are always placed in the same position in certain rooms, a permanent lighting booth may be constructed and equipped. Even smaller rooms need skillful light placement to improve visibility of screened presentations.

Lighting requirements for small rooms are simple; for large rooms and auditoriums they are more complex. Union regulations recognize this. Attendants are required for spotlight use, when the large rooms use stage lighting, and so on. They are usually not required for simple setups in small rooms. Don't forget to tell the client about union regulations and rates.

Dimmer switches on house lights are a must for meeting rooms. Delegates need partial illumination to take notes, while still being able to see the projection on the screen clearly.

Screens

Projection screens are often purchased by hotels. Larger ones must be tailor-made for the larger rooms, especially those hampered by low ceilings. The charts in figure 15.3 offer a guide to screen size selection under a variety of conditions and help you decide where to place the projection stands when setting up.

There are many types of screens available. The large screens, for ballroom and similar use, should definitely be stocked by the hotel. They last a long time when taken care of and represent a relatively minor investment. Local A-V dealers have a hard time supplying these huge screens, but little trouble supplying any number of small portable units.

Wall or *ceiling screens* come in a variety of sizes and are designed to be hung from hooks or lines or mounted on the wall or ceiling. They are inexpensive and the metal tube casings make for easy storage. They are activated like the old-fashioned window shades.

Tripod screens have a metal tube like the wall screen, but are mounted permanently on tripod stands so they can be placed anywhere. Light, portable, versatile, and inexpensive, they are extremely useful in smaller meetings.

There is a variety of screen fabric in use today. A favorite is *glass-beaded* (white), which offers great brilliance. Smooth white *matte*-surface screens offer

Fig. 15.3 Guide to screen size selection and seating distance from screen (Reprinted from *Basic Requirements for Meeting Room Facilities,* by permission of the Association of National Advertisers).

Choosing a screen size that takes full advantage of the specific type of projector and room size is as important as choosing the proper screen surface. Today's shorter projection lenses and larger rooms permit bigger, more lifelike projecting than ever. Now, for example, a 4" lens projects a 35mm slide to 60" height and width from a distance of only fifteen feet. And the new zoom projectors need big screens to make the most of their capabilities. The charts at the right are accurate guides to screen size selection. Make sure the screen selected is on the basis of the largest size slides or movies intended for projection.

8mm Movies

Lens Focal Length	Screen Width			
	40"	50"	60"	70"
3/4"	12'	16'	22'	25'
1"	17'	22'	29'	34'
1 1/2"	27'	34'	44'	53'

(Projection Distance)

35mm Slides

Lens Focal Length	Screen Width			
	40"	50"	60"	70"
3"	7'	9'	11'	13'
4"	10'	12'	15'	17'
5"	12'	16'	19'	22'
6"	15'	19'	22'	26'
7"	17'	22'	26'	30'
8"	20'	25'	30'	35'

(Projection Distance)

16mm Movies

Lens Focal Length	Screen Width			
	40"	50"	60"	70"
1"	9'	11'	13'	15'
1 1/2"	13'	17'	20'	23'
2"	18'	22'	26'	31'
2 1/2"	22'	27'	33'	38'
3"	26'	33'	40'	46'
3 1/2"	31'	38'	46'	54'
4"	35'	44'	53'	61'

(Projection Distance)

Super Slides

Lens Focal Length	Screen Width			
	40"	50"	60"	70"
3"	7'	8'	10'	12'
4"	9'	12'	14'	16'
5"	11'	14'	17'	19'
6"	13'	17'	20'	23'
7"	15'	18'	22'	27'
8"	17'	22'	27'	31'

(Projection Distance)

Audience Capacity

Furthest Seat 6 times screen width. First consideration when picking ideal screen for any room. (Assuming choice of lenses).

Closest Seat Equal to screen width.

Audience Capacity 6 sq. ft. per person after aisle space is deducted. (Assumes ideal seating arrangement.)

Screen Size	Furthest Seat from Screen	Closest Seat to Screen	Audience Capacity	Square Feet Seating Space
43" x 58"	30'	5'	88	531
54" x 74"	36'	6'	125	755
63" x 84"	42'	7'	169	1,018
72" x 96"	48'	8'	224	1,345
7 1/2' x 10'	60'	10'	350	2,100
9' x 12'	72'	12'	502	3,010
10 1/2' x 14'	84'	14'	684	4,110
13 1/2' x 18'	108'	18'	1,175	7,050
15' x 20'	120'	20'	1,400	8,400

Fig. 15.4 Angles indicate direction of maximum image reflection from different types of screens. The portion of the audience sitting outside those angles sees only a faint, unclear image on the screen. For example, beaded screens offer great brilliance, but should not be used if the screen has to be placed at an angle. (Reprinted by Permission of Minnesota Mining and Manufacturing Company and Copyright 1966 © by B. Y. Augur).

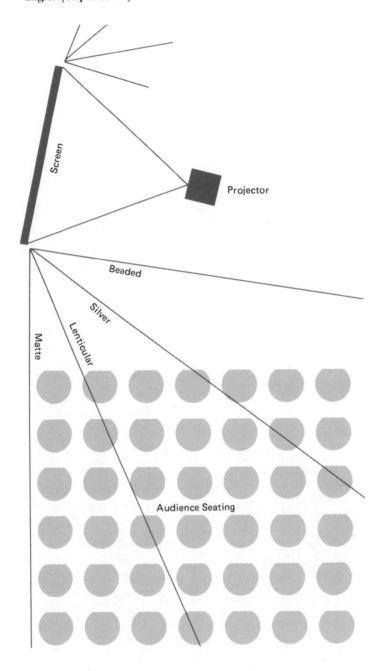

Screen

Projector

Beaded

Silver

Matte

Lenticular

Audience Seating

consistent brilliance from a wider angle, which is important in small rooms where some seats may be at a sharp angle to the screen. *Silver metallic* and *lenticular* surfaces combine the best features of both types, offering maximum brilliance and wide-angle light consistency (fig. 15.4). They are somewhat more costly than the others. Any local A-V dealer can assist you in selecting the proper ones for your facility.

Slide Projectors

Slide projectors have improved tremendously over the years. The upside-down or reversed slide has been virtually eliminated through the use of tray feed systems. Once a slide is positioned properly in the slide tray, it remains properly oriented and is not handled again. Of course, lack of rehearsals and careless tray filling still produce mishaps, but they are decreasing.

It is unfortunate that each brand of projector seems to take a different tray and the trays are not interchangeable. The situation is not as chaotic as it might seem because the Kodak Carousel slide projector is used by the vast majority of meeting presenters. It is extremely dependable and requires little maintenance and service other than lamp replacement. Spare lamps, fuses, and extension cords should be on hand.

If it chooses to stock any slide projector, a hotel should select this one. There are various models under the Carousel designation but all take a common tray. Should a presenter use another brand, he or she would have to specify it to an A-V dealer who may be able to supply it, or just unload the trays and reload into Carousel trays, which every A-V dealer has. This is a nontechnical chore needing no tools and taking but a few minutes.

Such projectors are called 2x2 or 35-mm size. They are so termed because they are designed for 35-mm slide film mounted in standard frames or mounts measuring two inches by two inches. Happily, this is the industry standard. You may occasionally get a call for a projector to handle large slide film like 2¼ inches by 2¼ inches or 3-by-4-inch lantern slides, but not frequently.

Figure 15.5 illustrates two slide projectors used in combination. This technique is widely used by meeting planners to avoid the light flash between slides when only one projector is used. When multiple slide projectors are used, a prerecorded magnetic tape may be synchronized with the slide sequence. The sound of the tape will activate the slide projector at the right moment.

350

Rearview projection

A relatively new technique in visual presentation that is receiving wide use is *rearview projection*. The term "rearview" is somewhat of a misnomer because the audience still views the picture from the front. The projector, however, is set up behind the screen. By using a curtain or similar room divider, hotels can cut off one part of a room from the other. The audience sits on one side of the partition, the projector on the other. A translucent rear-projection screen is framed by the curtain, and the projection equipment is hidden on the darkened rear side.

The primary advantage of this technique is that all projection equipment is hidden from the audience, eliminating the need for an aisle. The disadvantage is that the room cannot be fully used for seating.

Fig. 15.6 16-mm motion-picture projector. (By permission of the Eastman Kodak Company, Rochester, N.Y.).

Motion-Picture Projectors

When movies are shown at meetings, they are most frequently the 16-mm size (fig. 15.6). Fortunately, any 16-mm film, sound or silent, black and white or color, can be shown on any 16-mm projector. There are a number of brands on the market, and such variations as the slide trays discussed earlier are not found. The projectors can be used interchangeably. An organization may request a particular brand because its members are familiar with its operation; the leading brands are Bell & Howell, Eastman Kodak, Kalart-Victor, and Singer (Graflex).

The sound system built into motion-picture projectors is often poor; an independent subsidiary sound hookup should be used.

Use of a smaller film size, Super 8, is growing. You won't find it used at larger meetings, but there is an increasing application for small groups. It is used a great deal in sales and training presentations and therefore also used in such meetings.

Some manufacturers' projectors require special cartridges. Open reel types are interchangeable.

It is wise for the convention service manager to check out the room setup and the audiovisual equipment supplied before the meeting starts. He or she might check

1. the *screen,* to see if it is above the audience's heads and that all will be able to see clearly from where they sit
2. the *projector,* to see that it is secure on the stand and that an extra lamp is available
3. the *speaker,* to see if it is near the screen
4. the *electric cords,* to be sure they are out of the aisle and hidden

Overhead Projectors

Overhead projectors are very popular for instructional use. Figure 15.7 illustrates how a speaker may draw or write on blank forms as he talks to the audience. The projector is positioned at the speaker and projects behind him onto a screen. Overhead projectors handle any brands of transparencies up to nine by nine inches. Such units are relatively inexpensive, rarely break, and are in great demand. Popular brands are the 3M Company, Singer, Beseler, and many others.

There is often confusion between *overhead* projectors and *opaque* projectors. The overhead takes transparencies on film; the opaque reflects its image from paper material like a photo print or letter. Opaques are much bulkier to work with, but the copy does not have to be reproduced on a transparency. One big disadvantage of an opaque is that it must be used at the rear of a darkened room, while the overhead is used in the front. Opaques also get hot and must be cooled, often with a distracting motor.

Although most meeting planners are well versed in the layout of meeting rooms, occasionally the convention service manager will be called upon to advise in the placement of audiovisual equipment. Few things can destroy the effectiveness of a meeting more than the improper positioning of projectors and screens. No one wants to look down the back of someone else's neck while the speaker explains the visuals. Obscured views can be prevented with a simple understanding of A-V layout.

Figure 15.8 illustrates the proper positioning of an overhead projector so that the speaker does not block the audience's view. Figure 15.9 shows the best positioning of an overhead projector, a slide or filmstrip projector, and a movie projector. Review these illustrations thoroughly. Good visibility is foremost in communicating with visual techniques.

353

Fig. 15.7 With an overhead projector, there is no need for the speaker to look at the screen to see the image being projected. He can look at the visual on the projector stage and see it exactly as the audience sees it. This enables him to face his listeners and maintain the eye contact which stimulates audience reaction. (By permission of Minnesota Mining and Manufacturing Company).

Projector Stands

Projectors have to be placed on something. It may be a table or desk, but is it more versatile and convenient to have special projection tables or stands. These come in folding and rigid types. Some have casters for easy movement; with these stands projectors may be placed anywhere in a room.

Permanent projection booths are sometimes constructed for larger rooms. The screen chart in figure 15.3 will help you choose the proper lens to fill the screen from such a fixed position. Special ones with extra-long focal lengths for long pro-

354

Fig. 15.8 When using an overhead projector, the room should be arranged so that the audience's view of the screen is not blocked by the speaker and the projector. (Reprinted by Permission of Minnesota Mining and Manufacturing Company and Copyright 1966 © by B. Y. Augur).

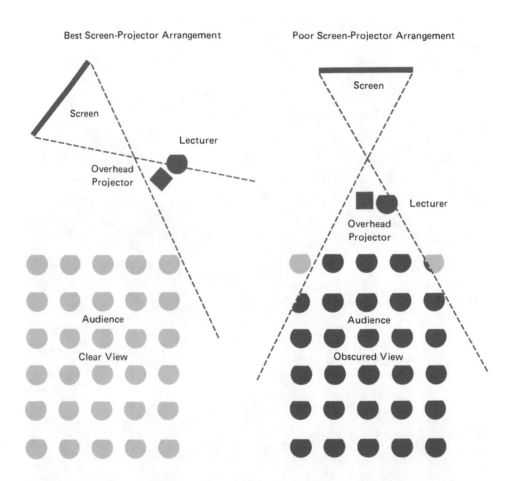

jection distance can be ordered from local A-V dealers. Check local fire and union regulations regarding projection booth operations.

Spare Parts

If you have your own projectors—slide, movie, or overhead—you should maintain a stock of spare lamps. Keep fuses at hand if the hotel is not wired with circuit breakers. Someone on the convention service staff should know how to select the proper lamps, replace burnt-out ones, and instruct others in the operation of the projectors.

355

Fig. 15.9   Best positions for overhead projector, slide or filmstrip projector, and movie projector in a U shape table arrangement. (Reprinted by Permission of Minnesota Mining and Manufacturing Company and Copyright 1966 © by B. Y. Augur).

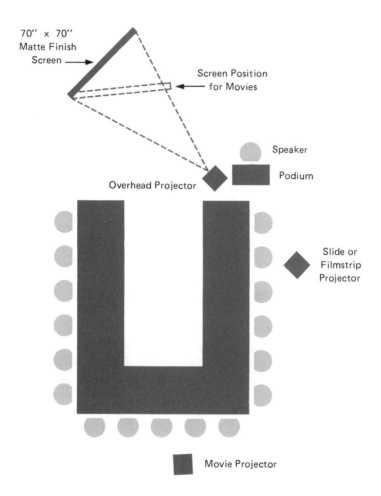

Other Presentation Devices

Not all presentation is done by film, of course. Many speakers use *chalkboards.* Some call them *blackboards,* but most of them are green these days. These may be permanently installed, hung on a wall, or used on a tripod easel. Make sure the chalkboard is washed clean and that chalk and *clean* erasers are supplied. It is the hotel's responsibility to provide the meeting planner with first-class chalkboards, blackboards, and easel charts. Such equipment that is in need of repair is unsightly and difficult to work with.

Paper easel pads or *flip-charts* are commonly used with broad soft-point pens, markers, or crayons. These are always portable, using handy tripod easels. There are special cabinets to house them. If you have rooms used extensively for training classrooms, you may find it convenient to mount such flip-charts. The Oravisual Company has a selection of these, which are readily available from audiovisual and art supply dealers.

Closed-circuit TV is becoming popular with large groups. It allows the audience to leave the meeting room. Ideally, the setup should be a two-way arrangement with facilities for sending back as well as receiving. Generally a live speaker is integrated with the TV program and will need a mike and other A-V equipment.

Videotaped cassettes are being used increasingly at training meetings. Audio cassettes have been around a long time, but the combination of audio and visual is new. A convention service manager should be familiar with this equipment. Speeches, events, sales presentations, and so on are taped for sight and sound and then played back. This training tool is similar to a live presentation but can be played over and over. The cassette is in the form of a cartridge that works like a small cassette player, with the visual shown on a TV monitor.

Pointers have become more sophisticated since the days of long wooden ones. Many speakers use metal pointers that telescope down to ball-point pen size. There are also electric ones that beam an arrowhead onto the screen in a darkened room.

Hotels are not expected to supply the gear for sophisticated A-V presentations such as multi-screen extravaganzas. These are usually handled by specialists. Local A-V dealers or service organizations can handle such needs if you get requests for such sources.

It is usually enough for hotels to be able to supply on short notice such basics as slide projectors, overhead projectors, 16-mm sound projectors, screens, chalk-boards, and easel pads. Beyond this, advance notice should be given and a specialist dealer called in. A meeting planner should supply a list of all A-V needs in advance.

To sum up, a hotel should have a good working relationship with a local audiovisual dealer/service organization. If such a company is not available, the hotel may decide to stock a department of its own. In either case, a hotel may choose to stock a minimum number of basic items and train staff people to maintain and operate them.

Charging for Audiovisual Equipment

No single rule can be established for how much a hotel should charge for A-V equipment. As seen in figure 15.1, hotels provide certain equipment free and charge for others. Competition, availability of outside firms, the number of guest rooms occupied, the extent of food and beverage functions, and the amount invested in equipment are some of the variables that must be considered in establishing a policy.

You should charge for some equipment; a list of the prices should be supplied along with your other prices. When outside services are used, a hotel may choose to pay the service company and bill the client, or it may ask the client to deal directly with the A-V supplier. Both practices are quite common.

A logbook should be used to control the rental of audiovisual equipment. The log should contain the date ordered, the item, the delivery date, the guest billed, and the banquet check number. If an outside agency is billing the hotel, each invoice should be approved by the convention service manager and recorded in the logbook before sending it to accounting.

Signs and Notices

Only the simplest meeting can make do without *signs* and *notices*. They are most obvious when absent. The convention organization has a great stake in making sure that all goes smoothly, and signs are a great help within the convention area. Many convention planners are inexperienced, so the hotel must stand ready to advise and supply. Unless you want to scramble at the last moment, you should remind the client of the need for such signs and notices and expedite the creation of them.

Hotel Rules

Hotels and convention facilities need rules about the use of signs to avoid damage to walls and doors by indiscriminate use of tape and tacks. It is a wise hotel that builds a sign holders in crucial areas of its convention space. (fig. 15.11).

The best kind are permanent frames on or near doors of meeting rooms that hold standard-sized card stock for signs. Bulletin boards and other movable signboards are handled easily on short notice. Those reliable tripod easels make great sign holders and are most versatile.

A printed form outlining hotel rules on signs should be submitted to convention organizers to be included in their convention manuals.

Hotel rules regarding distribution of notices also should be outlined clearly. Companies frequently request at trade conventions to distribute printed material at strategic points within the hotel or even to place them at the door of each delegate's room. Daily convention newspapers, newsletters, and advertising material are all distributed in this manner.

The hotel should inform the organization if it is willing and able to undertake

> All signs must be professionally printed or painted. Handwritten signs are not permitted.
>
> All signs must be displayed from easels
>
> Placement of signs are restricted to meeting room area.
>
> No signs allowed in main lobby or guest room corridors. The hotel has an electronic event board in the lobby for daily meeting room and registration information, as well as electronic signs outside of each function room.
>
> No pins, tacks, or adhesives of any sort are permitted on any hotel wall or door.
>
> No tape or glue permitted on painted walls. We realize that visual aids have to be displayed occasionally on vinyl walls of our meeting rooms, but please check with your convention service manager on the type of tape to use on vinyl walls.
>
> The hotel's staff will be happy to assist in hanging any banners or large signs. Please check with your convention service manager for any restrictions.
>
> Please be advised that you will be held liable for damages if the abovementioned policies are not adhered to.

such distribution and if it charges for the service. The convention organizer should be directed to inform the participants about the recommended procedure to follow for such service.

It is important to learn if the convening organization has any policy about signs or the distribution of newspapers, magazines, newsletters, advertising material, or any other printed notices. The policy should be aided by the hotel staff's compliance, and all such requests should be referred to the convention staff. Hotel personnel should either handle or supervise the hanging of posters or signs.

Sign Responsibility

It is the convening organization's responsibility to create signs. The convention service manager should be alert and advise when he or she notices that they are not being planned. A discussion of signs is helpful. The inexperienced meeting planner will appreciate it; the old pro won't mind the reminder.

The program indicates the need for signs. If the organization supplies them, the hotel is freed from the responsibility. We would suggest documenting that decision with a memo or letter. Most often, however, it is easier for the organization to have the signs made through the hotel to save the bother of transporting them.

Regardless of who accepts the responsibility of supplying signs, invariably a few more are needed at the last minute. Some arrangement must be made for such service. If the hotel cannot do the job in-house, a local sign painter must be on call. In view of the fact that setup usually is on weekends and evenings, it is a wise convention hotel that sets up in-house sign shops.

Price Schedule

Establish a price schedule for all sign work, whether the hotel has an in-house shop or farms the work out. A work order should be made out for each sign; its location, if predetermined, should be noted. No verbal orders should be taken. State whether the hotel will bill the organization or the group will deal directly with a local sign company.

Locations

The purposes of signs are to give information, direct pedestrian traffic and activity, and assure a smoothly flowing meeting. Thus signs are needed in logical locations. Trace the progress of attendees step by step to determine what signs are needed and where.

Start with the lobby. Large banners may be placed outside the hotel entrance or over the marquee. The goals are to prevent delegates from milling around and to direct traffic.

Notices on the bulletin board in the lobby, in elevators, and at crucial places in the corridors will help facilitate movement of people. The hotel staff also must be informed about events so it can answer questions intelligently. Such informed staff people should include the assistant manager, the bell captain, the doorman, and front desk personnel.

The Sheraton Waikiki has an in-house television system with the day's program for each convention in the hotel on one channel. When the guests awaken, they merely turn on the TV to find out the schedule of events planned for the day.

The checklist for signs and notices in figure 15.12 is most useful and could be part of the kit that hotels should supply to all meeting clients. They will appreciate the assistance and you will be spared a myriad of blunders and omissions.

Union Regulations

One of the biggest complaints of meeting planners is the influence that unions have on the operation of audiovisual equipment. When A-V equipment is ordered from outside firms, technicians often are part of the package. Projectionists, sound-re-

Fig. 15.11 Checklist for signs and notices to be given to a hotel's meeting clients. (Reprinted with permission from the *Convention Liaison Manual*, published by the Convention Liaison Council).

Checklist for Notices, Signs, Distribution of Materials

1. *Rules, regulations, policies, practices*
   - ☐ Organization
     Staff
     Registrants
     Hotel
     Convention bureau
     Outside business firms
   - ☐ Hotel
   - ☐ Convention bureau
   - ☐ Union contracts

2. *Preparation*
   - ☐ Sources
     Organization
     Hotel
     Convention bureau
     Outside business firms
   - ☐ Timing
     Advance
     On-the-spot
   - ☐ Charges
   - ☐ Ordered
   - ☐ Delivered

3. *Location*
   - ☐ Appropriate
   - ☐ Permissible
   - ☐ Visible
   - ☐ Accessible
   - ☐ Doorways clear
   - ☐ No bottlenecks

4. *Posting*
   - ☐ Bulletin boards
   - ☐ Easels, standards
   - ☐ Hanging facilities
     Equipment
     Labor

- ☐ Fastenings
  Accessible
- ☐ Permissible types
  Adherent tapes
  Thumbtacks, nails

5. *Sign display schedule*
   - ☐ Personnel instructed
   - ☐ Posting time
   - ☐ Period of display
     Convention period
     Specific function
     Special notices
   - ☐ Removal time

6. *Procedural setup*
   - ☐ Ordering
   - ☐ Delivery
   - ☐ Posting
   - ☐ Distribution
   - ☐ Payment

7. *Type*
   - ☐ Purpose
   - ☐ Size
   - ☐ Format
   - ☐ Readability
   - ☐ Quantity
   - ☐ Timing
   - ☐ Production method
   - ☐ Charges

8. *Purpose*
   - ☐ Publicity, advertising
   - ☐ Direction, identification
   - ☐ Personal identification
   - ☐ Information
   - ☐ Other

9. *Publicity, advertising*
   - ☐ Nature of business

Purpose
Services
Membership
Other
☐ Convention
General
Functions
Special events
Special services

10. *Direction, identification*

☐ Functions
Meeting rooms
Exhibits
Sessions
Food functions
Social events
Special events
☐ Special services
Information
Organization
Hotel
Convention bureau
Other
Registration
Ticket sales
☐ Headquarters
Office
Press headquarters
Hospitality
General
Ladies
Special groups

11. *Personnel identification*

☐ Method
Badges
Standard
Classified

Name cards
☐ Staff
Organization
Hotel
Convention bureau
Other
☐ Special service personnel
☐ Registrants

12. *Speaker identification*

☐ Timing
Convention period
When speaking
For conferences
☐ Method
Badge
Name card
☐ Now speaking signs
Name card
Time indicator
Placement of sign

13. *Distribution—time, place*

☐ Public areas
☐ Convention areas
Registration desk
Information desks
Headquarters
Office
Hospitality
☐ Meeting rooms
Placed on
Audience chairs
Display table, rack
Handed out
Entering
During
Leaving

14. *Distribution personnel—instructed*

☐ Staff
☐ Registration clerks
☐ Information clerks
☐ Hotel mail clerks
☐ Bell boys
☐ Special messengers
☐ Housemen
☐ Waiters
☐ Other
☐ Charges

15. *Special notices, materials*

☐ Personnel instructed
☐ Schedule of events
Ready time
Posting time
☐ Displays
☐ Messages
☐ Informational materials,
Records
Subject
Statistics
Finances, accounting

cording engineers, spotlight operators, and other specialists with expertise in complicated equipment are required. The problem arises when the services of a projectionist really aren't needed, but the union contract calls for such a person whenever the equipment is used.

One convention service manager told us, "One of the biggest complaints by convention groups coming to our city is the requirement to pay the high union scale for some person to sit idly by and run a machine that anyone could operate. In some cities the meeting planner or his people can't even plug the equipment in, but must wait for a union projectionist."

While this might seem a little farfetched, the situation is actually becoming more common. And it is unlikely that union restrictions will be eased. Hotels should inform meeting planners of such rigid union regulations; a violation can lead to work stoppage and a crisis in the convention.

Similarly, the creation and placement of signs and notices may come under union contract. In this case, the client should also be notified about any union jurisdiction to avoid difficulties.

Study Questions

1. In what cases would a hotel prefer an outside A-V specialist rather than coping with in-house service? List a likely inventory of in-house audiovisual equipment.

2. What is rearview projection? What are the advantages of overhead projection?

Distinguish between overhead and opaque projectors.

3. Discuss the problem of union restrictions in A-V presentations.

4. Comment on the importance of signs and notices in convention traffic flow. List the types of signs that might be used.

Outline

I. Admission Systems

    A. Convention Registration
    B. Convention Security
        1. Controlled Admission
        2. Ticket Arrangements
        3. Uncontrolled Admission
        4. Exhibit Security

II. Other Services

    A. Printing and Duplication
    B. Decorations
    C. Guest Packages
    D. Checkrooms and Parking
    E. Entertainment
    F. Telephones
    G. Convention Headquarters Room
    H. Convention Hospitality Suites

III. Women's Programs

    A. Building Women's Attendance
    B. Activities for the Women
        1. Women's Hospitality Suites
        2. Fashion Shows
        3. Shopping Trips
        4. Sightseeing and City Tours
        5. Beauty Demonstrations
        6. Guest Lecturers
        7. Wine Tasting
        8. Others

IV. Checklists

Admission Systems

The convening organization sets the admission policy. It is not the hotel's option to make such a decision, but it is its obligation to help the convention staff carry out the admission policy.

Admission at most conventions is controlled through convention registration of delegates. Admission is restricted for a variety of reasons, such as income, security, and exclusivity.

Convention Registration

Convention registration is not to be confused with room registration. As we discussed in chapter 11, when delegates register for guest rooms they are given room keys, and account folios for charges are assigned to them. But in the convention registration process, delegates receive packets outlining the convention program and pay their registration fees to the convention's sponsoring organization. In most cases, a convention registration desk is set up away from the room registration area.

The hotel's convention service manager has little control over convention registration, and yet it is extremely important to him or her that things run smoothly. Long lines mean long faces, and the delegate who has to wait may come away with a poor image of the hotel, even if it is not the hotel's fault.

Thus convention registration is a hospitality function, as well as a control function. The delegate's first impressions of the hotel are formulated at this desk.

Registration also serves as a source of information. Robert Paluzzi of Caesars Palace in Las Vegas, speaking before a class of ours, defined the convention registration desk as "the headquarter place for the meeting." A directory board, listing all the meetings of the day in chronological order, and a message board for memos and last-minute changes are both placed near this desk.

The convention service manager must be perceptive about the traffic flow and layout of this area. Seldom does the hotel actually get involved in the convention registration process, yet it is important for the service manager to understand the problems that the meeting planner might face. Poorly trained registration help; a shortage of supplies, such as badges or typewriters; and inadequate directional signs, causing traffic bottlenecks, are just a few of the potential problems. The convention service manager should try to keep these headaches from arising.

The registration area is generally broken into three areas: the packet pickup area, where the delegate receives the convention agenda; an area for the actual registration, where money changes hands and the delegate is given a badge; and an area where information and literature about tours and special services are available.

The packet pickup may occur in one of three ways. The hotel may distribute the packets at the front desk when the delegates register for their rooms. Or after preregistering and pre-assigning rooms, the hotel may leave the packets inside the guest rooms. But the most popular method is to distribute packets independently of the guest room registration. In this case, the packets are handed out at the convention registration desk.

Included in the delegate's packet are complete details of the convention and instructions for registering. A prudent convention service manager can make this packet really pay off for the hotel; it is an excellent method of informing and promoting in-house sales.

Among the paraphernalia the association might include in the packet are

a list of scheduled events
coupon tickets for all functions
an introductory letter stating the purposes and aims of the meeting
a list of officers and committees
information about speakers and entertainers

The hotel should also provide the meeting planner with material for inclusion, such as

the hotel facilities available to the guest
the times that hospitality suites and restaurants are open, and their locations
procedures for handling hotel bills and check-out
special favors such as notebooks and pens with the hotel's logo

The second area in the registration process, the point where the actual registration takes place, is handled almost exclusively by the meeting planner. Three to four secretaries are normally required with large groups. Many cities provide secretaries free of charge through their convention bureaus; at other times, the hotel may be requested to find registration help, or the association may bring its own.

Figure 16.1 shows a typical example of the third stop in the registration process, the tour and special service desk. City tours, trips to local attractions, exhibit setup instructions, and similar services are provided at this point.

Convention Security

Controlled Admission

Most conventions insist upon registering all attendees, even when there are no charges for admission. At the very least, good mailing lists are derived from the data collected at the registration desk.

Admission often is limited to people with particular jobs or professions.

People are screened at a central registration desk, fees are collected, and some sort of credential, usually a *badge*, is presented. The registrant's name and affiliation are typed, printed, or written on the badge, which then is usually placed in a plastic holder of some kind. Some holders are pinned to a garment; others clip or slip into a jacket pocket. Some conventions use a self-adhering badge for one-time use.

A more sophisticated type of badge is a plastic card embossed with the registrant's name and address, similar to a charge card. Exhibitors are supplied with devices that use these plastic cards to imprint the name and other data for mailing purposes after the convention. (Exhibitors use trade shows to develop new trade contacts, and follow-up of these new contacts may result in additional business. That's the system that feeds the exhibits, which usually support the entire convention.)

The convention service manager should be able to supply the names of local companies that stock different kinds of badges. However, it is generally not the hotel's responsibility to supply badges. This is the job of the convening organization. One innovative hotel, the Deshler-Wallick, in Columbus, Ohio, stepped over this rule and designed a combination convention badge-service directory as a give-away item. The badge-directory could be placed in a suit coat pocket. The top of the badge provided space for the delegate's name and organization, and the bottom had the directory of the hotel's services.

Badges are often color-coded to sort out the different categories of registrants. In some cases, all but exhibitors are barred from the exhibit area except during certain show hours, and the color-coding helps the security guards police this policy. Color-coding also helps the exhibitors recognize prospective customers.

Control by badge works out well enough for general admission, but it provides no clue to the actual number of people admitted to an event. When payment depends on the number admitted, ticket systems are used.

Ticket Arrangements

As we discussed in chapter 14, "Food and Beverage Service," tickets provide a simple way of presenting evidence on which to base charges. If the agreement is to charge ten dollars for each person served at a luncheon, each of those lunch tickets represents a ten-dollar bill. The tickets must be counted immediately after the affair, and the number verified by an authorized person from the convention staff.

Systems for collecting tickets are simple enough, but nothing should be left to the staff to improvise. Suggest one system.

If admission is to be by ticket, a small table or two, with chairs, is set up to handle the transactions. The table is especially needed if tickets may be purchased at the door and not merely presented. Sometimes tickets or badges are to be claimed at such a table. If you expect a crowd, you'll need several table stations. It is easier to bring up the subject and discuss it in advance than to scramble for tables and chairs at the last minute.

The tables and chairs may be placed just outside or just inside the door of the function room. Space is a consideration in deciding which place to put the tables.

Waiters collect tickets at a sit-down meal, while a hotel employee can collect tickets at the door for a buffet. It is worth repeating that a person on the convention staff should be at the door, too, to assist in troubleshooting and to identify and greet the VIP's. The tables also serve as a focal point for those who have questions, for notices to be placed, and for material to be picked up.

Tickets often are sold in advance by convention organizations. The associations make money from such functions in many ways. The price they charge might be more than what they pay the hotel. In addition, not every ticket for every function is used and no refunds are made. This happens especially when the convention sells a package of tickets for every event for a flat fee.

Lots of ruffled feathers can be avoided if the hotel staff meets with the convention staff to decide what to do when delegates lose or forget their tickets. Don't expect a security guard or a waiter to improvise in such cases. If a convention executive is authorized to approve admission at each function, make some provision for recording that number. The simplest way is for the convention executive to have extra tickets to supply when he or she sees fit to do so.

Sometimes, the count must be verified and the bill submitted to someone other than the convention organization. Many companies sponsor food functions as a way of helping an organization. The procedures are all the same except that you deal with another person. Arrangements should be made in advance to ascertain who should be billed—the convention organization or the sponsor. Arrangements for payment also should be spelled out.

Uncontrolled Admission

There are times when the doors are open to all who care to enter. However, this is relatively rare. But it is common to permit all who have badges to enter, allowing a free flow of people into and out of the meeting and exhibit areas. This is where color-coding helps a great deal. When admission requires only a badge, and the badge is readily available, a security guard or other hotel person, such as a captain, stationed at the door may be all that is needed.

In such uncontrolled arrangements, all liquor and food may be paid for with cash or coupons.

Exhibit Security

Conventions accompanied by exhibitions pose a number of potential problems that can be both embarrassing and costly to a hotel. Communication is needed between the convention service manager and the person responsible for security. Coordination and cooperation are necessary to provide the protection requirements.

When exhibitors are involved, the hotel's security force may have to be beefed up with outside help. The extra cost should be figured into the selling price and absorbed by the association. There are a number of national security companies that might be called in. However, many hotels maintain an on-call list of reliable off-duty policemen and firemen. They have been trained in the basic security procedures and are an excellent source of help.

All hotel security personnel, whether part-time or full-time, experienced or inexperienced, should go through a training session and orientation of the hotel's facilities. A job description such as that shown in figure 16.2 might be given to each guard. It outlines the guard's duties and responsibilities as an employee of the hotel.

Security in the modern hotel is becoming a more complex problem. There are four critical periods involved in security: move-in, open show hours, closed show hours, and move-out. Each has its own problems.

Move-in and move-out periods are the most critical times because of the many transitory, poorly identified persons who have access to exhibits and displays. People have been known to take anything from calculators to operating tables. Security personnel must be wary of anyone who looks suspicious. It might seem rather strange to see someone with an overcoat on when it is quite hot outside. The security guard should make tactful inquiries of such people immediately. Security guards must be alert and very observant to spot the unusual.

Tight security is essential at the loading docks and truck entries during move-in. Any materials or displays that go in or out of the door should have a pass-check from show management. Security personnel often encourage exhibitors during move-in to put their display goods in a "safe room," if one is available. If it is not available, they are encouraged to put their displays under their booths, away from the view of passing persons. This will help to eliminate theft.

It is advisable to have a roving officer rather than one who merely stands at the door; this more often is a psychological deterrent to would-be thieves.

During the show or exhibit much of the responsibility for guarding the booths falls on the exhibitors themselves rather than the security guards; this is especially true of large conventions, where it is hard to have a security guard at each exhibit. Exhibitors who decide to leave their booths should have replacements so the booths are not left unattended.

At especially large conventions, it is very desirable to keep the audience at a minimum because security is most difficult with huge audiences. Only members of the association or convention should have access. Badges are not the cure-all because many gate crashers think it is quite a challenge to steal someone else's badge

Fig. 16.2 A typical job description for hotel security guards.

Hotel Security Personnel Job Duties and Responsibility

The basic duty of a security guard is to protect the guest and the exhibits from criminals. In addition to these responsibilities, the security man has other duties.

1. *Help take care of an antagonist calmly.* Security must know how to take care of troublemakers through the use of logic or force without attracting too much attention from other guests.
2. *Watch for fire.* Security must know what to do about extinguishing small fires when fire trucks are still in transit.
3. *Report accidents.* A report must be presented to the hotel office for insurance purposes.
4. *Know how to take care of bomb threats.* Security must learn how to warn guests of bomb threats without making them panic.
5. *Emergency evacuation plan.* Security must know the hotel's exits so that in an emergency he can direct the people.
6. *Crowd control.* Security guards must know how to handle crowds during a mass panic.
7. *Policing loading areas.* Loading areas must be checked for stolen hotel property or stolen exhibits.

And in addition to these duties, a security man must have a law enforcement background and be familiar with local and state laws.

---

to get in. Nevertheless, badges certainly cannot be neglected as they are required at most conventions.

Burns Security Institute surveyed exhibitors and show personnel across the nation about exhibit hall security problems and practices; more than 200 responded. According to the survey, one of the primary problems in exhibit areas is internal pilferage, with both hall workers and exhibit workers taking advantage of management trust and stealing items.[1]

One of the most likely times for employees to steal is during dismantling. Security needs are crucial during this time because of the many activities going on in the hall. The employee knows the hotel, its hiding places, and the exits that are unguarded. Because of this, employee thefts are often successful.

Exhibits are also very vulnerable to theft during the evening when exhibitors are gone. Exhibitors often leave in a hurry to join the merriment without putting expensive exhibits in security rooms, if they are available.

1. Burns Security Institute, *National Survey of Exhibit Hall Security*, p. 4.

Electronic surveillance is a new feature of hotel security systems. Burglar alarms and closed-circuit television are used now, but not to the extent that people might believe. Certainly there is going to be better control with such equipment, but there will be a greater expense, which the association will have to bear. Thus many conventions will decide not to use such surveillance because of their tight budgets. If, however, the exhibition is a large one with highly valued items, this electronic equipment will be used.

Another security technique, canine patrol, is being used at some hotel conventions. The dogs are particularly effective when many exits to the convention hall are used.

Other Services

There are a number of other services that, while generally the responsibility of the convening organization, nevertheless will have to be executed by you. Advance planning will help carry them off more smoothly.

Printing and Duplication

Most printing is done by the organization before the event, but last-minute work is often needed. You should be able to supply the names of cooperative printers nearby who have proved their reliability. Some hotels have in-house print shops.

You should inform the convention staff of what types of duplication you can handle, what the lead time is, the costs, and the kinds of material you can handle. Have a fee schedule printed and presented beforehand or on display. You may have an in-house shop with offset printing capability, a stencil or spirit duplicator, or one of the more sophisticated models of office copiers. All of these can handle notices and the like.

Decorations

From time to time you will get calls for special draperies, flowers and plants, and special flags and banners. Exhibit decorators usually handle such items; they have the expertise and the trained personnel to take care of these things. (We'll discuss these people thoroughly in the next chapter.)

Hospitality suites may need floral decorations. You should have an arrangement with a florist to facilitate service and billing. Make clear to your clients whether they are to pay you or deal directly with the florist. Unless you have an arrangement with a florist for exclusive business, you really shouldn't care if they make their own arrangements. But most clients are only too happy to be steered to firms in the house or recommended by the hotel so that they can feel sure of prompt service.

Guest Packages

Convention exhibitors and convention delegates frequently bring samples and promotional material that they would like to distribute at the meeting. Procedures for accepting these guest packages must be determined and communicated to the employees involved. If adequate storage space is available, packages are generally stored free. But it should not be a hotel's practice to store large packages or any packages for an extended period of time.

A package logbook should be maintained, showing the date of receipt, where a package is stored, to whom it was released, and both the addressee and addresser.

Exhibitors occasionally misdirect packages to the hotel. Such packages should be referred to the decorator's warehouse for later delivery. If exhibitors ask the hotel at the end of the convention to wrap and send out packages, the service should be provided at a charge.

Checkrooms and Parking

Coat checkrooms are needed in intemperate climates. Arrangements for charges and gratuities should be worked out in advance, explaining any union regulations regarding the number of attendants and hours of straight time and overtime.

Three methods of charging for this service (when there are charges) are

1. letting individual guests tip the checkroom attendant
2. charging individuals on a per-coat basis
3. billing a lump sum or a per-coat charge to the banquet check

"Not Responsible for Loss of Article" signs should be permanently posted at all checkrooms.

Be aware of local traffic patterns when you consider parking problems. If you use valet parking, make sure you have enough attendants to handle the crowd. You can predict parking needs more accurately if the convention organizer can tell you of the expectations of attendance from the local area.

Entertainment

There are union regulations and tax liabilities to be considered when live entertainment is used. This varies from area to area and should be part of the general information included in the letter of agreement and discussed at the pre-event meetings.

Live entertainment will also affect your table and chair setups. Bands may call for raised platforms. Entertainers have difficult requirements, too. The entire stage area should be discussed to make sure you allow enough space and meet all specifications.

Hotels are often called upon to supply dressing rooms for entertainers. A problem is that entertainers prefer to rehearse on the scene, which may not be possible because the room may be in use for other convention events. This should be taken into consideration when the program is arranged and rooms selected. It may not be possible to honor such requests.

Telephones

Telephone service should be discussed with the convention staff before the event; it may be necessary to bring in the telephone company people.

Many conventions want provisions made for incoming calls to meeting rooms and exhibit areas. Outgoing telephone service from meeting rooms can be abused if it is not controlled. If outgoing service is requested, it must be planned. You should also discuss who is to pay and when.

Convention Headquarters Room

The administration of a large convention often requires a staff of five to ten people, so the association needs a room to work out of as an office. Hotels recognize this need and usually provide such a room free as a part of the package. Ideally, this room should be adjacent to the meeting rooms and equipped with tables, typewriters, duplicating machines, and perhaps a stenographer. Naturally, the hotel will charge for any such equipment supplied.

The Sonesta Hotel chain has gone a step further with what it calls a "Girl Friday" service. A secretary is assigned to large groups free of charge to work in the headquarters room. The secretary's functions might include typing, handling messages, and arranging show tickets, among others.

Convention Hospitality Suites

Planning something for the evening hours is sometimes a real problem for meeting sponsors. One solution a convention service manager might suggest to the client is a company hospitality suite. This calls for coffee, a bartender, card table, television—in general, a lounging atmosphere where the members can congregate informally. The advantage to the hotel is that the delegates stay in the hotel and spend their money there rather than being out on the town.

Another service provided by the hotel is what might be called "controlled hospitality suites." There is a tremendous demand for hospitality suites when a large convention and exhibition move into a hotel. Exhibitors rush for these rooms as places to entertain and transact sales. But the association executive also needs these suites for board and convention officials. When the demand for hospitality suites is greater than the number available, *the hotel's first obligation is to the meeting planner.*

Meeting planners are very specific about the assigning of suites. Ground rules often state that

1. exhibitors are not to have their hospitality suites open while meetings are scheduled
2. non-exhibitors will not be allowed to have hospitality suites.

There are other services called for in many conventions. Local model agencies, public stenographers, and similar services are called in when needed. Press facilities may have to be designated, and a source of typewriter rentals found for the convention staff. Most of these services do not require special handling, just advance notice and some thought.

Spouse's Programs

Many hotels have neglected a potentially profitable market in not promoting spouse attendance at conventions. The average convention delegate spends approximately $90 a day in the hotel. If the delegate brought his or her spouse the expenditures for both might well exceed $130 per day. This is added revenue for the hotel, and it does not require the selling of another guest room. For a 500-delegate convention, this could mean an *additional $20,000* a day in sales, no small sum for any hotel.

More often than not, attendance at today's conventions includes the spouse. And for some groups the annual convention has even become a family affair. Convention service people should make provisions for entertaining these additional guests. Special programs are usually arranged that are no different than any other program segment, as far as the hotel is concerned. It is a general conclusion that members stay longer and spend more money when the spouse is along; both result in more revenue for the hotel.

The first step, after recognizing the significance of attendance by spouses is to sell the idea to the meeting planner, who after all must increase the convention budget if spouse's programs are part of the plan. Point out that the presence of spouses may be healthy for the meeting. The attendee is less likely to come to the morning session blear-eyed after a late night on the town if his or her spouse is accompanying them. Sessions will probably be more businesslike and delegates more alert, attentive, and receptive.

Also suggest to the meeting planner that they often determine the attendance figure. If the spouse anticipates they'll have a good time, they may encourage the other to attend the convention. Another plus is that spouse's attendance at conventions fosters a close-knit family feeling, which improves a company's image.

In summary, if a poll were taken, it would probably show that the most successful meetings are those where both husband and wife attend.

Building Spouse's Attendance

Once the meeting planner is convinced of the value of inviting spouses, much can be done by hotels to promote their attendance. Working in conjunction with the association, the convention service manager should suggest ways to create interest and thus increase attendance. The following methods might be used:

1. Supply the association with the hotel's brochures and internal pieces and suggest that the meeting planner include them with group mailings. Include such items as menus, pictures of the hotel, and highlights of the city.
2. Taking this a step further, you might secure a complete and up-to-date membership mailing list from the meeting planner and send personalized letters describing the planned activities. Also tell them about the climate and offer suggestions on appropriate attire.
3. Suggest that the association designate a spouse's program chairperson. Offer to work with this person in arranging shows, sightseeing, and other interesting programs.
4. Advertise in the popular trade journals of the conferring group. Prepare an ad aimed at the delegate that extols virtues of having their spouse come along.

Activities for the Women

Hotels have recently taken positive steps to increase women's attendance; a few properties have even created women's service departments with directors to meet the needs of the women. Working alongside the convention service manager, the women's program director helps convention committees plan and coordinate interesting programs for the women.

Most hotels cannot afford to staff a special director for women, but every hotel dealing in group business should at least prepare a directory of possible activities for women. This directory should be freely distributed to meeting planners. Figure 16.3 shows such a list used by the prestigious Boca Raton Hotel and Club in Florida.

In preparing such a list, the question should be asked, What do women want? The American Hotel & Motel Association, recognizing the importance of women taking business trips with their husbands, commissioned the *Ladies' Home Journal* to conduct a study to answer this question.[2] The convention activities mentioned the most often as the most enjoyable were fashion shows, luncheons, and sightseeing tours. Activities that the women least enjoyed were the meetings, speeches, and business breakfasts. Asked whether they preferred the social-vacation aspects or attending meetings with their husbands, 75 percent said the socializing aspects.

These results are significant for both the convention service manager and the meeting planner. Everyone benefits when attendance is high and spouses are doing what they enjoy most. Bearing this in mind, let us take a look at the gamut of women's activities possible.

Women's Hospitality Suites

A women's hospitality suite at the Las Vegas Hilton is always open during the regular hours of the convention meetings, normally from 9 a.m. to 5 p.m. It is a room that can accommodate 150 people or more. The atmosphere is informal, and the purpose is to provide a place for the women to meet and socialize. Coffee and sweet rolls are provided by the hotel.

This idea has helped to increase attendance by wives, so the small added expenditure is easily justified by the additional revenue. Many times women find their hospitality suite an ideal place to plan their day's schedule.

Hospitality centers are not unique to the Las Vegas Hilton; most hotels use such a room as a congregating place. The room should be open all day. Some women may not want to participate in the planned trips and need a place besides their guest room to relax.

---

2. "Travel Study of Hotels and Motels," *Ladies Home Journal.*

Fig. 16.3 List of women's programs from the Boca Raton's convention brochure. (By permission of the Boca Raton Hotel and Club, Boca Raton, Florida).

Ladies Entertainment

Fashion Show—A very popular attraction for the ladies—and men also—is usually staged at the Cabana Club or Boca West Country Club at the conclusion of luncheon. A very fine show can be put on by the Hotel dress shop with eight or ten professional models.

Decorator's Symposium—Everything is free, including transportation—the ladies are transported to the Boca West Pavilion and are guided through the six (6) decorated models by an interior design expert, who will discuss techniques and answer questions. This event can be combined with luncheon at regular charges—the Boca West people will treat the ladies to champagne.

Bingo Game—An afternoon or evening bingo game for the ladies might be scheduled. The Hotel would supply the bingo equipment and boys to pass out cards, call numbers, etc. Prizes would be necessary and at least ten prizes would be sufficient.

Bridge and Canasta Party—An afternoon bridge and canasta party for the ladies is very enjoyable. This can be held at the Cabana Club or in the main hotel. The Hotel will supply card tables, score pads and pencils; the individual or association would supply the playing cards and tallies. The Hotel Social Director will assist.

Backgammon—Beginners' and advanced play. Matched play or Round Robin tournaments available upon request.

Brushless Painting Demonstration—A nationally known artist, lecturer and teacher, with a flick of her hands and arms creates graceful rhythmical and delicate shadings of color magic. This is an enjoyable as well as entirely different kind of entertainment which captures every audience—men as well as ladies. Most interesting as well as creative program. Original work done during demonstration will be given to members of the audience. The demonstration runs approximately 45 minutes. Arrangements can also be made for groups to participate or for private lessons in painting if desired. (Available December 1-April 1).

Golf and Tennis Clinics—Information available upon request.

Marlowe & Gray—Outstanding Numerologist and Astrologist demonstrations and lectures.

Frances Thomas—Lecture on Palmistry plus individual readings.

Flower Arrangement Demonstration—Hotel Flower Shop gives an excellent demonstration on flower arranging, which is always a delight to the ladies. This program runs approximately one hour.

Get Together Coffee—Another very popular event for the ladies, especially in the mornings in order to get better acquainted, the Hotel would serve coffee and Danish Pastry.

Boat Trip on Inland Waterway—Many groups plan a boat trip either north or south on the inland waterway. Various boats are usually available upon advance notice. A boat from Fort Lauderdale carries 400 persons. A musical combo may be taken along on one boat for dancing aboard. Bar and soft drinks are available.

Shopping Trip—Many ladies enjoy a shopping trip combined with luncheon. A trip can be arranged via air conditioned 41-passenger buses to Palm Beach with a stop for luncheon at one of the nice restaurants in Palm Beach, and a few hours shopping on beautiful Worth Avenue. Fashion symposiums, demonstrating what to do with scarves and accessories are available. Prices quoted on request. Such a trip would require one hour each way and another three hours for luncheon and shopping or a total of five hours.

The Flagler Museum—A complete tour of this famous museum located in Palm Beach. Luncheon arrangements can be made at one of the fine restaurants or hotels there.

Horse Racing—Spend a delightful afternoon complete with lunch at the world famous Calder Race Track. Arrangements can be made through the social hostess.

Arrangements for any of the above programs may be made through the Convention Sales Department, Boca Raton Hotel and Club.

Manicurists and beauticians are often staffed for women's suites. And occasionally, such activities and demonstrations as scarf tying and handicrafts are scheduled. If a hotel has difficulty in locating personnel, the local convention authority can frequently help with qualified hostesses.

Fashion Shows

A very popular event in the women's program is the fashion show. A well-planned fashion show with cocktails can be a memorable experience. Fashion shows are also frequently held in conjunction with luncheons. Hotel souvenirs or favors might be given away too.

The convention service manager should have a list of department and fashion stores that are willing to take part in such an event. Much community goodwill is built when hotels work with local businesses to sponsor and organize women's events. In other cases, the organizing responsibility is delegated to a specialized agency that is professionally involved in fashion show business. Either way, the fashions should be the latest available, and a wide price range should be shown. No woman wants to be intimidated with items out of her price range.

Don't repeat fashion shows too often. Check with the meeting planner on their frequency in past years. If there has been an abundance of fashion shows, another suggestion is probably in order.

Fig. 16.4 Guest lecturers are frequently used for women's programs. (Courtesy of Rankin Convention Consultants International for American Association of Orthodontists, speaker Clive David).

Shopping Trips

Another effort that promotes local goodwill is the shopping trip. Proper planning is very important. Normally, chartered buses take care of the transportation. A store guide should be scheduled to greet the women, and, if possible, they should be shown behind the scenes.

Timing is important. Often the women will break into smaller groups to go through different stores, so a rendezvous time could be clearly communicated. Also be sure that the women are back at the hotel in time to get ready for the evening's festivities.

Sightseeing and City Tours

Sightseeing and tours are also popular. A competent guide is paramount. The convention service manager should have a list of sightseeing and tour agencies contacted in advance.

All cities have points of interest: colleges, historic spots, gardens, and so on. One of the best-received tours is the home and garden type. Local women open their homes for conventioneer's wives, often in an effort to raise money for charity. Generally five homes for viewing is ample. As in the case of shopping trips, timing is important. Discourage the use of cars; go by buses to keep the group together.

Beauty Demonstrators

Most large convention hotels have plush beauty salons with the latest equipment and techniques, and the people who run them are truly professional. A session on beauty aid and care can be very complementary to the other events in the women's program. A visit to a beauty supply house might also be arranged.

Guest Lecturers

Many women's programs have speeches by professional people, such as doctors, lawyers, chefs, company executives, and psychiatrists; questions and answers follow. Perhaps there are local speakers you might suggest to the association. The range of these lectures is great, from flower arranging and dancing lessons to how to prepare a will.

Be conscientious about the times the meeting planner has scheduled the women's events. Many wives consider conventions as vacations and like to sleep in; they dislike being rushed from one activity to the next. Suggest that the planner schedule women's programs in the afternoons. Free time should be scheduled.

Wine Tasting

The Dunes Hotel in Las Vegas, recognizing women's programs as an integral part of a convention, has prepared two unique shows. The wine tasting session is a lecture on the selection of proper wines. A local wine distributor will often supply the wine free or at a special reduced rate.

The other program, called "the executive sweet show," points out how a woman can be a helpmate to her husband in his business or profession. Social graces, grooming, and self-identity are discussed.

Others

Certainly the list of possibilities is nearly inexhaustive. Other suggestions gleaned from our readings and discussions with convention service managers are theaters and concerts, special business meetings for wives only, and finale parties.

Checklists

The use of detailed checklists often brings to the surface the special services to be requested. The checklists also prevent the overlooking of many items.

There should be a checklist for the entire meeting and individual checklists for each part. After all, the function sheet is a kind of checklist and every hotel person knows how important that is. Make a point to save good checklists that you run across in your travels. Hotel people should make use of them and suggest them to clients, too. Figure 16.5 is the planning guide and checklist offered by the Sheraton Hotels.

Fig. 16.5 Convention checklist. (By permission of the Sheraton Corporation). Banquet checklist By permission of the Sheraton Corporation).

Convention Planning Guide and Check List

So many things go into planning a successful convention that no human being could keep all of them in mind at one time. This check list was developed to aid planners with this problem. With its help, perhaps you may be saved the headache of overlooking some item that might spoil an otherwise perfect convention.

Helpfully yours,

Sheraton Hotels & Motor Inns
A WORLDWIDE SERVICE OF ITT

1. ATTENDANCE

Total number of convention registrants expected

2. DATES

☐ Date majority of group arriving
☐ Date majority of group departing
☐ Date uncommitted guest rooms are to be released

3. ACCOMMODATIONS

☐ Approximate number of guest rooms needed, with breakdown on singles, doubles and suites
☐ Room rates for convention members
☐ Reservations confirmation: to delegate, group chairman or association secretary
☐ Copies of reservations to:....................

4. COMPLIMENTARY ACCOMMODATIONS AND SUITES

☐ Hospitality suites needed — rates
☐ Bars, snacks, service time and date
☐ Names of contacts for hospitality suites, address and phone
☐ Check rooms, gratuities

5. GUESTS

☐ Have local dignitaries been invited and acceptance received

☐ Provided with tickets
☐ Transportation for speakers and local dignitaries
☐ If expected to speak, even briefly, have they been forewarned
☐ Arrangements made to welcome them upon arrival

6. EQUIPMENT AND FACILITIES

☐ Special notes to be placed in guest boxes
☐ Equipment availability lists and prices furnished
☐ Signs for registration desk, hospitality rooms, members only, tours, welcome, etc.
☐ Lighting — spots, floods, operators
☐ Staging — size
☐ Blackboards, flannel boards, magnetic boards
☐ Chart stands and easels
☐ Lighted lectern, Teleprompter, gavel, block
☐ P. A. system — microphones, types, number
☐ Recording equipment, operator
☐ Projection equipment, blackout switch, operator
☐ Special flowers and plants
☐ Piano (tuned), organ
☐ Phonograph and records
☐ Printed services
☐ Dressing rooms for entertainers
☐ Parking, garage facilities
☐ Decorations — check fire regulations
☐ Special equipment

☐ Agreement on total cost of extra services
☐ Telephones
☐ Photographer
☐ Stenographer
☐ Flags, banners. Hotel furnishes, U.S. Canadian, State flags
☐ Radio and TV broadcasting
☐ Live and engineering charges
☐ Closed circuit TV

7. MEETINGS

(Check with property prior to convention)

☐ Floor plans furnished
☐ Correct date and time for each session
☐ Room assigned for each session: rental
☐ Headquarters room
☐ Seating number, seating plan for each session and speakers' tables
☐ Meetings scheduled, staggered, for best traffic flow, including elevator service
☐ Staging required — size
☐ Equipment for each session (check against Equipment and Facilities list)
☐ Other special requirements

(immediately prior to meeting, check)

☐ Check room open and staffed
☐ Seating style as ordered
☐ Enough seats for all conferees
☐ Cooling, heating system operating
☐ P. A. system operating; mikes as ordered
☐ Recording equipment operating
☐ Microphones; number, type as ordered
☐ Lectern in place, light operating
☐ Gavel, block
☐ Water pitcher, water at lectern
☐ Water pitcher, water, glasses for conferees
☐ Guard service at entrance door

☐ Ash trays, stands, matches
☐ Projector, screen, stand, projectionist on hand
☐ Teleprompter operating
☐ Pencils, note pads, paper
☐ Chart stands, easels, blackboards, related equipment
☐ Piano, organ
☐ Signs, flags, banners
☐ Lighting as ordered
☐ Special flowers, plants as ordered
☐ Any other special facilities
☐ Directional signs if meeting room difficult to locate
☐ If meeting room changed, post notice conspicuously
☐ Stenographer present
☐ Photographer present

(immediately after meeting, assign someone who will)

☐ Remove organizational property
☐ Check for forgotten property

8. EXHIBIT INFORMATION

☐ Number of exhibits and floor plans
☐ Hours of exhibits
☐ Set up date
☐ Dismantle date
☐ Rooms to be used for exhibits
☐ Name of booth company
☐ Rental per day
☐ Directional signs
☐ Labor charges
☐ Electricians and carpenters services
☐ Electrical, power, steam, gas, water and waste lines
☐ Electrical charges
☐ Partitions, backdrops

☐ Storage of shipping cases
☐ Guard service

9. REGISTRATION

☐ Time and days required
☐ Registration cards; content, number
☐ Tables; number, size
☐ Tables for filling out forms; number, size
☐ Chairs
☐ Ash trays
☐ Typewriters, number, type
☐ Personnel — own or convention bureau
☐ Water pitchers, glasses
☐ Lighting
☐ Bulletin boards, number, size
☐ Signs
☐ Note paper, pens, pencils, sundries
☐ Telephones
☐ Cash drawers, number, size
☐ File boxes, number, size
☐ Safe deposit box

(immediately prior to opening, check)

☐ Personnel, their knowledge of procedure
☐ Policy on accepting checks
☐ Policy on refunds
☐ Information desired on registration card
☐ Information on badges
☐ Ticket prices, policies
☐ Handling of guests, dignitaries
☐ Program, other material in place
☐ Single ticket sales
☐ Emergency housing
☐ Hospitality desk
☐ Wastebaskets
☐ Mimeograph registration lists

(if delegates fill out own registration cards)

☐ Set up tables away from desk
☐ Cards, pencils in place
☐ Instructions conveniently posted
☐ Tables properly lighted
(During registration, have someone available to)
☐ Render policy decisions
☐ Check out funds at closing time
☐ Accommodate members registering after desk has closed

10. MUSIC

For: ☐ reception   recorded or live
     ☐ banquet   "   "   "
     ☐ special events "   "   "
     Shows
     ☐ entertainers and orchestra rehearsal
☐ Music stands provided by hotel or orchestra

11. MISCELLANEOUS

(entertainment)

☐ Has an interesting entertainment program been planned for men, women and children
☐ Baby sitters
☐ Arrange sightseeing trips
☐ Car rentals

12. PUBLICITY

☐ Press room, typewriters and telephones
☐ Has an effective publicity committee been set up
☐ Personally called on city editors and radio and TV program directors
☐ Prepared an integrated attendance-building publicity program
☐ Prepared news-worthy releases
☐ Made arrangements for photographs for organization and for publicity
☐ Copies of speeches in advance

Sheraton Hotels & Motor Inns

A WORLDWIDE SERVICE OF ITT **BANQUET GUIDE and CHECK LIST**

Breakfast ... Luncheon ... Cocktail Party ... Dinner ... Dinner Dance

DATE _____

- ☐ Person to contact regarding the function, address, phone
- ☐ Function Room to be used, price
- ☐ Reception — hors d'oeuvres, canapes, decorations and music
- ☐ Covers to be set
- ☐ Covers guaranteed or date guarantee will be made
- ☐ Menu — cocktail, wine, fish alternate on Fridays
- ☐ Exact serving time
- ☐ Price including taxes and gratuities
- ☐ Gratuities how handled
- ☐ Seating style
- ☐ Number at head table
- ☐ Ticket collection
- ☐ Dinner or dinner dance
- ☐ Dancing after dinner: clear off?
- ☐ Extra services — costs
    - ☐ Special flowers, plants, candelabra
    - ☐ Lighted lectern — Teleprompter
    - ☐ Gavel
    - ☐ Extra Staging required
    - ☐ Waiting room for head table guests and line-up
    - ☐ Page Boy
    - ☐ Coat Rooms: who to pay gratuities
    - ☐ Cigars, cigarettes
    - ☐ Entertainers to be secured by hotel
    - ☐ Type
    - ☐ Fee
    - ☐ Photographer
    - ☐ Projection equipment and operator
    - ☐ Tape recorder
    - ☐ Flags, banners, signs
    - ☐ Lighting — spots, floods, etc.

- ☐ Record Player and Records—Operator
- ☐ P. A. system — microphones, type and number
- ☐ Table fountains
- ☐ Other extra services
- ☐ Who will pay for function and when
- ☐ Can deliver on all items promised
    (*immediately prior to function, check*)
- ☐ Chef, Maitre d' advised of any change in serving time
- ☐ Bar operating on schedule, if ordered
- ☐ Head table and seating style as ordered
- ☐ Proper number of seats and covers set
- ☐ Coat Rooms open and staffed
- ☐ Flowers, plants, candelabra as ordered
- ☐ Microphones as ordered and checked for operation
- ☐ Staging as ordered
- ☐ Temperature of room correct
- ☐ Special lighting as ordered
- ☐ Lectern, Teleprompter in place and working
- ☐ Water pitcher (*with water*) and glass at lectern
- ☐ Cigars, cigarettes as ordered
- ☐ Adequate ash trays, matches
- ☐ Recording equipment operating
- ☐ Projection equipment operating
- ☐ Flags, banners, signs in place
- ☐ Directional signs in place, room properly marked
- ☐ Other special requirements in place
- ☐ Member of executive staff designated to bid officials and guests farewell
- ☐ Place cards
- ☐ Distribution of souvenirs
- ☐ Photographer present
- ☐ Entertainers on hand, advised of schedule of appearances

Study Questions

1. Distinguish between controlled admission and uncontrolled admission.

2. What three methods are used in distributing delegates' convention packets?

3. Exhibit security is crucial. There are four critical periods identifiable in convention exhibit security. Identify them and cite methods for control of each.

4. Discuss the importance of the spouse's attendance at conventions and list possible programs for encouraging such attendance.

5. Review the convention planning guide and checklist used by the Sheraton Hotels. Design a similar checklist for a property you are familiar with and cite the benefits of such a checklist.

Outline

I. Exhibit Planning

    A. Decorators
    B. Scaled Drawings
    C. Photo File
    D. Layouts
    E. Timetable
    F. Labor Regulations
    G. Show Hours and Room
       Assignments

II. Exhibit Billing Procedures

    A. Decorator's Fee
    B. Hotel's Rental Charge

III. Convention Shipping and Receiving

    A. Exhibit Shipping
    B. Recommended Address
       Terminology
    C. Shipping Methods
    D. Incoming Shipping Costs
    E. Insurance

IV. An Overview

17

The exhibit is a very important part of the convention business. It is the key element in most trade conventions and a very important part of technical, scientific, and professional conferences as well. Associations revere exhibits both as a way to attract attendance and as a very essential revenue producer.

The exhibitors, in turn, consider exhibitions as unique opportunities to market their products. There is no other way they could reach so many buyers so quickly. Most of the association's decision makers are present at the shows, so lots of effort is put into exhibits as a tool of marketing.

We explained in chapter 4, "Selling the Association Market," that the association makes a profit from exhibits by charging exhibitors for booth space. Exhibits also offer the association a cash flow, which helps finance the convention planning. The exhibitor's reservation for booth space is usually accompanied by a check for half the cost of the space. The rest is sent in later, but still well in advance of the convention.

The association's only costs at this stage have been for promotion of the event and the payroll, a year-round burden. This advance money from exhibitors amounts to a great deal, and it literally finances the convention. The only additional revenue of any consequence comes from admission and registration fees. This is a much lesser amount, but it, too, is solicited in advance for the same reason.

The importance of the trade show is reflected in the development of hotels with considerable convention space. These hotels have had great success in going after conventions with exhibits.

It is a rare convention organizer who does not prefer to house the entire convention under one roof. When this is not possible, separate exhibit centers are often used in conjunction with neighboring hotels. The largest exhibits use huge convention centers like McCormick Place in Chicago, which has 1,248,000 square feet of space, and the Jacob Javits Convention Center in New York with 900,000 square feet.

Convention hotels with built-in exhibit areas are successful even in a city with a giant convention center. In Las Vegas, for example, the attraction of a one-house event brings lots of business to individual properties, even with the convention center available. While the very largest conventions would use the convention center and several hotels near it, a somewhat smaller event might turn to the Hotel Sahara (1,000 rooms and an exhibit area of 48,000 square feet), Bally's Las Vegas (2,832 rooms and 100,000 square feet of exhibit hall) or Caesars Palace (1,840 rooms and 101,000 square feet of exhibit space). All have the necessary supporting meeting rooms. And there are other hotels in the city set up for conventions with exhibits.

It is obvious why Las Vegas enjoys as much convention business as it does, what with its excellent convention facilities and tourist attractions. On a smaller scale, other hotels around the country use in-house exhibit areas as an asset in selling convention business.

Exhibit Planning

Decorators

It is customary for the hotel to furnish the basic exhibit area, perhaps with a floor covering, but perhaps with nothing. A *decorator* is hired to divide and drape the area into individual exhibit booths. The decorator, also called an *exposition* or *convention service contractor,* is contacted by the association, often through the recommendation of the hotel's convention service manager. The most common arrangement is for the association to contract with a decorator and pay the bill directly.

It is the decorator's job to organize, coordinate, and execute all the services required to set up the exhibit area. The old-time decorator was basically a window trimmer, carpenter, and sign painter, whose function was to construct eight-by-ten-foot booths. Decorators' work today is much more encompassing. They are in charge of labor, plumbing, electrical work, signs, cleaning, telephones, florists, booth hostesses, audiovisual information, and drayage (shipping).

In fact, decorators are key persons in the convention process. They work with meeting planners from the pre-show planning until the exhibit hall is cleaned and all the exhibitors' equipment is returned to the home offices. Decorators prepare floor plans for approval by local fire marshals. They contract with a number of suppliers, such as audiovisual dealers and florists, removing this task from the meeting planners. They provide floor managers to supervise and control the setup and dismantling of exhibit booths.

Equally important, they consult with hotel convention sales staffs in an effort to bring about understanding and acceptance of each other's procedures and responsibilities. This mutual understanding is best facilitiated through a pre-event meeting or a series of meetings between the decorator and the convention service manager.

Problem Areas

But decorators do find fault with hotels. Greyhound Exposition Services, a leading decorator with offices nationwide, has outlined the following ten hotel problem areas from actual convention situations:

1. *Poor Planning for Exhibit Layout*

   How many times has an exhibitor walked into his assigned booth space, to find a beautiful, gigantic and low-hanging chandelier right smack in the middle of the booth—or a column or similar obstruction. Reason? The Convention Sales personnel just pulled out a basic stock floor plan, and submitted it to the client—without consulting the Convention Service Contractor—and no place did the plan indicate the column or chandelier.

2. *Plumbing*

   Neither the plumbing contractor nor the exhibitors will ever be the same after this session—140 booths—130,000 sq. ft. of exhibit space . . . and two water and drain outlets from which to supply all of the plumbing lines and connections required by the exhibitors.

3. *Electrical*

   This was an electronics show; power load was so great existing equipment in the hotel was inadequate to provide half the required current. Additional lines had to be brought in by the Utility Company, at time of show move-in. An Electronics Show obviously involves a heavy power load, and the Hotel could have saved everybody a lot of headaches if this had been taken into consideration in booking the show—balancing requirements against electrical facilities available—then increasing the power in advance.

4. *Outdoor Tent or Patio Shows*

   No one at Greyhound mentions "Patio Shows" to our production supervisor who handled this one. The exhibit area consisted of canvas carport-type awnings, on the oceanside patio of the hotel . . . on the windiest day of the year. A case of man against the elements . . . and I'm afraid "man" came out a very poor second best. It can be done, but only on a cost plus basis.

5. *Labor*

   How many times have we set up a one hundred or two hundred booth show, all custom constructed displays, and found we would be allowed six hours for dismantle, pack-up and move out from the area. This unreasonable rush causes breakage and damage to property, mis-directed shipments, and worst of all, a non-happy and non-repeat client.

6. *Freight Move-in and Move-out*

   We handled a big show, involving snack food exhibits, which began dismantle at 5:00 p.m. with exhibitors for another show scheduled to begin set-up the following morning, in the same room, with different color booth drapery. The schedule actually didn't allow enough time for dismantle of the outgoing show, let alone taking into consideration the massive clean-up a food show involves with popcorn, hotdogs, mustard, ice cream and soft drink syrups on carpets and floors. We pulled out the carpet for cleaning, of course, but those slippery floors had to be scrubbed, and scrubbed thoroughly. After dismantle, recrating and move-out of all freight was complete. So we worked all through the night, and throughout the morning, while the impatient incoming exhibitors watched in fascination.

7. *Porter Service*

   That brings up another point. Aisles are generally cleaned by the hotel. Ex-

Fig. 17.1   Once the booths are set up, the crated exhibits are transferred to their assigned locations for construction. (Courtesy of Las Vegas Convention Service Co.).

hibit booths are generally cleaned by the Service Contractor . . . but who is responsible for the accumulated trash left behind from a gift show, premium show, food show, etc.? Are arrangements made in advance with the client so that he knows this must be paid for? As we have mentioned on many occasions, some of these small things are the most important, in the long run, and while the matter of porter service may seem insignificant in the overall picture, it can wind up losing future business for both the hotel and the Convention Service Contractor.

8. *Heavy Equipment*
Heavy equipment shows do not belong on ballroom floors, nor should this heavyweight material have to be moved over marble or plush carpet. Further, the live load limit of a floor is not equal to the static load limit. One of the machines, exhibited in this ballroom, weighed 12,800 lbs., in a single unit, 12′ long and 8′ wide. Not only that, but there was another part meant to be attached to the machine, weighing an additional 6,000 lbs. all by itself, which was to be

hoisted and attached to the top of the machine, to complete the unit, to a total height of 20′. Regret to say the hotel took a dim view of the whole operation, and refused to allow use of hoisting rig necessary to raise the 6,000 lb. attachment, so the show went on without it. A perfect show for a solid concrete floor, but never a ballroom.

9. *Crane and Hoisting*
   Here is a beautiful hotel, conceived as a convention facility, with no loading dock. The primary exhibit area is on the third floor, with freight access through a removable plate glass window, also three stories above the ground. This hotel is ideal for holding a gift show, where small freight can be moved in through the receiving room and service elevators, but our show consisted of construction materials. The only way to get the freight in was to park our loaded trailers right smack under the canopy, at the hotel's main entrance, unload the freight onto specially constructed sling platforms, and hoist it up into that third floor access window by means of a two-ton crane.

10. *Control of Dock*
    Here, we meet the Drayage Contractor's most serious problem. The most important single function of the Drayage Contractor is to get the exhibit freight in and out on schedule, a schedule not determined by him, for his convenience, but pre-determined by the Association and the Hotel. No hotel has unlimited facilities for receiving, storing and handling tons of exhibit freight. Most have limited dock space. Some much tighter than others, but none so extensive that they can accommodate miscellaneous common carriers, display house vans, and independent exhibitors' vehicles, out of control of the Official Drayage Contractor. The Official Drayage Contractor assumes the responsibility for prompt, orderly move-in and move-out of all freight for the show, and the only way he can fulfill this obligation is by being allowed absolute control of the loading dock, and with all freight movement through his hands.[1]

As we said, a meeting of the convention service manager and the decorator before showtime is a must. Most of the difficulties outlined above could be resolved through communication and joint cooperation.

Scaled Drawings

We have discussed the need for the hotel to have scaled drawings of its meeting rooms. Obviously, the same need exists for the exhibit area (fig. 17.2). Large, accurate drawings to scale should note the presence of columns, doors, windows, obstructions of any kind, the floor load capacity, and ceiling heights. The latter two

1. Manncraft (Greyhound Exposition Services), "Do's and Don'ts of Convention Planning," pp. 5-8.

Fig. 17.2   Detailed, scaled drawing of function space. Note that ceiling heights, sizes of door openings, and floor load limits are given. (By permission of the Boca Raton Hotel and Club, Boca Raton, Florida).

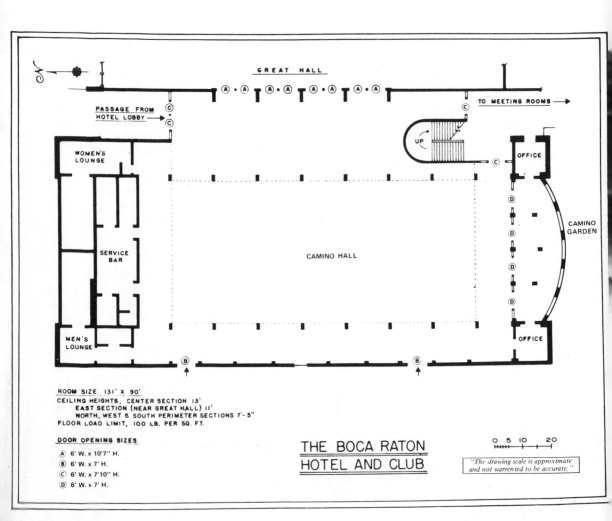

factors are essential because some displays rise high in the air and some merchandise is heavy indeed.

Supply the drawings to association clients in sizes that make good work sheets. It is important to keep drawings in scale. Many office copiers reduce the image to save paper or to increase sharpness. Some do it slightly; some, a great deal. But reduction destroys the key to the scale. If the scale is given as one-quarter inch equaling one foot, a *reduced* drawing carries such a notice, but a ruler laid across the drawing would give a false reading. Imagine setup day with a layout that was planned on the basis of such a false print!

Photo File

It is also helpful to maintain a file of photographs of conventions held previously in your establishment. The convention executive can check out aisle width, exhibit heights, and overall appearance from the photos. All too often, printed material shows only open rooms. Besides guiding the planner for his or her layout, the photos carry the endorsement of past patronage by convention organizations.

Layouts

You should also offer a convention planner a variety of layout schematics for a specific hall (fig. 17.3). An exhibit in a hall seemingly too large for it looks awful—it carries the stigma of failure on the part of the association to attract enough exhibitors. A different layout might provide wider aisles, or conference or rest areas; or perhaps the exhibitors could be spaced out to make for a better looking, more efficient exhibit. Screens (run-off drapes) or temporary walls could be used to block off unoccupied areas.

The schematics should be presented to the convention executive early enough to help him or her prepare convention solicitation brochures. After all, the executive sells exhibitors specific areas designated by numbers, not general space. It is difficult to change the layout after positions have been assigned. Decorators might be helpful in supplying these exhibit layouts for your hall.

The decorator must know the local fire regulations in regard to aisle width, room capacity, access to exits, and anything peculiar to the area. In many places, the local fire inspector must approve exhibit layout and setup.

Fig. 17.3 This material from the Bally Grand Hotel's convention brochure shows a variety of booth layouts for the same room. (By permission of the Bally Grand Hotel in Las Vegas).

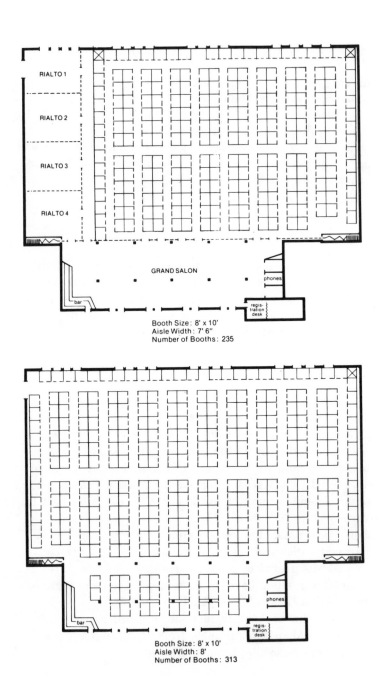

Booth Size: 8' x 10'
Aisle Width: 7' 6"
Number of Booths: 235

Booth Size: 8' x 10'
Aisle Width: 8'
Number of Booths: 313

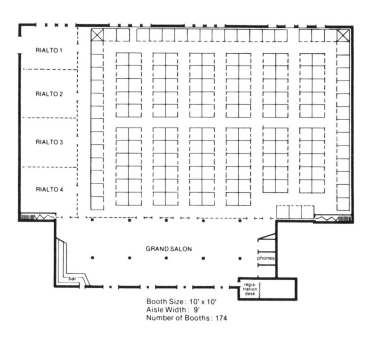

Booth Size: 10' x 10'
Aisle Width: 9'
Number of Booths: 174

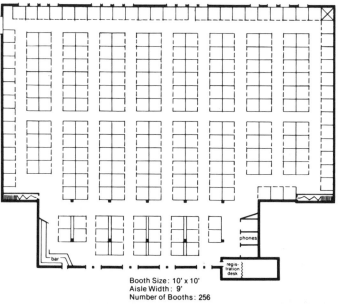

Booth Size: 10' x 10'
Aisle Width: 9'
Number of Booths: 256

Timetable

When planning for the exhibit, it is necessary to block out the time that each exhibit area will be in use. This includes the time needed to bring in the exhibit material, remove it from the crates, set it up, remove the packing cases, and clean up before the exhibit opens.

After the event, or more specifically, after the exhibit hours, the exposition contractor must plan the logistics of bringing in the packing cases, delivering them to individual booth areas, arranging for shipping or storage of the units, and cleaning up in time for the next exhibit to move in.

A day or two is needed for both setup and teardown with most exhibitions. Labor charges are important in this process. The most common complaint of exhibitors is the need to use high-priced labor at overtime rates. In an effort to negotiate the improvements they feel are needed, exhibitors have formed their own trade association, the National Trade Show Exhibitors Association (NTSEA).

Labor Regulations

The trend of trade shows beginning on Sunday has made it difficult to avoid night and weekend labor charges. This overtime, added to what many exhibitors consider already exorbitant labor rates, has caused some to reconsider their commitment to exhibitions. Whenever possible, a hotel shall allow exhibitors to set up early to avoid such charges.

Labor regulations in some cities prohibit exhibitors from even plugging in a projector or pounding a nail. The labor contractor does all the work, even the simple jobs that the exhibitor could easily do. Ed Johnson, past NTSEA president, says of this situation:

> Every show contract specifies an official contractor and spells out certain functions the official contractor will perform exclusively. Usually these services are limited to plumbing, electrical work and drayage, but some contracts include carpenters, model agencies and photographers. We believe the exhibitor should be able to select his own florist, photographer and models rather than be forced to use someone who may not suit his needs. (Often these subcontracted services lead to a kickback situation.) We want to make it very clear, however, that if we use someone besides the official contractor, he will be a bonafide contractor located in the show or convention city. Associations are afraid the exhibitor wants to bring in non-union help, and that just isn't true.[2]

2. June Chase, "Exhibitors Have Their Say," *Association & Society Manager*. Copyright by Barrington Publications, Inc., 825 S. Barrington Ave., Los Angeles, Calif. 90049.

Labor regulations vary a great deal throughout the country. Convention service managers should not close their eyes to the varying restrictions and trust to luck. Remind the association to alert its exhibitors to the labor regulations that apply in your hall. You must live with the labor contracts in your city. Most experienced convention executives are aware of the labor situations and have learned to live with them, but be wary of the inexperienced client.

Show Hours and Room Assignments

Two other common complaints of exhibitors are the hours the exhibit hall is scheduled to be open and the method in which guest rooms are assigned. Actually, both of these are determined by the association, not the hotel, but it is important for the convention service manager at least to be aware that there are complaints.

Exhibitors feel that exhibit hours should be shorter and that delegates should have free time from meetings during the day to browse through exhibit areas. Many are annoyed at the long days of sitting in their booths with little delegate traffic flow. They maintain that they are too tired after sitting all day and that there is too little time left to make their important business appointments, which is why they came to the convention.

How does all of this relate to the convention service manager? Bill Tobin of Caesars Palace said to a class of ours: "If I notice there is a particularly busy meeting and function schedule, I will tactfully point this out and encourage the meeting planner to give the exhibitors more exposure."

The assigning of guest rooms is the other source of exhibitor discontent. In the previous chapter we mentioned one of the services provided to the association by the hotel was "controlled hospitality suites," which means the association gets first choice on all the hotel rooms and suites it needs. After all, it is the association's meeting. Exhibitors would like to see less of this policy, however, because it leaves many of them in hotels other than the headquarters hotel. And when forced to stay in a different hotel than the delegates, the exhibitors naturally find it more difficult to transact, and close, those important evening sales.

So what can the hotel do? One possibility is for the hotel to rent its smaller meeting rooms to exhibitors for the evening hours. This arrangement would be mutually beneficial to delegates, exhibitors, and the hotel.

Exhibit Billing Procedures

What does the hotel charge for? There is no reason why a hotel cannot set its own policy regarding any aspect of the exhibit, providing, of course, that the client agrees to it. (fig. 17.4)

There are TWO CHARGES that you should be aware of for your budget purposes:

        a)   HOTEL EXHIBIT CHARGE
        b)   DECORATOR'S CHARGE

A.   HOTEL EXHIBIT CHARGE:

Sheraton-Waikiki exhibit charge is on a SLIDING SCALE PER ROOM BASIS.

SLIDING SCALE is based on a PER BOOTH BASIS PER ROOM PER DAY, AS FOLLOWS:

*WHEN WE USE THE TERMINOLOGY "BOOTH", WE ARE SPEAKING OF AN 8' X 10' AREA.

SLIDING SCALE:

NUMBER OF BOOTHS IN A ROOM RESPECTIVELY	PER ROOM RESPECTIVELY, KAUAI/MAUI/MOLOKAI/LANAI
35 - 44	$30.00 per 8' x 10' booth per day.
26 - 34	$35.00 per 8' x 10' booth per day.
18 - 25	$40.00 per 8' x 10' booth per day.
10 x 17	$60.00 per 8' x 10' booth per day.
05 x 09	$180.00 per 8' x 10' booth per day.

ALL FOYER BOOTHS $30.00 PER 8' x 10' BOOTH PER DAY.

*Entrance and exit days are full price on Fridays and Saturdays. One-half (1/2) price on Sunday through Thursday.

EXHIBIT PAVILION: $2000.00 EACH DAY, PLUS 4.16% TAX

                     * DAILY CHARGES INCLUDE SET-UP DAYS AND
                       EXIT DAYS.

* ALL ABOVE SUBJECT TO 4.16% SALES TAX.

    *There are two MONEY-SAVING OPPORTUNITIES contained in the above.

    a)   By careful planning of your entrance and exit dates
         and time, you can save money.

    b)   By containing your exhibits to the capacities that
         the respective rooms will hold offers money savings.

KAUAI ROOM	-	(44) 8' x 10' exhibits
MAUI ROOM	-	(44) 8' x 10' exhibits
MOLOKAI ROOM	-	(44) 8' x 10' exhibits
LANAI ROOM	-	(37) 8' x 10' exhibits
2ND FLOOR FOYER	-	(28) 8' x 10' exhibits

B.   <u>DECORATOR CHARGE</u>:

The decorator, when selected, also has a booth charge which includes rod and drape, electrical outlets and other specific equipment as negotiated between the decorator and the association.

The hotel agreement with the decorator is as follows:

    a)   The decorator will provide all chairs and tables negotiated with the association. The hotel cannot provide the tables and chairs for exhibits.

    b)   The respective booth electrical specifications including spotlights, are negotiated between the decorator and the association. The hotel is not involved.

    c)   Storage Equipment responsibility rests with the decorator. Equipment is stored in the decorator's warehouse prior to and after each convention.

    d)   Dryage - The decorator is responsible for the following:

        1.   Receipt of exhibits from the mainland.
        2.   Storing of goods.
        3.   Transfer to hotel.
        4.   Transfer to second floor exhibit area.
        5.   Removal of exhibits back to warehouse.
        6.   Shipping to mainland.

Common trade practice calls for the hotel to make a basic charge for the room. This charge may be a flat fee or it may be based on the number of exhibit booths sold. The booth unit fee is based on the minimum booth offered by the convention organization to exhibitors, usually an eight-by-ten-foot area. Large units are figured on multiples of the basic one.

This method of pricing is popular with convention executives because it protects them from a poor showing by exhibitors. Of course, it means that the hotel is locked into the convention's success, or lack of it, in selling exhibit space. And the hotel's role in such sales efforts is necessarily a passive one.

Decorator's Fee

The decorator usually receives a flat fee of fifteen to twenty-five dollars for setting up each booth, using pipe frame dividers and drapery for separation on back and side. The decorator charges the exhibitor extra for such furnishings as tables, chairs, and wastepaper baskets.

The fees the hotel charges for the room usually includes the overall lighting (but not that for individual exhibits), heating or air conditioning, and cleaning services. The individual exhibitor orders from the decorator and pays directly for extra lighting, booth decoration, the furnishings described above, electrical connections, water and gas connections, telephone service and installation, extra signs, graphics, floral decoration, and photography.

Hotel's Rental Charge

Hotels historically have been paid for guest rooms, food, and beverage, but only recently have they capitalized on the sale of exhibit space. Exhibitions more and more frequently are held concurrently with conventions, and hotels with adequate exhibit areas are in the best position to book these groups. Some hotels have not only been able to show profits from the rental of their exhibit areas, but they have also taken on the role of decorator, providing booths, furniture, drapery, and so on, for which there is an additional rental fee. This is not the rule, however; most associations use independent decorating firms.

There are two common types of exhibit arrangements for shows held within a hotel—the exhibit held concurrently with convention and the exhibit held as part of

a trade show. These categories require different considerations in determining rental charges.

The exhibit held concurrently with a convention is the more common type of arrangement, and rental charges vary to a greater extent. As we mentioned, it is a common hotel practice to make a basic charge for the exhibit area. Associations, which make a sizable profit reselling the space to exhibitors, are willing to pay a reasonable fee.

Hotels frequently establish a figure from which they are willing to negotiate. Each group must be analyzed individually. Various factors must be considered in arriving at an agreed rate, just as in determining the charges for meeting rooms (chapter 13). Here are some of the considerations.

1. What is the extent of the group's guest room commitment? Its meeting room commitment?
2. How much can the members be expected to spend for food and beverage?
3. Is there the possibility of repeat business with this group?
4. Are there any unusual problems in catering to this group (e.g., a large electronics show)?
5. How great is the demand from other groups for these particular days?
6. How much of the exhibit area will the group need?

The exhibit held as part of a trade show is often opened to the public, as in the cases of boat, gem, and antique shows. In other cases, such as the National Ski Show, the exhibit is restricted to dealers. Trade show organizers are primarily in the business for a profit and fully intend to make their profit from subleasing the hotel exhibit space.

Hotels can generally command a bigger rental charge for trade show exhibitions than those held in conjunction with conventions. Meeting rooms are seldom used by trade shows, and there is no assurance that attendees will stay in the hotel guest rooms. A case we know of is when antique dealers were booked into the Las Vegas Hilton. Most of the dealers were not financially able to pay the Hilton's high room rates, so they stayed in nearby budget motels.

Another consideration justifying a higher rental charge is the likelihood of damage to the hotel with the increased traffic flow. Such business, however, might well provide the hotel with increased food and beverage revenue in its public restaurants and lounges.

Convention Shipping and Receiving

The convention service manager can avoid many frayed tempers and difficulties by advising the convention organization about shipping procedures. Such advice should be given early enough for the convention executive to include it in mailings to exhibitors.

Exhibit Shipping

Many hotels do not have adequate storage space to receive and store exhibit material prior to the event, especially since they hope to have other exhibits both before and after the event. *Drayage companies* thus play an essential role in the flow of exhibit material.

Fig. 17.6 Exhibit shipping, handling, and storage responsibilities are generally delegated to decorators or drayage companies. (Courtesy of Las Vegas Convention Service Co.).

The drayage company receives all the exhibit material. It has adequate storage facilities in another part of town, probably where real estate is less expensive and zoning allows large warehousing operations. It also has adequate trucking equipment to move the material from its storage area to the convention site within a day or two of setup time. It is the aim of every exhibition hall manager to reduce to absolute minimum the time the hall is not used for an active exhibit. When setup day comes, the manager wants all the material moved in quickly.

Exhibit handling and storage are paid for by the convening organization. When the client doesn't understand that the drayage company is to store all material, cases start coming to the hotel. But if he drayage company is selected early enough, such shipments are rerouted to the drayage company facility. And the drayage company can have the convention coordinator include its facility as the proper shipping address for the exhibit crates. The exhibitor then ships directly to the drayage company, which accepts the material, stores it, and starts to deliver all the crates to the convention site on setup day. When the time comes to break down, the entire process works in reverse.

Frequently, the decorator will handle all the drayage. He will send the exhibitor labels for any freight that will be sent to the convention. The labels are pre-stamped with the name of the convention, to ensure that the service company gets the freight to the right show. The service company gives all exhibitors thirty days of free storage prior to the convention; this is to make sure all freight arrives in time.

Drayage material will be delivered to the booths prior to the show. After the convention the service company delivers the freight to a common carrier or other means of transportation, such as air or padded van.

It is important that the decorator know the truck line and invoice number of the shipment in order to trace freight if it is not received in time. Reforwarding instructions are also required by the service company.

Recommended Address Terminology

Proper address terminology facilitates handling and delivery of crates and parcels. If a drayage company is used it is much simpler to have all shipments addressed and consigned directly to its facility.

The *event* the shipment is intended for and the *dates* of the event should be marked clearly. This is essential even if in-house storage is provided. It is also important for small parcels sent through the mail, so there can be a logical grouping and storage within your hotel package room.

A convention service manager often will prefer to have the association address its material marked to his or her attention. Lost or misplaced crates create havoc; the first inquiries made by exhibitors are in regard to their crates and parcels.

It is important to set up a procedure on handling material addressed to the hotel. Even if the exhibitors' manual instructed that shipments were to be sent directly to the drayage company, you'll always get some sent to the hotel. How you handle such shipments depends on how much room you have at the hotel and how much time is left before the event.

Shipping Methods

You help your client and you help yourself if you indicate a preferred shipping method in your area, if there is one. From your vantage point, a preferred carrier or trucking company may mean smooth delivery of many shipments. And the client is assured of delivery with little trouble.

Local companies don't all offer the same degree of service. Some truckers may have larger installations in your city, or more trucks, or perhaps just a better, more concerned traffic manager. One desirable characteristic is delivery on weekends. Whatever the reason, recommended firms with consistently good performances ease the bottlenecks that appear on setup day. Good, local trucking arrangements help a great deal.

Incoming Shipping Costs

Some arrangement must be made to handle shipments that come in with postage or freight charges due. Drivers are not empowered to leave shipments when money is due. Without a clear arrangement a truck might remain at the loading platform, keeping others from unloading and generally causing havoc.

Exhibitors should be advised to prepay all shipping charges, but inevitably a number of cases and cartons arrive with some money due. A procedure should be set up to pay such charges and arrange for reimbursement. This responsibility clearly belongs to the convention organization, but the hotel should make sure that some sort of system is set up. When it isn't, the hotel is generally blamed as being unable to handle incoming shipments without trouble.

Outgoing shipments must be handled properly, too. One reason so many shipments come in with charges due is the ease of shipping that way, eliminating the need to weigh and evaluate shipping costs on the scene. If exhibitors prefer to ship that way when they leave your hotel, keep in mind that those shipments may not necessarily be heading back home. Many go on to other events. Similarly the exhibit cases you receive may be coming from another event freight-collect.

Working with good local shipping companies can ease your outgoing shipment problem. Alert them to the breakdown schedule of the show, and they can arrange for the trucks and drivers to be there. Those companies that work well with you to clear the cases out of your hotel are very likely the companies you'll be recommending for incoming shipments. Good local service companies are a comfort to a convention service manager, and they should be cultivated carefully.

Inform the convention staff of the time needed to set up the exhibit and to break it down. The specter of overtime charges works well with some exhibitors. Others rush to get ready for the exhibit but have to be prodded to get out quickly.

Insurance

Accidents do happen, and claims do come up, so insurance coverage is absolutely essential. It should be provided by the convening organization, and smart exhibitors will carry their own as well.

The convention organization should be encouraged to contact its own insurance agents to provide full coverage for liability, fire, theft, and breakage. In turn, if it is notified early, the convention staff should pass along such advice to exhibitors.

Too often the subject is not discussed until the need for coverage is at hand. Then someone says that he thought the hotel was covered. This is another area in which the hotel must be wary of inexperienced convention personnel.

For the protection of the hotel, each exhibitor should be presented with a contract releasing the hotel from liability should there be injury, losses, or breakage. And if exhibitors damage hotel property, they should be held liable for repair charges.

Lost shipments are always a problem. It is difficult for convention service managers to help when cases are lost en route, but they should do what they can to calm concerned and aggravated exhibitors. They of course should help exhibitors trace their shipments and expedite installation at the earliest moment after arrival.

The periods immediately before and immediately after the exhibit are crucial for the hotel's convention service personnel. They must be on hand to facilitate all the aspects of setup and breakdown. Most complaints by convention organizations and their exhibitor clients deal with these periods, so a good convention service manager can do much in these crucial hours to bring the organization back for repeat business.

A convention service manager must be a well-organized person who can work well with people under stress. His, or her, job is made easier if the convening organization staff is experienced, but he must be prepared to accept the additional work load that comes with inexperienced convention planners. He has to think ahead to anticipate the pitfalls and guide his clients through their events. No convention facility gains a good reputation without having a competent convention service manager.

An Overview

As a summary to this chapter we will provide an overview of the exhibit process in a step-by-step approach. First, it is important to look at the people involved.

Fig. 17.7   Example of insurance and hold harmless clause. (Used with permission.)

THE WESTIN BAYSHORE
Vancouver

EXHIBIT INSURANCE

The Group acknowledges that the Hotel and its owners do not maintain insurance covering property brought onto the Hotel premises by exhibitors and that it is the sole responsibility of the exhibitor to obtain insurance covering such losses. The Group shall give written notice of such to any exhibitors that it permits to use the function or Exhibit Space to be furnished by the Hotel.

EXHIBITS AND EXHIBITION INDEMNITY AND HOLD HARMLESS AGREEMENT

The Group assumes the entire responsibility and liability for losses, damages and claims arising out of injury or damages to displays, equipment and other property brought upon the Hotel premises, and shall indemnify, defend and hold harmless the Hotel, its owners, affiliated companies, agents, servants and employees from any and all such losses, damages and claims. Should the Group allow exhibitors to use the function space to be furnished by the Hotel, then the Group shall cause all such exhibitors bringing displays, equipment, and other property upon the Hotel premises to execute an Indemnity and Hold Harmless agreement in the form of this paragraph and thereby indemnify and hold harmless both the Group and the Hotel, its owners, affiliated companies, agents, servants and employees.

The Association Executive   When there is a large number of exhibits, the association may have an individual called the exhibit show manager who is responsible for soliciting exhibitors.

The Exhibitor   A company that exhibits at a number of shows will often have an exhibit supervisor on its payroll. This person is responsible for the company's exhibit. Both the association's exhibit manager and the company's exhibit supervisor will arrive at the hotel a few days early to work out any last-minute details.

The Decorator or Exposition Service Contractor   As previously mentioned, this person is hired by the association to organize and coordinate the exhibits.

The Convention Service Manager   This person's job, as it relates to exhibits, is to assist all the others involved in carrying out a successful exhibition.

With such a diverse group, close cooperation is needed if all parties are to benefit. Proper communication is the key. Problems are bound to arise if each party does not understand the total process and the role played by the others.

Now we'll summarize the process step by step.

Step No. 1: The association buys the exhibit space from the hotel   As we discussed, there are many variables that influence this charge. In some cases, the exhibit area may be provided free, but generally a fee is charged.

Step No. 2: The association contacts exhibitors and contracts for booth space   Figures 17.8 and 17.9 are the letter and contract, respectively, used by the National Restaurant Association in soliciting exhibitors for its annual show. This convention is held at the McCormick Place because of its large size, but the procedure would be the same for a hotel's exhibit hall. The association sells the space at a considerable markup from the price it paid the hotel.

Step No. 3: The association contracts with a decorator   Once a convention has decided to come to the hotel, the decorating company enters the picture. The hotel's service manager or salesperson recommends possible decorators, and the association contacts them and asks them for lists of their services. The association then decides which decorators are capable of servicing the convention and asks them to submit formal proposals. After reviewing all proposals, the association signs an official contract with the decorator of its choice. Appendix C shows a sample contract used by the Las Vegas Convention Service Co.

National Restaurant Association ■ One IBM Plaza, Suite 2600, Chicago, Illinois 60611 ■ 312/787-2525

January 17, 19XX

Dear Exhibitor:

A new year means new budgets and higher sales projections
for your company. The NRA Restaurant, Hotel-Motel Show
will be five of the most important sales days of the year
to attain these goals.

May 17-18-19-20-21, 19XX, are the dates for the Annual NRA
Show, to be held in Chicago at McCormick Place. Industry
attendees at this show have averaged over 85,000 for the past
three years, making this the largest, most important yearly
event in the foodservice and lodging field.

To help you join the growing list of 648 exhibitors who have
already contracted for exhibit space, we have enclosed for
your review a 19XX space sales brochure, which includes floor
plan and cost information relative to your company exhibiting.

Call us collect so that we may discuss exhibit locations
that are still available -- don't delay, do it TODAY.

Sincerely,

Gerald Roper
Convention Director

GJR:jt
Encl.

The National Leadership Association for the Foodservice Industry

Fig. 17.9   Contract between the National Restaurant Association and exhibitor. (By permission of the National Restaurant Association).

APPLICATION & CONTRACT FOR EXHIBIT SPACE

NRA Convention & Educational Exposition
McCormick Place, Chicago, Illinois, May 17-21, 19XX

SUBMITTED BY (Please Type)

IMPORTANT:

The company name, address and phone number shown below will be printed in the Official Exhibit and Buyers Guide distributed at the show.

Name _____

Title _____

Firm Name _____

_____

Street _____

City_____ State _____ Zip _____

Telephone: Area Code_____ Phone _____

Describe product line to be displayed: _____

_____

1. Please assign our company exhibit space measuring:

_____ ft. deep by _____ ft. wide (frontage)

for a total of _____ sq. ft.

In keeping with the above dimensions, our booth number preferences for both exhibit halls are:

_____ (1st choice)   _____ (3rd choice)

_____ (2nd choice)   _____ (4th choice)

2. Exhibit space rental charge is $7.00 per sq. ft. in all areas except "Hospitality Unlimited" where the rental is $8.00 per sq. ft. There is a $50.00 charge for each open corner. NOTE: There is an additional charge of $1.00 per sq. ft. for that portion of any island or perimeter booth used as a second floor or "double deck."

Price: _____ square feet $ $7.00 = $ _____

_____ square feet @ $8.00 = $ _____

_____ corners @ $50.00 = $ _____

_____ square feet @ $1.00 = $ _____

TOTAL $ _____

50% required deposit = $ _____

3. We do *not* want to be next to or across the aisle from:

_____

4. The following utilities are available *only in certain locations.* Exhibitors should indicate if such services will be needed.

☐ Water   ☐ Drain   ☐ Gas   ☐ Compressed Air

Standard electrical services are available at all locations—if heavy duty electrical services are needed, please check ☐

5. Will you be sampling products?   Yes ☐   No ☐

If yes, what type? _____

Note Item 9—Rules and Regulations: *Exhibitors must cease the distribution of samples of any kind whenever such action blocks the aisles or in any way handicaps nearby exhibitors.*

FOR OFFICIAL EXHIBIT AND BUYERS GUIDE LISTING

6. From the enclosed "List of Products, Equipment and Services" select the numbers of the categories which best describe the products to be exhibited. Indicate those numbers below. The amount of product listings allowed each exhibitor is noted on the Products List.

1. _____   4. _____

2. _____   5. _____

3. _____   6. _____

7. 50% of the total space rental cost must be enclosed with this application; balance due by **January 31st, 19XX.** We enclose our check made payable to the National Restaurant Association in the amount of $ _____ .

We agree to abide by all rules and regulations governing the Exposition as printed on the **reverse side** hereof and which are a part of this contract. Acceptance of this application by the National Restaurant Association constitutes a contract.

Authorized Signature _____

Title _____

IMPORTANT

Please sign and return all four copies to:

Gerald J. Roper, National Restaurant Association

One IBM Plaza, Suite 2600, Chicago, IL 60611

Upon assignment of space by the NRA, a copy of this contract will be returned to you.

FOR NRA USE ONLY

Date your application
and required payment received _____

BOOTH NUMBER ASSIGNED _____

Description of space assigned _____

_____

Measurement of space assigned:

_____ ft. deep by _____ ft. frontage

_____ sq. ft. @ $7.00 = $ _____

_____ sq. ft. @ $8.00 = $ _____

_____ open corners @ $50.00 = $ _____

_____ sq. ft. @ $1.00 = $ _____

TOTAL COST = $ _____

Payment Received = $ _____

Balance due January 31, 19XX = $ _____

ACCEPTED FOR NATIONAL RESTAURANT ASSOCIATION

By_____

Step No. 4: The decorator sends each exhibitor an "exhibitor's service kit." The decorator is given a mailing list of all the exhibitors responding to the association's solicitation. The decorator then sends each an exhibitor's kit, complete with information about all the services needed by the exhibitor for a successful convention. Figure 17.10 is a sample introductory letter used by Taylor and Son Decorating and Display Co. The service kit might include

1. information concerning all types of rental furniture and their prices
2. types of draping and floor coverings available, along with their prices
3. information concerning all available janitorial services
4. all electrical services, including power requirements, lighting, and labor
5. information for skilled laborers and the prices for rental of this labor
6. sign prices
7. the rental exhibits information, including sizes and prices
8. audiovisual information
9. telephone information, if the exhibitor requires one
10. information about models and florist if these services are needed
11. information about all of the aspects of freight and the prices pertaining to it

A major reason for sending out the exhibitor's service kits is to enable the exhibitors to order the items and labor they will need in advance. Advanced orders are very important to a good show. They enable the decorator to know the proper amount of furniture, drapery, carpeting, and so on that will be needed during the convention. Any orders that are made in advance are given special rates; this shows how important the advanced orders are to the service company.

Step No. 5: Booths are assigned and the floor plan is approved by the fire department The floor plan is an extremely important part of any convention. It must be done to scale, with the correct specifications to the room it will go in. The plan must be understood by both the service company and the show manager, and it must be approved by the local fire marshal.

To show how problems could occur, we cite a mistake we are familiar with that cost an association hundreds of dollars. A floor plan for a gift show was laid out so that the back walls lined up perfectly with the portable walls in the convention hall. The show manager believed he could close these walls to divide the booths into separate rooms. But he did not tell the service company this. After all the walls were up, the show manager wanted the walls closed, but the three feet needed to close the wall was occupied by the back wall of the booths. All of the booths had to be moved to make room for the walls. This was very costly and very unnecessary.

The layout of the floor plan is important in other ways. A good floor plan should be designed to get the most traffic by the convention attenders. It should be set up so that there is plenty of room in the registration area and so people attending will be required to flow smoothly through the hall.

Study Questions

1. Discuss the role of the decorator in the convention process and the problem areas defined by Greyhound Exposition Services.

2. Review figure 17.2, noting the detail of Boca Raton's scaled drawing. Why is such a drawing a great sales tool?

3. Describe the two types of exhibit arrangements for shows held within the hotel.

4. Summarize the exhibit process, including a discussion of the roles played by the association executive, the exhibitor, the decorator, and the convention service manager.

Outline

I. Convention Billing

    A. The Master Account
    B. Time of Payment
    C. Guest Credit
    D. HSMA's Suggested Payment Schedule
    E. Gratuities

II. Post-Convention Review

    A. Comparison with Projections
    B. Function Attendance
    C. Special Services
    D. Individual Comments
    E. Match-up
    F. Final Appraisal

Convention Billing

Billing policy is often established months before the group gets into the hotel, not at the end of the convention. As with most aspects of convention planning, the time to avoid billing problems is in the beginning and not at the end.

After the booking has "gone definite," the convention service manager begins to collect information from the meeting planner about various aspects of the convention so he or she can prepare the specification sheet. (As we explained in chapter 12, the specification sheet is the major internal means of communication for hotel personnel involved in the convention.) There are three basic areas that every convention service manager looks at as he or she puts together the specification sheet: reservations, program, and billing.

Open and honest communication is paramount in this process. Many questions about billing need to be answered.

1. What areas does the master account cover?
2. How are the delegate's charges to be handled?
3. Will there be more than one master account?
4. Who is authorized to sign?
5. What about gratuities?
6. How should early arrivals and late departures be handled?
7. Should the hotel or the group be billed by outside service companies like florists and audiovisual suppliers?
8. What are the charges for the various types of guest rooms? Meeting rooms? Exhibit area?
9. What are the arrangements for food and beverage?
10. How are transportation charges to be handled? How are special events, such as golf tournaments and tours, to be priced?
11. What are the arrangements for audiovisual, electrical, and phone charges?
12. Will there be a charge for security and other labor provided by the hotel?
13. How does the meeting planner want the bill broken down?
14. Are deposits required?
15. Who will prepare and collect chits? Tickets? Banquet checks?

All these aspects need to be prearranged, with each detail clearly spelled out. Billing requirements for each function should be clearly outlined in the specification sheet (fig. 18.1). The accounting department, as well as the other service departments in the hotel, wants explicit instructions on the billing procedure.

417

Fig. 18.1 Billing instructions from actual specification sheets for a corporate convention and an association convention. (By permission of the Arizona Biltmore Hotel and Caesars Palace).

EXAMPLE I—Arizona Biltmore Hotel, Phoenix
_____ Corporation

CONTROLLER: Corporation will guarantee all personal checks up to $250 for all members.

Reserve suites 67-66-63-62-61-60-59-58 from 4/2-8. Charge 6 to Master Account—other 2 to be complimentary.

BILLING: MASTER ACCOUNT to cover American plan room rate, tax and service charge of all guests.

Master Account also to cover: receptions, surcharges, recreational activities on tournament day, breakfast trail ride, cowboy hats, bandanas, coffee breaks, entertainment, hostesses, etc.

PREPARE INCIDENTAL FOLIO for each guest. Post all incidental charges to their respective account. To be paid prior to departure.

(LIST IN ACCOUNTING OFFICE OF ENTIRE ACCOUNTS TO BE TRANSFERRED TO M/A).

NIGHT AUDITOR: NOTE: extend $4.50 inclusive credit per person for those taking shopping tour on 4/4 or leaving prior to luncheon on 4/5. MUST NOTIFY CASHIER 24 HOURS IN ADVANCE IN ORDER TO RECEIVE THIS CREDIT.

THIS CREDIT GOES TO MASTER ACCOUNT—*NOT INCIDENTAL ACCOUNT*.

EXAMPLE II—Caesars Palace, Las Vegas
_____ Association

MASTER ACCOUNT: All group functions should be added to the master account. Mr. _____ and Ms. _____ will be the authorized signers.

NOTE: Please post a charge in the total amount of $250.00 to this group's master account. This charge is for the purchase of 250 CAESARS PALACE medallions at a cost of $1.00 per medallion.

MASTER ACCOUNT 2: A second master account is to be set up. To this master, charge the entire accounts of all _____ Association Directors and Staff. Mr. John M. _____ will be the authorized signer.

INDIVIDUAL ACCOUNT: Rooms, tax, and incidentals to be paid by the individuals.

The Master Account

A master account is generally set up to facilitate billing to the convention organization. The hotel executive and the convention executive should discuss the charges that should be billed to this account. All other charges are billed to the guests on their individual accounts. (fig. 18.2)

Additional master accounts may be set up for individual program segments upon request. Sometimes a participating company will sponsor a program event such as a luncheon or a cocktail party, and a separate master account is set up for this affair.

It is imperative that the convention organization put down in writing all people authorized to charge to the master account. These usually are the convention staff personnel. If *all* their charges are to be allowed on the master account, say so. The understanding is that these people are also authorized to sign charges. If this area of authority is to be limited in any way, it too should be spelled out.

Failure to detail the event of charges to the master account can lead to difficulties in the cases of convention guests, such as industry notables, association board members, speakers, and program presenters. The hotel really doesn't care who pays what or how, so long as it is made clear who is to pay. It is the convention staff's responsibility to inform its guests about the extent of the hospitality, but it is your desk clerk or cashier who must face these people when they check out.

Ask the convention staff to inform you, as well as the guests, who will pay for rooms, food, beverage, telephone, valet charges, and other incidentals. It helps to inform the guest when he or she checks in that the room charges will be paid for by the association, but many hotels feel that this is the convention staff's task. Unfortunately, it is surprising how infrequently the convention staff follows through to tell its guests the extent to which they are responsible for charges. Bringing the matter to the attention of convention executives will at least alert them to potential embarrassing problems and maybe move them to set policy.

Such arrangements apply to corporate meetings as well as association conventions, since corporate meetings may be attended by persons other than company employees. The arrangements should be spelled out completely. Actually, this applies to corporate personnel too. Some companies pay *all* charges through the master account, while some pay only room and food charges, with the rest paid through individual expense accounts. All variations will be encountered.

The hotel should have no policy of its own, but should merely follow the *clear* instructions of the company meeting planner. These instructions should be in writing. Generally speaking, if you get the meeting planner to spell it out to you in writing, the corporate personnel stand a better chance of receiving instructional memos telling them how to check out.

Fig. 18.2 Master Account Billing Authorization and Speciman Rates Bulletin used with permission of the Insurance Conference Planners Association.

The biggest problem when working with master account billing is probably unclear communication. The Insurance Conference Planners recently prepared a guide to be used by meeting planners and hoteliers alike, providing possible solutions to problems usually associated with master account billing.

Two forms from this guide are illustrated here. The first, a Master Account Billing Authorization Form, provides a comprehensive set of instructions on: (1) how the hotel charges are to be posted (master account or individual guest's room folio; (2) the limit of financial responsibility the meeting group will accept and (3) the names and specimen signatures of those who are authorized to sign for any master account expense item. The second, The Rates and Charges Bulletin, communicates to the convention attendees the specific rates for rooms, meals, incidental charges and billing procedures as agreed to by the convening group and the hotel. The bulletin is sent to the convention attendees one month prior to the convention date. Use of this communication bulletin reduces disputes and speeds guest check-out.

Time of Payment

Methods and time of payment vary a great deal, depending on the policy of the hotel, the credit and reputation of the convening organization, past history, the frequency of group business, and other factors.

Master accounts can add up to a considerable amount of money, and it is hard to blame hotel managers if they try to get as much of it as possible up front. This is not only because of concern about being paid, but also because of a desire to accelerate time of payment and to ease the hotel's cash flow.

The usual practice in the trade is a payment when the contract is signed, a pre-convention payment at an agreed date, on-the-scene payments, and a final one. The final payment can be broken into two parts—one at the end of the event, and a final settlement later.

Hotels have been known to be flexible about payments, depending on what they know about the client. Political organizations certainly should not be allowed to run up large bills because payment may be uncertain or delayed. But a prestigious local corporation that has dealt with you many times may cause your comptroller little concern about the bill.

Many meeting planners insist upon talking with someone from the hotel's accounting department before the convention begins. The standard policy for the Americana Hotel chain is to take the meeting planner to the accounting office at the first mutually convenient time to go over the billing procedure. The under-

SPECIMEN RATES AND CHARGES BULLETIN

To: Convention Attendees

The following rates and charges, which have been agreed to by ABC Company and the XYZ Hotel, will

be in effect during your stay at the XYZ Hotel. The rates listed in this bulletin represent the maximum

you should be charged for the listed services during the length of your stay at this convention.

DAILY ROOM RATE: - Modified American Plan (2 Meals)

Twin Occupancy	Single Occupancy (of twin room)
$70.00 Per Person, per day	$115.00 Per Person, per day

plus   5.50 Per Person, daily
               service charge*
	plus 5.50 Per Person, daily
	                 service charge*

plus 2.27 Daily state tax, (3%)	plus 3.62 Daily state tax, (3%)
$77.77 Daily Total	$124.12 Daily Total

These Rates: Include   Lodging, breakfast & dinner-daily, and gratuities for maids
                                    and MAP dining room personnel.

               Don't Include   Bellman, doormen, or limo driver gratuities, parlor charges,
                                    or incidental charges.

MAP CREDITS:

Tavern Room	-	A credit of $8.00 per person will apply and the balance would be charges at a la carte prices.
Golf Club	-	Dinner in Golf Club carries a surcharge depending on items selected.
Main Dining Room	-	A few items are a la carte, depending on items selected.
All Extra Meals	-	(A la carte) charges will be billed to your individual hotel account.
Room Service	-	A room service charge of $2.00 per person ($2.50 in cottages), will apply to all room service orders.

NOTE: MAP includes dinner on check-in day, and breakfast on check-out day. Should you dine in a group,
        be certain that all room numbers are listed, or only that person who signs will get the total charges
        for the group.

TRANSPORTATION:

Airport to Hotel   - $ 6.50 per person
                               $ 3.25 per person -- (Small children)

                          * Applicable if the hotel imposes a Service Charge.

ICP MASTER ACCOUNT BILLING AUTHORIZATION _____ (HOTEL) _____

CONVENTION
NAME: _____
DATES: _____
FOOD PLAN: _____

NOTE: Please post charges as indicated below. Master Account charges noted here apply only on meeting dates.
See separate letter for exceptions and additional Master Account information.

	MA	IND
ROOM & FOOD PLAN		
Room & Tax		
MAP (FAP) * Guest		
MAP (FAP) * Spouse		
Other		
FOOD & BEVERAGE		
Restaurant - Food		
Restaurant - Bar		
Room Service - Food		
Room Service - Bar		
Bar Charges		
Cover Charge		
Other		
BANQUET CHARGES		

	MA	IND
HOTEL SERVICES		
Telephone - Local		
Telephone - Long Distance		
Parking		
Valet & Laundry		
Bellmen		
Maids		
Pool/Beach Attendants		
TV Movies		
Beauty Salon		
Barber Shop		
Merchandise Shops		
Other		
MISCELLANEOUS		
Airport Transfers		
Other		

	MA	IND
SPORTS		
Golf Greens Fees		
Golf Lessons		
Golf Driving Range		
Golf - Caddie Fee		
Golf - Cart Rental		
Golf - Club Rental		
Tennis - Court Fees		
Tennis - Lessons		
Tennis - Racquet Rental		
Sports Merchandise		
Spa/Health Club		
Stables		
Other		
TOURNAMENTS		
Refreshments		
Club/Racquet Rental		
Golf/Tennis Balls		
Greens Fees		
Cart Rental		
Caddie Fees		
Court Fees		
Other		

* Including tax & Service charge, in any.

The _____ Company
(Sponsor Organization)

1. (Is/Is not) responsible for payment of delinquent charges posted to individual accounts.

2. (Will/Will not) guarantee payment of its attendees hotel bills whether paid by check or charge card.

3. (Will/Will not) guarantee personal checks cashed by its attendees up to $ _____

4. Some persons (list attached) will have entire room and incidental accounts posted to Master. These persons should be pre-registered and will not check themselves out. Their room bills will be reviewed and signed by the sponsor organization's planner.

5. Authorizes these signatures _____ (Type)
    for its M.A. charges _____ (Sign)

The hotel should consider these billing instructions definite and authorized by _____

_____ (Planner)   _____ (Date)   (____) _____ (Telephone Number)

9

standing agreed upon earlier is reinforced and problems are solved before the service is performed.

It is in the interest of both parties to present the final bill as soon as possible. Convention organizers frequently complain that hotels cannot present the final accounting at the end of the event, while the convention staff is still on the premises and memories are fresh. The master account should be presented before the organizers leave. If complete billing is not ready, they can still review the charges and initial approval. Some charges lag, but at least the bulk of the account can be settled.

Trouble often arises over some charges. The hotel doesn't want the entire account held up while a relatively minor matter is adjudicated, of course. One suggestion is to set this amount aside pending further investigation and/or discussion while the rest of the bill is settled. Some meeting planners ask that a certain amount be held back after the event to handle any adjustments. The amount of money held back and the time allowed should be part of the letter of agreement or other correspondence. Otherwise, the entire bill might be held up and perhaps used unfairly for leverage.

At some conventions, a considerable amount of cash is generated through registration and ticket sales. Some arrangement should be made to count this money and keep it safe. If such cash is applied against the master account, receipts should be issued for all such payments. And if agreed-upon payments have been made on schedule, organizations may request checks from the hotel in return for such cash. Such arrangements should be cleared with the hotel comptroller.

One of the major advantages the computer (chapter 11) brings to the hotel is increased speed in billing convention groups. Of course, not all hotels can afford the benefits of a computer, but more and more properties are making the investment. With computer systems, the bill can be broken down for each function and quickly tallied to provide the total charge within an hour of the last meeting. Confusion and long hours of labor are minimized, and the bill can be reviewed and finalized while details are still fresh in the minds of the hotel people and the meeting planner.

Guest Credit

Another matter to be discussed by the hotel staff and the meeting planner is guest credit. With national credit cards, it is simply a matter of saying which cards the hotel will accept. If the hotel limits the cards it will take, this information should be given in time for inclusion in the convention brochure so that guests will be forewarned. But most national and international cards are accepted in most hotels, so this seldom constitutes much of a problem.

The extension of credit directly to the guest is more of a risk. The convention executive should be told if this is contrary to hotel policy. Then the recommended procedure by which a guest could establish credit with the hotel might be outlined.

The hotel should also state its policy about cashing checks for guests. Maximum amounts should be made clear. Cashing checks for people with no established credit is a courtesy, not an obligation. Many associations, and certainly corporations, guarantee the checks cashed for members or employees. A maximum limit, if any, should be indicated.

HSMA's Suggested Payment Schedule

The Hotel Sales Marketing Association has prepared a list of standardized billing procedures which should greatly reduce the snags in convention accounting. Following are the guidelines:

1. Establish a formal procedure for the hotel and the meeting planner to review periodically the room block arrangements before the meeting. The recommended schedule: up to one year before the meeting; six months before; then every month; and, with one month to go, weekly. The use of rooming lists is encouraged.
2. Meeting room usage and charges should be thoroughly reviewed before the meeting.
3. In general, use of credit cards should not be encouraged. The hotel should specify clearly what cards will be accepted and the maximum that can be charged.
4. A master statement of all functions should be organized daily. Single folios are to be used for all attendees' charges.
5. Night auditors and cashiers should be instructed about the details of posting convention charges.
6. It is desirable to have corporate meeting planners guarantee all attendees' bills. The hotel should inform the company of any delinquent accounts after thirty days.
7. A representative from accounting, the head cashier, and perhaps the accounts receivable department head should attend the preconvention meeting.
8. The specification sheet and individual function forms are to be supplied to the meeting planner before the convention; charges to be clearly specified in advance.

9. At the conclusion of each function a copy of the master statement and supporting vouchers should be furnished to the meeting planner for his signature.
10. It is recommended that the master account be submitted in full no more than five days after the meeting. Prepayment of a portion of the master statement is encouraged.[1]

The overriding emphasis of this checklist is communication. Clear, concise information on every aspect of billing must be communicated to the accounting department.

Gratuities

> The end of tipping is a long way off in America. I feel the planner should settle the gratuities subject in advance. If he feels uncomfortable with the amount expected, he should go to another hotel. Likewise, if he feels there is dissatisfaction with the amount of his gratuities, he should think twice before returning to that hotel. Most of the problems with gratuities are the result of not discussing the subject with the hotel convention staff—in the beginning, when everything else is being settled. Nobody should ever feel strange about asking the hotel for advice on this matter.[2]

Gratuities are a generally accepted part of convention costs. They are covered in all sales proposals and later in the letter of agreement. Yet, few areas of convention management seem to cause as much controversy.

Meeting planners are often confused about how much to tip, who should be tipped, and when the tip should be given. Hotels frequently are approached for advice on the amounts considered fair. A good hotel, anticipating this need, should be able to suggest tipping guidelines. However, wisdom should be used. Meeting planners are naturally offended by the suggestion that their gratuities are a form of remuneration rather than an expression of appreciation for good or exceptional service.

Gratuities can be categorized into four distinct groupings.

1. Tips for hotel hourly personnel, such as bellmen, waiters, maids, doormen, etc.
2. Tipping for group functions and banquets. These tips are normally figured as a percentage of the bill and added onto the check.

1. Barry Kushner, "Meeting's Over: How Do You Settle the Bill?" *Successful Meetings.* Reprinted with permission from *Successful Meetings*, copyright 1975, Bill Communications, Inc.

2. Roger Sonnabend, chairman of the Sonesta Hotels, quoted in 3M Business Press, *The Hotelman Looks at the Business of Meetings*, p. 67.

3. Blanket tips. The gratuity is added into the room charge and delegates are not encumbered with further tipping.
4. Special tips given to management personnel, such as the convention service manager, banquet manager, and head housemen.

Association Management, a leading trade publication, has surveyed hotels and meeting planners on the question of gratuities. The following general guidelines were suggested by the hotels surveyed for tipping hourly service personnel, our first classification:

bellmen—anywhere from fifty cents to one dollar per piece of luggage. (Las Vegas hotels commonly specify seventy-five cents in and seventy-five cents out.)
waiters, waitresses and room service—15 percent of the check is most common.
housekeepers—fifty cents to one dollar per person per day.
doormen—twenty-five cents per bag; fifty cents for valet parking service.[3]

Gratuities for group meals and banquets, our second classification, seem to present the most problems. Many meeting planners justifiably decry the practice of a 15 percent tip regardless of the quality of the service. However, the hotel is often following a union contract. The flat percentage gratuity is 15 to 17 percent in most cities. In the initial negotiations with the meeting planner, the convention service manager should clear the air by explaining this.

When there is a flat percentage on food and beverage setups, the hotel normally distributes the tip among the service personnel. A breakdown for a 15 percent tip might be 12 percent divided among the waiters and busboys and 3 percent for supervisory personnel such as captains and maître d's.

Blanket gratuities, our third classification, are becoming increasingly common. Meeting planners and delegates often favor this form of tipping, since they tip only once, when they register, and are not faced with the decision again. American plan resorts have used this method for years, and now commercial convention hotels are trying the system. The American plan of pricing has a single charge for room, meals, and gratuities. The more common European plan prices rooms, meals, and tips separately.

To help clarify blanket tipping, we will outline the policies of two well-known resorts.

If a blanket tipping policy is to be used, this must be communicated to the delegates. Often the meeting planner will point out the policy in the registration

---

3. "Guidelines for Handling Convention Gratuities," *Association Management.*

1. *The Greenbrier*
   White Sulphur Springs, West Virginia
   In lieu of gratuities for housekeeping and Modified American Plan food service personnel, a service charge of $5.00 per person is added daily to guests' accounts. Bellmen, doorman, and others who render personal services are not included in the service charge.
2. *Boca Raton*
   Boca Raton, Florida
   For the convenience of the convention group, the hotel adds $4.50 per day per person to cover the following hotel personnel:
   a. front door and parking attendants
   b. handling of luggage on arrival and departure
   c. chamber maids
   d. dining room personnel for meals served under the meal plan

   For a la carte food and beverages an automatic gratuity of 15 percent is added to the check. Other personnel are tipped at the convention group's discretion.[5]

packet. Notices declaring "Your gratuities are completely covered in the room charge; do not tip hotel personnel" are common. Similarly, the hotel should communicate this procedure to its employees, discouraging them from accepting tips. Again, the specification sheet is the medium whereby tipping policy is communicated internally.

The final type of gratuity is that used in rewarding special personnel. Meeting planners may ask the hotel about the accepted practice and internal policies for giving such tips. Hotels that do recommend tipping for special services will offer a suggested minimum scale, such as that shown in figure 18.3.

In conclusion, the handling of gratuities, as with all the elements of convention management, should be carefully reviewed and understood by both the meeting planner and the convention service manager. Even though tipping is a touchy area, no difficulties should arise if guidelines are clearly established at the outset.

4. Used with the Greenbrier's permission.
5. From the hotel's convention brochure. Used with permission.

Post-Convention Review

In any type of work, it is wise to review a job when it is completed. Much can be learned from this. Such a review should be done with an eye toward constructive comments; it helps not at all to review merely to lay blame on some individual—generally someone else. The purpose of a review is to evaluate performance during the event and the forecasting and planning that preceded the convention. All this is undertaken with the goal of improving technique so that the next event will go even smoother.

A convention service manager interviewed by us about post-convention meetings said, "A good, thorough preconvention meeting can lead to a very short and satisfying post-convention wrap-up." Good advice, and certainly an important point to remember in preparing for the event (chapter 12).

We recommend two review sessions. The first should include the hotel sales manager, the convention service manager, and the department heads who were involved. The purposes of this intra-staff meeting are to review all the meeting's rough spots, to discuss how the event could have been expedited, and to recognize any efforts that went well as examples for the future.

The second meeting should involve the convention executive and staff, or all he or she might invite. The convention bureau and decorator also might be included.

This is also held to go over all the many things that happened at the convention while they are fresh in everyone's mind. A good time to hold this meeting is when the master account gets a final review and approval. Everyone is in the hotel and relaxed after the great effort.

But don't duck discussions about the rough spots. Talk them out and try to agree on how they can be handled in the future. Both teams learn much from these inter-staff meetings.

It is also a time to begin the pitch for more business. Too many hotel staff people are reluctant to start selling at this time, but if all went well, it's the best time to make the pitch. This may not be a bid for the convention itself, but associations hold other types of meetings, too. Corporations hold meetings all the time, and you should make your bid for more of their business.

Every aspect of the meeting should be reviewed and discussed candidly. Association executives should feel free to express their views on the staff's service and performance. Meeting planners appreciate having the opportunity to share their comments. If they sense the hotel is honestly concerned about improvement, they will more readily book future business.

Fig. 18.3 Gratuity structure for special hotel personnel based on a survey of meeting planners. Used with permission of *Meetings News*.

Gratuities Vary Based On Hotel Staff Positions

Q. Assume that the following hotel personnel have been equally attentive. Indicate whether you would give them a gratuity, and if so, how much:

PERSONNEL	YES	NO	HIGH	LOW	AVERAGE
Convention Service Director (main contact)	75%	25%	$500	$25	$125
Food and Beverage Manager	68%	32%	$500	$15	$ 88
Assistant Convention Services Director	65%	35%	$150	$15	$ 58
Setup Crew Supervisor	62%	13%	$200	$10	$ 44
Hotel General Manager	0%	100%	—	—	—
Convention Sales Manager	10%	90%	$200	$35	$ 69
Account Executive on your convention	17%	83%	$400	$15	$ 80
Catering Manager	63%	37%	$400	$20	$ 78
Front Desk Supervisor*	69%	31%	$100	$10	$ 36
Head Banquet Waiter**	82%	18%	$125	$10	$ 42
Audio Visual Operator	41%	59%	$200	$ 5	$ 44
Switchboard Operator***	39%	61%	$ 50	$10	22

* Other gratuity: candy (1)
** Other gratuity: $10 per event (1); $20 per function (1)
***Other gratuity: $10 for each operator (1); $250 to PBX Fund (1); $150 to include operators (1); candy (4); and gift (1)

Mentioned By 10 Or Fewer Respondents	Average Amount
Accounting Manager	$ 23
A/V Supervisor	$ 25
Banquet Captains	$ 40
Bell Captain	$ 33
Chef	$ 90
Sales, Convention Services & Catering Secretaries	$ 38
Executive Suite Maid	$ 20
Front Desk Personnel	$ 25
Group Reservations Coordinator	$ 75
Head Housekeeper	$ 33
Maids for Staff Rooms	$ 20
Master Account Coordinator	$ 50
Package Room Supervisor	$ 37
Pastry Chef	$ 25
Reservations Assistant	$100
Reservations Manager	$163
Reservations Personnel	$ 5
Room Service Supervisor	$ 75
Sous Chefs	$ 35
Tennis and Golf Pros	$ 62
Transportation Director	$ 25

Comparison with Projections

Compare what happened with what was expected to happen. Compare the number of guest rooms originally blocked out with the number actually used. Review the flow into and out of the hotel, with an eye toward having adequate help on hand to receive the guests. Were no-shows a problem? Did you overbook? If so, how did you handle it? Compare attendance with that of other years.

Early departures wreak havoc with hotel income. Yet they generally reflect at least as much on the convention programing as on hotel attractions. If early departures were greater than in previous years, the program could be at fault; but the hotel still might give some thought to what it can do to make its facilities or area more inviting.

If this convention continually has a problem with early departures, the executive should make some effort to get members to estimate their stays more accurately and honestly. Most convention executives realize that healthy hotels are their concern, too.

Late departures create a different problem when they interfere with other group commitments that are beginning. There is enough evidence of intentional overbooking by hotels that late departures add fuel to the fire. Late departures are a problem, of course, only when the house is overfilled. Otherwise, it's a pleasant bonus.

Resort properties often have problems with early arrivals and late departures when they book back-to-back conventions divided by a weekend. This calls for careful attention to reservation systems.

The entire projection of arrival and departure patterns should be reviewed thoroughly. The mix of rooms used—singles, doubles, twins, and suites—should be compared with what was blocked out in order to polish the technique for the next time. Compare the pattern with the work schedule of your front desk people and other personnel needed for heavy arrival traffic.

Function Attendance

Both the hotel people and the convention executive are most interested in how actual attendance at special functions compared with expectations. Guarantees at food functions don't tell the whole story. If actual attendance fell below the guarantee, the convention executive still has to pay for the full number guaranteed or try to persuade the hotel to accept payment for only those served. On the other hand, if more than an extra 10 percent showed up, the hotel is hard-pressed to seat and serve them. The convention organization is chagrined not to serve its members; the hotel is undeservedly shown in bad light.

Also take another look at function room allocations. It is difficult to conduct an impressive meeting in a room only 30 percent filled. A smaller room would have helped, if one were available. If not, dividers and screens could have helped. Perhaps the larger room could have been used for something else.

Special Services

Feedback on the hotel's services also is of great interest. Each convention is different, but the hotel can learn from each one about room service, the restaurants, the play at the athletic facilities, the elevator service. Keep a vigilant eye on these services because hotel reputations depend on them.

It is an interesting phenomenon that the people who shape the image in the hotel business are the ones who get the least pay. The telephone operator and the front desk people probably have more contact with hotel guests than anyone else of the staff. If they have been congenial throughout the convention, the customer probably will carry away a good image of the hotel.

Individual Comments

A very different picture may emerge if you take the trouble to invite comments from your own staff, as well as from guests. Staff members have a different vantage point than the sales manager or the convention service manager. Ask the bellmen and the maids and the front desk people how they think the convention went.

Stand near the cashier at check-out time to get candid comments from guests. Some hotels make post-event mailings to guests. Questionnaires are sent requesting how the hotel might better serve its guests. The benefits are twofold: the hotel projects a sincere desire to render good service, and it is often able to detect unspotted problem areas.

Figure 18.4 is the service evaluation form used by Doubletree Inns which quizzes the respondent on all service aspects of the meeting. This procedure has proved very advantageous in booking repeat business.

Whatever your approach, some effort should be made to determine the staff's and guest's feelings about how the event went and how the hotel fared.

Match-up

After it is all over, give some thought to how well the meeting matched up with your convention facility. From the hotel's viewpoint, how high a priority would you give this particular convention or meeting? Such a rating will help you select prospects for future sales efforts. The convention executive is thinking along similar lines. If you matched his needs and performed well, he will be more receptive to returning in the future.

This match-up review involves many of the factors that went into the group's original selection of your hotel and your decision to go after the business. It is a re-evaluation of all the hotel facilities and group needs, with the benefit of experience, and taking into consideration the suitability of the meeting rooms, number and kinds of guest rooms, other attractions in and around the hotel, the area, and so on.

Both groups reappraise each other, and their conclusions affect the decision to do business again.

The Hotel Sahara in Las Vegas uses a Group and Convention Performance Report as a post-convention tool for assessment and evaluation (fig. 18.5). Information is collected about the group's spending habits and room commitment, among other data. Such a form serves as a research tool, with projections measured against actual numbers. An analysis gives the Sahara an indication of the types of groups it should be soliciting.

Appendix B is a similar, but more comprehensive, post-convention report used at the Disneyland Hotel in Anaheim, California. This gives the hotel a permanent record of the activities, so that a complete summary is available when a future sale is discussed. The servicing of repeat conventions is facilitated because the hotel can quickly review the group's needs and requirements.

The Boca Raton Hotel follows up on convention executives after they return home, sending them a complete report of the principal convention events. Included are the number in attendance, the costs involved, and other pertinent details that might be helpful to the executives in making up their own reports. The hotel feels this service saves the meeting planners many hours of labor and provides a cross-check for their figures.

Finally, many convention bureaus ask local hotels to provide them with statistics on conventions. A confidential convention report distributed by the Anaheim Visitor and Convention Bureau is pictured in figure 18.6. This report provides over-all data on the convention and aids the bureau in structuring its files.

433

DOUBLETREE INN

SERVICE EVALUATION

COMPANY/GROUP NAME _____

EVALUATOR'S NAME _____

FRONT OFFICE	Exlt	Good	Fair	Poor	Comments
Registration					
Bellman Service					
Telephone Service					
Desk Clerk Service					
Employee's Attitude					

RESTAURANTS & LOUNGE					
Coffee Shop					
Food & Beverage Quality					
Food & Beverage Service					
Dining Room					
Food & Beverage Quality					
Food & Beverage Service					
Lounge					
Entertainment Quality					
Beverage Quality					
Beverage Service					
Room Service					
Food & Beverage Quality					
Food & Beverage Service					

HOUSEKEEPING					
Guest Rooms					
Restaurants & Lounge					
Public Areas					
Meeting & Banquet Rooms					

MEETING & BANQUET FACILITIES					
Room Set-up					
On Time?					
Banquet Meal Service					
Food & Beverage Quality					
Food & Beverage Service					
Coffee Breaks					
Employee Attitudes					
Sales/Catering Staff					
Service Staff					
Air Conditioning/Heat					
Lighting					
Necessary Equipment Provided					

MISCELLANEOUS					
Courtesy Car Service					
Parking					

ADDITIONAL COMMENTS _____

_____

FUTURE RESERVATIONS:

Are there future meeting or banquet dates presently in the planning stage? _____

Can dates be held on tentative basis? _____

I would like additional information on Doubletree facilities in the following cities: _____

987-5

Fig. 18.5 The Sahara Hotel in Las Vegas uses its Group and Convention Performance Report to evaluate its conventions and as a research tool. (Reprinted with permission of Sahara Hotel).

HOTEL SAHARA

GROUP & CONVENTION PERFORMANCE REPORT

NAME OF GROUP _____

SALES ACCOUNT EXECUTIVE _____

RATES _____

NUMBER OF ROOMS BOOKED _____ SUITES _____

METHOD OF HANDLING
ROOM RESERVATIONS _____

ACTUAL ROOM UNITS PICKED UP

TOTAL ROOM NIGHTS

DATES										
DAYS										
BLOCKED										
OCCUPIED										

PARLORS (INCLUDED IN ROOM UNITS)

BLOCKED										
OCCUPIED										

COMMENTS: _____

_____

_____

_____

PREPARED BY: _____

DATE: _____

435

Fig. 18.6 Post-convention report issued by the Anaheim Visitor and Convention Bureau to local hotels. (By permission of the Anaheim Visitor and Convention Bureau).

@naheim

CONFIDENTIAL CONVENTION REPORT

Date_____

Organization_____

Regular or Special Meeting_____Annual,Semi-Annual,Other_____

If Regional or District, Name States or Area_____

Executive in Charge_____ Title_____

Address_____

Dates of Meeting_____Hdq. Hotel_____

Reg. Attendance_____Total Att._____Pre-Reg._____

Daily Reg.: Sun_____Mon_____Tues_____Weds_____Thurs_____Fri____Sat____

No. in Hotels_____Rms. in Hdq. Hotel_____Suites_____

No. Spouses_____Comp Rms._____Travel Agent (yes)_____ (no)_____

Meeting Rooms: Attendance_____Capacity_____Rental_____Simul.____

Exhibits Held: Hotel_____Center_____Net Space_____Rental_____

Duration of Exhibit: Move In_____ Show Days_____ Move Out_____

Meal Functions: No. and Type_____Attendance_____

_____

No. Simul._____ Hotel_____Center_____Cost_____

Future Definite Convention Cities & Dates:

19_____   19_____

19_____   19_____

Newly Elected Officers and Addresses:

_____

_____

Additional information:

By_____

VISITOR & CONVENTION BUREAU 800 WEST KATELLA AVENUE/ANAHEIM, CALIFORNIA/92802/(714) 533-5536
EASTERN SALES OFFICE/1629 K STREET, N.W./WASHINGTON, D.C./20006/(202) 872-1178

Final Appraisal

Could you do a better job if the clock could be turned back to give you another chance? That question should be considered with complete frankness in the cold light of post-convention experience. If the answer discloses areas of difficulty, you should take steps to eliminate the problems in the future. The problems could deal with personnel or facilities. Solving them could help the sales manager set priorities on the kind of business you want and can handle. If the answers please you, don't forget to send a thank-you letter to the meeting planner, and to put that name in your follow-up file for some time in the very near future.

Study Questions

1. Discuss the statement "As with most aspects of convention planning, the time to avoid billing problems is in the beginning and not at the end." What procedures are recommended for avoiding billing problems?

2. Outline the HSMA's suggested payment schedule.

3. List the four groupings for service gratuities, and distinguish between blanket gratuities and special tipping.

4. Comment on the importance of a post-convention review. Who should attend the post-convention meeting? What should be included in the post-convention report?

5. Compare the post-convention forms used by Doubletree Inns, Disneyland Hotel, and the Hotel Sahara. What are the benefits of such a report?

Convention Liaison Manual
Convention Liaison Council
1575 Eye Street, N.W.
Washington, D.C. 20005

Convention Management and Service
by Frank W. Berkman, CHSE,
   David C. Dorf, CHSE and
   Leonard R. Oakes, CHSE
The Educational Institute of the American Hotel & Motel Association
1407 South Harrison Road
East Lansing, MI 48823

The Executive's Guide to Meetings, Conferences & Audiovisual Presentations
by James R. Jeffries and
   Jefferson D. Bates
McGraw-Hill Book Company
1221 Avenue of the Americas
New York, NY 10020

500 Guest Service Ideas
Edited by Charles Nolte
Innkeeping World
P.O. Box 84108
Seattle, WA 98124

How To Make Meetings More Productive
by Myron Gordon, Ph.D.
Sterling Publishing Company
Two Park Avenue
New York, NY 10016

How To Make Meetings Work
by Michael Doyle and David Starus
Jove Books
51 Madison Avenue
New York, NY 10010

How To Organize Meetings
by Martin Jones
Beaufort Books
9 East 40th Street
New York, NY 10016

Meeting Management: A Professional Approach
by James E. Jones
Bayard Publications, Inc.
695 Summer Street
Stamford, CT 06901

Meetings, Conventions & Incentive Travel: (4,349 Ideas & Money Saving Tips)
by Helen Adam
Helen Adam & Associates
Benjamin Fox Pavilion
Jenkintown, PA 19046

The Practice of Hospitality Management I
Edited by Abraham Pizam, Ph.D.
R.C. Lewis, Ph.D., and
P.B. Manning, Ph.D.
AVI Publishing Company
P.O. Box 831
Westport, CT 06881

The Practice of Hospitality Management II
Edited by Robert C. Lewis,
Thomas J. Beggs, Margaret Shaw, and
Steven A. Croffoot
AVI Publishing Company
P.O. Box 831
Westport, CT 06881

Professional Meeting Management
by The Professional Convention Management Association
PCMA
100 Vestavia Office Park, Suite 220
Birmingham, AL 35216

Selling Out: A How-To Manual on Reservations Management
The Educational Institute of the American Hotel & Motel Association
1407 South Harrison Road
East Lansing, MI 48823

Appendix A   Directory of Trade Organizations and Customer Publications

American Hotel & Motel Association (AH&MA)
888 Seventh Avenue
New York, NY 10106
(212) 265-4506

American Society of Association Executives (ASAE)
1575 Eye Street N.W.
Washington, DC 20005
(202) 626-2723

American Society for Training and Development (ASTD)
1630 Duke Street
Alexandria, VA 22313
(703) 683-8100

American Society of Travel Agents (ASTA)
4400 MacArthur Boulevard N.W.
Washington, DC 20007
(202) 965-7520

Association & Society Manager (Publication)
1640 5th Street
Santa Monica, CA 90401
(213) 395-0234

Association Management (Publication)
1575 Eye Street N.W.
Washington, DC 20005
(202) 626-2711

Association of Independent Meeting Planners
5103 Wigville Road
Thurmont, MD 21788
(301) 271-4222

Best's Insurance Convention Guide (Publication)
Ambest Road
Oldwick, NJ 08858
(201) 439-2200

Business Travel News (Publication)
600 Community Drive
Manhasset, NY 11030
(516) 365-4600

Convention Liaison Council (CLC)
1575 Eye Street N.W.
Washington, DC 20005
(202) 626-2764

Convention World (Publication)
500 Summer Street
Stamford, CT 06901
(203) 327-0800

Corporate & Incentive Travel (Publication)
488 Madison Avenue
New York, NY 10022
(212) 888-1500

Corporate Meetings & Incentives (Publication)
747 Third Avenue
New York, NY 10017
(212) 418-4108

Convene (Publication)
100 Vestavia Office Park
Birmingham, AL 35216
(205) 823-7262

Corporate Travel (Publication)
1515 Broadway
New York, NY 10036
(212) 869-1300

Exhibit Designers and Producers Association (ED&PA)
1411 K Street N.W.
Washington, DC 20005
(202) 393-2001

Exposition Service Contractors Association (ESCA)
1516 So. Pontius Avenue
Los Angeles, CA 90025
(213) 478-0215

Health Care Exhibitors Association (HCEA)
5775 Peachtress-Dunwoody Road
Atlanta, GA 30342
(404) 252-3663

Hotel Sales & Marketing Association International (HSMAI)
1400 K Street N.W.
Washington, DC 20005
(202) 789-0089

Institute of Association Management Companies (IAMC)
5820 Wilshire Boulevard
Los Angeles, CA 90036
(213) 937-5514

Insurance Conference Planners Association (ICPA)
18 Chestnut Street
Worcester, MA 01608
(617) 793-5828

Insurance Conference Planner (Publication)
500 Summer Street
Stamford, CT 06901
(203) 327-0800

International Association of Auditorium Managers (IAAM)
500 N. Michigan Avenue
Chicago, IL 60611
(312) 661-1700

International Association of Conference Centers (IACC)
45 Progress Parkway
Maryland Hts, MO 36043
(314) 469-9093

International Association of Convention & Visitors Bureau (IACVB)
1809 Woodfield Drive
Savoy, IL 61874
(217) 359-8881

International Association of Fairs & Expositions (IAFE)
P.O. Box 985
Springfield, MO 65801
(417) 862-5771

International Communication Industries Association (ICIA)
3150 Spring Street
Fairfax, VA 22031
(703) 273-7200

Medical Meetings (Publication)
63 Great Road
Maynard, MA 01754
(617) 897-5552

Meeting Manager (Publication)
1950 Stemmons Freeway
Dallas, TX 75207
(214) 746-5222

Meeting News (Publication)
1515 Broadway
New York, NY 10036
(212) 869-1300

Meeting Planners International (MPI)
1950 Stemmons Freeway
Dallas TX 75207
(214) 746-5222

Meetings & Conventions (Publication)
500 Plaza Drive
Secaucus, NJ 07094
(201) 902-1700

National Association of Exposition Managers (NAEM)
334 East Garfield Road
Aurora, OH 44202
(216) 562-8255

National Passenger Traffic Association (NPTA)
516 Fifth Avenue
New York, NY 10036
(212) 221-6782

Official Meeting Facilities Guide (Publication)
500 Plaza Drive
Secaucus, NJ 07094

Pacific Area Travel Association (PATA)
228 Grant Avenue
San Francisco, CA 94108
(415) 986-4646

Professional Convention Management Association (PCMA)
100 Vestavia Office Park
Birmingham, AL 35216
(205) 823-7262

Religious Conference Management Association (RCMA)
1 Hoosier Dome
Indianapolis, IN 46225
(317) 632-1888

Sales & Marketing Executives International (SMEI)
Statler Office Tower, Ste 446
Cleveland, OH 44115
(216) 771-6650

Sales & Marketing Management (Publication)
633 Third Avenue
New York, NY 10017
(212) 986-4800

Society of Company Meeting Planners (SCMP)
2600 Garden Road
Monterey, CA 93940
(408) 649-6544

Society of Government Meeting Planners
1133 15th Street N.W.
Washington, DC 20005
(202) 232-6883

Society of Incentive Travel Executives (SITE)
271 Madison Avenue
New York, NY 10016
(212) 889-9340

Successful Meetings (Publication)
633 Third Avenue
New York, NY 10017
(212) 986-4800

Tradeshow & Exhibit Manager (Publication)
1640 5th Street
Santa Monica, CA 90401
(213) 395-0234

Trade Show Bureau
P.O. Box 797
East Orleans, MA 02643
(617) 240-0177

Travel Industry Association of American (TIA)
1899 L Street N.W.
Washington, DC 20036
(202) 293-1433

Western Association News (Publication)
1516 S. Pontius Avenue
Los Angeles, CA 90025
(213) 478-0215

Appendix B   Post-Convention Report

Following is the post-convention report used by the Disneyland Hotel in Anaheim, Calif. (used with permission).

File # _____

DISNEYLAND HOTEL
POST-CONVENTION REPORT

ASSOCIATION: _____

_____

DATES: _____

CONTACT: _____ TITLE: _____

ADDRESS: _____

TOTAL GUEST ROOMS COMMITTED: _____

TOTAL GUEST ROOMS RESERVED: _____

TOTAL ROOM NIGHTS: _____ , OVER THE DATES OF _____

OVERFLOW HOUSING: _____ , ROOMS AT _____

HOUSING (handled by):   HOTEL _____ V & C _____

RATES:

COMPLIMENTARY ROOMS: _____

_____

_____

GUEST ROOMS

ACTUAL OCCUPANCY: _____

DAY OF WEEK: _____

DATE: _____

OCCUPANCY: _____

_____

DAY OF WEEK: _____

DATE: _____

OCCUPANCY: _____

TOTAL ROOM-NIGHTS: _____

PUBLIC ROOMS:

ROOM RENTALS: _____ AMOUNT: _____

EXHIBITS:

ROOM: _____ NUMBER OF BOOTHS: _____

TOTAL CHARGE: _____ TOTAL SQUARE FEET _____

@ _____ PER NET SQ. FT., FOR _____ SHOW DAYS.

SECURITY CHARGES:

NUMBER OF HOURS: _____ @ _____ PER HOUR = _____

ADDITIONAL MICROPHONE CHARGES:

NUMBER OF ADDITIONAL MICROPHONES USED: _____ @ _____

EACH = _____

Use of: Dining Rooms   LOW _____ MEDIUM _____ EXCELLENT _____
         Room Service   LOW _____ MEDIUM _____ EXCELLENT _____
         Public Bars   LOW _____ MEDIUM _____ EXCELLENT _____

CITIES OR AREAS UNDER CONSIDERATION FOR NEXT CONVENTION:

Year _____ City _____

Year _____ City _____

How, when and where will decision be reached: _____

_____

_____

_____

Decision will be made by: _____

_____

Thank you letters written to:

_____ By: _____

_____ By: _____

_____ By: _____

SPECIAL NOTES:

_____

_____

_____

_____

_____

Disneyland Hotel Salesman: _____

Disneyland Hotel Catering: _____

Disneyland Hotel Banquet: _____

Disneyland Hotel Convention Coordinator: _____

Appendix C   Sample Contract

Following is a sample contract of the kind used by the Las Vegas Convention Service Co. (used with permission).

LAS VEGAS CONVENTION SERVICE CO.

___(date)___

Name _____
Title _____
Assn. _____
Address _____
City & State ____

Re: ___(name of show)_____
        ___(dates)_____
        ___(site)_____

Dear _____:

(INTRODUCTION PARAGRAPH USUALLY DICTATED, INCLUDING DECORATING AND DRAYAGE SERVICES IN THIS PARAGRAPH)

(1)   The Las Vegas Convention Service Company agrees to install, maintain, and remove the required number of 8' x 10' or 10' x 10' standard gold draped exhibit booths for a total rental price of $_____ per booth, plus $2.50 for a 9" x 44" booth identification sign stating the exhibitor's name, city, and state. The above-quoted costs are subject to 3.5% Nevada Sales and Use Tax.

(2)   Additional services such as rental furniture, labor to install and dismantle exhibits, special booth decorations, table skirting, special sign service, electrical and material handling will be provided through our service center at prevailing rates.

(3)   The first 18' of registration counter, if needed, will be furnished at no charge, and additional counters will be supplied at $_____ per foot, including standard sign copy. Special copy will be furnished upon request. The above-quoted costs are subject to 3.5% Nevada Sales and Use Tax.

LAS VEGAS CONVENTION SERVICE CO.

Mr. _____
     (date)
_____
Page 2 _____

(4) Items listed below ordered by Show Management for use by the
     Association from exhibitor service rate sheets will be sub-
     ject to the following discounts:

Furniture	50% Discount
Table Drape	25% Discount
Signs	10% Discount

(5) We would like to recommend that you use Global Productions
     for all of the audiovisual and video equipment needed for
     your forthcoming meeting. Global Productions is a subsidiary
     of the Las Vegas Convention Service Company and services the
     majority of meetings in the Las Vegas area. They have a vast
     inventory of the latest audiovisual and video equipment
     appropriate for almost any situation. The equipment is avail-
     able on a rental basis, by the day or week and undergoes
     a rigid performance check before delivery. Also, they are
     familiar with the profiles of all meeting rooms and can assure
     you of technically compatible installations.

(6) If you have need for additional meeting services, Global
     Productions provides multi-media presentations, set and stage
     designs and construction, special graphic effects, signs, a
     complete photography department, welding, carpentry, electrical
     work, special lighting effects, video taping, tape recorders
     to tape large or small meetings, theatre sound systems and
     many more.

(7) As a follow-up to this agreement, we are asking Global Produc-
     tions to contact you or your meeting coordinator to discuss
     your basic meeting needs. They would welcome the opportunity
     to present suggestions to make your meeting more successful.

(8) Through our transportation division we agree to provide your
     Association and your exhibitors complete convention freight
     handling including pre-show storage, move-in, handling of
     empty containers to and from the booth, and move-out.

(9) Storage and handling in the amount of 1,500 pounds of Associ-
     ation registration materials and/or Association exhibit will
     be provided at no cost to the Association. The Las Vegas
     Convention Service Company will allow a 25% reduced rate on
     material weights over 1,500 pounds.

LAS VEGAS CONVENTION SERVICE CO.

Mr. _____
        (date) _____
Page 3 _____

(10) Please be advised the rates contained in our exhibitor service kit
      (refer to enclosed sample), unless previously guaranteed, are
      subject to change and offered only as a sample with the understand-
      ing that rates in effect at the time of your show will prevail.

(11) The following services will be provided at no additional charge to
      Show Management:

      (A) Supply sufficient number of exhibitor service kits for
           mailing to confirmed exhibitors;

      (B) Procure advance clearance with all unions involved in policies
           and operating procedures in order to avoid any jurisdictional
           embarrassment to the exhibitor or Show Management;

      (C) Submit all estimates where required on all extra work ordered
           by Show Management;

      (D) Assist in drawing up rules and regulations as they apply to
           the _____ Hotel;

      (E) Prepare floor plans of booth layout;

      (F) Lay out floor prior to booth setup;

      (G) Staff, equip, and operate a service center during installa-
           tion, show time and dismantling, with experienced personnel;

      (H) Handle all orders and technical matters during show days;

      (I) Supervise subcontractors such as florists, models, etc., if
           desired by Show Management. Items in this category ordered
           by Show Management will be billed by subcontractors at
           prevailing rates; should you desire these items to be billed
           by Las Vegas Convention Service Company, a 15% handling charge
           will apply;

      (J) Consult and meet with Show Management whenever and wherever
           requested;

      (K) Protect you with regular insurance coverage on property damage
           and public liability.

1624 Mojave Road   •   P.O. Box ███ 42569 Las Vegas, Nevada ███ 89104   Telephone: (702) 457-5075

LAS VEGAS CONVENTION SERVICE CO.

Mr._____

_____(date)_____

Page 4_____

(12) Should any emergency arise, of any nature, previous to the opening
      date of_____which would prevent
      its scheduled opening, destruction or damage to the exhibit building
      by fire, wind, storm, strikes, acts of God, etc. reimbursement is
      to be made only to the extent of actual costs as reflected by labor
      time cards and special materials purchased for use in your show.
      Time and expense for preparatory work, plans, meetings are not to
      be reimbursed regardless of time of cancellation.

(13) For your convenience, we are submitting this proposal in duplicate.
      If the above meets with your approval, please acknowledge one copy
      and return for our files.

      Sincerely,

      LAS VEGAS CONVENTION SERVICE CO.

      Your name_____

      Title_____

      HRN:ac
      Enclosure: 1 Service Kit

ACCEPTED BY:_____ DATE:_____

1624 Mojave Road   •   P.O. Box ▮▮ 42669   Las Vegas, Nevada ▮▮ 89104   Telephone: (702) 457-5075

Appendix D   Sample Proposal Letter

Following is a sample proposal letter of the kind used by Caesars Palace in Las Vegas (used with permission).

3570 LAS VEGAS BOULEVARD, SOUTH

LAS VEGAS, NEVADA 89109

AREA CODE 702—731 7110

November 29, 19

Mr. John Smith
President
John Smith Incorporated
201 First Street
New York, New York

Dear Mr. Smith:

It was good to hear that the JOHN SMITH INCORPORATED is considering Las Vegas for a future convention. We wish to extend to you, your officers and members a genuinely sincere invitation to headquarter this meeting at CAESARS PALACE.

DATES

Your preferred dates are available and will be held for you on a tentative basis pending a final decision or until such time as another association requests the same set of dates:

November 7-11, 19

RATES

Special convention rates will be extended as follows:

      $_____per room daily, single or double occupancy, European Plan, plus 6% county room tax, net, non-commissionable.

SUITE RATES
$_____ - Petite Suite
$_____ - One-bedroom Deluxe Suite
$_____ - One-bedroom Royal Suite

Two-bedroom suites are also available.

Mr. John Smith
November 29, 19
Page Two

<u>ROOMS</u>

It is my understanding that you anticipate the use of approximately 500 sleeping rooms.

All of the accommodations at CAESARS PALACE are tastefully
decorated with shades of color that befit the Roman Era.
All rooms are equipped with color televisions and radios.

AS A SPECIAL ADDED FEATURE, IN EACH ROOM FIRST RUN MOVIES
ARE AVAILABLE AT NO COST, COMMENCING AT 12:00 NOON TO
6:00 A.M., WITH SPECIAL FEATURES FOR CHILDREN ON SATURDAYS
AND SUNDAYS STARTING AT 6:00 A.M.

<u>COMPLIMENTARY SERVICES</u>

IN ADDITION TO THE SALES DEPARTMENT OF CAESARS PALACE, THE
FOLLOWING PERSONNEL ARE AVAILABLE ON A FULL-TIME BASIS TO
ASSIST YOU, AT NO ADDITIONAL CHARGE, DURING NORMAL WORKING
HOURS:

CONVENTION COORDINATOR - MICHAEL C. MONAHAN, 702/731-7200
            CONVENTION SET-UP SUPERVISOR*
            SOUND TECHNICIAN*
            CONVENTION PORTERS*

        *AVAILABLE ON PAGE.

We will be happy to provide one COMPLIMENTARY unit (either
bedroom or parlor) for every 50 units actually used. This
complimentary policy will apply only during the dates of
your meeting with us. These complimentary units may be
assigned at your discretion.

We are happy to provide personalized return reservation
cards for distribution to your members at no charge
whatsoever. We will also assist you in the promotion
of your meeting with envelope size color hotel brochures
(in reasonable quantities, of course).

Among some of the niceties offered by CAESARS PALACE is
unlimited free ice for your room. Merely call Room Service
(extension 421) for your delivery. Also CAESARS PALACE
maintains a Guest Relations Desk to assist hotel guests
in making show reservations throughout the city. Our

Mr. John Smith
November 29, 19
Page Three

Bell Captains are available and most happy to make reservations
for those delegates wishing to enjoy the many tours of the
area.

Our Las Vegas Convention & Visitors Authority services include
publicity material, badges and badge holders, personnel for
the registration desk, bulletin typewriters and information
sheets. . . .all free of charge. You may obtain these
services by contacting the Las Vegas Convention & Visitors
Authority at 702/735-2323.

MEETING & BANQUET SPACE

The Colosseum, our main ballroom, will seat 6,000 persons
theatre style or 4,000 banquet style (round tables of 10).
The Colosseum may be divided into seven smaller rooms by
the use of electrically operated, soundproof walls, capable
of operating independently with sound and lights. The
Imperium, Majestium, Regalium and Atrium Rooms may be
divided into even smaller rooms when the need arises. In
addition, we feature two permanent convention registration
desks, three interconnecting Association headquarter offices
(located directly behind our 46' permanent convention desk),
and two Board of Directors Conference rooms. Also, the adjoining South Wing contains 12 studio rooms which easily convert
into small meeting rooms, capable of handling 15 persons
conference style or 25 persons theatre style. This same wing
contains a one-bedroom Association Executive Suite. There is
a total of 35 meeting rooms, seating from 15 to 1,200 persons
each.

PLEASE MAKE CAREFUL NOTE THAT WE DO NOT CHARGE FOR THE USE
OF OUR MEETING AND BANQUET SPACE.

EXHIBIT SPACE

The Colosseum, our main ballroom, is also an ideal exhibit
area. This ballroom, completely carpeted, is located on the
ground floor with direct truck access openings into two
separate loading doors. West entrance measures 18' x 36',
capable of airplanes passing through without the removal of
wings. The South entrance measures 10' x 12'. Floor load
is unlimited. This area will hold 288 - 8' x 10' booths.
The overall area will accommodate 365 - 8' x 10' booths.

CAESARS PALACE will provide sufficient microphones for your
use in our meeting rooms at no charge. Other sound equipment, projectors, screens, cordless mikes, etc. may be

Mr. John Smith
November 29, 19
Page Four

obtained from the Nevada Audio-Visual Services in Las Vegas,
702/876-6272, on a rental basis. If you wish, you may
deal directly with our Convention Coordinator on this item
also.

You may deal directly with our fine local firm, Las Vegas
Convention Service Company, 702/457-5075, for booth set-up
or through our Convention Coordinator.

In addition to the above, the Circus Maximus (our showroom)
is available for daytime use up to 4:30 p.m. This room,
with its elaborate stage, perfect acoustics and unobstructed
view, is capable of seating upward to 1,100 persons schoolroom style or 1,500 persons theatre style.

ALL OF THE MAIN CONVENTION ROOMS ARE CONCENTRATED IN ONE
PRIVATE AREA AND ON ONE LEVEL, COMPLETELY ISOLATED FROM
ALL OUTSIDE DISTRACTION.

PLEASE MAKE CAREFUL NOTE THAT WE DO NOT CHARGE FOR THE USE
OF OUR EXHIBIT SPACE.

GROUP FUNCTIONS

Our Catering Department will work directly with you concerning the specifics on your food and beverage requirements.

    CATERING MANAGER - JEANNE SCHROEDER
    ADMINISTRATIVE ASSISTANT CATERING MANAGER -
      VICKI MC GURK
    PHONE NUMBER FOR BOTH: 702/731-7207

DINING/ENTERTAINMENT

The spectacular Palace Court gourmet restaurant, open 7:00 p.m.
to 1:00 a.m., overlooking the Garden of the Gods, features
the finest in French cuisine dining. Also included in this
delightful setting is the Palace Court Lounge with music and
dancing from 7:00 p.m. to 3:00 a.m. Bacchanal Restaurant,
in lavish Roman decor with pillars and statues, is open
6:00 p.m. to midnight with gourmet entrees. Ah-So, a
Japanese Steak House in an Oriental garden atmosphere with
water-lily ponds and waterfalls, is open 6:00 p.m. to
midnight. An informal Italian restaurant, Piazza, is
open 5:30 p.m. to 11:30 p.m. Cleopatra's Barge, with a
replica of Cleopatra's trysting ship, is open 9:00 p.m.

Mr. John Smith
November 29, 19
Page Five

to 4:30 a.m. with a live band for dancing. Our Circus Maximus
showroom presents top-name entertainers such as Frank Sinatra,
Tom Jones, and many other stars, twice nightly. Caesars
Forum, our gambling casino, is open 24 hours daily.

TENNIS

CAESARS PALACE now boasts four indoor and eight outdoor
championship tennis courts with head professional, Pancho
Gonzales. The courts are located on the premises and are
available for play, both day and night. Tournaments can
be arranged. There is no charge for the use of these
courts.

SWIMMING

In our Garden of the Gods, CAESARS PALACE boasts one of
the most spectacular swimming pools to be found anywhere.
This Olympic-sized pool is attended by legions of Caesar's
lifeguards and Roman Goddesses, who will serve you your
favorite "nectar of the Gods".

GOLF

Arrangements can be made to play golf at any one of eight
championship courses in the area. The nearest course is
directly across the street, just two or three minutes
walking distance from CAESARS PALACE.

MEN'S AND WOMEN'S HEALTH CLUBS

Handball courts, along with squash courts, sauna baths,
whirlpools, steam rooms with masseurs and masseuses in
attendance, indoor and outdoor sunbathing areas, separate
television lounge areas for men and women are the latest
luxuries for guests of CAESARS PALACE. These excellent
facilities are located in the private area of the roof
garden on the 15th floor.

Located in the same roof garden area, award-winning
beauticians are at your beck and call to pamper your
every wish in the Beauty Salon. Also, in the same area,
our barbers are available, by appointment, for hairstyling.
Each shop enjoys a commanding view of the Las Vegas Strip
and the surrounding areas.

Mr. John Smith
November 29, 19
Page Six

We have a number of very fine shops on our first floor
arcade including a Men's Shop, Dress Shop, Fur Shop,
Jewelry Shop, Toy Shop, and Gift Shop.

PHOTOGRAPHY

Arrangements for complete photographic coverage can be
made with Cashman Photo Enterprises, Inc., 702/735-0131,
which is located on our premises. In the event the
services of Cashman are unavailable, we also recommend
our comprehensive local firms, Photography by Ron Tomlin,
702/734-2421, and Allen Photographers, 702/735-2222. You
may deal directly with these companies for your photographic requirements.

GROUP BUS MOVEMENTS

We suggest the use of Gray Line Tours. You may call them
directly at 702/384-1234.

Last, but not least, if you are planning to use a ground
handler for your arriving delegates, we would be more than
happy to assist you in the selection of this company.

Mr. Smith, we hope all of the above sounds exciting to
you and meets with your approval. Any comments you might
have in mind regarding this proposal will be appreciated.

However, the real proof of the pudding would be a personal
visit to CAESARS PALACE for a few days, as our guest, and
see for yourself the wonderful facilities of CAESARS
PALACE in the glamorous setting of Las Vegas.

Kind regards,

CAESARS PALACE

Charles J. Monahan
Vice President - Sales & Marketing

CJM:ls
Enclosures

Appendix E   Marketing Plan

I.   Commercial Business
   A. Special Rates
      1. A twenty percent discount off all rack rates will be allowed for all commercial accounts. This policy will be advertised and promoted to local as well as national concerns.
   B. Car-rental Agreement
      1. A room-car package will be offered to commercial guests. An agreement has been negotiated with a local rental firm. This agreement specifies unlimited mileage for a flat rate to include rental car and guest room. Front desk personnel will be informed and trained in promoting this package at check-in time.
   C. V.I.P. Services
      1. The assistant manager will be responsible for greeting all special guests. Fruit baskets and complimentary beverages will be provided in the guest roms of all V.I.P.'s.
   D. Establish Local Commercial Accounts
      1. The area is a major industrial center and the home office for a number of major corporations. Many branch personnel arrive and depart daily. Efforts will be made to reach this commercial business and a special position will be designated for this market. The responsibilities of this position will include development of promotion information, follow-through and reservations and room control for commercial accounts. Corporate secretaries will be sent direct mail prices regarding commercial rates and special services.
II. Tour and Travel Business
   A. Group and Tour Packages
      1. A Get-a-way week-end package has been developed. The plan calls for a three day, two night package to include full access to golf course, tennis courts and other recreation amenities. The package will be priced at the single rate and will be promoted as a "two for the price of one."
      2. Negotiations are underway with Greyhound World Tours. Weekly motorcoach tours are anticipated to begin in the summer. Promotion of the package is to be shared with eighty percent of the costs covered by Greyhound.
   B. Agency Business
      1. A list of travel agencies specializing in travel to our area will be prepared. These agents will be given personal calls by our representatives. Follow-up printed materials will then be supplied.
      2. Familiarization tours will be scheduled for agents and a special room rate will be extended to all walk-in travel agents.
      3. A fly-drive package is being negotiated with Tradewind Tours. The wholesaler is working with an airline, rent-a-car firm and ourselves in packaging this program. The package will be marketed through travel at a 7% commission.

461

III. Convention and Banquet Sales
    A. Exhibitions
        1. We will exhibit at the following conventions; American Society of Association Executives and Incentive Travel Managers.
    B. Direct Mail
        1. The direct mail program will be continued. Our prices however will be up-dated and a series of three letters stressing our convention facilities will be mailed to our list of meeting planners.
    C. Trade Publications
        1. We will advertise in the following trade magazines; *Meetings and Conventions, Association Management* and *Incentive Travel Manager.*
    D. Tip Sheets
        1. Data-bank services will be purchased. This service will provide our convention sales personnel with timely tip sheets on convention groups meeting in our area.
    E. Sales Personnel Objectives
        1. All salespersons are being asked to outline a specific plan of action for the year. This outline will include personal objectives and is to be reviewed by the Director of Sales. Areas to be included are outside calls, personal visits, number of phone contacts made, new business, repeat business and personal performance goals.
    F. Banquet Sales
        1. The catering department is to develop a banquet menu. All sales persons should familiarize themselves with this menu and actively promote group banquet business.

IV. Walk-in and Individual Business
    A. Local Promotion
        1. We will work closely with the Chamber of Commerce, information centers and service stations to encourage recommendation of our property.
    B. In-House Promotion
        1. Of utmost importance is the service attitude of our employees. On going training sessions are to be conducted by management. Criss-cross advertising, directional signs and in-house billboards will be used to inform the quest of the hotel's facilities.

Glossary A   Convention and Meeting Terms

All business depends strongly on accurate communication. The convention business is no exception. In fact, communication may be an even more vital factor here because every convention is a custom production.

Experience has shown that trouble is avoided when all parties use common terminology. Hotel staff people should make an effort to employ the correct designations and to encourage their clients to do so too.

Many of these terms and definitions are reprinted, with permission, from the *Glossary of Hotel/Motel Terms* by Frank W. Berkman, published by the Hotel Sales Management Association, International.

BANQUETS AND FUNCTIONS

A la carte   A meal with each item on the menu priced separately (run of the menu).

Cash bar   A private room bar setup where guests pay for drinks. Sometimes called a **COD bar** or an **a la carte bar,** this type of bar is usually set up by the hotel for large groups.

Covers   The number of persons served at a food function.

French service   Each food item individually served on a plate at the table by a waiter, as opposed to serving a completely setup plate.

Guarantee   The figure given by the function planner to the hotel at least twenty-four hours prior to function for the number of persons to be served. Most hotels are prepared to serve at least 5 percent over the guaranteed figure. Payment is made on the basis of the guaranteed number of covers or the total number served, whichever is greater.

Host bar   A private room bar setup where drinks are prepaid by a sponsor (sometimes called a **sponsored bar**).

Open bar   A private room bar setup where guests do not pay for drinks. A host bar is a form of open bar.

Paid Bar   A private room bar setup where all drinks are prepaid. Tickets for drinks are sometimes used.

Plus-plus   A term to indicate that taxes and gratuities must be added to the stated rate.

Table d' hote   A full-course meal with limited choice.

EUROPEAN HOTEL DESIGNATIONS

Deluxe   Finest type hotel, private bath, and full service.

First class   Medium range, usually with private or semi-private bath.

Hotel garni   A hotel without dining facilities (except breakfast).

Tourist or economy   Commercial type hotel, usually without private bath.

EXHIBITS

Booth   Space allotted to exhibit or on contract, usually 8 by 10 feet.

Drayage   Transportation of material from point of arrival to exhibit area.

Floor load   Weight per square foot that exhibit floor can safely accommodate.

Loading dock   Entrance to area where exhibit shipments are received.

Net square feet   Net salable exhibit space.

FOOD PLANS

Continental breakfast   Consists of juice, toast, roll or sweet roll, coffee, tea, or milk (in some countries, coffee and roll only).

Continental plan   Rate includes breakfast and room. Commonly called **bed and breakfast.**

Demi-pension   Rate includes breakfast, lunch or dinner, and room.

European plan (EP)   No meals included in room rate.

Full American plan (AP)   Rate includes three full meals and room. Full board or full pension.

Modified American plan (MAP)   Rate includes breakfast, dinner, and room.

MEETING ROOM EQUIPMENT (AUDIOVISUAL)

Cordless mike   A small portable microphone that operates without direct electrical connection.

Easel   A three-legged stand used to hold blackboards, cork boards, magnetic boards, posters, stands, etc.

Flip-chart stands   A large pad, usually twenty by twenty-four inches or larger, on a tripod stand used by speaker for illustrative purposes.

Lavaliere mike   A small portable microphone that hooks around the neck by a ribbon or cord; commonly known as a **necklace, lapel, neck,** or **pendant mike.**

Motion-picture sound projector   Most commonly in 16-mm film size, but now available in the smaller Super-8 size. The 16-mm motion-picture sound projector is the standard for larger meetings; the smaller Super 8 is growing in use in small group sessions.

Opaque projector   Equipment that projects image of opaque object, such as printed material.

Overhead projector   Equipment that projects an image from a large transparency (up to nine by nine inches). Speaker or operator can write on transparencies as they are projected.

Public address system   The sound system, portable or built-in, available for amplification in one or more rooms.

Roving mike   A hand microphone on a long electrical cord for speaker who roams around the stage or audience.

Standing mike   A microphone attached to a metal stand from the floor. It is adjustable to height of speaker.

Table mike   A microphone on a short stand that is placed on a table for seated speakers.

2×2 slide projector   Also called 35-mm slide projector. Equipment that projects image from transparencies in mounts measuring two inches by two inches. The most popular is the Kodak Carousel, which utilizes a special round slide tray.

MEETING ROOM SETUPS

Auditorium or theater style setup   A series of chairs set up in rows, with aisles, facing the head table, stage, or speaker.

Board of directors setup   A series of tables set up in a rectangular shape, with chairs on both sides and the ends. It can also be set up with oval ends.

Dais   A raised platform on which the head table is placed.

E shape setup   A series of tables set up in the shape of the block letter E, with chairs usually on the outside of the closed end and on both sides of each leg.

Floor or standing lectern   A full-size reading desk that rests on the floor; sometimes mistakenly called a floor podium.

Hollow circular setup   Same setup as **horseshoe,** except both ends are closed and chairs are set up only on the outside.

Hollow square setup   Tables set up in a square with the middle hollow and chairs on each of four sides, outside of square.

Horseshoe setup   Tables set up in the shape of a horseshoe. Chairs usually go around the outside but may be placed inside as well.

Podium   A raised platform or stage on which the speaker stands; sometimes called a **rostrum.**

Schoolroom perpendicular setup   Same as **schoolroom** setup, except that tables are perpendicular to the head table and chairs are placed on both sides of the tables.

Schoolroom setup   Tables six feet by eighteen inches are lined up in rows on each side of a good-sized center aisle. Usually there are six chairs to two tables; all tables and chairs face the head table.

Schoolroom V setup   Same as **schoolroom** setup, except that tables and chairs are tilted like the letter V, with the base of the V at the center aisle; also called **schoolroom-herringbone** style.

Senate style setup   Same as **auditorium,** except chairs are set up in a semicircular fashion facing the head table; sometimes referred to as **auditorium, semicircular.**

Setup and breakdown time   The time needed before and after a function to arrange and rearrange the facility.

T shape setup   A series of tables set up in the shape of the block letter T, with chairs usually on the outside of the top of the T and on both sides of the leg.

Table lectern   A raised reading desk which holds the speaker's papers and rests on a table; sometimes mistakenly called a table podium.

Tablet armchair setup   A series of armchairs with attachable writing tablets set up in **auditorium** or **theater style.**

U shape setup   A series of tables set up in the shape of the block letter U, with chairs usually on the outside of the closed end and on both sides of each leg.

V shape setup   Same as **auditorium,** except chairs are set up in the shape of the V, with the base of the V at the center aisle; also called **auditorium-herringbone style.**

NEGOTIATIONS AND ARRANGEMENTS

Commitment   The detailed arrangements hotel and/or buyer have agreed upon. Same as proposal or agreement but not used in the legal sense.

Cutoff date   The designated day when the buyer (upon request) must release or add to function room or guest room commitment. With certain types of groups, rooming lists should be sent to the hotel at least two weeks prior to arrival.

Letter of agreement   Letter from the buyer accepting the proposal. This may be the hotel's proposal initialed by the buyer. No legal agreement exists unless both sides have exchanged letters or duplicates of letters have been okayed.

Option date   The date agreed upon when a tentative agreement is to become a definite agreement by the buyer and seller.

Proposal   First letter sent by the hotel outlining the understanding between the buyer and the hotel.

Rooming list   A list of names submitted by the buyer of guests who will occupy the previously reserved accommodations.

ROOM ACCOMMODATIONS

Adjoining rooms   Two or more rooms side by side without a connecting door between them. Rooms can be adjoining without being connecting.

Cabana   A room adjacent to pool area, with or without sleeping facilities, usually separate from hotel's main building.

Connecting rooms   Two or more rooms with private connecting doors permitting access between rooms without going into the corridor.

Double   A room with one large bed for two persons.

Double bed   A bed large enough to sleep two. The industry standard measures 53 inches wide and 75 inches long.

Duplex   A two-story suite (parlor and bedroom[s]) connected by a stairway.

Efficiency   An accommodation containing some type of kitchen facility.

Function room   A room suitable for group use for meetings, exhibits, entertaining, etc. No sleeping facilities.

Hospitality   A room used for entertaining (cocktail party, etc.); usually a function room or parlor.

Hospitality suite   A parlor with connecting bedroom(s) to be used for entertaining.

Junior suite   A large room with a partition separating the bedroom furnishings from the sitting area.

King-size bed   An extra large double-type bed measuring 76 inches wide by 80 inches long. An **extra-long king-size** is 84 inches long.

Lanai   A room overlooking water or a garden balcony or patio (resort hotels mainly).

Parlor   A living or sitting room not used as a bedroom (called a **salon** in some parts of Europe).

Roll-a-way beds   Extra mobile beds that can be placed in a room for extra

persons occupying the room, usually at a nominal charge.

Sample room   A display room for showing merchandise, with or without sleeping facilities.

Single   A room to be occupied by one person.

Studio   A one-room parlor setup having one or two couches that convert to a bed (sometimes called an executive room).

Suite   A parlor connected to one or more bedrooms. When reserving a suite, always designate the number of bedrooms needed.

Twin   A room with two single beds for two persons. (Beds can be adjoining with one common headboard.)

Twin double   A room with two double beds for two, three, or four persons; sometimes called a **family room** or a **double-double.**

ROOM OCCUPANCY

Check-in   The hotel day starts at 6 A.M.; however, occupancy by arriving guests may not be possible until after the established check-out time (usually 1 P.M.). Guests are required to sign hotel's registration card.

Check-out   All guests should advise hotel cashier upon departure and follow the agreed upon procedure for payment. If room is required by the guest beyond hotel's posted check-out time, approval must be given by the hotel management.

ROOM RESERVATIONS

Commercial rate   A flat rate agreed upon by a company and the hotel for any individual room reservations, regardless of rack rates.

Confirmed registration   An oral or written confirmation by the hotel that a reservation has been accepted (written confirmations are preferred). There is usually a 6 P.M. (local time) check-in deadline. If the guest arrives after 6 P.M. and the hotel is filled, the assistant manager will make every effort to secure accommodations in another hotel. This does not apply to guests with confirmed reservations where a **late arrival** time has been specified.

Day-rate Usually one-half the regular rate of a room for use by the guest during a given day up to 5 P.M. Sometimes called a **use rate.**

Deposit reservation A reservation for which the hotel has received cash payment for at least the first night's lodging in advance and is obligated to hold the room regardless of the guest's time of arrival. The hotel should preregister this type of guest. **Cancellation procedure:** This type of reservation should be canceled as early as possible, but a minimum of forty-eight hours prior to scheduled date of arrival in a commercial type hotel. For resort hotels the customer should verify cancellation policy when making the reservation.

Flat rate Specific room rate for a group agreed upon by hotel and group in advance.

Guaranteed payment reservation A room is set aside by the hotel, at the request of the customer, in advance of the guest's arrival. Payment for the room is guaranteed and will be paid by a company or organization even though the guest may not arrive—unless the cancellation procedure in effect in each property is adhered to. Company or organization should receive from the hotel a cancellation code or name of the person accepting the cancellation.

Housing bureau The local convention bureau will act (for certain convention groups) as a housing bureau and assign rooms in participating hotels in the city or area. In some parts of the world, a **hotel clearing house** is a semi-official organization that assigns rooms in hotels for individuals and/or groups seeking accommodations.

No-show A confirmed reservation that has not been fulfilled or canceled by the customer.

Preregistration The guest is preassigned a room by the hotel to be available upon the guest's arrival. This procedure is also used for some types of group business. Some hotels have a special **preregistration desk** or rack near the front desk.

Rack rate The current rate charged for each accommodation as established by the hotel's management.

Run of the house rate An agreed upon rate generally priced at an average figure between minimum and maximum for group accommodations for all available rooms except suites. Room assignments usually made on a **best available** basis.

TYPES OF MEETINGS

Clinic Usually face-to-face small groups, but may have general sessions where staff provides most of the training resources to train in a particular subject.

Colloquium A program in which the participants determine the matter to be discussed. The leaders then construct the program around the most frequent problems. Usually attended by thirty-five or fewer persons, with equal emphasis on instruction and discussion.

Conference Usually general sessions and face-to-face groups with high participation to plan, get facts, and solve organization and member problems.

Congress More commonly-used European designation for convention (mainly international in scope).

Convention Usually general sessions and committee meetings; mostly information-giving, and generally the accepted traditional form of annual meeting.

Exposition A public exhibition or show, put on with or without an accompanying meeting.

Forum A panel discussion, with experts in a given field taking opposite sides of an issue, liberal opportunity for audience participation.

Institute General sessions and face-to-face groups discussing several facets of a subject. Primarily a substitute for formal education, with staff providing most of the training resources.

Lecture A formal presentation by an expert, sometimes followed by question-and-answer period.

Panel Two or more speakers stating their viewpoints, with discussion between speakers. Discussion is guided by a moderator.

Seminar Usually one face-to-face group sharing experiences in a particular field under the guidance of an expert discussion leader. Attendance is generally thirty or fewer persons.

Symposium A panel discussion by experts in a given field before a large audience; some audience participation, but appreciably less than a forum.

Trade show An exhibition with displays, generally held within a trade, industry, or discipline. May be held independently or in conjunction with a convention.

Workshop Usually a general session and face-to-face groups of participants training each other to gain new knowledge, skills, or insights into problems. Attendance generally no more than thirty to thirty-five participants.

Index

Name Index

Subject Index